# Juvenile Justice System in India

# Juvenile Justice System in India

Manish Dwivedi

ADHYAYAN

ADHYAYAN PUBLISHERS & DISTRIBUTORS

New Delhi-110002

*Published by*
**ADHYAYAN PUBLISHERS & DISTRIBUTORS**
4378/4B, 105, J.M.D. House, Murari Lal Street
Ansari Road Darya Ganj, New Delhi - 110002
Ph.: 011-23263018, 011-23277156, Fax: 23280028
Email: adhyayanpublishers@yahoo.com

*Juvenile Justice System in India*


Edition 2011
ISBN 978-81-8435-283-2



Printed in India

Published by Harish Chandra Yadav for Adhyayan Publishers & Distributors, Delhi. Laser Typesetting at Jain Computers and Printed at Tarun Offset Printers. Delhi

# Preface

Despite eight years of a separate Act meant to deal with juvenile delinquency, the situation on the ground has not changed much. India's juvenile justice system calls for complete overhauling to tackle the sluggish pace of judicial processes and lack of proper care at observation homes.The ***Juvenile Justice (Care& Protection of Children) Act 2000*** is the primary legal framework for juvenile justice in India. The Act provides for a special approach towards the prevention and treatment of juvenile delinquency and provides a framework for the protection, treatment and rehabilitation of children in the purview of the juvenile justice system. This law, brought in compliance of Child Rights Convention, repealed the earlier Juvenile Justice Act of 1986.

JJ Act is considered to be an extremely progressive legislation and Model Rules 2007 have further added to the effectiveness of this welfare legislation . However the implementation is a very serious concern even in year 2010.

The first legislation on juvenile justice in India came in 1850 with the *Apprentic Act* which required that children between the ages of 10-18 convicted in courts to be provided vocational training as part of their rehabilitation process. This act was transplanted by the *Reformatory Schools Act*, 1897, the *Indian Jail Committee* and later the Children Act of 1960. The Juvenile Justice Bill was first introduced in the LokSabha on 22 August 1986.

This Act, further amended in 2006 and is now known

as the Juvenile Justice (Care and Protection) Act, 2000.Section 21 of the Juvenile Justice (Care and Protection of Children) Act, 2000 (56 of 2000) as amended by the Juvenile Justice (Care and Protection of Children) Amendment Act, 2006 (33 of 2006)., states that: "Prohibition of publication of name, etc., of juvenile or child in need of care and protection involved in any proceeding under the Act-(1) No report in any newspaper, magazine, news-sheet or visual media of any inquiry regarding a juvenile in conflict with law or a child in need of care and protection under this Act shall disclose the name, address or school or any other particulars calculated to lead to the identification of the juvenile or child shall nor shall any picture of any such juvenile or child shall be published: Provided that for any reason to be recorded in writing, the authority holding the inquiry may permit such disclosure, if in its opinion such disclosure is in the interest of the juvenile or the child. (2) Any person who contravenes the provisions of sub-section (1), shall be liable to a penalty which may extend to twenty-five thousand rupees".

Hon'ble Supreme Court vide Judgement in Hari Ram Versus State of Rajasthan gave restrospective effect to Juvenile Justice Act , 2000.In Maharashtra there are 46 observation homes that cater to over 9,000 -10,000 children from both categories. These homes are run independently by the State Department for Women and Child Welfare, or in collaboration with voluntary organisations.

The Juvenile Justice Act has established two bodies - the Child Welfare Committee (CWC) to specifically address the needs of 'children in need of care and protection' and the Juvenile Justice Board to look into matters concerning 'children in conflict with the law'.

In the case of 'children in conflict with the law', the Act mandates that after being apprehended the child must be brought before the Juvenile Justice Board (JJB) within 24 hours, or a metropolitan court that may be holding charge of the JJB.

Children who are detained in observation homes are

from typically poor families; they have had few opportunities to attend regular school. They have already experienced a great deal of marginalisation in their lives. Many have faced abuse and exploitation; some have been severely neglected by their parents causing them to leave their families and resort to crime.

Therefore when these children are brought to the observation home they are in immediate need of care and guidance.

**System needs reform**

Despite the Act, however, observation homes have not achieved the objectives for which they have been set up. For instance they still lack adequate facilities for children in conflict with the law.

A normal day for the children goes somewhat like this. The boys live in a big dormitory that they rarely move out of. This is where they eat, sleep, and occasionally play games.

A bell rings at noon and they are served lunch. After this they are left to entertain themselves within the confines of the hall, with a caretaker watching over them all the time.

"They allow the other boys (non-offenders) to play, attend school and go out on excursions. They don't allow us to do anything. We are not permitted to leave this hall at all."

"The children are not a priority as they are not voters. They are poor and illiterate and hence people get away with providing inadequate facilities. The feeling that they deserve what they get is still rampant," he says.

What's worse is that there is hardly any segregation of children in conflict with the law and children in need of care and protection.

Children in need of care and protection have regular visitors and are often allowed to go out with them. They also have access to education, sports and a library; some have even won scholarships. On the other hand, children in conflict with the law are usually not from the same city and so rarely have any visitors. The boys, mostly between the ages of 13 and 18, sit huddled together watching television the whole day.

Another area of serious neglect is the shockingly slow justice system. At the time of writing this article there were over 3,500 cases pending with the juvenile justice court. The two 'non-judiciary' members have to be present at the time of the hearing; the judge cannot sign the deposition in their absence.

There are also delays due to witnesses not turning up in court and delays in cross-examination.

Add to this the fact that very often members of the Juvenile Justice Board are not well-versed in the Act itself. "We are not clear ourselves. We have asked them to give us training, but it hasn't happened," according to most of the members of the JJBs.

Caught in the midst of unending bureaucracy and indifference are young boys and girls whose future hangs in the balance. As Pune-based social worker PoornimaGadia says: "The situation cannot be reversed unless there is a change in attitude at all levels."

Finally, I hope that this book will be certainly very useful for all those dealing with the subject. I thankful to Mr. Harish Chander Yadav, Adhyayan Publication and Distributors, New Delhi for publishing this book in a very short span of time.

**Manish Dwivedi**

# Contents

# 1

# Introduction

Throughout the world, children who come into conflict with the law as a result of being accused or suspected of committing a crime are at greatest risk of having their fundamental rights violated. For this reason, the Convention on the Rights of the Child (CRC) has established the following as the core guiding principle for the treatment of children in conflict with the law:

> State Parties recognise the right of every child alleged as, accused of, or recognised as having infringed the penal law to be treated in a manner consistent with the promotion of the child's sense of dignity and worth, which reinforces the child's respect for the human rights and fundamental freedoms of others and which takes into account the child's age and the desirability of promoting the child's reintegration and the child's assuming a constructive role in society.[1]

To this end, States parties are required to establish laws, procedures, authorities and institutions specifically applicable to children alleged as, accused of, or recognised as having infringed the penal law. This Report seeks to assess the progress made by South Asian countries in meeting these obligations. National juvenile justice systems, both laws and practices, are assessed against the key requirements of the CRC and the UN guidelines on juvenile justice: the UN Rules for the Protection of Juveniles Deprived of their Liberty (JDLs);[2] the UN Guidelines for the Prevention of Juvenile Delinquency (Riyadh Guidelines);[3] and the UN Standard Minimum Rules for the Administration of Juvenile Justice (Beijing Rules). The first Part of this Report offers a snapshot of the juvenile justice systems across the region. This is followed by more detailed Country Profiles.[4] Annex 1 contains a regional comparative chart based on the Implementation Checklist contained in UNICEFs Implementation Handbook for the Convention on the Rights of the Child.

**Juvenile Justice Legislation and Procedures**

With the exception of Bhutan, every country in the region has separate legislation governing procedures for children in conflict with the law.[5] In all cases, this legislation deals with both children in conflict with the law and children in need of protection, often with a lack of differentiation between these two groups. Although there has been significant impetus for reform in recent years, no country in the region has established a fully separate system of justice for children that ensures they are separated from adults at all stages of the criminal proceedings. Legislative reform is currently underway in Nepal, Sri Lanka and Maldives, and is being considered in Bhutan.

**Jurisdiction and Scope**

(a) *CRC and UN Guidelines:* The CRC requires all State parties to establish special laws, procedures, authorities and institutions specifically applicable to all children in conflict with the law. A "child" is defined as a person under the age of 18. State parties must also establish a minimum age below which children are presumed not to have the capacity to commit a crime.[6]

(b) *Regional Assessment:* With the exception of Afghanistan, the minimum age of criminal responsibility in all countries in the region is below international standards, ranging from seven (India, Pakistan and Maldives) to 12 (Afghanistan). Bangladesh has recently raised the age from seven to nine, and in Bhutan and Nepal it is 10.[7] The UN Committee on the Rights of the Child has repeatedly expressed concern about this issue in its Concluding Observations to each country's Periodic Report.[8] Afghanistan, Bhutan, India, Maldives and Pakistan extend juvenile justice protections to all children under the age of 18.[9] In Nepal, Sri Lanka and Bangladesh a juvenile is defined as a person under the age of 16.[10]

In most countries there are additional restrictions on the applicability of juvenile laws, and special protections do not apply universally to all children alleged to have committed an offence. In India, juvenile justice legislation does not apply in Jammu and Kashmir.[11] In Pakistan, it has not been extended to the Federally Administered Tribal Areas or the Provincially Administered Tribal Areas.[12]

In Sri Lanka and Nepal, children who are jointly charged with adults are subject to adult proceedings. Sri Lanka also does not extend special protections to children charged with certain serious offences (murder, attempted murder and robbery).[13] In Bangladesh, special laws override juvenile justice protections and children above 16 years could be subject to stringent laws which allow life imprisonment and death penalty.[14]

## Inter-agency Coordination, Monitoring and Reporting

All countries in the region currently have ongoing juvenile justice reform initiatives. However, a lack of clear strategic focus and inter-agency coordination mechanism has resulted in many interventions being disjointed and unsustainable.

In Afghanistan, Bangladesh and Nepal, high-level juvenile justice task forces have been established to provide greater coordination across the justice sector, and Maldives has drafted a comprehensive, inter-agency strategic plan for juvenile justice reforms. Monitoring children's rights in general, and the rights of children in conflict with the law in particular, remains weak throughout the region. In all countries, an agency has been designated to monitor implementation of the rights of the child, and to report on progress to the UN Committee on the Rights of the Child. However, data collection remains a challenge, and no country in the region has established a comprehensive set of juvenile justice indicators to monitor and evaluate the situation of children in conflict with the law. Some progress has been made on the development of indicators in Bhutan, India and Pakistan based on global indicators developed by UNICEF. India is introducing a web-enabled database to collect data on child protection throughout the country, and Pakistan has piloted the global indicators in selected provinces. The lack of effective mechanism to monitor the treatment of children by police and in detention is cause for concern. No country in the region has a fully-functioning system to regularly inspect all places of detention. Judges and magistrates reportedly conduct regular visits to institutions in Afghanistan, Pakistan, Bangladesh, Maldives and India, but this is largely dependent on individual initiative. In Afghanistan, Pakistan, India, Bangladesh and Nepal some independent custody monitoring is conducted by national human rights commissions or by local NGOs.

In fact, it is doubtful whether the dominant rule of law (ROL) paradigm pursued by many international agencies should be the main means for integrating law and development. An alternative approach often is preferable: legal empowerment—the use of legal services and related development activities to increase disadvantaged populations' control over their lives. Legal empowerment is not the only alternative, but it merits serious consideration as a major vehicle for poverty alleviation.

The dominant paradigm—or "rule of law orthodoxy"—takes a "top-down," state-centered approach through which development agency personnel design and implement law-oriented projects in cooperation with high government officials. As principally practiced by multilateral development banks, which are major sources of ROL aid, it concentrates on law reform and government institutions, particularly judiciaries.

The banks aim to build more business-friendly and investment-friendly legal systems that presumably help spur economic growth and poverty alleviation. Other development organizations sometimes use ROL orthodoxy to promote such additional goals as good governance and public safety, whether as ends in themselves or as steps toward reducing poverty. The problems with the paradigm are not these economic and political goals, per se, but its questionable assumptions, unproven impact, and insufficient attention to the legal needs of the disadvantaged.

As a specific strategy, then, the dominant paradigm comprises a series of assumptions, a chain of reasoning, and a group of activities that promote the rule of law to presumably achieve economic progress. As a set of programs that similarly take a top-down, state-centered approach to achieve a diversity of additional goals, however, ROL orthodoxy cuts an even broader swath through the field of law and development. This wide array of initiatives tends to exclude supporting civil society or building the legal capacities and power of the poor.Thus, some bilateral, multilateral, and privately funded organizations that eschew the banks' development philosophies nevertheless pursue similar practices through their law programs in many countries. And while some of the banks and other aid agencies are laudably undertaking more civil society initiatives and other creative endeavors through their law-oriented work, these generally pale in view of their agencies' orthodox orientations and funding priorities.

In contrast with the dominant paradigm, legal empowerment is more balanced in nature. It is grounded in grassroots needs and activities but can translate that community-level work into impact on national laws and institutions. It generally strengthens civil society and the legal capacities and power of the poor in order to address their priorities, but wherever possible involves cooperation with government. This alternative approach also addresses a central reality that ROL orthodoxy overlooks. In many developing countries, laws benefiting the poor exist on paper but not in practice, unless the poor or their allies push for the laws' enforcement.

Legal empowerment differs from ROL orthodoxy in at least four additional ways: (1) attorneys support the poor as partners, instead of dominating them as proprietors of expertise; (2) the disadvantaged play a role in setting priorities, rather than government officials and donor personnel dictating the agenda; (3) addressing these priorities frequently involves non-judicial strategies that transcend narrow notions of legal systems, justice sectors, and institution building; (4) even more broadly, the use of law is often just part of integrated strategies that include other development activities.

Legal empowerment is not only an alternative to ROL orthodoxy; it should be an element of many mainstream socio-economic development efforts (regarding, for example, public health, gender, rural development, irrigation, education) that generally do not address ROL or the legal needs of the poor. For instance, the field of natural resources management often witnesses the unfortunate phenomenon of "parks on paper"—zones whose protected status means little in reality. Especially when undertaken in conjunction with conservation, protection, and livelihood activities, strengthening the legal capacities of the disadvantaged can help convert these parks from legal fictions into actual protected areas. Nevertheless, I do not maintain that legal empowerment is the correct path to pursue under all circumstances. Nor is the dominant paradigm always inapplicable. Furthermore, the two are not mutually exclusive. But we do know enough to raise questions, and that is precisely one point of this paper: ROL orthodoxy's numerous problematic features make the prevalent devotion to it a remarkable state of affairs. There is a clear imbalance in the international development community's use of resources. Many development agencies that profess pro-poor priorities invest far more in building up government legal institutions and elites than in fortifying impoverished populations' legal capacities and power. In the process, they often insufficiently heed the priorities of the poor, the experience of successful efforts to empower them, and the need to build-up civil society if governments and their legal systems are to become responsive and accountable.

The great resources poured into the dominant paradigm, to the relative exclusion of alternatives, represent a great gamble—or, as McAuslan puts it, "an act of faith."[8] Today's heavy emphasis on judges, lawyers, and courts is analogous to what the public health field would look like if it mainly focused on urban hospitals and the doctors staffing them, and largely ignored nurses, other health workers, maternal and public education, other preventive approaches, rural and community health issues, building community capacities, and nonmedical strategies (such as improving sanitation and water supply).

In contrast, a growing array of qualitative and quantitative research suggests that legal empowerment has helped advance poverty alleviation, good governance, and other development goals. This alternative paradigm offers the added value of putting community-driven and rights-based development into effect by offering concrete mechanisms, involving legal services, for advancing the rights of the poor. Legal empowerment accordingly merits substantially increased financial and political support, whether directly or under the rubrics of ROL or mainstream socio-economic development initiatives.

Legal empowerment both advances and transcends the rule of law. It advances ROL in the sense that where the poor have more power they are better able to make government officials implement the law and influential private parties abide by it. Such power also enables disadvantaged groups to play a greater role in local and national law reform. In these crucial respects, it builds good governance.

But legal empowerment also is about far more than ROL or governance: It is about poverty alleviation, broadly defined to include empowerment as well as material improvement. Many of its goals and results vindicate or expand the rights of the poor, whether framed in terms of local, national, or international law. But this is not always the same as their gaining greater control over their lives—sometimes dramatically, but often in subtle or apparently minor ways that nevertheless mean a great deal to people scraping to get by.Thus, the key concept in legal empowerment is not law; it is power.

The upshot of all of this is the need to scrutinize ROL orthodoxy, examine alternatives such as legal empowerment, and pursue a paradigm shift in integrating law and development.

## RULE OF LAW ORTHODOXY: A PROBLEMATIC PARADIGM

### Key Features of Rule of Law Orthodoxy

The rule of law orthodoxy embraced by much of the international donor community should not be confused with the rule of law itself. In the view of the World Bank.

While defined in various ways, the rule of law prevails where

*(i)* the government itself is bound by the law,
*(ii)* every person in society is treated equally under the law,
*(iii)* the human dignity of each individual is recognized and protected by law, and
*(iv)* justice is accessible to all.

ROL orthodoxy, by contrast, is a set of ideas, activities, and strategies geared toward bringing about the rule of law, often as a means toward ends such as economic growth, good governance, and poverty alleviation. This paradigm comprises a mélange of goals, assumptions, activities, and strategies. Many of these vary according to context, are ill-defined, or are only implicit. úμe characterization offered here, then, seeks to distill some common traits without identifying them with anyone institution, project, or country.

The paradigm's programs and goals are not confined to the economic sphere, though that often is most salient in development discourse and among the multilateral financial institutions that today are major sources of funds for ROL programs.This central stream of ROL orthodoxy considers the rule of law essential for long-term development because it provides security for foreign and domestic investment, property and contract rights, international trade, and other vehicles for advancing economic growth.

Martinez accordingly asserts that "the liberalization of market economies...requires a legal order that is fair, efficient, easily accessible, and predictable." This line of thought further holds that properly functioning courts and other legal institutions nurture a favorable business climate by protecting investments and by enforcing contracts and property rights. Foreign and domestic enterprises are more likely to establish and expand operations that manufacture goods and provide services under such circumstances, the reasoning goes. Among other benefits, this in turn provides jobs, increases the output of goods and services, yields a ripple effect of additional business for and employment by local enterprises that serve expanding domesticand foreign firms, brings about technology and skills transfer, and increases foreign exchange reserves.

As a strategy for presumably alleviating poverty by promoting business and investment, ROL orthodoxy is substantially linked to globalization. It seeks to further the national adoption of international legal standards and practices, as well as the integration of national economies into the world economy.

ROL orthodoxy has an even wider reach, however, as a set of programs that emphasize top-down, state-centered approaches for pursuing a diversity of goals, beyond building better business environments. It infuses many law programs supported by the U.S. Agency for International Development (USAID), for example, which seeks to advance the rule of law as part of its democracy and governance (DG) program. Much of the law-oriented work of the United Kingdom's Department for International Development (DFID) emphasizes state institutions as vehicles for promoting the poor's personal safety, security of property, and access to justice (SSAJ).

USAID and DFID do not pursue orthodox approaches exclusively or everywhere (nor do other aid agencies that focus on state legal institutions). In a number of countries, both of these donors fund legal services for the disadvantaged. Furthermore, DFID's SSAJ program explicitly aims to address the poor's urgent legal needs. In prioritizing personal safety, for instance, the program certainly responds to many disadvantaged populations' vulnerability to criminal violence. But it mainly works through the state in doing so.This is despite the fact that informed, organized citizens may be as essential as training or pay raises to deterring police misconduct or encouraging police professionalism. A rural resident whom law enforcement personnel extort rather than serve when he seeks their help is in a far better bargaining position if he belongs to a well-connected, well-informed farmers' association. More generally, the point is that law projects undertaken under the rubrics of DG, SSAJ, and other rationales nevertheless manifest ROL orthodoxy where they exhibit its top-down, state-centered emphases, even though the underlying justifications differ from those of the multilateral banks.

To be fair, international aid agencies increasingly consult with the disadvantaged and civil society in setting priorities, and a few are broadening their perspectives on legal systems. DFIDs policy papers, for example, emphasize how crucial it is to ascertain the legal needs of the poor and the multifaceted ways in which dysfunctional legal systems perpetuate their poverty. But civil society consultation is far different than supporting civil society to serve the disadvantaged and build their legal capacities. DFID, USAID, and a limited number of other organizations also have expanded their characterizations of the justice sector to embrace traditional dispute resolution mechanisms. However, they still tend to exclude administrative agency and local government decisions that boil down to matters of law and that the poor often consider crucial matters of justice.

In short, key features of ROL orthodoxy include:

- A focus on state institutions, particularly judiciaries.
- This institutional focus is largely determined by the legal profession, as represented by a nation's jurists, top legal officials, and attorneys, and by foreign consultants and donor personnel.
- As a result, a tendency to define the legal system's problems and cures narrowly, in terms of courts, prosecutors, contracts, law reform, and other institutions and processes in which lawyers play central roles.
- Where civil society engagement occurs, it usually is as a means toward the end of state institutional development: consulting non-governmental organizations (NGOs) on how to reform the (narrowly defined) legal system, and funding them as vehicles for advocating reform.
- A reliance on foreign expertise, initiative, and models, particularly those originating in industrialized societies.

These features translate into funding a distinct array of activities, including:

- courthouse construction and repair;
- purchase of furniture, computers, and other equipment and materials;

- drafting new laws and regulations;
- training judges, lawyers, and other legal personnel;
- establishing management and administration systems for judiciaries;
- support for judicial and other training/management institutes;
- building-up bar associations; and
- international exchanges for judges, court administrators, and lawyers.

**Questionable Assumptions**

ROL orthodoxy is built on a number of questionable assumptions. Not all are necessarily wrong or automatically inapplicable in all contexts. Taken together, however, they form an unstable foundation on which to base the dominant paradigm for integrating law and development. Even if only some of them are flawed, we need to reassess our faith in the orthodox approach.

ROL's Impact on Poverty Alleviation: A Lack of Evidence.The bottom line for assessing the dominant paradigm must be its impact on the poor. Poverty alleviation is the main goal of many development organizations. Reducing poverty is the greatest reason why tax-payers, governments, and international institutions pour substantial funds into the legal field. But so far, at least, there has been a paucity of proof that the rule of law necessarily reduces poverty. There is evidence that ROL goes hand in hand with favorable development indicators, such as lowered infant mortality and higher incomes and literacy.[15] What such evidence does not demonstrate is cause and effect: whether strengthened rule of law brings about poverty alleviation, or *vice versa.* There is some historical evidence and analysis arguing for a causal connection between the establishment of the rule of law and overall socio-economic development, not least Weber's linking of law and legal systems to the growth of capitalism in Europe. But, why assume that what (presumably) transpired in Europe several centuries ago applies to Asia or Africa or Latin America today? As North points out, "Economic (and political) models are specific to particular constellations of institutional constraints that vary radically both through time and cross sectionally in different economies."[16] A fundamental tenet of development principles and practice is that the elements of success in one society do not necessarily translate into success elsewhere—particularly where the gap between the two comprises several centuries, thousands of miles, and vastly different political, economic, and cultural contexts.Thus, as Perry argues in summarizing literature challenging the notion that developing countries must adopt Western laws and legal institutions, "Law reform projects seem to be based on the unspoken Weberian assumption that because a particular legal system is found in countries which are developed, that legal system will help countries to be developed.There is no proof of this."[17] She also notes that those projects "ignore evidence [such as businesses' informal commerce-facilitating and development-promoting practices] which demonstrates, as a matter of fact, that there are limits to the importance of law in economic transactions."[18]

In a separate summary of relevant research, Messick similarly finds that "the question of the direction of causality" has not been settled by cross-country regression analysis.[19] Reviewing what we do not know about law and development, Carothers sees "a surprising amount of uncertainty [about whether]...promoting the rule of law will contribute to economic development and democratization...[and] about how the rule of law develops in societies and how such development can be stimulated."[20] Other sources agree that we lack evidence to know whether legal reform and legal systems improvement spur development,[21] or suggest that such legal change may be an effect of development rather than a cause of it.[22]

Actual experience in today's developing and transitional societies also undercuts the Weberian model. Several nations that have achieved significant economic growth and attendant poverty alleviation in recent decades have done so in the absence of Western-style rule of law. China is a leading example.[23] Indonesia, Thailand, and South Korea also thrived for years—and were hailed as success stories by international institutions—before the 1997–98 Asian economic crisis (which was brought on by factors other than the flawed legal systems of these countries).[24]

Indeed, the success of the East Asian model was rooted in good policy decisions and other factors, not the rule of law. And even as recently as a decade ago, some observers argued that authoritarian governments, regimes often quite abusive of the rule of law, are inherently better than democracies at implementing successful economic policies. Haggard laudably challenges that conclusion, but it is noteworthy that ROL does not figure in his analysis.[25] In a study for the Asian Development Bank, Pistor and Wellons suggest that law (both on the books and in actual practice) is more a dependent than causal variable, asserting that it is "embedded in culture" and that "to be effective law has to be embedded in the overall economic policy framework."[26]

Perry's case study of foreign enterprises in Sri Lanka, which includes a survey of those enterprises, disputes an important element of the "rule of law alleviates poverty" argument: the assumption that ROL is a crucial factor affecting foreign direct investment (FDI). She concludes that "the role of legal systems as a determinant of FDI is neither straightforward, nor proven, nor uniform."[27] Drawing in part on his work as a practicing lawyer in Eastern Europe, Hewko agrees. He asserts that "the existence of real business opportunities and the overall visceral perception...of a host country" are much more important to many foreign investors than extensive ROL reforms.[28] Hewko argues, in fact, that once such investors set up operations on the ground they can identify specific FDI-facilitating changes better than can foreign aid institutions and their consultants.[29] At the very least, it would seem that the supposed link between ROL and investment has not been demonstrated.

Some maintain that to move further forward, China and other countries need to get their legal houses in order. Others might contend that the world has changed in ways that require fully functional legal systems for development to unfold, even if they were not necessary before. Upham counters such arguments by pointing out that neither the United States nor Japan, two leading examples of relative prosperity, embody what he calls "formalist rule of law—that is, regimes defined by their absolute adherence to established legal rules and completely free of the corrupting influences of politics."[30] In fact, the inconsistent and inequitable operations of the U.S. legal system are "not a failure of execution, the inevitable falling short of an ideal. On the contrary, it is the result of...conscious choice" reflected in federalism, the political selection of judges, the jury system, and inadequate access to justice for many Americans.[31] Operating in an equally intentional manner, "the Japanese system kept the formal legal system out of economic policy making...Additionally, the settlement of individual disputes occurred through a broad system of informal mechanisms that kept most disputes out of the court system altogether."[32]

Without necessarily advocating the Japanese approach, Upham nevertheless suggests that "if one had to choose [between the U.S. and Japanese models], it would be the informal systems of Japan that would seem most useful to developing countries."[33] He maintains that the U.S. model, in many respects the system propagated by ROL orthodoxy, is far more expensive to adopt and far more likely to undermine functional indigenous institutions.Echoing Perry's point about viable but informal business practices, Upham even posits that "formalist rule of law could actually inhibit foreign investment in developing countries, since doing business in courts could be more expensive than using effective, informal systems of dispute resolution."[34] Though we should be aware of the gender and other biases infecting many informal systems (not to mention many formal ones), we still can recognize that ROL orthodoxy tilts heavily—and perhaps counterproductively—toward formalism.

***ROL Promotion's Weak Track Record.*** Even if the rule of law does help reduce poverty, this does not mean that intentional foreign efforts to build ROL will do so. It could be that ROL and its attendant benefits might only flow from a society's internal changes rather than external inputs such as foreign aid for ROL promotion.

What, then, is the impact of those foreign efforts? There is no evidence of poverty alleviation and little evidence of other results that would necessarily lead to reducing poverty or advancing other development goals. External reviews of ROL aid efforts have been highly critical. The U.S. General Accounting Office found serious flaws in USAID's largely state-oriented ROL work in parts of Latin America.[35] In a book on various Latin American countries' progress in (often donor-supported) judicial reform, Prillaman offers a bleak assessment of all except Chile, which he views as having a mixed record.[36] Summing up the track record of U.S. government work with judiciaries across the globe, Carothers asserts that "what stands out about U.S. rule-of-law assistance since the mid-1980s is how difficult and often disappointing such work is."[37]

As critical as Prillaman and Carothers are, there are respects in which they may be too charitable in their assessments. Prillaman sees Chile as a partial, favorable exception to the rule of collapsing reform efforts. Yet Chile and other partial success stories, such as Costa Rica, may be exceptional not because of donor efforts, but rather because of underlying, enduring legal cultures that transcend reform strategies or even regimes. For his part, Carothers concludes that "some learning is occurring, particularly among aid officials and consultants working in Latin America, the region in which the United States has labored most intensively on rule-of-law aid."[38] Whether that learning is translating into actual impact on Latin Americans' lives is a matter he does not substantially address. In addition, it is worthwhile to ask whether the foreign "aid officials and consultants," rather than domestic actors, do most of the learning under orthodox ROL programs (I return to this issue of intellectual ownership below).

Blair and Hansen's USAID-commissioned study of rule of law assistance in six Latin American and Asian countries advises against a "legal system strengthening/institution building strategy"—and implicitly, against ROL orthodoxy, which resembles that strategy—unless a number of elements already are in place in a country.[39] The most fundamental of these elements are the absence of rampant corruption in its justice system and the absence of major human rights violations in the society. Where such abuses are prevalent, they argue against any ROL assistance.

Blair and Hansen more specifically advise against the orthodox, institution-oriented strategy where a country's political leadership lacks the will to pursue reforms. They further find that this crucial political will is missing in most situations. They reluctantly maintain that in many countries "constituencies and coalitions may be so fragmented and fractious, and the political environment may be so inimical to judicial reform (perhaps even to the notion of ROL), as to eliminate any effective program activity."[40] These conclusions—that ROL assistance will prove unproductive under many circumstances and (implicitly) that ROL orthodoxy is inappropriate in even more situations—both weigh against the dominant paradigm.

Despite this bleak assessment, there may be respects in which Blair and Hansen, like Prillaman and Carothers, may be too optimistic about the prospects for ROL programs producing large-scale change. Even the greatest amount of political will is sometimes insufficient to implement lasting legal system reforms in the face of recalcitrant bureaucracies and improper but powerful external influences.

Hammergren's subsequent USAID review in effect seeks to rebut elements of the Blair/Hansen study but essentially is much more a thoughtful "how to pursue reform" document rather than a documentation of impact.[41] She asserts that by addressing more technical and politically manageable issues, practitioners of ROL assistance can establish progress, credibility, and insights that help them tackle more fundamental obstacles to reform.[42] In effect, they can build political will even where it is missing. This is a credible argument, but whether it will prove true in practice in many places, particularly to help alleviate poverty, is questionable. It optimistically implies that foreign reformers will outlast and outsmart domestic opponents in a process that can take many years or will cultivate domestic partners who can sustain change in challenging contexts. It also represents a programmatic gamble on the ability of reformers to cultivate local political will. The consulting firm Management Systems International (MSI) recently undertook for USAID an explicitly achievement-oriented assessment of USAID's ROL programs.[43] In addition to describing some support in some countries for civil society and legal services for the poor, the study reports apparent progress with state institutions—the kind of results Hammergren refers to as "system changes [such as shifts from written to oral testimony in court cases] or first level behaviors number of bankruptcies filed and settled following the passage of a new law, reduction in time to judgment, etc.)."[44] Other changes are more a matter of outputs than outcomes—cross-border cooperation and training involving the U.S. and Mexican judiciaries, for example.[45]

Though the assessment represents a thorough effort to tackle a daunting task, various sources' analyses cast doubt on whether many of the beneficial changes it detects are truly significant or lasting. Prillaman sees a downward spiral in Latin American judicial reform, MSI's favorable findings about USAID's work in that region notwithstanding. Bohmer implicitly differs with MSI's conclusions concerning Argentina, criticizing the "many top-down approaches to legal reform" in that country's history, "which focus entirely on government institutions" but which have largely ignored the country's legal culture and the anti-reform incentives in those very institutions and the legal community.[46] And as described below, Blackton's perspective on the Egyptian judiciary and the impact of his work on a USAID-supported project in that country is much more critical than that of the MSI assessment. Finally, as Carothers suggests in generally commenting on USAID's ROL efforts, beneficial changes may pale in comparison with enduring realities: limited access to justice, vested interests devoted to the status quo, corruption, clientelistic appointments, etc.[47]

Carothers is not alone in this critique. Other observers imply or assert that the kind of impact ROL orthodoxy achieves may not address the fundamental problems plaguing many countries' legal systems. In one of the most in-depth scholarly studies of a given judiciary's operations—a scrutiny of the civil courts in the Indian state of Uttar Pradesh—Moog concludes that the "conventional explanations for the functioning of the district-level courts [too few jurists, insufficient funding, inadequate rules of court, overly complex legislation, excessive litigiousness] are largely unsatisfactory."[48] He points instead to a host of external and internal forces that constrain the courts' performance.

Kauffman similarly "challenge[s] the prominence given to the traditional 'long list' of obstacles to proper rule of law/judiciary performance in the literature and in practitioners' writings—such as the conventional focus on budgetary resource constraints, cumbersome procedures, process delays, caseload management, traditional training approaches, study tours, and the like."[49] He asserts that "there are forms of corruption (such as state capture) which rather than being a symptom of more fundamental weakness, can in themselves be the cause of a dysfunctional judiciary"[50] [emphasis in original]. The upshot of these analyses is that ROL orthodoxy's impact might reflect winning some battles but losing the war—or even perhaps fighting the wrong battles.Thus, what is seen as progress in terms of ROL orthodoxy does not automatically translate into more general advances for development. For instance, USAID boasts of its role in helping to increase judicial budgets in parts of Latin America. Yet an application of the analyses of Moog and Kauffman suggests that in at least some settings this is an inappropriate focus. The funds might be better devoted to other needs outside the legal field (such as education or health), within it (legal services for the poor), or issues that straddle legal and other fields (such as targeting the widespread problem of violence against women). The more general point is that working with the courts is not necessarily the most effective, efficient, or viable method of addressing the legal needs of the disadvantaged in ways that alleviate poverty or serve other development goals.

In addition, with the exception of support to legal aid and related services for the disadvantaged, the MSI-documented impact on the actual lives of the poor ranges from scattered to indiscernible. To be fair, as Hammergren correctly points out, "the impact [of law projects] on economic variables, whether of the growth or poverty type, is really hard to trace...We are not even terribly clear about how improvements in court performance will affect the poor or any other economic group."[51] And as the World Bank's Legal Vice Presidency notes, "the [law and justice] sector poses certain special problems for measurement, not the least of which are the lack of any consensus on what a well-functioning system looks like, uncertainties as to the extent of its impact on extra-sectoral goals, and the fact that a large part of its success ultimately comes down to what it deters (conflict, illegal behavior), not what it does."[52] These are valid points. But if "lack of consensus" on the nature of a well-functioning justice system and uncertainty of "its impact on extra-sectoral goals" (such as poverty alleviation) are the case, they are problems not just for measuring impact but for undertaking ROL orthodoxy at all. The presence of so much uncertainty weighs in favor of diversifying the international community's approaches to integrating law and development.

***Altar of Institutionalization.*** The rationale for ROL orthodoxy also has intellectual roots in a general emphasis on the roles of institutions in development. The general notion in the development literature is that institutions are so fundamental that they must be addressed by international actors for development to unfold.[53]

But there is a difference between how the concept of institutions is considered in development literature and how it is applied in development practice, at least in the legal field. North defines institutions as "the rules of the game in a society, or...the humanly devised constraints that shape human interaction...both formal constraints—such as rules that human beings devise—and informal constraints—such as conventions and codes of behavior."[54] He further distinguishes between institutions as "the underlying rules of the game" and organizations (legislatures, regulatory bodies, firms, universities, unions, etc.) that both influence and are influenced by institutions.[55] In ROL programs, however, the emphasis on institutions typically reflects how the term commonly is used—including how I use it here: institutions as organizations, with a particular focus on state institutions/organizations such as judiciaries. This is not to suggest that a divergence between development theory and practice is at play in ROL orthodoxy, hinging on a semantic distinction. But the way in which this matter plays out in the legal sphere merits attention. The programmatic focus of the dominant paradigm is on the judiciary and other state organizations, as well as laws as institutions. The result is that the paradigm places great faith in a narrow view of the legal field: worshipping at the altar of institutionalization, as it were.

In contrast, a full-fledged scrutiny of how the rules of the game affect the poor would consider the historical, cultural, social, and political factors that shape both the formal and informal manifestations of how the poor interact with the law and would take both formal and informal types of law into account. That analysis might in turn learn from and apply strategies that enable the poor to affect the rules of the game and how they potentially can do so. Formal laws and state organizations of course would play important parts in this analysis. But the view of how they operate—and whether and how they can be reformed—would only be part of the picture. Underlying factors that shape their operations and alternative strategies that do not wholly or mainly rely on state organizations would be taken into account.

An additional difficulty with the focus on state institutions is that it ignores the institutional flaws in the very international development agencies that maintain this focus.

As a USAID colleague remarked to me several years ago, "Given the way this institution works, I can't believe we're in the business of institutional development." Critics of the World Bank, some with experience working there, offer comments such as There's a big disconnect between World Bank operations and World Bank research," and "You get the sense that the left hand doesn't know what the right hand is doing at the World Bank."[56]

Of course, such problems are not confined to the development community: One can find insiders making analogous comments about the U.S. Congress, the Pentagon, many corporations, and a host of other entities. Furthermore, personnel at USAID, the World Bank, and other aid organizations can justifiably boast of organizational strengths and successes, despite institutional flaws. But it is ironic and perhaps a bit self-deluding to aim for sweeping reforms in developing countries' legal institutions when many funding agencies are themselves so resistant to change.

A final problem with the focus on state institutions is that it ignores the opportunity costs of pursuing alternative strategies, such as focusing directly on the poor as a means of improving justice delivery (with related impact on poverty alleviation and other goals). Where donors provide support, civil society can and does play a central role in such strategies. Under ROL orthodoxy, however, civil society is seen as an adjunct, at most, to state-oriented institutionalization: useful for building up constituencies for reform so that the "real work" of changing legal institutions can take place. The NGOs, community-based organizations (CBOs), informal institutions, and religious institutions can facilitate the delivery of justice is minimized. Similarly, the actual and potential roles of media and elements of the private sector are relegated to supplementing state-centered initiatives.

***Supposed Centrality of the Judiciary.*** A key assumption of ROL orthodoxy is that the judiciary is central to serving society's legal needs: Unless we fix the courts, many other legal reforms will fail. As the World Bank's Legal Vice Presidency puts it, The rule of law is built on the cornerstone of an efficient and effective judicial system."[57] Applying similar reasoning that many development organizations use in many countries, the Asian Development Bank asserts that "although a daunting task, Cambodia has no alternative other than to overhaul the current judicial system if it is to lay a strong foundation for the nation's future development."[58] These claims tie in with related assumptions that neither alternative roads to justice nor dysfunctional judiciaries are usable. This package of assumptions, however, is fatally flawed.

Even within the realm of formal legal systems, and assuming ROL's (unclear) causal link to development, there are many nonjudicial institutions and processes that affect economic progress.These include administrative law, national and local governments' legislation and legal decisions, and the many arrangements through which international trade and investment disputes are handled by forums outside developing countries.

Moreover, as a review for the Danish Agency for Development Assistance (Danida) of its judicial and related aid concludes, support for the formal legal system "does have important limitations and trade-offs: the majority of the population is often not in a position to access the formal legal system for various cultural, linguistic, financial or logistical reasons . . .Their access to justice largely depends on the functioning of informal systems, which have been neglected in terms of external support."[59] Although the report stops short of challenging Danida's attention to the formal system, it nevertheless finds "little connection between the justice, constitution and legislation assistance and the overriding poverty orientation of Danish assistance."[60]

## BEYOND RULE OF LAW ORTHODOXY 16

DFID concurs with the Danida evaluation's assertion about the limits of the formal system, estimating that "in many developing countries, traditional or customary legal systems account for 80 percent of total cases."[61] This clearly is not a precise calculation. But taken together with the many disputes and other legal matters handled by formal but ncn-judicial forums, one can reasonably conclude that perhaps 90 percent or more of the law-oriented problems involving the poor are handled outside the courts in much of the developing world. One could argue that judiciaries are nevertheless more important than these alternatives—an assertion that, to make a very long debate short, might be true in some respects and false in others.The point simply is to put the courts in perspective, particularly the perspective of the poor.

Interest in informal systems is slowly growing. DFID recently completed a multicountry study of the subject, which should soon be available online.There is a stirring of interest in the matter within the World Bank. Some donors are supporting NGO efforts to use and reform these mechanisms in countries such as Bangladesh.[62] But although informal systems are the main avenues through which the poor access justice (or injustice), such systems remain programmatic stepchildren to the judiciary and other official institutions.

Furthermore, as described below in the discussion of legal empowerment, the actual experience of the poor comprises numerous issues that as a matter of law or strategy should be handled outside the courts. Some issues involve informal systems, some formal but nonjudicial forums.

Even flawed judiciaries offer opportunities for the poor to address some issues in some countries. The very fact that a battered woman has a lawyer advising her, or even other community women backing her, can deter her husband from continuing to abuse her. Like most people in most disputes everywhere, he may have an avid desire to avoid courts. The likelihood that the courts are gender-biased does not spare him from the expenses involved and does not guarantee him a favorable outcome.

In addition, even where judicial operations need drastic improvement, experience indicates that public interest litigation can still score major victories. Such litigation is not the poor's first choice in most countries, nor even a viable choice in many, but this has far less to do with operational inadequacies than with the conservative orientations of the judges. The point is that a dysfunctional judiciary is not an automatic bar to securing justice for the poor, often outside the courts but sometimes even through them.

*Judicial Reform as an End in Itself.* Some advocates of court-centered programs might argue that a functional judiciary is necessary for a modern society.[63] The goal may not be poverty alleviation or even the rule of law, but improving judicial performance as an end in itself. Who could argue against the desirability of this?

This argument, however, bumps up against the need to set priorities. It would be one thing to pursue judicial reform in a world of unlimited resources. It is quite another matter to invest so heavily in the courts when there are many other legal options for serving the poor, particularly in view of the opportunity costs of excluding those options out of preference for judiciaries. The opportunity cost problem becomes all the more acute in view of the questionable track record of judicial assistance programs.

Moreover, the notion of such programs as ends in themselves conflicts with the explicit goal of many development institutions: poverty alleviation. Entering the World Bank lobby, one sees large, stirring words about its vision for a world free of poverty, not a world free of judicial delay.

***Underestimating the Obstacles, Overestimating the Potential.*** The faith in state institutions partly stems from donors' devotion to the notion that they can bring about society-wide impact despite the huge obstacles they face and the relatively limited resources they possess. In certain contexts the international community may be up to this challenge. But those situations are exceptions to the rule.

So it may be possible for a UN force of several thousand foreign police officers to stabilize Kosovo and train a new local police force, given that the United Nations was able to start with a clean slate (in the sense that it did not need to work with a preexisting institution and leadership) and administrative control over a population of less than two million—though the ultimate effectiveness of that effort remains to be seen. The typical development or transitional context, however, involves far larger polities, no administrative control by international agencies (though such control would not guarantee wise or successful programs by any means), and deeply ingrained forces dictating the operations of judiciaries, police, and other justice institutions. As Anderson notes, "Constitutionalism and the rule of law depend upon sustained political support."[64] Such support is lacking in many societies, not least among those persons responsible for upholding the rule of law.

Thus, in addition to depicting widespread corruption and favoritism, Blackton's summary of the Egyptian judiciary's proclivities paints a picture of a self-serving institutional culture in the developing country that receives the largest amount of U.S. aid, including substantial ROL assistance:

One area in which the [Supreme Judicial] Council is very active is in protecting the "family guilds" within the Egyptian judiciary...

The council is cautious in approving disciplinary actions against the "sons of counselors" and sympathetic to requests for multi-year leaves of absence and overseas secondments for these favored members of the judicial family...

Family influence and gratuities are significant elements in the assignment process, first at the Ministry where assignment lists are prepared and later amongst members of the Supreme Judicial Council where the log-rolling is intense and the final lists are approved...

The Ministry of Justice and the Judges Clubs are institutional mechanisms for accessing scarce government resources—apartments in Cairo, villas on the Mediterranean and the Red Sea, subsidized automobile loans, free medical care in Europe or America for a judge or a judge's family member.[65]

Half a world away, in the Philippines, Soliman similarly portrays an institutional culture whose undue influences similarly transcend widespread corruption:

A chief obstacle to judicial independence is the pervasive culture of personalism, and the repetitive cycle of debt-of-gratitude (*utang na loob*) that besets public service. Personalism refers to decision-making based on personal, kinship, familial or other ties (coming from the same province, ethnolinguistic group, sorority, fraternity or social club), rather than on the merits of the case, the evidence presented and the impersonal application of the law on the facts. Personalism is aggravated by perceived debts-of-gratitude, extended to persons who have helped the judge along his professional career...Personalism is further reinforced by feelings of guilt, shame or embarrassment (*hiya*) when the judge does not render a decision in favor of the person to whom he owes the debt-of-gratitude. Filipino social norms dictate that the proper behavior is to return the favor (pagbigyan) to persons to whom we owe such "debts."[66]

Where problems run so deep, reforms may themselves prove problematic. A UN Development Program (UNDP) paper finds reported corruption in the Indonesian court system "so pervasive that proposals have been put forward recently to dismiss the entire judiciary," with other justice sector institutions similarly infected.[67] Recent reform efforts have perpetuated or exacerbated the problem. Rather than improving its performance, a judicial independence law instead served to insulate the institution from accountability. And "the new commercial courts, which were intended to serve as a model in which cases are handled competently, expeditiously, transparently and with integrity are developing a reputation for delivering similar standards of justice as those elsewhere in the court system."[68]

Some donor personnel and agencies simply overlook such problems by virtue of viewing legal systems development in a purely technical, rather than a political, manner. They undertake superficial international exchanges, such as high-profile conferences of Supreme Court justices, whirlwind tours for top officials, and consultancies that involve boilerplate transfer of laws from industrialized societies to developing ones.

It would be grossly unfair, however, to lump all proponents of the dominant paradigm's programs into this category. Where they focus on putting in place basic procedures, training, and procurement of supplies, they understandably argue that this technical approach is necessitated by the reality that judiciaries must walk before they can run. This point is true as far as it goes but begs the question of whether these technical improvements put a dent in corruption, bias, and other undue influences, not to mention the opportunity costs of this course or the sustainability of technical improvements once foreign aid for them ends.

Other ROL orthodoxy proponents recognize the tremendous forces at play and correctly portray them in political and not just legal or technical terms. Yet they may still underestimate the power of those problems, ignore how they shape their organizational and individual partners, and overestimate their own capacities to analyze and overcome the obstacles. Proceeding with the best intentions, they nevertheless may skate along the surface of how a foreign society operates.

Soliman highlights this issue in pointing out that "the sources of judicial interference [in the Philippines]...may not be openly opposing the reform measures (in fact, nobody in his right mind would dare oppose these measures). It is just that these measures will be disregarded or slowly be implemented, to the point that it becomes meaningless."[69]

Many development practitioners can tell tales of misplaced faith in local partners who paid lip service to reform. My own experience includes work by my (then) office with Filipino judicial reformers subsequently identified with criminal conduct—in one case a supreme court justice was forced to resign and in another a trial judge was involved with covering up violent assaults by a relative (the son, in fact, of a former chief justice). In evaluating work with the Cambodian judiciary, I was told by a U.S.-based NGO of its great progress with courts in a particular province, only to have independent Western and Cambodian sources volunteer (without prompting) that those courts were particularly corrupt. Although technical progress can take place even in the face of undue influences, where such influences are widespread they tend to trump the value of the technical change.

Perhaps the most illuminating illustration of this point, however, comes from a different international field: drug control. For a good part of the late 1980s and early 1990s the U.S.



Government's efforts to staunch the flow of illegal drugs from Mexico relied considerably on that country's top officials. That confidence culminated in U.S. drug policy chief Barry McCaffrey praising Mexico's top anti-drug enforcement officer as "an honest man and a no-nonsense field commander."[70] The commander was arrested eight days later and subsequently charged with having protected a top drug lord. In such a high priority arena and with all of its intelligence resources at its disposal, the U.S. Drug Enforcement Agency could not detect the true nature of its hero. Operating with much less information and funding, what are the prospects for practitioners of ROL orthodoxy to know the real intents of the government officials who are their local partners? This is particularly challenging when the real issue is not whether such officials are corrupt—in many or most instances they are not—but whether they really are dedicated to reform. Although the same can be said of NGO personnel, it is often easier to observe their direct work with the disadvantaged than it is to assess high officials' dedication to reforms that constitute only a part of their jobs.

There are certainly numerous honest, sincere chief justices, attorneys general, and other justice sector officials across the globe. But in working with them, even those donors that acknowledge the shortcomings of an institution-centered approach still tend to underestimate the problem: The challenge is not just the institutional culture itself, but also the societal milieu from which the institution springs. Egyptian and Philippine judges frequently favor their relatives and others with special connections because that is what one does to be a good family or community member in Egypt and the Philippines. Personal probity or even sincere dedication on the part of a high official may not be sufficient to outlast or outwit influences that are societal, rather than organizational, in nature. Thus, strengthening the Indonesian judiciary's independence and organizing a new commercial court there do not reform that judiciary's injustices out of existence.

The tendency to underestimate the obstacles to institutional reform is mirrored by an inclination to overestimate the potential impact. The dominant paradigm promises the realization of the rule of law. Yet it is unclear how the multilateral development banks' business-promoting version of the paradigm can even theoretically bring about the equal treatment, dignity, and access for all that the World Bank's definition of ROL promises. Furthermore, even proponents of ROL orthodoxy grant that this is inevitably a slow, problem-plagued process.

Of perhaps even greater importance, there is often less than meets the eye in the nominal successes along the way. The adoption of a new law or new rules of court may be hailed as a great step forward, but the reality in many developing and transitional societies is that laws and rules are only rarely enforced. Training of judges might seem an important endeavor, unless of course most judges make little use of their new knowledge. Simply working with a national institution such as the judiciary can become confused with bringing about national changes in its operations or can trigger changes that do not necessarily benefit the poor. Thus, reforming a law or ostensibly revamping a judiciary offers the allure of national impact but in reality may affect few judges, cases, or citizens.

*Myths of Sustainability.* An important argument for investing in state legal institutions is that only such a course can offer sustainable development. The assumption is that, once reformed, the institutions will deliver improved services without continued donor input. The converse assumptions are that NGOs and other civil society groups do not merit ongoing development support because they are inherently unsustainable organizations or that they must generate funding themselves after a few years of donor financing.

The DFID Bangladesh (DFIDB) office accordingly illuminates a tension and assumption that many development agencies struggle with in many countries:

> ...a striking conclusion is that there are few DFIDB projects with government that are making a higher-level impact for poor people...Thus, DFIDB faces a dilemma; it can achieve a more direct impact on poor people in the short-term (possibly up to 2015) by working outside government, but for the long-term only sustained improvement in delivery of public services will reach the majority of the population. A balance needs to be struck between the short and long-term goals.[71]

At least as applied to the legal field, three development myths account for this understandable but questionable assumption about the nature of sustainable change. The first is that support for state legal institutions will yield self-sustaining reforms and enduring improvements in services. As already suggested, however, the underflow of societal forces may undo promising changes: If legal systems' operations are in fact more the effect than the cause of social conditions, many systems that experience temporary improvements may revert to form. In addition, the chief justices, ministers of justice, and other officials who lead or agree to reforms often come and go rather rapidly—ironically, more rapidly than the leaders of supposedly unsustainable NGOs. The dedication to reform sometimes resides in those officials, not their institutions.

Often, however, even that personal dedication is not present. Commenting on a USAID project's short-term cuts in delay in pilot courts in Egypt, consultant and former USAID official John Blackton asks:

> Will that hold up when we leave? Will our changes move from our court clusters to the nation as a whole? Have we brought about a genuine change in judicial culture—one in which reducing case delay is valued? I fear that the answer will, three years after, we are gone, be "no" to most if not all of my questions. The expat and Egyptian professionals organized within the construct of "the project" are the ersatz substitute for political will and a new judicial culture. We [the project team] are in fact, variables in the experiment. Our presence strongly impacts the results. Donors don't like to admit how much this is true, but in justice projects in settings like Egypt, I believe it is significantly so.[72]

This problem often manifests itself from the very outset of projects, with donor organizations and personnel, rather than those of recipient countries, initiating and driving ROL programming. It is not as though chief justices, ministers of justice, and their staffs typically analyze their legal systems' problems on their own and present resulting proposals to funding agencies. More frequently, the agencies initiate the dialogue, commission the consultants, and design the projects. Of course, donors often have access to the intellectual capital that can undertake these tasks. And recipient institutions' personnel certainly are consulted and in some cases become very engaged in the planning and implementation of projects. But to return to Blackton's point, the funding agencies often supply "the ersatz substitute for political will and a new judicial culture." The result is a lack of intellectual ownership among recipients.

Proponents of ROL orthodoxy sometimes acknowledge that short-term reforms may hinge on persons rather than institutions and that intellectual ownership is an issue, but they legitimately argue that legal systems development must be seen as a long-term process. It accordingly will take many years or even decades before it becomes clear whether and to what extent sustained impact transpires. Fair enough, but this argument exposes a second sustainability myth: the notion that government initiatives should always be seen as potentially sustainable and that civil society efforts should not. If state institutions merit such ongoing support, especially with highly uncertain outcomes, then why exclude civil society from the long-term mix?

In reality, legal services NGOs and other civil society groups can outlast the appointments of the personnel heading and staffing many government agencies and acquire a greater knowledge of their fields. Over the course of many years, such NGOs often develop track records that enable them to obtain funding from a range of donors. It is even conceivable that long-term societal changes could generate in-country resources for them in some countries, whether from their governments or private sources. With support from the Ford Foundation and other sources, over the past several years the Asia Foundation has pursued an initiative to encourage the growth of indigenous philanthropy in many Asian nations.

The third sustainability myth is that, such philanthropy-promoting efforts aside, legal services and related NGOs in many developing nations must have the potential to become wholly self-supporting if medium-term outside support is to be justified. In fact, NGOs engaged in challenging the status quo may always depend on foreign sources for funding in many parts of the developing world, just as equivalent groups depend on foundations and other outside sources in many far more affluent industrialized societies. It is questionable whether developing country NGOs should even seek government or private money in many contexts, in view of the strings and uncertainty that could come attached.

This does not mean that a given under should automatically commit itself to many years of support to a given NGO. But it should be open to the possibility of such ongoing assistance if the recipient shows sufficient promise and impact. It does mean that donors and other development agencies should move beyond repeatedly uttering the "NGOs must make themselves sustainable" mantra and take more responsibility for assisting worthwhile partner organizations to move toward sustainability. This can include providing support that expands the fund-raising and financial management capacities of civil society groups, as well as connecting such groups with industrialized society donors that otherwise would be logistically unable to support overseas development.[73] Yet another mechanism is self-sustaining endowments. Organizations such as the Ford Foundation, USAID and most recently the ADB have established such funds for selected high-impact organizations and important fields in certain countries.[74] The endowment approach merits further, broader consideration as a mechanism for ensuring ongoing funding of civil society efforts in the legal field.

We also need to rethink what we mean by sustainability. Rather than organizational sustainability, which biases funding toward often ineffective state institutions, a key consideration should be sustainability of impact. If a given legal services NGO serves enough people, or builds enough capacities for the poor to effectively assert their own rights, or affects enough laws—such impact is sufficient to justify past and future donor investment. It would be unfortunate for such an organization to cease operating down the line, but its existence would still be validated by the poverty it has helped alleviate and the justice it has helped secure. This patient approach has implicitly guided some of the better donor support for NGO legal services and has enabled recipient NGOs to build expertise and experience that translate into impact over time.

## Other Bases of the Paradigm

Given the problematic nature of this series of assumptions, it is important to ask why the dominant ROL paradigm has taken hold so strongly. Some reasons lie in the assumptions themselves, of course. Many individuals and organizations operating in this field manifest a sincere dedication to the paradigm because they believe in many or most of its premises. But it would be misleading to attribute ROL orthodoxy's predominance to these intellectual factors alone.

It is important to identify other influences, which are at least as important as the intellectual bases, to start to move beyond the paradigm.

*Rule of Lawyers.* ROL orthodoxy assumes the centrality of the judiciary in particular and other formal legal institutions (for example, ministries of justice, prosecutorial services, police) more generally because the main actors involved in rule of law aid are lawyers and judges. Unlike development professionals in some other fields, many Western ROL practitioners have little or no prior experience in developing and transitional societies before entering this arena through the legal door. They naturally see the problems and prospects for legal systems development in terms of their experience in their own countries, experience that typically features the courts and other forums through which they work with legal colleagues. The single greatest category of funding, then, focuses on assistance for judiciaries.

The upshot for the field is the "rule of lawyers." It carries with it the powerful tendency to minimize, usually not intentionally, the many other factors and actors that affect legal systems development and that can be brought to bear to improve it. Attorneys and judges are not blind to such considerations, but their perspectives and experience undercut giving non-lawyers and non-legal tools the full weight they deserve. This contributes to such phenomena as the fixation on courts and other institutions, and working with fellow lawyers and judges.

The rule of lawyers also overlooks the ways in which attorneys are sometimes part of the problem rather than part of the solution. Bar associations in some societies are self-serving guilds that effectively limit access to justice, or that work against social and economic equity. These associations may vocally advocate political freedoms and judicial independence, but be much less sensitive to the needs and priorities of the poor, particularly where those priorities challenge the interests of prosperous clients or the attorneys themselves.

Of course, we all tend to view the world through the lens of prior experience and professional orientation, so lawyers and judges are by no means unique in this regard. The impact, nevertheless, is that ROL orthodoxy is guided by a perspective that is either blind to the many influences and possibilities that lie beyond a narrow institutional perspective, or that can see such factors only dimly. Ironically but not coincidentally, some of the best people involved with funding agencies' law-oriented programs are non-lawyers. The Ford Foundation, for example, has used a number of such individuals as program officers engaged in its human rights and social justice work.

This is not to dismiss the roles of lawyers and judges, of course. They are crucial for an array of purposes pertaining to the poor, not least as part of legal empowerment mechanisms discussed below. They serve a vast array of other societal purposes. But the development community does, after all, prioritize poverty-alleviation, pro-poor programs, and community-driven and rights-based development to various degrees. This is not reflected in the programmatic rule of lawyers.

***Bureaucratic Inertia.*** Another influential factor fueling ROL orthodoxy is bureaucratic inertia. As with most institutions in most fields, initial programs, personnel, and perspectives can lead to similar subsequent initiatives, regardless of whether they are appropriate to new contexts (or were appropriate in the first place). Thus, USAID focused on judicial operations and other state legal processes in Latin America in the 1980s. Though initially driven by political forces swirling about controversial U.S. policies concerning Central America, USAID's law program gradually took on a life of its own.

The impact of the Latin American roots of USAIDs ROL program is instructive. The personnel who accumulated the early experience in this field were based in Latin America and accustomed to seeing the ROL through the lenses of judicial and state-centered operations. They have acquired considerable expertise in the process, but for some it has come at the expense of a broader perspective on law and development.

Of course, many funding institutions have taken similar approaches, without the legacy of this geographical focus. Even so, as an early and major actor in this field, USAID may have influenced them by virtue of its example.

More generally, institutional inertia may play a role even for the many organizations on which USAID has no influence. In many cases, other funding agencies commissioned lawyers and judges to offer advice and design programs as the agencies initially explored work in this field. The legacy of their initial rule of lawyers, then, was to set in place programs and personnel that continue to shape priorities and perspectives.

*Improper Incentives.* Though many development practitioners talk in terms of "getting the incentives right" in developing country governments and systems, an irony of ROL orthodoxy is that it is substantially a product of improper incentives in funding institutions. In some cases, career rewards are more closely linked to initiating programs—loans in the case of the multilateral banks—than whether the programs benefit the poor.

A related improper incentive, perhaps particularly at the banks, is that the dominant paradigm can easily consume large amounts of money and that this is considered a good thing. A colleague working with a problematic judiciary once described it to me as a "black hole" for funding. Though this was a complaint, the problem can also be an asset for donor personnel. Although criticism in some quarters of ROL orthodoxy's allegedly boilerplate approach may be overheated, the approach nevertheless involves a standard set of activities that make it easier to move money.

Some funding agencies also present their personnel with de facto "use it or lose it" requirements. That is, a given field office's or division's future resources hinge partly on whether it spends all of what it has been allocated during the fiscal year. Many activities supported by ROL orthodoxy—constructing court houses, buying computers, training judges, retaining consultants, and the like—can be funded in ways guaranteed to exhaust annual allocations. This creates an additional incentive to pursue this approach.

Political pressure also drives ROL programming. Particularly in the wake of wars or transitions from dictatorships to democracies, there are demands from high officials in donor governments to help new leaders turn around their nations' ineffective legal institutions. Those officials may evince little patience for sound programs that take proper account of constraints and opportunities. This typically translates into a "don't just stand there, do something" perspective, even in situations where, realistically, there is little to do.

***Structural Biases.*** Various structural biases built into aid organizations also push ROL assistance toward the dominant orthodoxy. Due to explicit mandates and governing structures, some organizations view national governments as their partners, rather than the poor. It is no coincidence, then, that some of the more effective multilateral agencies, such as the U.N. High Commissioner for Refugees and the U.N. Children's Fund (UNICEF), focus on serving particular populations, rather than governments.

The multilateral development banks labor under an additional, obvious structural burden: Recipient governments naturally require control over how their loans are spent. Most governments are much more prone to use these resources for state projects and personnel, rather than having them diverted to potentially troublesome civil society groups. In addition, policy parameters dictate that development banks sometimes can more easily fund capital projects or offer lower rates on loans for such projects.

In reality, the situation of the banks is a bit less rigid than their loan-making nature implies. They have access to grant funds, largely from bilateral donors, that can complement loans in a flexible manner. They also have some leeway in negotiating loans with recipient governments, not least because of many loans' heavily discounted nature and repayment terms. Whether they are prepared to use the grant funds and leeway to move beyond ROL orthodoxy is another matter, of course.

Another structural bias stems from constraints on taking a political approach to development work. The World Bank is supposed to focus on economic issues. It is prohibited from considering political factors in its policies and projects. The other multilateral banks are similarly restricted. In reality, as the staffs of these institutions acknowledge, their work is politically charged in countless ways. And over the past decade the World Bank and, to varying degrees, the other multilateral banks have begun to grapple explicitly with issues such as corruption and human rights that were previously taboo. But the economic focus nevertheless acts as a brake on confronting some of the most pervasive problems plaguing ROL.

Yet another structural shortcoming is the project approach, the way many development agencies plan how to spend their funds. Tremendous amounts of time and resources go into designing projects, often leaving too little flexibility to respond to new developments or to learn and apply lessons as the projects unfold. This is an issue that reaches far beyond the legal field, but it strongly resonates in this field. Once a project has started, it is very difficult to back away from work with chief justices or government ministers even if they fail to demonstrate the desired political will. Barring extreme circumstances, the funding organization is "locked in," both politically and financially.

A related bias stems from what might be called "the view from the hotel window." Particularly during project development, when the very nature of the project is decided, many agencies rely on visiting consultants rather than in-country staff. This can lead to a superficial analysis of what ails a legal system and what legal issues confront the disadvantaged. To put the point mildly, a society seen from a hotel is far different from one experienced every day.

As a consultant myself, I may be in the position of the person living in a glass house (or hotel) throwing stones at its windows. But the visiting consultant bias is exacerbated when taken together with the other influences that steer ROL work toward a state-centered approach. Because ROL orthodoxy is geared toward working with state institutions, the visitors' meetings with NGOs and representatives of disadvantaged populations (to the degree that such meetings take place at all) focus on how to fund such institutions, rather than whether to do so and what alternative initiatives might be possible. The typical judicial administration consultant, for example, does not go tromping through the boondocks to learn how the poor perceive the judiciary, what their lives are like, what legal problems they face, or how they handle those problems.

A fundamental structural barrier involves the sectoral walls that divide much development work. Even though development issues often transcend sectors such as irrigation, natural resources management, urban housing, education, and the like, there is relatively little cross-fertilization of ideas, not to mention integration of approaches. Again, this is not unique to the legal field but severely constrains integration of law and development.

***Lack of Applied Research.*** One final consideration merits mention because it is so crucial: In many organizations that support law-oriented work, there often is a reluctance to support research that will scrutinize whether and how such work is doing any good or that will otherwise inform its efforts.[75] It is ironic, in fact, that some organizations that fund extensive research on legal systems or human rights conduct virtually none on the impact of their own law-oriented programs. It can be far more rewarding to report anecdotal progress to the higher levels of an institutional hierarchy than it is to undertake the kinds of in-depth quantitative and qualitative inquiries that might contribute to learning and impact, but that also might yield negative results. This is not confined to ROL orthodoxy, but it is most striking in view of the resources it consumes.

In fairness, as discussed above, constructing studies that would probe the successes, failures, and lessons of ROL initiatives is no easy task. And as the aforementioned divisions within the World Bank demonstrate, there is no guarantee that applied research will actually inform programs. Until such research is valued as contributing to progress even if it reveals problems, law-oriented work will lag behind other development fields in terms of both sophistication and impact.

## LEGAL EMPOWERMENT: AN ALTERNATIVE APPROACH

### The Nature of Legal Empowerment

Legal empowerment is the use of legal services and related development activities to increase disadvantaged populations' control over their lives. It is consistent with a more general concept used by the World Bank: "In its broadest sense, empowerment is the expansion of freedom of choice and action."[76] The distinguishing feature of legal empowerment is that it involves the use of any of a diverse array of legal services for the poor to help advance those freedoms. At the same time, this legal work is often only a part (and not necessarily the most important part) of an integrated strategy that features other development activities—group formation, literacy training, or livelihood development, for instance.

In contrast with ROL orthodoxy, a strategy of fostering legal empowerment typically involves:

- An emphasis on strengthening the roles, capacities, and power of the disadvantaged and civil society.
- The selection of issues and strategies flowing from the evolving needs and preferences of the poor, rather than starting with a predetermined, top-down focus on judiciaries or other state institutions.
- Attention to administrative agencies, local governments, informal justice systems, media, community organizing, group formation, or other processes and institutions that can be used to advance

the poor's rights and well-being, rather than a focus on a narrowly defined justice sector.

- Civil society partnership with the state where there is genuine openness to reform on the part of governments, agencies, or state personnel, and pressure on the state where that presents an effective alternative for the disadvantaged.
- Great attention to domestic ideas and initiatives, or experience from other developing countries, rather than Western imports.

*Legal Services.* As defined here, legal services for the poor include:

- counseling, mediation, negotiation, and other forms of non-judicial representation;
- litigation, both on an individual basis and through public interest lawsuits designed to affect policies, effect precedents, or otherwise benefit large numbers of people;
- enhancing people's legal knowledge and skills through training, media, public education, advice, and other mechanisms;
- development of services by paralegals (lawpersons, often drawn from the groups they serve, who receive specialized legal training and who provide various forms of legal education, advice, and assistance to the disadvantaged); and
- advocating, advising on, and building the poor's capacities regarding legal, regulatory, and policy reform.

In many country contexts, litigation is only one of numerous options used by legal services organizations, and often constitutes a course of last resort. As discussed above, most legal issues affecting the poor are handled not by judiciaries but by administrative law, local governments, alternative dispute resolution, and informal processes. And even where the courts are an option, the poor often prefer these alternatives because they are far more accessible (both geographically and financially) and comprehensible.

***Related Activities.*** The "related activities" in legal empowerment's definition are any that complement legal services, but which themselves are not inherently law-oriented in nature. They include community organizing, group formation, political mobilization, and use of media. They may also involve development-oriented endeavors, such as livelihood development, micro-credit provision, literacy training, reproductive health services, and natural resources management.

Legal services can in and of themselves constitute and produce legal empowerment, but experience indicates that greater impact frequently flows when they are integrated with related activities. Some links may be indirect, implicit, or initially unplanned, as in the case of a group formed for another purpose (such as micro-credit) that later makes use of legal services.

***A Process and a Goal.*** Legal empowerment is both a process and a goal. As a process, it involves activities aimed at increasing disadvantaged populations' control over their lives. As a goal, legal empowerment refers to their actual achievement of that control. Thus, the process can take place even if the goal has yet to be achieved.

***Nexus with Poverty Alleviation and Other Goals.*** Legal empowerment ultimately is about poverty alleviation, both in the narrow and broader meanings of the term.

It contributes to poverty alleviation, narrowly defined, by improving material standards of living and accordingly addressing what is often called "income poverty." Thus, women may be less poor and have more control over their lives if they gain the right to work (and resulting employment) or a fair share of inheritances. The same applies to farmers and urban populations who respectively obtain land ownership and secure housing.

UNDP and most of the development community also view poverty alleviation more broadly, however, often using the term human poverty and reflecting the fact that the poor "often define their own lot not so much in terms of 'lack of money' as an absence of empowerment."[77] Poverty alleviation accordingly includes increasing the capacities (such as legal knowledge and skills), participation, opportunities, and, most fundamentally, power of the poor concerning actions and decisions that affect their lives. Women are less poor and have more control to the extent that they affect government or family decisions, whether effecting gender equity or halting domestic violence. Minority groups similarly may benefit where their cultures are respected or they influence majority perspectives and policies. Legal empowerment helps achieve those goals.

Legal empowerment should also be viewed in the context of evolving thinking that illuminates how empowerment, human rights, freedom, development, and poverty alleviation blend in practice: Reaching one such goal often equals achieving another. In Development as Freedom, Sen addresses the processes through which people assume increasing control over their lives.[78] UNDP has similarly linked human development, human rights, and seven essential freedoms.[79] The World Bank advocates "facilitating empowerment" as a key means of attacking poverty.[80] Thus the notion of control contained in the definition of legal empowerment is equivalent to both freedom and power for the poor.

A number of donors have in effect endorsed the kind of cross-sectoral integration represented by legal empowerment, though carrying it out in practice has been more problematic. A USAID study found that the linkages of its democracy and governance sector (which includes law programs) "with other sectors are an emerging development success story."[81] DFID policy guidance highlights how its justice sector work can pursue entry points through public health, rural livelihood, or urban development projects.[82]

The potential benefits of legal empowerment work are implied in various academic studies that point to the importance of civil society capacity building, organization, or political influence in improving the lives of the disadvantaged.[83] Other research identifies vibrant NGOs' roles in successful development efforts, especially when they are able to engage or collaborate with government.[84] By building the poor's legal capacities, organization, and NGO links, legal empowerment may be particularly promising in connection with views of community-driven development articulated by Gupta et al.[85] For instance, it can help forge useful links with higher level government officials in situations where their local subordinates serve local vested interests. This can enhance project monitoring, accountability, and performance and of course serve broader development goals.

*Central Role of Civil Society.* Civil society usually plays a central role in legal empowerment for a diversity of reasons. This is reflected in both the aforementioned research and the fact that the most successful and creative legal services for the poor across the globe generally are carried out by NGOs, often in partnership with CBOs, or occasionally by law school programs that effectively function as NGOs.[86] This does not absolutely preclude a central role for the state: Sufficiently motivated government units also can carry out legal empowerment programs. However, civil society groups typically demonstrate more dedication, flexibility, and creativity than state institutions and personnel. Despite the best intentions of many such personnel, various actors and factors, not least their co-workers, may block them from doing their jobs properly. Related considerations that frustrate government responsiveness to the poor's legal and other needs include inappropriate resource allocation, excessive bureaucracy, corruption, patronage, gender bias, and general resistance to change.

My aim here is not to replace ROL orthodoxy with a similarly rigid civil society paradigm that naively glorifies NGOs as a panacea for poverty or presents them as universally altruistic and honest. It is crucial for donors to separate the wheat from the chaff in supporting civil society. Where civil society is weak, it is important to put in place long-term programs that help build it. Furthermore, legal empowerment is often about good governance; state institutions are extremely relevant. Legal empowerment can involve NGOs in building the capacities of state institutions and their personnel, through training and other devices.

What NGOs and their partner populations can do far more effectively than donors, simply by virtue of civil society efforts to extract cooperation from state institutions, is identify government agencies and personnel who manifest dedication, working with them and around their reform-resistant colleagues. In this way, civil society acts as a supportive force for cooperative elements in the state and as a countervailing force against anti-reform elements. Legal empowerment catalyzes this progress in the many contexts where legal knowledge and action are important parts of reformist strategies.

Again, this certainly is not to suggest that all development NGOs are effective, competent, and dedicated. Some are far more interested in developing their own resources than in helping the populations they purportedly serve. Others are so small as to limit their effectiveness (though we should not underestimate the ability of modestly staffed legal services NGOs to generate ripple effects of impact through paralegal development, working in partnership with other civil society elements, and contributing to policy and law reform advocacy coalitions). But where these constraints apply, they constitute arguments for such steps as involving responsible international NGOs, expanding the pool of persons who could sincerely engage in legal empowerment work (through law school programs, for example), and gradually building up civil society reach and capacities.

In some wartorn, politically oppressed, or particularly impoverished societies, the presence, power, and capacities of NGOs that could engage in legal empowerment are limited. One would not expect assertive advocacy of women's rights, for instance, in areas controlled by many Afghan warlords. How development agencies might cautiously support legal empowerment under such circumstances is a matter to which I will return in this paper. For now, suffice to say that the same obstacles constricting the work of legal services NGOs in problematic contexts similarly limit the prospects for building effective judiciaries and other legal institutions. Precluding support for the former while pushing ahead with the latter is a lopsided approach to justice and development.

***Nexus with a Rights-Based Approach to Development.*** Among its other applications, legal empowerment should be seen as a strategy for implementing a rights-based approach to development. As the Office of the High Commissioner for Human Rights (OHCHR) has noted, "There is no single, universally agreed rights-based approach, although there may be an emerging consensus on the basic constituent elements."[87] The OHCHR expands on this to suggest that "while a State is primarily responsible for realizing the human rights of the people living within its jurisdiction, other States and non-State actors are also obliged to contribute to, or at the very least not to violate, human rights."[88] It also highlights empowerment, participation, international human rights' universality, and numerous other concepts and activities as key elements of the approach.

In a crucial way, legal empowerment is a rights-based approach: It uses legal services to help the poor learn, act on, and enforce their rights in pursuit of development's poverty-alleviating goal. And as indicated above, the realization of empowerment, freedom, and poverty alleviation typically equals enforcement of various human rights.

Yet as I emphasized earlier in this paper, legal empowerment is about power and freedom even more than it is about law. True, in practice the goal of advancing the rights of the poor often is one and the same as alleviating their poverty. And much activity toward this end is rights-based in nature: teaching them relevant laws; building their capacities to use those laws themselves; providing legal representation where necessary; drawing on such rights as freedom of speech, assembly, and association. But legal empowerment also often involves related development activities such as community organizing, group formation, livelihood development, and literacy training. Thus, legal empowerment uses various mechanisms, many rights-based but some not, as means toward the end of making human rights a reality for the poor.

**Impact and Activities**

An expanding array of studies document legal empowerment's impact in both qualitative and quantitative terms. Most of that impact falls under the broad rubric of poverty alleviation. But as noted above, in many instances it also can be framed in other general terms (such as justice, human rights, freedom, and, of course, empowerment) or more specific goals (such as improved governance, gender equity, or environmental protection).

***Multi-country Documentation of Impact.*** In recent years, a few international studies have illuminated legal empowerment's manifold approaches and types of impact. A seven-nation, year-long examination of legal empowerment, conducted by the Asia Foundation for the Asian Development Bank, concludes that this work "helps to advance good governance and to reduce poverty in both substantial and subtle ways."[89] The documented benefits range from the constitutional and consumer protection reforms to implementation of Pakistani women's voting rights and access to credit.

A multi-country review for the World Bank describes the poverty-alleviating impact of legal services NGOs and, by implication, of legal empowerment.[90] It highlights, inter alia, how such NGOs help enforce social and economic rights, facilitate the poor's engagement with local governance, assist women to reform laws that bar them from participating in development, and promote recovery in post conflict countries.

Finally, the Ford Foundation's eighteen-month review of legal services and related work by its grantees across the globe finds considerable positive impact on equitable and sustainable development, as well as on human rights, civic participation, and government accountability.[91] The resulting book describes the impact of university-based legal aid clinics, paralegals, public interest litigation, and law-related research, even in China, Eastern Europe, and other areas where civil society is relatively weak.

**National Impact.** The picture I so far have sketched of legal empowerment mainly depicts community-oriented work, but legal empowerment can build on that work to have national impact (as well as impact on the state and province level, which in some countries is where important policy and legal decisions are made). The Ford Foundation, World Bank, and Asia Foundation/ADB reports, as well as other sources, document that impact to various degrees, describing numerous instances in which legal empowerment has helped generate such macrolevel reform.

For example, the approximately two dozen Philippine legal services NGOs collectively known as Alternative Law Groups (ALGs) have contributed to scores of national regulations and laws concerning agrarian reform, violence against women, indigenous peoples' rights, environmental protection, and a host of other issues.[92] Arguably, they have played roles in the bulk of such pro-poor reforms over the past decade, providing legal expertise and other assistance for coalitions of NGOs, national federations of poor people's organizations, and (sometimes) religious groups.

The ALGs derive their expertise and credibility from working on a grassroots level, where they make the most of existing laws while learning what reforms might make sense and, most crucially, what reforms the disadvantaged might want. They heavily engage in paralegal development, community training, and advocacy. Typically partnering with CBOs—and strengthening those groups' internal cohesiveness in the process—ALGs help farmers to avail themselves of land reform; fishing associations to guard their waters against outsiders' environmentally destructive practices that cut into their catch; community associations to understand and participate in local budgeting and governance; and other disadvantaged groups to act on local needs and priorities. So much of their work involves helping the disadvantaged interact with local elected and administrative officials that it is appropriate to think of the ALGs in terms of governance as well as law.

The ALGs largely have not worked through the Philippine courts for several reasons: judicial conservatism and corruption; the suitability of administrative, legislative, and other non-court mechanisms to address partner populations' needs; and the fact that these populations are more legally self-sufficient when non-court approaches are used.

Nevertheless, legal empowerment strategies can effectively use the Public Interest Litigation (PIL) in those circumstances where there are prospects of winning and implementing favorable decisions, where it does not exclude the disadvantaged from decision making, and where its use does not preclude complementary approaches. This approach can be found in South Africa, where PIL has built on a base of community and political activism. This has yielded a string of landmark court victories stretching over more than two decades, both vindicating South Africans' rights and increasing their control over their lives.

Under apartheid, the Legal Resources Centre (LRC), the university-based Centre for Applied Legal Studies (CALS), and their allies used PIL to undermine restrictions on blacks' residence and travel rights, abuse of prisoners in detention, and the state policy of establishing black "homelands" in resource-poor parts of the country. In recent years, newer legal services NGOs have joined with LRC and CALS to have significant impact on housing, land, and health rights and a host of other issues. Similarly oriented NGOs in neighboring countries, such as Namibia's Legal Assistance Centre, have also had notable success in this vein.

It is important to emphasize, however, the degree to which public interest litigation draws on and works with community concerns, not least in the identification of clients and cases. As explained by the head of LRC's Constitutional Litigation Unit:

We work closely with community advice offices, which are sometimes an important focus for community organization, public education and advocacy.

Our clients are often a community—for example in land restitution claims or a large eviction case.

We work in partnership with other NGOs which themselves are involved in supporting community organization—most classically [under Apartheid], when we supported communities resisting forced removal from their land, we worked very closely with...Black Sash [an NGO that provides grassroots paralegal assistance and training], which used community workers and field workers.

We represent organizations which are themselves the focus for a social movement—for example, the Treatment Action Campaign, which is mobilizing and leading the campaign for the provision of anti-retroviral drugs to prevent transmission of HIV, and to treat HIV/AIDS.[93]

Though activist, sophisticated civil society certainly facilitates both grassroots and national legal empowerment initiatives—witness South Africa and the Philippines—legal empowerment can have national impact even in less conducive settings. The Sustainable Use of Biological Resources Project (SUBIR) in Ecuador, undertaken by the international NGO CARE in collaboration with local Afro-Ecuadorian groups in the remote northwest part of the country, has generated national reforms and local benefits. The government banned division of communal land into individual lots in response to these groups' identifying such changes as threatening their identity and way of life. The communities also successfully lobbied for Afro-Ecuadorian recognition in the national constitution, including protection for their collective rights as indigenous peoples.[94]

As with the Philippines and South Africa, the national impact of this legal empowerment initiative in Ecuador has built on a base of localized work and impact. These community-level results include:

- The paralegals have formed, and themselves joined, higher level organizations focused on conflict management, land titling, and community advisory services.

- Fifty communities have obtained legal status, a prerequisite to formal recognition of property rights.
- Some three dozen communities have secured title to approximately 50,000 hectares of their traditional lands.[95]

In a far different context, Senegal, UNICEF provided financial and communications support that helped local NGOs and village women mobilize against Female Genital Mutilation (FGM). The efforts facilitated the women learning about both their rights and the health implications of FGM. The result was the parliament's adoption of legislation banning the practice.[96]

Once again, the national reform was linked to local mobilization, in this case:

> ...teaching women first about their human rights, followed by other modules related to problem solving, health and hygiene...Although the project had originally targeted 30 villages...project organizers, facilitators and participants succeeded in expanding its reach. In November 1999 approximately 80,000 people from 105 villages participated in a ceremony during which they issued a public declaration ending the practice..."[97]

To return to a general point about legal empowerment, even where foreign initiative has been involved in these cases, it seems to respond to local needs and priorities. In contrast, whatever the justifications for most ROL orthodoxy endeavors, it would not seem that the poor would see better courthouses or judicial administration as issues to rally around.

The Ecuador and Senegal experiences indicate that where local civil society requires assistance, international organizations can play important facilitating roles regarding legal empowerment. In the end, this work must respond to community priorities, perhaps even more so when the implications are national rather than local. And preferably, the only foreign support that is needed is financial. But as with other development initiatives, there is room for other assistance (such as capacity building) where necessary.

At the same time, it is important not to become too enthralled with national impact, for the reasons suggested above in the critique of ROL orthodoxy: Changes in laws and policies mean little to the poor if they are not enforced, and enforcement is the exception rather than the rule in most developing countries. Both the Ford Foundation and Asia Foundation/ADB studies emphasize implementation of reform and not simply reform per se for this reason. A value of legal empowerment is that it can constitute a feedback loop, through which grassroots experience feeds legal and regulatory change, which further grassroots work in turn converts from reform on paper to reform in practice.

**Quantitative Research Indicating Impact**

With the caveat about national impact in mind, it is useful to turn to survey research, sometimes complemented by focus groups and other mechanisms, that documents legal empowerment's community-level results. A World Bank assessment of an NGO legal services program it supported for poor women in Ecuador found, inter alia, that as compared to demographically similar non-client populations, clients experienced significantly less domestic violence, higher rates of child support payments, and enhanced self-esteem.[98] These results have powerful, positive implications for poor women and children. For instance, above and beyond its immediate damage, the poverty-exacerbating impact of violence against women has been well documented by the World Bank and other sources.[99] Reducing the violence yields numerous benefits.

The Asia Foundation/ADB study similarly used quantitative inquiries in two of the seven countries it covered, with similarly favorable results. Survey research, focus groups, and interviews with government officials in the Philippines all indicated that farmers who received NGO capacity-building and related legal services—from Kaisahan, one of the aforementioned ALGs—brought about more successful implementation of a government agrarian reform program than did farmers who did not receive such services. The research also suggested follow-on impact, in terms of greater productivity, income, farm investment, and housing quality among those recipients of legal services.[100]

In Bangladesh, the Asia Foundation/ADB study determined that two broad-based NGOs that integrate legal services with mainstream development work achieved manifold poverty-alleviating impact. Based on comparisons between their member populations and demographically similar control groups, these results included: restraining the widespread but illegal practice of dowry;[101] successful citizen participation in joint actions and in influencing local government decisions; fostering positive community attitudes toward women's rights and participation in governance; use by the poor of government-managed lands that local elites otherwise seize; and dramatically less reliance on those elites for dispute resolution. The same research found that a third NGO, a legal services group that specializes in community-level mediation, achieved modest impact in some of these regards and an even greater impact on reducing elite dominance of dispute resolution.[102]

Finally, quantitative research on a USAID-funded Women's Empowerment Program in Nepal similarly suggests the value of integrating legal and socio-economic development work. The program combined literacy classes, arithmetic education, micro-enterprise development and training, micro-credit access, non-formal legal education, and advocacy-oriented group strengthening for 100,000 women. An impact study found that women involved with this project benefited in several ways when compared to control populations. They initiated eight times as many actions for "social change" (such as community development and health projects, and campaigns against domestic violence, alcohol, and gambling by men), participated 30 percent more in family and independent income allocation decisions, and better understood the importance of keeping their daughters in school.[103] A subsequent review concluded that literacy was a key element in the women's empowerment but reaffirmed the value of integrating legal and quasilegal (advocacy-oriented) components with the literacy training and other mainstream development activities.[104]

The findings of these various studies should be approached with some caution, because the methodologies may well benefit from refinement in the future. These inquiries, therefore, should be seen as modest initial forays into issues that merit far more scrutiny. Still, the results suggest the possibility of a powerful impact that affects poverty more directly and cost-effectively than does the dominant ROL paradigm. Those results also indicate that legal empowerment holds great potential for mainstream socioeconomic development efforts.

***Paralegal Development as a Multifaceted Resource.*** Though this paper cannot detail the many forms that legal empowerment takes, paralegal development merits special mention because it transcends many societies and sectors. As noted above, paralegals are laypersons, often drawn from the groups they serve, who receive specialized legal training and who provide various forms of legal education, advice, and assistance to the disadvantaged. Their education also includes learning through experience, often by soliciting advice from NGO lawyers or other NGO personnel (themselves paralegals) as concrete issues arise. Perhaps, then, the notion of paralegal training should give way to one of "ongoing paralegal development," including but not limited to training.

Depending on their level of sophistication and the needs of the populations they help, paralegal activities may range from providing basic information and advice on the one hand to representation in administrative processes and assisting litigation on the other. The training similarly is pitched to the paralegals' sophistication and levels of prior education.

Toward the more basic end of the paralegal skills

spectrum, then, in India, the Karnataka Women's Legal Education Program:

> mainly works through what are known as sanghas (collectives) to provide women with paralegal training. A sangha, typically composed of twenty to twenty-five community members, often is formed by a small local NGO in order to help it address livelihood, family planning, or credit needs. [The Program] conducts paralegal workshops for both selected sangha members and NGO personnel.

A fundamental feature of sangha training in India is the emphasis on attitudinal change. Given the deeply ingrained feelings of inferiority that the culture inculcates in both dalits (untouchables) and women, NGOs seek to broaden their perspectives. [The Program] does this, in part, by emphasizing gender considerations such as the value of women's reproductive and household work.[105]

Drawing on this legal training and attitudinal change, the women report that they are able to band together against domestic violence in their communities. Armed with basic knowledge of minimum wage laws, they also negotiate better farm wages from local landlords—not necessarily as high as legally required, but better than what they previously were paid.

At the more sophisticated end of the spectrum, South Africa's Black Sash Trust, an NGO, uses professional paralegals to assist citizens with a diversity of problems, such as obtaining government benefits to which they are legally entitled and detecting illegal conduct by government personnel. It also trains volunteer, community-based paralegals. Black Sash builds on both kinds of experience to pursue policy advocacy and press for government accountability on national and state levels, often in partnership with other groups. Its work contributes, for example, to public interest litigation launched by LRC.

A recent review of Kenyan access to justice projects supported by DFID summarizes three key elements of how paralegal operations further the empowerment of disadvantaged individuals and groups in Kenya:

> Paralegal Networks are an important component of community empowerment. They are unique in the [Access to Justice] Sector in that they seek to achieve the objective through setting up a local resource-base of knowledge and seek to facilitate action by local communities to resolve their own problems in a sustainable manner. The focus in this assessment is on three main categories of paralegal work...

[1] Paralegal workers are playing an important and relevant role in the civic education process, especially in relation to promoting rights awareness...

[2] For rights to be meaningful and for people to adhere to and to trust in the rule of law, the ordinary person must have access to the formal legal system. In the context of the communities within which the paralegals operate, however, the informal legal system (those run by the chiefs and other administrators and the elders and other community-based leaders and informal group mechanisms) are just as important as the formal ones in terms of addressing day-to-day issues...

[3] The empowering influence of rights awareness is a catalyst for social organization and community-driven development. The activist function recognizes that legal rights...can often [best] be achieved working outside of the [formal, narrowly defined legal system] and particularly through articulation of rights using advocacy and lobbying in an activist manner. The point is that the legal system itself can sometimes work against the best resolution of a particular problem.[106]

One could quibble with that final point, by positing a broad definition of the legal system, embracing the impact of advocacy and lobbying on rights and government decision making. Regardless, the substance of the insight remains the same: paralegal efforts (and other activism) sometimes achieve the most when they transcend conventional confines of legal systems and legal work.

Although on initial reflection it might seem that the circumstances of prisoners militates against legal empowerment—they hardly can benefit in the ways described by the DFID Kenya review and by definition they do not control their circumstances—experience indicates that paralegal development can help even this kind of population.

More specifically, in Malawi, a Paralegal Advisory Service (PAS) organized by Penal Reform International (PRI), four national NGOs, and the Malawi Prison Service operates in the country's four main prisons, where 75 percent of the country's 8,500 inmates reside. Providing basic legal information, advice, and assistance to the prisoners, PAS particularly focuses on:

...remand prisoners who have overstayed or are being held unlawfully or inappropriately. Priority is given to vulnerable groups (women, women with babies, young people in conflict with the law, foreign nationals, the mentally and terminally ill, and the elderly). Paralegals assist prisoners in filling out bail application forms and then lodge them with the relevant court, and advise convicted prisoners who wish to appeal against their sentence...

In 2002 an independent evaluation report found that prisoners had become more sophisticated in their understanding of the law and court procedure. In addition, the PAS facilitated the release of over 1000 prisoners, whether through bail, discontinuance or discharge...

According to the evaluation report...since they do not seek to find fault with individual agencies in the system, but to assist the system as a whole to function better, [the paralegals] are valued by the police, courts and prisons.[107]

The project assumes greater salience, given that inadequacies in many criminal justice systems cause innocent individuals to be imprisoned or guilty persons to be jailed longer than is legally warranted. The paralegal services become all the more valuable in view of these realities.

Of course, not all paralegals can achieve the array of results described here. Their effectiveness often hinges on their levels of education, the degrees to which their communities are organized, the extent to which government is responsive, and the overall political milieu within which they operate. But even modest initial achievements can set the stage for more dramatic impact down the line, as conditions and capacities develop.

***Integration and Mainstreaming.*** Legal empowerment often operates best when it integrates various activities so that the whole is greater than the sum of the parts. This takes place in two ways. The first involves the integration of different kinds of legal services, so that public education, community training, paralegal development, negotiation, mediation, legal advice, litigation, and law reform reinforce one another.

For instance, paralegals engaged in negotiation or mediation can call on lawyers to take cases to court as a last resort; litigation is not usually used but increases the negotiating power of the parties being assisted by the paralegals. Even where a judicial system is terribly flawed, the possibility of going to court can alleviate the power imbalances that usually tip against women and the poor.

The other type of integration takes place where legal services blend with group formation, community organizing, and other activities pursued under the rubric of "mainstream" socio-economic development fields—for example, rural development, public health, reproductive health, housing, natural resources—and address the goals and concerns of those fields. Most of the above illustrations involve such mainstreaming. The work of the Philippines ALGs, for example, is sometimes called "development lawyering" or "developmental legal services" for this reason.

But it is not only legal services NGOs that take the lead in this work. Other NGOs conduct legal empowerment work, sometimes in combination with legal services groups but also on their own. Banchte Shekha, a women's movement based in rural Bangladesh, has improved its members' capacities and well-being through a combination of literacy training, rights education, livelihood development, consciousness raising, organizing, and alternative dispute resolution (ADR). By building on all of these other activities, the Banchte Shekha ADR—a reformed version of a traditional dispute resolution process called shalish—both addresses mistreatment of women and ameliorates the power imbalances that often tilt ADR against them. The Asia Foundation/ADB survey research cited above documents the NGO's positive impact on dowry, women's status, and other issues.

A regrettably short-lived, USAID-supported initiative in the 1990s further illustrated the value of integrating law and mainstream development, in this instance legal and family planning services. Communities whose members were already familiar with reproductive health NGOs readily accepted the integrated programs. In introducing legal services, those NGOs drew on the goodwill established through many years of contact with the communities. An evaluation of the project confirmed the mutually beneficial relationship of the two kinds of work.[108]

One of the more significant forms of mainstreaming takes place where legal services facilitate agrarian reform and other land tenure improvements for the disadvantaged (for example, helping women with land claims stemming from divorce or inheritance). As the aforementioned Asia Foundation/ADB study demonstrates, NGO lawyers and paralegals can contribute to the success of agrarian reform programs. The Rural Development Institute (RDI) similarly documents the positive contribution of legal services to such programs.[109] It also highlights the roles civil society can play more generally, urging aid donors to "provide technical assistance and financial support to indigenous non-governmental organizations, labor organizations, and other broad-based groups that are able to conduct essential grassroots education and organizing on the land reform issue."[110] The manifold benefits of agrarian reform include poverty-alleviating increases in crop production, nutritional welfare, and incomes; ripple effects on economic growth; and contributions to democratic development and stability.[111]

***Law Students: Expanding Legal Empowerment's Pool of Attorneys.*** Although this paper has discussed certain respects in which lawyers play supportive rather than leading roles regarding legal empowerment, they of course are essential for a number of activities that strengthen disadvantaged populations' control over their lives. The best way to engage attorneys in this kind of work is to expose them to such activities and perspectives while they are in law school, through clinical legal education and related activities.[112] Beyond expanding legal services to the poor, this approach expands the students' perspectives, experience, and contacts in ways that enable many to work with the disadvantaged over the long haul.

In South Africa, the University of Natal-Durban's Campus Law Clinic, which operates much like an NGO, tackles many cases and issues that represent the interests of groups rather than individuals. Through both classroom instruction and actual practice, it familiarizes students with legal issues outside the ambit of the traditional curriculum.

Support by the Open Society Institute, the Ford Foundation, and USAID for clinical legal education in Eastern Europe and the former Soviet Union appears to be contributing to the growth of public interest law in those transitional societies. In Poland and some other countries, this includes building up a nucleus of future attorneys dedicated to progressive legal practice.

The Philippines may be particularly noteworthy because many of the attorneys leading and staffing the ALGs first received exposure to development work while in law school. The Ateneo Human Rights Center, an NGO based at a leading law school, has been particularly instrumental in this regard. But other law schools' programs, as well as ALGs' paid positions and internships for law students, have also contributed to sustaining this integration of development and law.

Coincidentally, the University of Dhaka Faculty of Law is now running a similar program for leading law students from across Bangladesh, immersing them in field research that exposes them to the lives and legal needs of disadvantaged populations. A number of alumni of this effort, and of a clinical legal education program that provides brief placements with NGOs, have gone on to staff legal services groups after graduation.

Finally, the integration of law and development in law schools is also taking hold in some programs in Latin America. As the Dean of Argentina's University of Palermo Law School notes, "the economic crisis in Argentina put us in a new situation where we could not just do public interest litigation, for we could not assume that the bankrupt state could respond to [the court decisions]...so we need to work with grassroots and poverty organizations in additional ways" that include paralegals and basing legal service lawyers in poor neighborhoods.[113]

## TOWARD A PARADIGM SHIFT

### Building a Legal Empowerment Program

Though detailing a legal empowerment program is far beyond the parameters of this paper, it is possible to sketch some potential elements. A "model" program would comprise a mix of features: prioritizing the needs and concerns of the disadvantaged; emphasizing civil society, including legal services and development NGOs, as well as community-based groups; using whatever forums (often not the courts) the poor can best access in specific situations; encouraging a supportive rather than lead role for lawyers; cooperating with government wherever possible, but pressuring it where necessary; using community organizing or group formation; developing paralegal resources; integrating with mainstream socioeconomic development work; and building on community-level operations to enable the poor to inform or influence systemic change in laws, policies, and state institutions.

This model program inevitably gives way to the reality that legal empowerment work must vary from country to country, issue to issue, and even community to community. In the Philippines, this multifaceted work has featured community organizing and typically deals with administrative law and local governance; in Bangladesh, alternative dispute resolution and informal justice systems; in South Africa, public interest litigation and broad-based mobilization. Paralegal development and law reform cut across numerous legal empowerment initiatives, but there are many exceptions to this rule and many locally determined ways of undertaking these activities.

Legal empowerment programs should take a long-term perspective: It can take at least a few years to start producing impact and even longer for that impact to broaden and deepen. A long-term approach also involves building a public interest bar by supporting law school and NGO programs that engage law students and young attorneys in legal services and that teach them the skills and perspective of development lawyering: how to both teach and learn from the poor; how to view them as partners rather than (subservient) clients; how to analyze problems politically, culturally, and from a gender perspective, rather than just legally; and how lawyers can advance social change. Conversely, exposing other development fields' young professionals to human rights and legal empowerment considerations could expand their capacities to integrate law and development in their work. In-country and international exchanges also can open up vistas for disadvantaged populations' leaders, NGO lawyers, law students, law professors, development practitioners, and government officials to learn from pertinent experience elsewhere.

Regardless of the exact nature of a legal empowerment program, it can be undertaken under at least three rubrics: (1) as aid specifically directed at legal empowerment; (2) in conjunction with ROL promotion; or (3) as part of mainstream socioeconomic development work.

The program's effectiveness will hinge not just on what work is supported, but how it is supported. NGOs that show sufficient progress and potential merit ongoing core funding that enables them to pursue their own agendas in accordance with evolving circumstances and partner populations' priorities, rather than in response to sometimes rigid donor requirements. Similarly, it is best for funding agencies to take a flexible, foundation-like approach. This approach involves gradually identifying grantees, making grants, and building programs as situations evolve. It is in contrast to the project approach that tends to lock in activities at the outset. This is not to say that bilateral and multilateral donors can or should restructure to resemble foundations. But they should set up foundation-like assistance windows for supporting legal empowerment.

This can involve channeling bilateral aid funds to local and international NGOs familiar with grant making, legal empowerment, civil society or grassroots development, as well as to those multilateral development agencies whose mandates and operating styles aim to serve the poor rather than their host governments. Funding for legal empowerment work should not be administered by aid agencies that are constrained by their policies or orientations to work through official channels rather than civil society, unless they can open appropriate funding windows or otherwise modify their operations. Although it would be a great step forward for multilateral banks to mainstream legal empowerment work into their socioeconomic development projects, the funds for that work should be grants rather than loans under most circumstances and should flow through organizations that can best take a foundation-like approach.

## Striking a Balance in Rule of Law Aid

Despite this paper's critical tone toward ROL orthodoxy, it does not aim to dismiss all assistance to state legal institutions. The objective, instead, is to press for a more skeptical stance and a better balance in ROL aid. The best intentions of some donor and government officials notwithstanding, state institutions often are burdened by counterproductive incentives and constraints that outweigh or outlast efforts to ameliorate them. These include entrenched bureaucratic structures, inefficient use of resources, corruption, patronage, gender bias, general aversion to change, and other factors that work against, rather than for, the disadvantaged. Many aid organizations' law programs either do not address the legal priorities of the poor or do so ineffectively because of excessive reliance on state institutions and top-down approaches. Though precise calculations are beyond this analysis, some international agencies could be spending as much as 90 percent of ROL funds on activities that address only 10 percent of disadvantaged populations' greatest legal problems.

In view of the dominant paradigm's problematic assumptions and track record, it is best to raise the bar in deciding where and to what degree to work with state legal institutions. The political will for reform should be strong, not simply acquiescent. We should be modest about our expectations for generating and sustaining that political will where it is lacking. Even to the extent that long-term cultivation and support of local reformers in state institutions makes sense, this also weighs in favor of long-term funding of civil society forces that act on their own justice agendas, hold those state institutions accountable, and help them do their jobs whenever possible.

With legal empowerment's accomplishments and potential in mind, it should be the sole focus of some law-oriented programs and a core component of most others. This translates into substantial support for legal services and capacity building for the poor, toward the dual ends of both implementing and reforming laws. Where legal empowerment is the sole focus of a law program, it could be organized around general themes such as gender or agrarian issues, or could more comprehensively support pro-poor legal services. Regardless, a guiding principle is responsiveness to disadvantaged populations' legal needs, rather than a top-down focus on a narrow range of legal institutions. This emphasis is also guided by the fact that domestic civil society's homegrown analyses of problems and solutions are often better informed than those of foreign donors.

As a core component of law programs, legal empowerment can complement work with state institutions. This can take the form of collaboration with both upland populations and ministries of natural resources regarding environmental matters, for example. It can also involve strengthening the knowledge, capacities, and organization of those upland groups (or of farmers, or of women) regarding not just the legal issues specific to them but also the conventional justice sector. For instance, legal services for farmers who are originally organized around agrarian concerns may constitute an important complement to state-oriented efforts to improve police professionalism, where those farmers have sufficient legal knowledge and connections (with lawyers, higher level law enforcement personnel, other officials, politicians, NGO staff) to call police to account. Certainly, vibrant civil society is a valuable, even crucial, resource in promoting police accountability. Law enforcement personnel who are prone to abusive, corrupt conduct require outside, organized groups to ensure that state efforts to reorient them prove sustainable. Those groups typically exist for purposes other than police monitoring per se.

The bottom line, then, is not that government is always the problem and civil society the solution. Rather, part of the necessary paradigm shift is to view the justice sector more broadly, which necessarily results in greater support for civil society efforts that address a broader assortment of legal issues and that help or pressure government to do its job better. This can yield not only greater agrarian, gender, and environmental justice, but a greater likelihood of effecting safety, security, and access for the poor even within narrow notions of the sector.

## Mainstreaming

Another important component of the paradigm shift—potentially more far-reaching than adjusting the balance within the ROL field—is to mainstream legal empowerment into socio-economic development projects (for example, natural resources management, irrigation, rural development, public health, gender). Educating and enabling the disadvantaged to deal with legal matters immediately affecting them would positively impact human rights, good governance, and project performance. It could also open doors to their positive involvement with other issues important to them. Filipino farmers and Bangladeshi women organized around agrarian reform and gender concerns, respectively, have been better able to participate in local governance, for example.

One potentially powerful approach to mainstreaming is to build on the group formation that occurs in many socio-economic development fields. Pulling together disadvantaged persons for purposes of micro-credit, livelihood, reproductive health, public health, forest use, irrigation, or literacy training addresses their immediate priorities. It also may be tolerated or even welcomed by local leaders who might resist an initial focus on women's or farmer's rights. Once the group achieves some cohesion and acceptance in the community, members can start discussing legal issues that affect them, with paralegal development and legal activism following further down the line.

If legal services are to be mainstreamed into socio-economic development, it will be necessary to overcome the sectoral divisions that hinder development effectiveness. One place to start would be the most basic sorts of workshops within development agencies. At these sessions, legal practitioners and those from other disciplines could share experiences about specific projects and resulting lessons. Those in the legal field would have more to learn than to teach about conducting impact-oriented research. On the other hand, they might bring to the table perspectives about ways of advancing rights and alleviating poverty simultaneously, perhaps fleshing out the concept of a rights-based approach to development.

Aid agencies should adopt structural changes to make mainstreaming possible. Their headquarters should launch cross-sectoral working groups to learn about existing civil society efforts and impact concerning legal empowerment, convert these lessons into guidance for field offices, and provide an impetus for those offices to consider launching legal empowerment initiatives.

A related process should take place in these agencies' country offices, with water or forest sector staff, for example, exploring how legal services might benefit their partner populations, as well as their current and potential projects. Conversely, justice sector staff (or governance sector colleagues, who handle law-oriented programs in some organizations) could examine how a broader, cross-sectoral approach could benefit their work. To avoid a top-down approach, these efforts not only should involve consultation with partner groups but also should consider relevant efforts already under way in the country, particularly those of civil society, with a view toward possibly supporting or building on them. The end result of these processes would be initiatives that feature or include legal empowerment.

**Reaching the Poorest of the Poor**

What of the many situations in which civil society, legal services, and the basic capacities of the poor are torn by war, crushed by repression, stunted by severe poverty itself, or in the early stages of recovering from any of these situations? Admittedly, legal empowerment works best in the presence of a vibrant civil society. Is it beyond the reach of the poorest of the poor? Legal empowerment (or, for that matter, state legal institutions) should not automatically be included in the initial mix of development efforts. Sometimes basic socioe-conomic recovery initiatives should be the priority.

Still, despite these constraints, the building blocks of legal empowerment can be put in place. As discussed above, group formation around basic socio-economic needs can provide an entry point for mainstreaming subsequent law-oriented work. A long-term strategy of building-up a rights-oriented civil society can benefit both development and human rights.

Local conditions permitting, the long road toward the poorest of the poor achieving control over their lives can include introducing them to the very notion that they have rights and the ways in which those rights can benefit their daily existence. Training them regarding these matters should take account of their priorities, their levels of education, and the nature of the laws most relevant to them. This generally translates into the use of interactive, "popular education" methodologies rather than law lectures, and a focus on domestic laws rather than international human rights treaties (unless of course the domestic laws repress rather than serve the poor).

International NGOs may play leading roles in these efforts where local conditions or insufficient capacities bar domestic NGOs and community-based groups from doing so. A goal, course, is to build those domestic capacities over time.

**Filling the Informational Vacuum**

This paper concludes where it began, both asserting the need for a paradigm shift and acknowledging that those of us concerned with law and development do not know enough to pinpoint the precise contours of that change. Rule of law orthodoxy is characterized by questionable assumptions, unproven impact, and insufficient attention to the legal needs of the disadvantaged. Legal empowerment constitutes an appealing alternative that has contributed to poverty alleviation, good governance, and other development goals. But the legal field remains far behind other development fields in documenting and learning from impact. Along with more general research on law and development, we need to better understand the dynamics underlying legal empowerment, the challenges it faces, and the impact it achieves.

A legal empowerment program, then, should include rigorous research that can help determine the most effective strategies and activities, as well as contribute knowledge to governance, ROL, and socio-economic development work. Quantitative and qualitative tools such as survey research and rapid rural appraisals should be used to scrutinize the dynamics that contribute to (or constrain) successful legal empowerment work, so as to derive lessons that will help human rights and development organizations build on that experience. At the same time, it is important to avoid becoming consumed by short-term indicators and other bureaucratic mechanisms that can counterproductively dominate monitoring and evaluation.

USAID (in Nepal), the Asia Foundation and ADB (in the Bangladesh and the Philippines), and the World Bank (in Ecuador) have begun to use research to fill the large informational vacuum. But we need more ambitious and varied studies across the globe if the international community is to most effectively integrate law and development so as to benefit the poor.

## REFERENCES

1. Convention on the Rights of the Child, Article 40.
2. Adopted by General Assembly resolution 45/113 of 14 December 1990.
3. Adopted and proclaimed by General Assembly resolution 45/112 of 14 December, 1990.
4. Adopted by General Assembly resolution 40/33 of 29 November, 1985.
5. Pakistan Juvenile Justice Systems Ordinance 2000, Section 247; Hudood Laws, 1979.
6. Sri Lanka Children and Young Persons Ordinance, 1936, Sections 4 and 88.
7. Public Safety Act 2000; Special Powers Act, 1974.
8. Convention on the Rights of the Child, Articles 39 and 40(2).
9. UN Standard Minimum Rules for the Administration of Juvenile Justice, Articles 10 and 12.
10. Bangladesh Children Act, Vangrancy Act, 1943, Code of

Criminal procedure, Article 54, and Suppression of Violence against Women Act, 2000; Pakistan Punjabi Youthful Offenders Act, 1952 and Sindh Children's Act, 1955; Nepal Public Offences and Punishment Act, 2000; Sri Lanka Children and Young Person's Ordinance, 1936 and Vagrants Ordinance, 1841; Bhutan Code of Civil and Criminal Procedure.

## NOTES

1. This paper is primarily based on researchl conducted under the generous and much-appreciated auspices of an Open Society Institute Individual Projects Fellowship. It also draws on studies and consultancies that I have conducted for other institutions, such as the Ford Foundation, the U.K.'s Department for International Development and the World Bank. Foremost among these studies is a research project for the Asia Foundation and Asian Development Bank: Stephen Golub and Kim McQuay, "Legal Empowerment: Advancing Good Governance and Poverty Reduction," in Law and Policy Reform at the Asian Development Bank, 2001 edition (Manila: Asian Development Bank, 2001), available at www.adb.org/Documents/Others/Law_ADB/lpr_2001. For better or worse, however, all analysis and conclusions in this paper are my own and should not be attributed to any of these institutions.
2. Although such organizations as the U.K.'s Department for International Development (DFID), the Asian Development Bank, and the Asia Foundation have started to use the term legal empowerment, I use it here to also include a range of initiatives (some described in this paper) that fit the definition but that go by other names—or by no specific title at all.
3. The term rule of law orthodoxy was coined by Frank Upham in his Mythmaking in the Rule of Law Orthodoxy, Carnegie Endowment Working Paper No. 30, Rule of Law Series, Democracy and Rule of Law Project (Washington, D.C.: Carnegie Endowment for International Peace, September 2002). Upham characterizes ROL orthodoxy as contending "that sustainable growth is impossible without the existence of the rule of law: a set of uniformly enforced, established legal regimes that clearly lay out the rules of the game" (p. 1). I expand the definition so that it includes not just this underlying rationale, but the set of ROL programs and activities geared

toward achieving sustainable growth and other goals. In this paper, then, ROL orthodoxy is the same as the dominant paradigm for integrating law and development, and not just the intellectual basis for the paradigm.

4. In ascribing certain orientations to the multilateral development banks and other aid institutions, I of course am generalizing about organizations that have different units proceeding in different ways, some in more creative and less orthodox manners than others.
5. I use the term disadvantaged populations in the legal empowerment definition because it could be considered a broader class of persons than the poor concept includes the poor, but also those who face discrimination or abuse as a result of their gender, race, ethnicity, or other personal attributes. Still, as discussed in this paper, the consensus characterization of poverty has broadened to include lack of opportunity and power, so that it comes closer to the notion of disadvantaged persons. To avoid further splitting of definitional hairs, however, I use the terms "poor" and "disadvantaged" interchangeably in this paper.
6. Here, the term mainstream socio-economic development efforts refers to the many fields that are organized around the concept of directly improving the social and economic well-being of the poor and that consume the bulk of development funding.
7. For instance, the World Bank's Africa Region Gender and Law Program has laudably implemented a program of matching grants for state and civil society institutions to implement legal services for women, but its funds are very limited and insecure in comparison with what the institution spends on judicial reform. World bank's Legal and Judicial Reform Practice Group has commendably started to undertake support for legal services for the poor, but the effort is constrained by the relative paucity of funds devoted to such services: less than $400,000 of a $10.6 million judicial reform project in Ecuador, for instance, and even this project was an exception to the rule. See World Bank, Impact of Legal Aid: Ecuador (Washington, D.C.: World Bank, February, 2003).
8. Patrick McAuslan, "Law, Governance and the Development of the Market: Practical Problems and Possible Solutions," in Good Government and the Law: Legal and Institutional Reform

in Developing Countries, ed. Julio Faundez (London: Macmillan, 1997), 25–45, at 30–1.

9. World Bank, Legal and Judicial Reform: Observations, Experiences, and Approach of the Legal Vice-Presidency (Washington, D.C.: World Bank, July 2002), 1.

10. Nestor Humberto Martinez, "Rule of Law and Economic Efficiency," in Justice Delayed: Judicial Reform in Latin America, ed. Edmundo Jarquin and Fernando Carrillo (Washington, D.C.: Inter-American Development Bank, 1998), 3.

11. See www.usaid.gov/democracy/index.html. DG programs' link to ROL is reflected in the fact that the name of the USAID unit that originally promoted the rule of law in the 1980s was the Office of Administration of Justice and Democratic Development. However, although USAID's DG goals are not inherently business-oriented, one assumption is that good governance creates the proper environment for business to flourish.

12. See, for example, DFID, DFID Policy Statement on Safety, Security and Accessible Justice (London: DFID, 2003).

13. See, for example, DFID, Justice and Poverty Reduction (London: DFID, 2000).

14. For a thoughtful but nevertheless narrow list of the main components of the justice sector, see DFID, Safety, Security and Accessible Justice: Putting Policy into Practice (London: DFID, July 2002), 12.

15. See, for example, Daniel Kauffman, Misrule of Law: Does the Evidence Challenge Conventions in Judiciary and Legal Reforms? Draft for discussion, July 2001, at www.worldbank.org/wbi/governance/pdf/misruleoflaw.pdf.

16. Douglass C. North, Institutions, Institutional Change and Economic Performance (Cambridge, U.K.: Cambridge University Press, 1990), 110.

17. Amanda Perry, "International Economic Organizations and the Modern Law and Development Movement," in Making Development Work: Legislative Reform for Institutional Transformation and Good Governance, ed. A. Seidman, R. B. Seid-man, and T. Walde (New York: Kluwer Law International, 1999), 19–32, at 28.

18. Perry, "International Economic Organizations," 26.
19. Richard E. Messick, "Judicial Reform and Economic Development: A Survey of the Issues," World Bank Research Observer, Vol. 14, No. 1 (February, 1999), 117–36, at 122.
20. Carothers, Promoting the Rule of Law Abroad: Problem of Knowledge, Carnegie Endowment Working Paper No. 34, Rule of Law Series, Democracy and Rule of Law Project (Washington, D.C.: Carnegie Endowment for International Peace, January 2003), 3.
21. See, for example, McAuslan, "Law, Governance," 30–1.
22. See, for example, Richard Posner, "Creating a Legal Framework for Economic Development," World Bank Research Observer, Vol. 13 (Washington, D.C.: World Bank, 1998).
23. China is not an unalloyed example of success, however, in that growing prosperity for hundreds of millions citizens is partly offset by economic insecurity and even deprivation stemming from loss of jobs and the removal of the "iron rice bowl." Positive and negative developments are products of the shift from socialism to capitalism, however, rather than any efforts to institute the rule of law.
24. For an analysis that places responsibility for the crisis mainly on U.S. government and International Monetary Fund decisions rather than East Asian nations' laws and institutions, see Joseph E. Stiglitz, Globalization and Its Discontents (New York: W.W. Norton and Company, 2002), Ch. 4, 89-132. Stiglitz, recipient of the 2001 Nobel Prize for Economic Science, was World Bank chief economist during the crisis.
25. Stephan Haggard, Pathways from the Periphery: Politics of Growth in the Newly Industrialized Countries (Ithaca, NY: Cornell University Press, 1990).
26. Katarina Pistor and Philip A. Wellons, Role of Law and Legal Institutions in Asian Economic Development: 1960–1995 (New York: Oxford University Press, 1999), 19.
27. Amanda Perry, "An Ideal Legal System for Attracting Foreign Direct Investment?" American University International Law Review, Vol. 15, No. 6 (2000), 1627–57.
28. John Hewko, Foreign Direct Investment: Does the Rule of Law Matter? Carnegie Endowment Working Paper No. 26

Rule of Law Series, Democracy and Rule of Law Project (Washington, D.C.: Carnegie Endowment for International Peace, April 2002), 4.

29. Hewko, Foreign Direct Investment, 5.
30. Upham, Mythmaking, 7.
31. Upham, Mythmaking, 19.
32. Upham, Mythmaking, 1.
33. Upham, Mythmaking, 32.
34. Remarks summarized from a roundtable on the rule of law at the Carnegie Endowment for International Peace, September 5, 2001, at www.ceip.org/files/events/events.asp?p=1&EventID=380.
35. U.S. General Accounting Office (GAO), Foreign Assistance: Promoting Judicial Reform to Strengthen Democracies, Report GAO/NSAID-93-140 (Washington, D.C.: GAO, 1993).
36. William C. Prillaman, Judiciary and Democratic Decay in Latin America: Declining Confidence in the Rule of Law (Westport, CT: Praeger, 2000).
37. Carothers, Aiding Democracy Abroad: Learning Curve (Washington, D.C.: Carnegie Endowment for International Peace, 1999), 170.
38. Carothers, Aiding Democracy Abroad, 176.
39. Harry Blair and Gary Hansen, Weighing in on the Scales of Justice: Strategic Approaches for Donor-Supported Rule of Law Programs, USAID Development Program Operations and Assessment Report No. 7 (Washington, D.C.: USAID Center for Development Information and Evaluation, February 1994).
40. Blair and Hansen, Weighing in, 51.
41. Linn Hammergren, Rule of Law: Approaches to Justice Reform and What We Have Learned: A Summary of Four Papers, USAID Center for Democracy and Governance (Washington, D.C.: USAID, April 1998). Another thoughtful report in this vein, as reflected in its title, is Madeleine Crohn and William E. Davis, eds., Lessons Learned: Proceedings of the Second Judicial Reform Roundtable Held in Williamsburg, Viriginia, May 19-22, 1996 (Washington, D.C.: National Center for State

Courts, USAID, Inter-American Development Bank, November 1996).

42. Hammergren, Rule of Law.
43. USAID, Achievements in Building and Maintaining the Rule of Law, Occasional Paper Series, Office of Democracy and Governance, USAID (Washington, D.C.: USAID, November 2002).
44. E-mail correspondence from Linn Hammergren to author, December 16, 2002.
45. USAID, Achievements in Building, 79.
46. Martin Bohmer, "Access to Justice and Judicial Reform in Argentina," in Columbia University Budapest Law Center/ Public Interest Law Initiative, Open Society Justice Initiative, and Fundacja Uniwersyteckich Poradni Prawnych, Fifth Annual Colloquium on Clinical Legal Education, 15–16 November 2002 (Warsaw, Poland: 2002), 32. In fairness, the MSI report briefly notes apparently modest USAID support for civil society in Argentina (p. 35), though this seems limited to civic education and public information about judicial performance.
47. Carothers, Aiding Democracy Abroad, 170.
48. Robert S. Moog, Whose Interests are Supreme? Organizational Politics in the Civil Courts in India (Ann Arbor, MI: Association of Asian Studies, 1997), 63.
49. Kauffman, Misrule of Law, 2.
50. Kauffman, Misrule of Law, 2.
51. E-mail correspondence from Linn Hammergren to author, December 16, 2002.
52. World Bank Legal Vice Presidency, Legal and Judicial Reform: Observations, Experiences, and Approach of the Legal Vice Presidency (Washington, D.C.: World Bank, 2002), 65.
53. Although there is some movement by DFID and other donors toward a sector-wide approach in the legal field, this promising development often translates into a focus on specific state institutions.
54. North, Institutions, Institutional Change, 3–4.
55. North, Institutions, Institutional Change, 5.

56. Former World Bank official William Easterly and Scott Pegg, respectively, in Daphne Eviatar, "Striking It Poor: Oil as a Curse," *New York Times,* June 7, 2003, at www.nytimes.com/2003/06/07/arts/07BANK.html.
57. World Bank Legal Vice Presidency, Legal and Judicial Reform, 5.
58. Asian Development Bank (ADB), Cambodia: Enhancing Governance for Sustainable Development (Manila: ADB, October 2000), 44, at www.adb.org/Documents/Books/Cambodia_Enhancing_Governance/chap_04.pdf.
59. Danish Ministry of Foreign Affairs, Danida, Evaluation: Danish Support to Promotion of Human Rights and Democratisation, Volume 2: Justice, Constitution and Legislation (Copenhagen: Evaluation Secretariat, Ministry of Foreign Affairs, 2000), vi.
60. Danish Ministry of Foreign Affairs, Danida, Evaluation.
61. DFID, Safety, Security and Accessible Justice, 58.
62. See, for example, Stephen Golub, "From the Village to the University: Legal Activism in Bangladesh," in Many Roads to Justice: Law-Related Work of Ford Foundation Grantees around the World, ed. Mary McClymont and Stephen Golub (New York: Ford Foundation, 2000), 127–58.
63. Aforementioned Danida evaluation, for example, more generally asserts that "a well-functioning, formal legal system is a pre-requisite for establishing a 'modern' society." Danish Ministry of Foreign Affairs, Danida, Evaluation, vi.
64. Michael R. Anderson, Access to Justice and Legal Process: Making Legal Institutions Responsive to Poor People in LDCs, IDS Working Paper 178 (Brighton, U.K.: Institute of Development Studies, February 2003), 12, Box 4.1.
65. John Blackton, "Egypt Country Report," pp. 6-8, unpublished background paper prepared in 2000 for USAID and International Foundation for Election Systems (IFES), Guidance for Promoting Judicial Independence and Impartiality, Revised Edition (Washington, D.C.: USAID Office of Democracy and Governance, January 2002).
66. Hector Soliman, "Philippines Country Report," p. 3, unpublished background paper prepared for USAID and IFES, Guidance for Promoting Judicial Independence.

67. UNDP, Status of Governance in Indonesia: A Baseline Assessment, draft report produced on behalf of the Partnership of Governance Reform in Indonesia, October 2000, p. 11.
68. UNDP, Status of Governance in Indonesia, 12.
69. Soliman, "Philippines Country Report," 5.
70. Tim Golden, "Mexico and Drugs: Was U.S. Napping?" New York Times, July 11, 1997, at A1, A11.
71. DFID Bangladesh (DFIDB), Country Strategy Review: 1998–2002 Bangladesh (Dhaka: DFIDB, August 2002), 22.
72. Written interview with author, May 8, 2001.
73. Save the Children, CARE, and other development and relief groups are well-known for their efforts in this regard, but in recent years other organizations, such as the Asia Foundation, have taken on such facilitating functions.
74. In connection with an approximately $330 million loan to Pakistan, the ADB is establishing a $24 million endowment for an Access to Justice Development Fund. Although two-thirds of the annual interest income will go to conventional judicial development activities, from 15 to 20 percent will be spent on a Legal Empowerment (Sub-)Fund (largely for legal services and public awareness activities). Smaller sub-funds will support legal and judicial research and legal education innovations. See ADB, Report and Recommendation of the President to the Board of Directors on Proposed Loans and Technical Assistance Grant, RRP: PAK 32023 (Manila: ADB, November 2001), 60–64.
75. One partial exception to this rule can be found within the World Bank's Poverty Reduction and Economic Management Network (PREM), which actively facilitates and disseminates very useful research on legal systems development experience (as well as many other topics).
76. Available at www.worldbank.org/poverty/empowerment/whatis/index.htm.
77. Stephen Browne, "Governance and Human Poverty," Choices (September 2002), at www.undp.org/dpa/choices/2001/september/essay.pdf.
78. See Amartya Sen, Development as Freedom (New York: Alfred A. Knopf, 2000).

79. See UNDP, Human Development Report 2000 (New York: Oxford University Press, 2000).
80. See World Bank, World Development Report 2000/2001 (New York: Oxford University Press, 2000), 7.
81. USAID Center for Development Information and Evaluation, Linking Democracy and Development: An Idea for the Times, USAID Evaluation Highlights No. 75 (Washington, D.C.: USAID, December 2001), 1.
82. DFID, Safety, Security and Accessible Justice, 15.
83. See, for example, Michael Edwards, "NGO Performance—What Breeds Success? New Evidence from South Asia," World Development, Vol. 27, No. 2 (1999), 371; P. Evans, "Development Strategies across the Public-Private Divide," World De-velopment, Vol. 24, No. 6 (1996), 1033–7; J. Fox, "How Does Civil Society úµicken? Political Construction of Social Capital in Rural Mexico," World Development, Vol. 24, No. 6 (1996), 1089–103.
84. See, for example, David Brown and Darcy Ashman, "Participation, Social Capital, Intersectoral Problem Solving: African and Asian Cases," World Development, Vol. 24, No. 9 (1996), 1467–79: Kathryn Smith Pyle, "From Policy Advocate to Policy Maker: NGOs in Recife," Grassroots Development Journal, Vol. 21, No. 1 (1997); Maria Maia, "NGOs as Mediators: Role in Expertise, Language and Institutional Exemption in Urban Development Planning," Working Paper No. 77 (London: Development Planning, University College, May 1996), 12.
85. Monica Das Gupta, Helene Grandvoinnet, and Mattia Romani, Fostering Community-Driven Development: What Role for the State? World Bank Policy Research Working Paper 2969 (Washington, D.C.: World Bank, January 2003).
86. See, for example, Golub and McQuay, "Legal Empowerment"; Daniel Manning, Role of Legal Services Organizations in Attacking Poverty (Washington, D.C.: World Bank, September 1999); and Mary McClymont and Stephen Golub, eds., Many Roads to Justice: Law-Related Work of Ford Foundation Grantees around the World, available at www.fordfound.org/publications/recent_articles/manyroads.cfm.
87. Office of the High Commissioner for Human Rights (OHCHR),

"Rights-Based Approaches: Is Only One Rights-Based Approach?" at www.unhchr.ch/development/approaches-05.html.

88. OHCHR, Draft Guidelines: A Human Rights Approach to Poverty Reduction Strategies, para.13, at www.unhchr.ch/development/povertyfinal.html.
89. Golub and McQuay, "Legal Empowerment," 12.
90. Manning, Role of Legal Services Organizations.
91. McClymont and Golub, Many Roads to Justice, 5.
92. "Alternative" in their name reflects their development-oriented perspectives and how their operations differ from private legal practice and traditional legal aid in the Philippines.
93. E-mail correspondence from Geoff Budlender to author, January 7, 2003.
94. CARE, "CARE Ecuador's Subir Project," unpublished summary produced by CARE International's Ecuador office, October 2000.
95. CARE, "CARE Ecuador's Subir Project."
96. Available at www.unicef.org/newsline/99pr1.htm.
97. International Center for Research on Women and the Center for Development and Population Activities, "Report-in-Brief," Promoting Women in Development Program (Washington, D.C.: 1999), 1–2.
98. World Bank, Impact of Legal Aid: Ecuador (Washington, D.C.: World Bank, February 2003), 11–12.
99. See, for example, Lori L. Heise with Jacqueline Pitanguy and Adrienne Germain, Violence against Women: Hidden Health Burden, World Bank Discussion Paper No. 255 (Washington, D.C.: World Bank, 1994); and Andrew Morrison and María Beatriz Orlando, "Social and Economic Costs of Domestic Violence: Chile and Nicaragua," in Too Close to Home: Domestic Violence in the Americas, ed. Andrew Morrison and María Loreto Biehl (Washington, D.C.: Inter-American Development Bank, 1999).
100. See "Appendix 1: Impact of Legal Empowerment Activities on Agrarian Reform Implementation in the Philippines," in Golub and McQuay, "Legal Empowerment," 135–49.

101. Dowry is the payment of money, livestock, or other material goods by the bride's family to the family of the groom, in order to secure a marriage. After the agreed payments are made and marriage occurs, the dowry demands by the groom's family frequently escalate and are accompanied by violence or other abuse against the wife.

102. See "Appendix 2: Impact of Legal Empowerment on Selected Aspects of Knowledge, Poverty, and Governance in Bangladesh: A Study of úµree NGOs," Golub and McQuay, "Legal Empowerment," 135–49.

103. Rajju Malla Dhakal and Misbah M. Sheikh, Breaking Barriers—Building Bridges—A Case Study of USAID/Nepal's Women's Empowerment Program (Washington, D.C.: Asia Foundation, 1997).

104. Gwen úµomas and Ava Shrestha, Breaking New Ground: A Case Study of Women's Empowerment in Nepal, Women's Empowerment Program (Kathmandu: USAID/Nepal, 1998).

105. Stephen Golub, "Nonlawyers as Legal Resources for úµeir Communities," in McClymont and Golub, Many Roads to Justice, 309.

106. South Consulting, "Kenya Civil Society Programme: Review of Access to Justice Projects," Final Draft (Nairobi: South Consulting, 2001), 28–29.

107. Adam Stapleton, "Energising the Criminal Justice System: Malawi's Paralegal Advisory Service," Id21insights: Communicating Development Research, at www.id21.org/insights/insights43/insights-iss43-art06.html.

108. Karen L. Casper and Sultana Kamal, "Evaluation Report: Community Legal Services Conducted by Family Planning NGOs," a report prepared for úµe Asia Foundation's Bangladesh office, Dhaka, 1995.

109. See, for example, Leonard Rolfes Jr. and Gregory Mohrman, Legal Aid Centers in Rural Russia: Helping People Improve ú°eir Lives, RDI Reports on Foreign Aid and Development No. 102 (Seattle: Rural Development Institute, February 2000).

110. See, for example, Roy L. Prosterman and Tim Hanstad, Land Reform in the 21st century: New Challenges, New Responses, RDI Reports on Foreign Aid and Development No. 117 (Seattle: Rural Development Institute, March 2003), 24.

111. Prosterman and Hanstad, Land Reform, 4–7.
112. See, for example, Columbia University Budapest Law Center/ Public Interest Law Initiative, Open Society Justice Initiative, and Fundacja Uniwersyteckich Poradni Prawnych, Fifth Annual Colloquium.
113. Interview with the author, July 15, 2003.

# 2

# Juvenile Justice System in India: An Overview

Care and protection of children is recognized as basic to the survival and growth of the human fabric. Children are found in the most vulnerable situations and professional approach to amelioration is mandatory for any society. The expectation not only stems from International commitments by way of the UN Convention on the Rights of Child and the Optional Protocols, but also as a course correction and way-forward for the Indian Society, determined, as it is, to handover the baton to children when they grow to adulthood.

Juvenile Justice System in India can be briefly traced to initial Children Acts of some States in pre-Independence Era. The central legislation on children - The Children Act was enacted in 1950, which governed the administration of care and protection of children till 1986, when the ambit and nomenclature was changed to widen it to juveniles as well. The Juvenile Justice Act, 1986 also addressed the need for a mechanism of handling children and juveniles in institutional care.

The Beijing Rules on Standard Minimum Rules for Administration of Juvenile Justice, 1985 set the tone for addressing the problem of juvenile delinquency as an independent issue, with a need to revisit social policy ramifications. The idea of addressing this vexing problem, away from adult justice, meant rethinking and re-jigging welfare measures as well as prepare the administration to handle juveniles as a separate category. This ideal ethos and hope is well exemplified in the numerous perspective documents of both the UN agencies and Government of India (A World Fit for Children - UNICEF, India; National Plan of Action, 2005 etc.).

Juvenile Justice System is an emerging subject. The three decades - from 1986 to 2006 has seen India move towards the goals set in UNCRC. Many facets of juvenile justice have been addressed - protection of children and young persons, mechanisms for awareness among adults and care-givers of the rights of children, establishing systems and mechanisms for administration of juvenile justice, sensitization of the allied systems to the need to treat children and young persons differently and tenderly, an emphasis on mainstreaming rather than separation through institutional approach to juvenile justice, counseling of all stakeholders, proactive policy measures by Governments to prevent abuse, protect, and provide for re-integration into society etc.

The latest legislation had moved closer to fulfill international aspirations by providing a wider definition to the term juvenile, apart from being up to the age of 18 years of age. Many categories of children facing some form of threat and abuse in their realm have been included. The process of juvenile justice through the twin institutions of Juvenile Justice Boards (JJBs) and Child Welfare Committees (CWCs) has been further strengthened to provide for speedy disposal of cases. The re-integration of children into society is furthered by proactive mechanisms for adoption. The attainment of goals set in UNCRC assumes significance as the Amendment Act has set time-frame for its' implementation by States.

Citizen awareness and acceptance of children and young persons is paramount in the administration of juvenile justice. While the Juvenile Homes provide temporary succor, eventually, it is only the family that can provide care and love to the growing individual. Thus, repatriation and re-integration can only repair the damage to the psyche and prepare the person for adult roles. As the Standard Minimum Rules state, "Sufficient attention shall be given to positive measures that involve the full mobilization of all possible resources, including the family, volunteers and other community groups, as well as schools and other community institutions, for the purpose of promoting the well-being of the juvenile, with a view to reducing the need for intervention under the law, and of effectively, fairly and humanely dealing with the juvenile in conflict with the law."(1.3)

The Juvenile Justice Act, 2000 and its Amendment Act 2006 defines a child as all persons up to the age of 18 years.

The juvenile justice system in India is designed to trace two categories of children, those in conflict with law, and those in need of care and protection, which includes children who are begging, in prostitution, neglected children, abandoned children, abused children and street children, all of them with different needs and vulnerabilities (HAQ, 2005). However, India has had interventions on Juvenile Justice consensus 1856. The first through the National Children's Act enacted in 1960 followed by the Juvenile Justice Act, 1986 and presently the Juvenile Justice (Care and Protection of Children) Amendment Act 2006. Way back in 1985, even standard minimum rules for the administration of juvenile system, also known as Beijing rules articulated the global consensus on humane and sensitive handling of the children who come in conflict with law.

A subsequent document, even rules for the protection of juveniles lays down with juvenile institutions, need to have a required arrangements for returning the child to the community. In this regard, UN Convention on the Rights of the Child, 1989 is notable and has influenced the evaluation of juvenile justice throughout the world. In a developing country like India, the range of ethnic, cultural, economic and social problems is rather large. Undoubtedly, children do not remain inserted from these. In varying degrees they come to have individual and group biases.

**Juvenile Home**

Facilities include : Shelter, child-care facilities, counseling, education, medical care and vocational training.

In-puts for enhancing quality of facilities and services.

- Joyful surroundings colourful and pictorial paintings
- Gardens, tree plantations.
- Play equipment in the playground/indoor games.
- Training/orientation of staff-house parents, superintendent, watch and ward staff.
- Improving first aid/medical facilities, installing couple of beds for segregation of sick children.
- Basic health education for children.
- Appointment of a counselor.
- Coaching for education—for children who are scholastically backward/learning disability.
- Provision of teaching learning materials.
- Library.
- Vocational training facilities for imparting skills relevant to market demand.

**Staff**

- House-parents/care-takers.
- Manager/Superintendent.
- Vocational Training Instructor.
- Person in charge of recreational, social, cultural and community activities.
- Counselor.
- Social Worker : for community resource mobilization, for facilitating community participation/involvement in home management, promoting interaction between children in the home and children in the community; promoting access to vocational training facilities to children from the community, placement of children under apprenticeship in small established/private sector, providing educational coaching facilities for children in the neighborhood along with children of the home.

- Probation Officers – increase of numbers of probation officers to facilitate early reunion of child with the family.
- Watch and ward to be sensitized on dealing with the children.
- Crèche attendant to manage the crèche, a facility for poor working women of the neighborhood.

However, even as the law exists, implementation remains weak and invisible, which is reflected in the situation of the children. One of the biggest problems in the implementation of Juvenile Justice Act lies in the narrow understanding of civil society regarding the use or jurisdiction of the law. Since the very beginning the word 'juvenile' has come to be synonyms as 'delinquency'. With the inclusion of child in need of care and protection the understanding of the ambit of the law has somewhat in place.

**Children in Conflict with Law**

Children in conflict with law or the child offenders are most commonly referred to as juveniles or juvenile delinquents. Covered under the Juvenile (Care and Protection of Children) Act, 2006, the number of such children has increased over the years, from 17,203 in 1994 to 32,145 in 2006. The crimes committed by juveniles have also seen an increase in the same period from 8,561 to 21,088. While part of this increase in juvenile crimes may be attributed to the inclusion of boys aged 16-18 years in the definition of child in the revised juvenile justice law of 2000 and 2006, the fact remains that the rate of juvenile crimes is fairly high and more and more and more children in the 16 – 18 years category are coming in conflict with law.

Once the crime is committed and the child is apprehended, the case comes before the Juvenile Justice Board (JJB). Till the inquiry is pending the child is kept in an observation home, unless otherwise released as per the law. On conviction, the child is sent to the special home or place of safety.

**Juvenile Apprehended under IPC and SLL Crimes by Sex (1994-2006)**

| *Sl. No.* | *Year* | *Boys* | *Girls* | *Total* | *Percentage of Girls* |
|---|---|---|---|---|---|
| 1. | 1994 | 13,852 | 3,351 | 17,203 | 19.5 |
| 2. | 1995 | 14,542 | 4,251 | 18,793 | 22.6 |
| 3. | 1996 | 14,068 | 5,030 | 19,098 | 26.3 |
| 4. | 1997 | 14,282 | 3,514 | 17,796 | 19.7 |
| 5. | 1998 | 13,974 | 4,969 | 18,923 | 26.2 |
| 6. | 1999 | 13,088 | 5,372 | 18,460 | 29.1 |
| 7. | 2000 | 13,854 | 4,128 | 17,982 | 23.0 |
| 8. | 2001 | 31,295 | 2,333 | 33,628 | 6.9 |
| 9. | 2002 | 33,551 | 2,228 | 35,779 | 6.2 |
| 10. | 2003 | 30,985 | 2,335 | 33,320 | 7.0 |
| 11. | 2004 | 28,878 | 2,065 | 30,943 | 6.7 |
| 12. | 2005 | 30,606 | 2,075 | 32,681 | 6.3 |
| 13. | 2006 | 30,375 | 1,770 | 32,145 | 5.5 |

*Source:* Crime in India 2007.

*Note:* As per revised definition of Juveniles in the Juvenile Justice (Care and Protection of Children) Act, 2000, Boys in the age group of 16-18 years have been included.

**Incidence and Rate of Juvenile Delinquency Under IPC (1994-2006)**

| *Sl. No.* | *Year* | *Incidence of* | | *Percentage of Juvenile Crime to Total Crimes* |
|---|---|---|---|---|
| | | *Juvenile Crimes* | *Total Cognizable Crimes* | |
| 1. | 1994 | 8,561 | 16,35,251 | 0.5 |
| 2. | 1995 | 9,766 | 16,95,696 | 0.6 |
| 3. | 1996 | 10,024 | 17,09,576 | 0.6 |
| 4. | 1997 | 7,909 | 17,19,820 | 0.5 |
| 5. | 1998 | 9,352 | 17,78,815 | 0.5 |
| 6. | 1999 | 8,888 | 17,64,629 | 0.5 |

| *Sl. No.* | *Year* | *Incidence of* | | *Percentage of Juvenile Crime to Total Crimes* |
|---|---|---|---|---|
| | | *Juvenile Crimes* | *Total Cognizable Crimes* | |
| 7. | 2000 | 9,267 | 17,71,084 | 0.5 |
| 8. | 2001 | 16,509 | 17,69,308 | 0.9 |
| 9. | 2002 | 18,560 | 17,80,330 | 1.0 |
| 10. | 2003 | 17,819 | 17,16,120 | 1.0 |
| 11. | 2004 | 19,229 | 18,32,015 | 1.0 |
| 12. | 2005 | 18,939 | 18,22,602 | 1.0 |
| 13. | 2006 | 21,088 | 18,78,293 | 1.1 |

*Source:* Crime in India 2007.
*Note:* As per revised definition of juveniles in the Juvenile Justice (Care and Protection of Children) Act, 2000, Boys in the age group of 16-18 years have been included.

As can be gathered from the above table, with increase in the age of boys covered by juvenile justice law from 16–18 years, the burden of pending cases and the pressure on the Juvenile Justice Boards has clearly increased. Number of convictions is high as compared to acquittals, which can be seen from the number of children sent to special homes and those acquitted. Those who are pending disposal are either kept in observation homes or may have been released on bail. Till date no information has been collected on number of children released on bail. The Juvenile Justice Boards as well as the concerned administrative authority are usually shy of sharing such information with public.

## Factors Responsible for Children Coming in Conflict with Law

There are several social and economic factors that push children to committing crimes. In the year 2006, out of the total juveniles involved in various crimes, 7975 were illiterate and 12,688 had education up to primary level. These two categories have accounted for 64.28 percent of the total juveniles arrested during the year 2006. Children living with parents/guardians 24,990 have accounted for 77.7 percent of the total juveniles arrested. The share of homeless children who were involved in various crimes was just 6.8 percent.

A large chunk of juveniles (72.3%) belonged to the poor family whose annual income was up to Rs. 25,000. The share of juveniles hailing from middle income group (Rs. 50,000–2,00,000) was 7.5 percent. The share of juvenile from upper middle income (Rs. two lakh to three lakh) and upper income (above Rs. three lakh) was considerable low at 0.16 percent and 0.18 percent respectively.

In 1999, the National Crime Records Bureau had observed 'As expected, low income and education, poor economic set up is generally the main attributes for delinquent behavior of the juveniles'.

At the same time, we cannot ignore the impact of media on children. Violence in today's cinema, acceptable aberrations shown in TV serials, advertisements, fashion show, reality TV showing. Crime related episodes, all of these have a negative impact on the minds of children.

On the other hand, some children in conflict with law are actually victims of crimes, particularly when they are used, trafficked and forced into begging, drug peddling, prostitution etc. Unfortunately, the law does not even recognize child beggars as children in need of care and protection.

The contribution of growing consumerism and other pressures of a neo-liberal economy, domestic violence and a total lack of a protective environment in pushing children to commit crimes is fairly significant and calls for attention from the policy-makers.

Inadequacy of law and the behavior of police add to the woes of children. It has been found that children, often innocent ones, are rounded up by the police for theft and robbery so that the police can claim that can show some action on the cases reported by them.

**Areas of Concern**

The co-ordination and interaction between different wings of the juvenile justice delivery system is poor. Lateral linkages with other sectors and Ministers/Departments such as health, Nutrition, education and vocational training, sports and youth affairs, law enforcement, including railway police etc. need to be strengthened to stop any violation or denial of basic human rights of children in conflict with law and ensure

> **Identified Justice delivery System for Children in Conflict with Law**
>
> - Juvenile Justice Board - Magistrates and Social Workers;
> - Probation Officers;
> - Police and Special Juvenile Police Unit;
> - Observation Home Staff/Special Home Staff/After Care Homes;
> - NGOs;
> - State Advisory Committee/Board;
> - District/State Rehabilitation Committee;
> - Railway Police;
> - State Monitoring Committee;
> - Ministry of Women and Child Development Department;
> - Department of Education;
> - Department of Higher Technical Training;
> - Ministry of Home Affairs;
> - Department of Finance;
> - State Human Rights Commission.

proper rehabilitation and reformation. Coordination is also missing between the states and juvenile justice mechanisms set up the different states. This is important particularly if a case of a child in conflict with law needs to be shifted or transferred to his native state. This also requires adequate investment of human and financial resources to transport the child and hence coordination between the local police in the two states as well as the railway police and the concerned JJBs.

2. With the share of juvenile crimes doubling over the past decade i.e. from 0.5% to 1.0% in relation to total crimes it is evident that the infrastructural and administrative support has to increase proportionately to address the issue related to children in conflict with law.

3. Impediments in the Administration of Justice Institutionalization has to be the last resort. However, in the present situation, children are deprived of their right to be properly defended, denied bail even when they have committed petty offences or are first time offenders, and hoarded in institutions, in conditions detrimental to their growth, development and protection.

Amongst most children in conflict with law, those that remain out of the possibility nof protection under the juvenile justice system are child beggars. These children continue to be governed by the Bombay Prevention of Begging Act. As a result, their cases are dealt with in the Beggars Courts and they are also held in the beggar's homes, which is for both adult and child beggars.

There are several other concerns concerning administration of juvenile justice that need elaboration. These include:

### *Denial of Bail*

Bail is a right of every child offender and the spirit of the juvenile justice legislation clearly suggests that children in conflict with law should be released on bail except on three conditions: *(a)* the child will be exposed to moral, physical and psychological danger or, *(b)* the release will defeat the ends of justice or, *(c)* release is likely to bring him in association of any known criminal. It has been found that children are often denied bail on these grounds, without clearly establishing the name of persons from whom the child is likely to be in danger or the name of criminals with whom the child is likely to be associated. Moreover, to seek bail children need to be legally represented before the Board. For those who can afford, finding a good lawyer is not a problem. But most others have to rely on the poor and sub-standard legal aid services. As a result, not only does the number of cases pending disposal goes up and the institutions receiving such children remain overcrowded, but the child's right to be heard have a say in his own disposition stands jeopardized.

### Inadequate Social Investigation Reports

Another hurdle in helping these children access their right to bail or be released under other provisions in the law is the Special investigation Report prepared by the Probationary Officers for every child, which forms an important and significant basis for the JJB's decision to grant or deny bail. A social investigation report is meant to be based on home visits made by the probationary officers and inquiry from the child's, relatives etc. Given the increase in the number of cases of crimes committed by children and shortage of probationary officers, such in-depth inquiry has never been possible. As a result, there is no real assessment of the child's situation and circumstances and his/her family environment. Even a good case of bail gets rejected in the absence of a fair social investigation report.

### Poor or Non-existent Probation Services

A fairly significant number of children in conflict with law are released on probation. However, a good probationary service program, where the child is supervised, monitored and provided support on being released on probation, does not exist in India. Neither are there any successful experiments available to provide a model for developing effective probationary service programs. This is an area that needs urgent and utmost attention to ensure a reformative approach to juvenile justice rather than a punitive approach.

## Inhuman Conditions in Institutions

Violence and abuse faced by children in conflict with law, from the time they are apprehended till they are released, tells a lot on the existing system and its inadequacies. Children in conflict with law face abuse and other human rights violations during arrest, interrogation and detention, including arbitrary arrest, physical abuse during interrogation, and routine harassment and physical abuse by police and by private security guards. They are held in overcrowded and unsafe conditions, denied basic sanitary facilities, and sometimes commingled with adults. They are also denied family visits, religious services, and other important contacts with their communities and even adequate food at times. There is complete deprivation of the right to liberty in total disregard of international juvenile justice and protection standards. Even when education is guaranteed as a fundamental right for 6–14 year olds, for those held in institutions, this right stands violated. The facilities where they are detained fail to provide adequate medical care, mental health intervention, or rehabilitative services. Drug and substance abuse, sexual abuse, physical punishment and inhuman treatment are rampant and often reported in the media. In many states, these children are still kept with adults inside the prisons.

There is no age-specific segregation and treatment of children inside the observation homes and special homes. Smaller children being physically and sexually abused by the older ones is often reported and found to be true. Perhaps the spaces and facilities for children in conflict with law need to be separated to cater to different age groups and their needs.

Currently, rehabilitation options for children held in institutions are very limited. Traditional and conventional vocations are taught under the vocational training programs without really assessing what kinds of skills have a viable market. As a result children end up learning tailoring or book-binding and the likes, virtually left with no skills that can help them earn a decent livelihood on being released. In fact, there is acute shortage of staff and personnel to take up the vocational training courses and often children are found idling away their time in the institutions, taking to drugs and becoming unproductive for the rest of their life.

## Unfriendly Atmosphere in the JJB

The trend observed over a period of time shows that children are deprived of the variety of rehabilitative dispositions that are available in juvenile proceedings either due to the low awareness/interest of the presiding magistrates or due to stated resource crunch. The whole atmosphere in the JJBs is unfriendly to the child. While JJBs were created under the juvenile justice system to be a child-friendly mechanism, they continue to function like any other adult court. Though training is mandated for the JJB members, it does not happen in most cases. There is limited use of non-institutional options for rehabilitation and social integration. Due to heavy pressure on the JJBs with regard to the number of cases handled in a day, children have to wait long hours till they are called in. In fact, they have to be there the whole day, often without food, water and proper toilet facilities as they are all brought together from the institution in the morning and taken back together at the end of the day.

The age of commission of crime occurs within the impressionable early and late adolescent period. This indicates that till child protection is not given the same emphasis as other issues concerning children and unless it is integrated with every other sectoral intervention for preventing children from falling into vulnerable situations and protecting them when required, all rights for all children can never be met.

## Policy Commitment/Implementation of JJ Act

Juvenile justice administration is the subject of detailed international standards. These standards cover a vast and complex range of issues from prevention through early intervention, judicial process, conditions of detention and social reintegration, involving a wide range of actors.

**Summary of International Instruments Relevant to Juvenile Justice Administration**

| *Child-specific instruments* | *Non-Child specific instruments* |
|---|---|
| UN Convention on the Rights of the Child | UN International Covenant on Civil and Political Rights (ICCPR) |
| UN Guidelines for the Prevention of Juvenile Delinquency (the 'Riyadh Guidelines') | UN International Covenant on Economic, Social and Cultural Rights |
| UN Standard Minimum Rules for the Administration of Juvenile Justice (the Beijing Rules') | UN Convention against Torture and Other Cruel, Inhuman or Degrading Treatment or Punishment |
| UN Rules for the Protection of Juveniles Deprived of their Liberty (JDL) | UN Convention on the Elimination of Racial Discrimination |
| | UN Convention on the Elimination of All Forms of Discrimination Against Women (CEDAW) |
| | UN Minimum Rules for Non-Custodial Measures: 'the Tokyo Rules' (11990) |
| | UN Standard Minimum Rules for the Treatment of Prisoners |
| African Charter on the Rights and Welfare of the Child | African Charter on Human and People's Rights |
| European Convention on the Exercise of Children's Rights | European Convention for the Protection of Human Rights and Fundamental Freedoms (and Protocols) |

| *Child-specific instruments* | *Non-Child specific instruments* |
|---|---|
| | American Convention on Human Rights and additional ?rotocol in the Area of Economic, Social and Cultural Rights. |
| SAARC Convention on Regional Arrangements for he promotion of Child Welfare in South Asia (2002) | SAARC Decade of the Rights of the Child (2001–2010) |

The primary instrument guiding the development of juvenile justice is the United Nations Convention on the Rights of the Child (1989). This instrument is seen as the overarching framework for a child rights approach. It contains an elaborate set of guidelines for maintaining human rights standards in juvenile justice systems and for the administration of juvenile justice itself.

The table shows some of the principles and rights which need to underpin the intervention relating to children in conflict with the law.

| *Principal* | *Explanation Supported by CRC article* |
|---|---|
| Diversion | (3) In all matters concerning a child, the child's best interest should be a primary concern. |
| Empowerment | (2) All children should have equal access to services regardless of race, sex language or other status. |
| Cultural Appropriateness | (8) Consideration should be given to dealing with children in a manner consistent with their culture. |
| Best Interests of the Child | (37) Alternative solutions should be sought before arresting or detaining a child. |

| *Principal* | *Explanation Supported by CRC article* |
|---|---|
| Deprivation of Liberty a Last Report | (40) Efforts should be made to avoid children going through the formal justice system where possible. |
| Non-discrimination | (40) The resourcefulness of each child and their family should be promoted. |
| Restorative Justice | (12) Children should have a say in all matters that affect them. |
| System Accountability | (5) A child's family should be involved in the making of decisions affection a child and wherever possible regard should be given for the views of the family. |
| Child's Participation | (40) Efforts should be made to restore the damage caused to all parties affected by the offence. |
| Family Participation | Everyone intervening with children and their families should be held accountable to/for them. |
| Re-integration | (40) Efforts should be made to re-integrate children into their communities and to assist them to play a positive rile in the community. |

Table showing Relevant Articles form the Convention on the Rights of the Child:

| *Principal* | *Explanation Supported by CRC article* |
|---|---|
| Best interests of the child | (3) In all matters concerning child, the child's best interest should be a primary concern. |
| Non-discrimination | (2) All children should have equal access to services regardless of race, sex language or other status. |

| *Principal* | *Explanation Supported by CRC article* |
|---|---|
| Cultural Appropriateness | (8) Consideration should be given to dealing with children in a manner consistent with their culture. |
| Deprivation of Liberty a Last Resort | (37) Alternative solutions should be sought before arresting or detaining a child. |
| Diversion | (40) efforts should be made to avoid children going through the formal justice system where possible. |
| Empowerment | (40) The resource/fullness of each child and their family should be promoted. |
| Child's Participation | (12) Children should have a say in all matters that affect them. |
| Family Participation | (5) A child's family should be involved in the making of decisions affecting a child and wherever possible regard should be given for the views of the family. |
| Restorative justice | (40) Efforts should be made to restore the damage caused to all parties affected by the offence. |
| System Accountability | (All) Everyone intervening with children and their families should be held accountable to/for them. |
| Re-integration | (40) Efforts should be made to re-integrate children child into their communities and to assist them to play a positive role in the community. |

*Source:* Training on Juvenile Justice, UNICEF.

## LITERATURE REVIEW

**1. Azeez, Mudassir. (1998)**

A study of psycho-social and health aspects of inmates in Juvenile homes. Mysore: Government Medical College, Dept. of Community Medicine, 150 p.

**Abstract:** A study of 421 juveniles in the 4 Juvenile Homes of Bangalore and Mysore (out of a total of 21 in Karnataka) was carried out to study the psychological factors of the juveniles prior to their admission, to assess their health status, self-esteem, adjustment problems and to examine provisions under the Juvenile Justice Act, 1986 and its relevance in the present-day context. Results, through physical examination and interviews, revealed that most of the juveniles (70%) were in the 12-16 years age group and were from large nuclear families. More than 90 percent of the parents were illiterate and were from low socio-economic class. 58 percent of the inmates came from broken homes. Only 92 (21.85%) juveniles were suffering from some morbidity at the time of the study. Communicable diseases, nutritional deficiencies, diseases of eyes, ears, skin and dental caries were the common conditions seen in children living in over crowded institutions. The common offences committed by delinquents were ticketless travel (38%), stealing (22%), begging (12%) and wandering (9%). Only boys were involved in gambling (7.24% of total children; 13.5% boys) and only girls were involved in prostitution (4.34% of total children; 9.37% girls). 77 percent inmates agreed that they harboured some sort of alienation, and the alienation was more among girls than boys. The Juvenile Homes provided accomodation, education, recreation and rehabilitation facilities. Education was given upto 7th Standard, and for those children who had no inclination for studies, vocational training like tailoring, weaving, carpentry, bakery, etc. was given. Television, books, magazines were provided, festivals were observed, creative arts such as teracota, doll-making, painting, music and karate were also taught to interested inmates. Regular health check-up was conducted once a month. Academically inclined students were sent to high schools and thereafter sent to after care homes to complete their graduation. Juvenile homes for girls were in a better condition, as they took initiative to keep the premises spick and span. The study recommended that parents should be counselled regarding positive approach in disciplining their children and size of the family should be small so that parents could give child-centred care to their children. Review and modification of the existing acts dealing with problem children was also recommended. Rehabilitation should be more meaningful and suited to modern day trades and skills. Preventive and corrective measures within the available resources were suggested to solve the social problem of delinquency.

**Key Words** : 1. CHILDREN IN DIFFICULT CIRCUMSTANCES 2. INSTITUTIONALIZED CHILD 3. HEALTH STATUS 4. JUVENILE DELINQUENT 5. JUVENILE HOME 6. JUVENILE JUSTICE ACT 7. INSTITUTIONAL CARE

**2. Joglekar, Adhiraj and Patel, R R. (1997)**

Usefulness of V code diagnosis : neglected child and juvenile delinquents. Mumbai : BYL Nair Children's Hospital. Dept. of Psychiatry, 11 p.

**Abstract:** The study was undertaken in Mumbai in 1997 with the following objectives : To find out if there is a need for a separate category called Neglected Juveniles; to compare the delinquents and the neglected children with respect to their – intellectual abilities, personality profiles and psychiatric morbidity and to discuss the implications of the differences between the two groups. The sample under study consisted of 60 children from the streets. Children were divided into two groups – delinquents and neglected (as per the definition of Justice Act 14). A semi-structured interview schedule was used to gather preliminary data and reach a psychiatric diagnosis as per DSM IV. The results revealed that more number of respondents in the delinquent group fall in the categories of mild mental retardation and border line intellectual functioning [66.6%] compared to 0 percent and 46.6 percent of the neglected group. The neglected children were found to be affected more by feelings and were more emotional. The same group was found to be more humble and conforming and relaxed than the delinquents. The delinquents were found to be more expedient and have a tendency to evade rules suggesting a weak super ego. Study suggested that there is a definite need to give more importance to the entity called Neglected children and further it suggested that the children in observation home should not be looked at with a bias and must be screened at the earliest in order to separate the neglected children from the delinquents as the former may become deviant through observation.

**Key Words**: 1. DESTITUTE CHILD 2. INSTITUTIONALIZED CHILD 3. JUVENILE DELINQUENT 4. NEGLECTED CHILD 5. INSTITUTIONALISED CHILD 6. INSTITUTIONAL CARE 7. STREET CHILDREN 8. OBSERVATION HOME.

**3. Wankhede, Nilkantha S. (2003)**

Study of medico social problems of inmates of Government Observation Home for Boys, Nagpur. Nagpur: Indira Gandhi Medical College, Dept. of Preventive and Social Medicine. ~120 p.

**Abstract**: Family is a crucial guiding influence in the child's personality development. Any faulty familial, environmental, socio-cultural conditions could maladjust the child. In the past five decades, a large majority of Indian children continue to remain in distress and turmoil despite hectic planning of welfare programs, legislation and administrative actions. According to Juvenile Justice Act 2000, Juvenile is defined as "a person who has not completed 18 years of age". The problem of juvenile vagrancy is more acute in urban communities and especially in industrial areas.

This study was carried out at Government Observation Home for Boys, Nagpur. The study design was comparative cross-sectional study. 5000 subjects were included in this study of whom 250 study subjects were inmates of Government Observation Home. It was observed that the maximum number of subjects (25.2%) were in the 10-16 years age group and a few 7.6 percent were below 10 years of age. Majority of the delinquents (75.71%) were above 14 years of age and a few (73.6%) were below 14 years of age. It was observed from the study that 6.4 percent parents of study subjects were skilled workers as compared to 19.2 percent of comparison subjects, and 13.2 percent parents were unemployed as compared to 2.8 percent of comparison subjects. It was found that 80.7 percent delinquents belonged to urban areas as compared to 73.6 percent neglected children in urban areas. When delinquents and neglected juveniles were compared with each other, it was observed that 72.14 percent delinquents belonged to nuclear families compared to 64.55 percent neglected children. About 5.6 percent study subjects belonged to upper middle socio-economic class, 18.0 percent study subjects to lower middle socio-economic class and 20.2 percent belonged to upper lower socio-economic class. It was observed that stealing was the commonest reason for their apprehension in all ages (36.8%), followed by vagrancy (29.2%), begging (12.4%), fighting and quarrelling (9.2%), murder (3.2%), etc. 56 percent study subjects were apprehended for various serious criminal acts, and 44 percent were admitted due to child neglect and abuse by parents and relatives. About 31.2 percent parents of study subjects were illiterate as compared to 7.2 percent of comparison subjects. Around 30.8 percent study subjects were illiterate as compared to 3.2 percent comparison subjects. School dropout rate was higher after 5$^{th}$ Standard. 3.2 percent parents of study subjects had an over protective attitude compared to 4.8 percent parents of comparison subjects. Haemoglobin level of 4.8 percent study subjects was normal, 24.4 percent had mild anaemia, 38 percent had moderate anaemia, and 16.8 percent had severe anaemia. Overcrowding was observed in institutions and cleanliness was not maintained. Immunization status of study subjects was significantly lower as compared to comparison subjects in respect of BCG immunization. At every Observation Home there should be a full time qualified physician. Facilities like toilets, and washing and cleaning facilities should be provided to maintain cleanliness within the premises. Institutions should have facilities for recreation and education. Health education and counseling aimed at reducing the behavioural problems among inmates of juvenile correction centres should be imparted.

**Key Words** : 1. DESTITUTE CHILD 2. INSTITUTIONAL CARE 3. OBSERVATION HOMES 4. INSTITUTIONALIZED CHILD 5. JUVENILE DELINQUENT 6. NUTRITIONAL STATUS JUVENILES 7. HEALTH STATUS JUVENILES.

**4. Chandra Shekara, T.S., Poornima, B.K. and Manjunatha, P.S. (2001)**

A Study on Child Care Institutions in Karnataka. Bangalore : NIPCCD, Regional Centre Bangalore. ~100 p.

**Abstract**: The study found that child care institutions run by the Government or private bodies have been playing an important role in providing services to children who are deprived of a natural family. The objectives were to study the functioning of child care institutions with reference to infrastructure, their procedures, rules and regulations concerning admission and discharge of children; understand the views and experiences of child inmates; and offer suggestions for enhancing the quality of functioning of child care institutions. 44 institutions run by the Department of Women and Child Development, 99 under Backward Classes and Minorities Department, and 18 private institutions were included, covering 21 districts. 160 inmates (children) were selected for the study, 32 inmates from government institutions, 93 from grant-in-aid (GIA) and private institutions. 75 staff members, 13 from Government, 44 from GIA and 18 from private institutions were interviewed, in addition to 6 members representing the management. Findings revealed that infrastructure facilities available in child care institutions differed significantly from institution to institution. Private institutions had relatively better infrastructure facilities. Variations were observed in the delivery of services like education, vocational training, recreation and rehabilitation. GIA institutions were slightly better in providing these facilities. Facilities for sports were available in majority of the institutions. Counselling and therapeutic services were lacking in Government institutions. Television was found to be the major source of recreation for children. Government institutions followed the prescribed rules. Some private institutions ran child care centres independently and had their own bye-laws. Child care institutions in the Government, grant-in-aid and private sector did not have up to date information on numbers and addresses. It was found that the training of staff on issues concerned with administration of child care institutions was not a priority. Inmates stayed in the institutions for more than 5 years. A majority of inmates (56%) had relatives/ parents either living separately or divorced, and in any case were not taking care of the child. 29 percent of them had a single parent only. Only 15 percent had both parents deceased. All the 75 institutions studied had board and lodging facilities. Out of 160 children, a majority 110 (69%) were accommodated in dormitories and the remaining were provided rooms. Government run institutions had better hostel facilities and kitchens. Kitchen was very important in view of its role in preparing and serving good food cooked in hygienic conditions. Breakfast, lunch, dinner and special diet was offered to all the children during festival days and on Sundays. They were also provided bed tea/ coffee (56%) and evening coffee/tea (53%), specially in Government institutions. The satisfaction rate was relatively higher for lunch and special diet, compared to breakfast and dinner. The food provided in private institutions wasbetter compared to GIA and Government institutions. It was recommended that child care institutions should develop good liaison with social service organizations, philanthropists, religious institutions and other clubs/associations. Schools may be motivated to provide concessions to children coming from child care institutions. Running institutions solely on Government grants may be discouraged. The quality of food in Government run institutions should be improved.

**Key Words**: 1. DESTITUTE CHILD 2. INSTITUTIONAL CARE 3. CHILDREN IN DIFFICULT CIRCUMSTANCES.

**5. Pagare, Deepti et al. (2004).**

Sexual abuse of street children brought to an observation home. New Delhi : Maulana Azad Medical College, Dept. of Community Medicine. 6 p.

**Abstract**: WHO estimates that globally 8 percent boys and 25 percent girls below age 18 suffer sexual abuse of some kind every year. Sexual abuse of children in India occurs across all socio-economic classes and is widespread among boys and girls, both in rural and urban areas. Perpetrators of sexual abuse find their victims in wide ranging situations, and homeless boys, living in an unprotected environment on streets, make easy prey for sexual abuse. The study was conducted at an Observation Home for Boys in Delhi where non-delinquent male juveniles aged 6-18 years are temporarily detained. All the boys admitted for the first time to the Observation Home between May to October 2002 were included. The boys were requested to undergo examination in a separate room by the Medical Officer, based on the Guidelines of American Medical Association (AMA, 1985) for Primary Care Physicians for diagnosis of suspected sexual abuse. All the boys were assured confidentiality and none was forced to undergo physical examination against his will. A total of 202 boys were willing for clinical examination, but the final sample consisted of 189 boys. Among the 178 subjects living away from families, 62.9 percent had left home between 6 to 10 years of age. Overall, 38.1 percent boys reported sexual abuse, with use of force ranging from 4.8 percent to 23.8 percent. Over 15 percent boys reported penetrative sexual abuse. The maximum proportion of abuse was reported in the age group of 8-10 years (42.9%). The mean age at abuse was reported as $9.13 \pm 2.4$ years. Most children (93.2%) reported the incident to be within 2-3 weeks of leaving home. All boys reported single episode of sexual abuse except four. The maximum proportion of incidents occurred during late evening or at night (59.2%). 22.2 percent cases occurred during the day. Most children (76.2%) were abused at railway stations, about 4 percent were abused at the work place, and 1.4 percent at some other Observation Home. Among the 72 abused children, 44 (61.1%) had some physical sign of abuse while 29 (40.2%) showed behavioural signs of sexual abuse. 18 boys had signs suggestive of sexually transmitted diseases, and this also increased their vulnerability to HIV infection. The problem of sexual abuse among inmates of Observation Homes is grave and requires urgent remedial action. The period of detention at Observation Homes may be utilized for identification of the victims and their proper medical, social and psychological rehabilitation to prevent further abuse. Concerned authorities should take appropriate action and make efforts to create safe living conditions for all children, including street children.

**Key Words**: 1. DESTITUTE CHILD 2. CHILD SEXUAL ABUSE 3. SEXUAL ABUSE BOYS 4. ABUSE IN INSTITUTIONS 5. INSTITUTIONAL CARE 6. STREET CHILDREN 7. EXPLOITATION OF CHILDREN 8. OBSERVATION HOMES 9. DELHI.

# 3

# Infrastructure and Manpower at Child Care Institutions

The vision behind all of the UN human rights treaties is promoting respect for the dignity of each person, for instance, the right to life, freedom of expression, freedom from torture, the right to education, and the right to an adequate standard of living. In view this principle, a child centred system recognizes the child as subject to fundamental rights and freedoms and ensures that all actions concerning the child are to be guided by his/her best interests.

To provide for the care, protection, treatment, development and rehabilitation of neglected or delinquent juveniles and for the adjudication of certain matters relating to, and disposition of, delinquent juveniles the Juvenile Justice Act, 1986 (53 of 1986) was enacted by Parliament. Several provisions of the Constitution including clause (3) of article 15, Clauses (e) and (f) of Article 39, Articles 45 and 47 also impose on the State a primary responsibility on ensuring that all the needs of children are met and that their basic human rights are fully protected. On 20th November, 1989 General Assemble of the United Nations adopted the Convention on the Rights of the Child wherein a set of standards to be adhered to by all State partied in securing the best interests of the child has been prescribed. The

**The Juvenile Justice (Care and Protection of Children) Amendment Act, 2006**

An Act to consolidate and amend the law relating to juveniles in conflict with law and children in need of care and protection, by providing for proper care, protection and treatment by catering to their development needs, and by adopting a child-friendly approach in the adjudication and disposition of matters in the best interest of children and for their ultimate rehabilitation [and for matters connected therewith or incidental thereto]

**Source**: Subs. By Act 33 of 2006, Sec. 2, for "through various institutions established under this enactment" (w.e.f. 22.8.2006)

Convention emphasis social re-integration of child victims, to the extent possible without resorting to judicial proceedings. The Government of India, having, ratified the Convention, has found it expedient to re-enact the existing law relating to juveniles bearing in mind the standards prescribed in the Convention on the Rights of the Child, the United Nations Standard Minimum Rules for the Administration of Juvenile Justice, 1985 (The Beijing Rules), the United Nations Rules for the Protection of Juveniles Deprived of their Liberty (1990), and all other relevant international instruments. To achieve this objective the Juvenile Justice (care and Protection of Children) Bill was introduced in the Parliament[1].

### Status of the Implementation of the JJ Act, 2006: A Situational Analysis

A review of the working of the Juvenile Act, 1986 (53 of 1986) had indicate that much greater attention is required to be given to children in conflict with law or those in need of care and protection. The justice system as available for adults is not considered suitable for being applied to juvenile or the child or anyone on their behalf including the police, voluntary organizations, social workers, or parents and guardians, throughout the country. There is also an urgent need for creating adequate infrastructure necessary for the implementation of the proposed legislation with a larger involvement of informal systems specially the family, the voluntary organization and the community. However, for the present assessment an attempt has been made to cover all the homes of 27 States/UTs. The distribution of the target numbers and actually assessed/visited by the study team is given in Table 3.1. It is evident that a substantial number of different types of homes were visited and details were obtained by the enumerators. A total of 1135 children homes are created under the Juvenile Justice Act out of which 69.25 percent were covered. Although Special and After Care Homes were less in number but 93.55 percent and 49.06 percent respectively were covered for the present assessment. More than two-third (69.25%) Observation Homes were assessed by the team members.

**Table 3.1**

**Children Institutions Created under the JJ Act (Targeted and Actually Selected/Assessed)**

| *Sl. No.* | *Institution* | *Target Nos.* | *Actually selected/assessed* | *% to Target* |
|---|---|---|---|---|
| 1. | Observation home | 284 | 195 | 68.66 |
| 2. | Special home | 62 | 58 | 93.55 |
| 3. | Children home | 531 | 369 | 69.49 |
| 4. | Shelter home | 205 | 21 | 10.24 |
| 5. | After care home | 53 | 26 | 49.06 |
| 6. | Other homes | 355 | 117 | 32.96 |

The setting up of the juvenile justice is in recognition of the vulnerabilities of children, and the responsibility on the state for setting up systems for the welfare and development of children. Keeping this in view, an attempt has been made to find out the latest status of the

**Table 3.2**
**Status of the Implementation of the JJ Act, 2006 in the States/UTs**

| Sl. No. | States/UTs notified | Rules Fund on (Date) | JJ Districts set up (Y/N) | No. of Body | Statutory SJPU | | No. of Act created | No. of Children Home Created under JJ | | | | | |
|---|---|---|---|---|---|---|---|---|---|---|---|---|---|
| | | | | | No. of CWCs | No. of JJBs | | Observation Home | Special Home | Shelter Home | Children/Juvenile | After Care Home | Others |
| 1. | 2. | 3. | 4. | 5. | 6. | 7. | 8. | 9. | 10. | 11. | 12. | 13. | 14. |
| 1 | Andhra Pradesh | 8.5.2003 | Yes | 23 | 23 | 23 | 23 | 9 | 6 | 0 | 9 | 1 | 1-Child Guidance Bureau |
| 2 | Arunachal Pradesh | 16.1.06 | No | 16 | 8 | 8 | - | - | - | - | 1 | - | - |
| 3 | Assam | Under Process | No | 27 | 27 | 27 | 27 | 4 | Under process | - | 3 | Under process | - |
| 4 | Bihar | 1.9.2003 | No | 38 | 5 | 32 | 40 | 10 | 1 | 2 | 3 | 2 | - |
| 5 | Chhattishgarh | 16.12.06 | Yes | 18 | 6 | 6 | 16 | 6 | 2 | - | 11 | 2 | - |

| 1. | 2. | 3. | 4. | 5. | 6. | 7. | 8. | 9. | 10. | 11. | 12. | 13. | 14. |
|---|---|---|---|---|---|---|---|---|---|---|---|---|---|
| 6 | Goa | 22.7.2004 | No | 2 | 1 | 1 | 1 | 01(B) 01(G) | 2 | 2 | 2 | - | - |
| 7. | Gujarat | 31.12.2003 | No | 26 | 25 | 25 | 25 | 24 | 13 | 23 | 66 | 14 | 8 |
| 8. | Haryana | 11.10.2002 | Yes | 20 | 20 | 20 | 20 | 3 | 1 | 2 | 2 | 1 | - |
| 9. | Himachal Pradesh | 4.5.2002 | Yes | 12 | 12 | 2 | 12 | 1 | 1 | 11 | 7 | 2 | - |
| 10. | Jammu & Kashmir | N.A | N.A | N.A | N.A | N.A | N.A | N.A | N.A | N.A | N.A | N.A | N.A |
| 11. | Jharkhand | N.A. | No | 24 | 11 | 21 | 24 | 7 | 1 | - | 2 | - | - |
| 12. | Karnataka | 26.9.2002 | Under process | 29 | 28 | 22 | 27 | 22 | 2 | 45 | 5 | 5 | 1- Shishu Mandir |
| 13. | Kerala | 21.1.2003 | Yes | 14 | 10 | 5 | 14 | 14 | 2 | 12 | 9 | 3 | - |
| 14. | Madhya Pradesh | 15.7.2003 | Yes | 48 | 30 | 30 | 48 | 18 | 3 | 1 | 3 | 2 | Shishu Greh |
| 15. | Maharashtra | 3.4.04 | No | 35 | 29 | 29 | 28 | 60 | 4 | - | 190 | 4 | 1 |
| 16. | Manipur | 19.5.2004 | No | 9 | 9 | 9 | - | 3 | 2 | 1 | 9 | - | - |
| 17. | Meghalaya | 8.12.04 | No | 7 | 7 | 7 | - | 03 Cum Spl. Home | Cum Spl. Home | 1 | - | - | - |

| 1. | 2. | 3. | 4. | 5. | 6. | 7. | 8. | 9. | 10. | 11. | 12. | 13. | 14. |
|---|---|---|---|---|---|---|---|---|---|---|---|---|---|
| 18. | Mizoram | 1.8.03 | Yes (2.5 lacs) | 8 | 2 | 2 | 39 | 2 | 2 | - | 5 | - | - |
| 19. | Nagaland | 1.3.06 | No | 11 | 1 | 1 | - | 1 | 1 | - | 1 | 1 | - |
| 20. | Orissa | 1.4.06 | Yes | 30 | 25 | 30 | 17 | 12 | 3 | 4.6 | 46 | - | - |
| 21. | Punjab | 8.12.2003 | Under process | 20 | 5 | 19 | 15 | 4 | 2 | - | 7 | 2 | - |
| 22. | Rajasthan | 23.7.2002 | Yes | 33 | 16 | 32 | 33 | 32 | 1 | - | 32 (B) 8 (G) | 1 | - |
| 23. | Sikkim | 13.3.2003 | No | 4 | 4 | 4 | - | 1 | - | - | 5 | - | - |
| 24. | Tamil Nadu | 14.2.2002 | Yes | 31 | 18 | 8 | 31 | 8 | 2 | 5 | 31 | 3 | - |
| 25. | Tripura | 23.3.2002 | Yes | 4 | 1 | 4 | Yet to be created | 1 | 1 | - | 6 | - | - |
| 26. | Uttar Pradesh | 31.3.2004 | Y(25 lacs) | 71 | 9 | 17 | 40 | 17 | 2 | 6 | 14 | 4 | - |
| 27. | Uttrakhand | N.A. | No | 13 | 13 | 13 | - | 7 | 1 | 4 | 1 | - | - |
| 28. | West Bengal | Under process | Yes | 19 | 15 | 11 | under process | 7 | 4 | 42 (18= Govt) | 42 | 5 | -15 |
| **Total (States)** | | | | **592** | **360** | **408** | **480** | **278** | **59** | **203** | **520** | **52** | **355** |

| 1. | 2. | 3. | 4. | 5. | 6. | 7. | 8. | 9. | 10. | 11. | 12. | 13. | 14. |
|---|---|---|---|---|---|---|---|---|---|---|---|---|---|
| 29. | A & N Island | 11.7.2002 | | | | | | | | | | | |
| 30. | Chandigarh | 15.3.2002 | No | 1 | 1 | 2 | 1 | 1(B), 1(G) | - | 1 | - | Shared with observation Home | |
| 31. | D & N Haveli | | | | Children are being sent Navsari & Surat of Gujarat | | | | | | | | |
| 32. | Daman & Diu | 20.6.2002 | No | 2 | 1 | 2 | | Navsari & Junagarh (Gujarat) | | | | | |
| 33. | Delhi | 19.8.2002 | Yes | 10 | 4 | 2 | | 2 (B), 1 (G) | 2 | - | 10 | - | - |
| 34. | Lakshadweep | | | There is no no problem relating to juveniles in the Territory. However, they have earmarked a room in working Women's Hostel at Kavaratti to accommodate such cases, if required | | | | | | | | | |
| 35. | Pondicherry | 22.3.2002 | No | 1 | 1 | 1 | 1 | 1 | 1 | 1 | 1 | 1 | - |
| **Total (UTs)** | | | | **14** | **7** | **7** | **2** | **6** | **3** | **2** | **11** | **1** | **-** |
| **Total (All-India)** | | | | **606** | **367** | **415** | **482** | **284** | **62** | **205** | **531** | **53** | **355** |

**Source**: Concerned Department of State Governments.

implementation of the Juvenile Justice (Care and Protection of Children) Act, 2006 in the States/UTs and the information in this regard is given in Table 3.2.

**Implementation Status of JJ Act in States/UTs**

| | |
|---|---|
| • State Rules formulated and notified after JJ Act, 2000: | 29 |
| • State Rules formulated and notified after JJ Act, 2006: | Nil |
| • State Rules being finalized: | 31 |
| • States/UTs with CWCs/JJBs: | 32 |
| • States/UTs Created JJ Fund: | 13 |
| • States/UTs where creation of JJ Fund is under process: | 02 |
| • States/UTs created SJPU: | 22 |
| • UTs not requiring any Home: | 03 |

The implementation of the Juvenile Justice Act requires the formulation of state rules and the setting of the juvenile justice system machinery, mainly the Child Welfare Committees (CWCs) and the Juvenile Justice Boards (JJBs). As per the JJ Amendment Act, 2006 (Section-1 of the principal Act) the words "commencement and application" shall be substituted. Meaning thereby the state should formulate rules within one year after the notification of central model rules. It may be mentioned that Central model Rules vide G.S.R. 679(E), dated 26th October, 2007, published in the Gazette of India. But after that, none of the State/UT has formulated state rules for implementation of the Juvenile Justice (Care and Protection of Children) Act, 2006 (Table 3.2). Almost all have mentioned that formulation of rules are under process. Majority of the States/UTs have set up JJ fund and number of CWCs/JJBs has also increased considerably. It is interesting to note that majority of the States/UTs have created Special Juvenile Police Unit (SJPU).

**Type of Institutions**

The amended JJ Act extends to the whole of India except the state of Jammu and Kashmir. The Act seeks to consolidate and modify the law relating to juveniles in conflict with the law and children in need of care and protection, by providing for proper care, protection and treatment by catering to their development needs, and by adopting a child-friendly approach in the adjudication and disposition of matters in the best interest of children and for their ultimate rehabilitation. This could be through various institutions (Government or NGO) established/recognized under this enactment or through non-institutional services such as adoption, foster care, and sponsorship. An attempt has been made through this enactment to make up for the lacunae in the existing adoption laws by permitting persons belonging to all religions to adopt.

There is a classification and separation of delinquents on the basis of their age and the nature of offences committed by them. The five types of institutions provided under the Act are as follows:

- Juvenile homes
- Special homes
- Observation homes
- After-care homes
- Fit persons / Institutions

**Table 3.3**
**Type of Homes**

| *Homes* | *Run By* | | | *Supported By* | | |
|---|---|---|---|---|---|---|
| | *State Govt.* | *NGO* | *% of Homes run by State* | *MWCD* | *State Govt.* | *Other* |
| Observation home | 157 | 38 | 80.41 | 43 | 124 | 28 |
| Special home | 45 | 13 | 77.97 | 15 | 30 | 13 |
| Children home | 190 | 179 | 51.49 | 81 | 236 | 52 |
| Shelter home | 11 | 10 | 52.38 | 4 | 11 | 6 |
| Aftercare home | 22 | 7 | 73.07 | 7 | 18 | 1 |
| Others | 55 | 62 | 47.00 | 12 | 66 | 39 |
| **All India Total** | 477 | 309 | 60.68 | 162 | 485 | 139 |

The State Government may establish and maintain as many juvenile homes as may be necessary under this Act. The State Government may, by rules made under this Act, provide for the management of juvenile homes, including the standards and the nature of services to be maintained by them and the circumstances under which, and the manner in which, the certification of a juvenile home may be granted or withdrawn. However, some of these institutions were private institutions also run voluntary organizations. A total of 786 institutions were visited and detailed information was obtained in a questionnaire developed for the purpose (Table 3.3).

It is evident from Fig. 3.1 that a substantial number of children institutions were being run by the state government. However, a total of 309 institutions were also run by the voluntary organizations. It was found that maximum number (179) Children Homes were run by the voluntary organizations. Even other types of homes (62) like; *Shish Grih, Balak Sadan* etc. were run by the voluntary organizations.

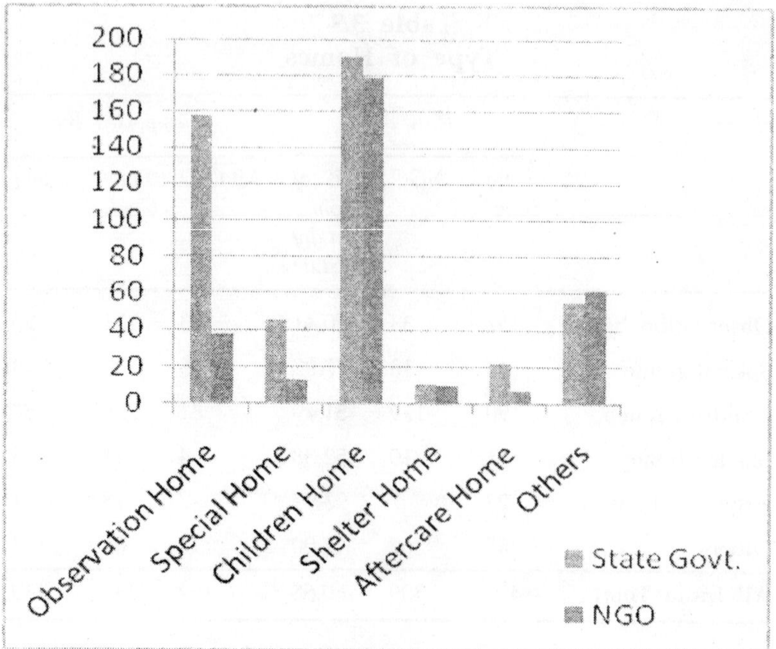


**Fig. 3.1: Type of Homes**

It can be seen in Table 3.3 that maximum number (485) homes were supported by state government. There were 162 homes supported by MWCD, govt. of India.

### Physical Set up of Institutions

Physical set up of different child care institutions such as accommodation, other infrastructural facilities, sports facilities etc. were assessed by the research team who visited different Homes. Data regarding availability of accommodation at different Homes is presented in Table 3.4 on next page.

It is evident from table that on an average per Observation Home 3 dormitories, 4 classrooms, 5 bathrooms, 7 latrines and 3 store rooms were available whereas corresponding figure for Special Homes was 1, 5, 6 and 1. It has been noticed that a substantial number of classrooms (10), dormitories (5), kitchens (5), recreation rooms (7), bathrooms

**Table 3.4**

**Availability of accommodation and infrastructure at different Child Care Institutions**

| Sl. No. | All India | Observation Home | | Special Home | | Children Home | | Shelter Home | | Aftercare Home | | Other | | Total | |
|---|---|---|---|---|---|---|---|---|---|---|---|---|---|---|---|
| | | No. | Capa-city | No. | Cap-acity | No. | Capa-city | No. | Capa-city | No. | Capa-city | No. | Capa city | No. | Capa-city |
| 1. | Dormi-tories | 610 | 31039 | 147 | 7413 | 1867 | 153809 | 85 | 1632 | 94 | 5897 | 228 | 5189 | 3031 | 204979 |
| 2. | Class-rooms | 860 | 2187 | 649 | 370 | 3836 | 7770 | 48 | 364 | 8 | 50 | 105 | 2485 | 5506 | 13226 |
| 3. | Sick room/First aid room | 73 | 1331 | 41 | 27 | 248 | 6656 | 15 | 335 | 9 | 12 | 51 | 157 | 437 | 8518 |
| 4. | Kitchen | 191 | 4505 | 57 | 108 | 1923 | 5538 | 24 | 953 | 25 | 95 | 82 | 888 | 2302 | 12087 |
| 5. | Dinning Hall | 110 | 4225 | 44 | 2960 | 266 | 8516 | 22 | 710 | 18 | 225 | 66 | 857 | 526 | 17493 |
| 6. | Recreation room | 77 | 2964 | 31 | 150 | 2490 | 8937 | 16 | 1960 | 9 | 170 | 45 | 758 | 2668 | 14939 |
| 7. | Library | 47 | 652 | 17 | 0 | 768 | 2005 | 13 | 460 | 7 | 42 | 223 | 130 | 1075 | 3289 |
| 8. | Counselling | 83 | 229 | 16 | 0 | 164 | 2825 | 8 | 425 | 6 | 0 | 27 | 237 | 304 | 3716 |

| Sl. No. | All India | Observation Home | | Special Home | | Children Home | | Shelter Home | | Aftercare Home | | Other | | Total | |
|---|---|---|---|---|---|---|---|---|---|---|---|---|---|---|---|
| | | No. | Capa-city | No. | Capa-acity | No. | Capa-city | No. | Capa-city | No. | Capa-city | No. | Capa city | No. | Capa-city |
| 9. | Office Rooms | 266 | 2226 | 87 | 10 | 735 | 6830 | 38 | 425 | 124 | 78 | 109 | 275 | 1359 | 9844 |
| 10. | Work-shops | 144 | 367 | 48 | 10 | 380 | 4705 | 31 | 775 | 7 | 0 | 54 | 294 | 664 | 6151 |
| 11. | Bath-rooms | 965 | 1856 | 296 | 391 | 2339 | 4166 | 124 | 291 | 91 | 290 | 368 | 821 | 4183 | 7815 |
| 12. | Latrines | 1356 | 1361 | 375 | 406 | 2885 | 4057 | 134 | 291 | 110 | 315 | 585 | 941 | 5445 | 7371 |
| 13. | Store room | 541 | 1418 | 68 | 0 | 730 | 3052 | 35 | 475 | 29 | 11 | 91 | 475 | 1494 | 5431 |
| 14. | Play-Ground | 108 | 5585 | 36 | 0 | 1939 | 38643 | 19 | 2146 | 2510 | 250 | 59 | 431 | 4671 | 47055 |

(6) and latrines (8) were available in per Children Home. These facilities in Shelter Homes and After Care Homes were lagging behind. In fact, capacity and strength in the dormitory section gives the strength of children based on the 40 sq.ft. norm per child. State-wise details can be seen in Annexure-2. The bathroom and latrines have been calculated based on the guidelines of one bathroom for 10 children and one latrine for 7 children. But most of Homes do not adhere to these guidelines. It has also been observed that most of the Homes did not have the infrastructure to segregate children according to their age. In most of the cases, white washing was done when budget was available.

As per the guidelines laid down in the Juvenile Justice Amendment Act, 2006 there is provision to provide sanitary pads, cloths etc. invariably to all girls. Data in this regard shows that it was grossly inadequate in all the Homes.

**Clothing for Girls**

| *Sl. No.* | *Article* | *Quantity to be provided per child* |
|---|---|---|
| 1. | Skirts & Blouse or Salwar Kameez or Half Sari with blouses and petticoats | 5 sets per year for girls depending on age and regional preferences |
| 2. | Banyans (1 Metre each) | 6 per year for younger girls |
| 3. | Brassiers | 6 per year for older girls |
| 4. | Panties (1 Metre Cloth each) | 6 per year |
| 5. | Sanitary Towels | 12 packs per year for older girls |
| 6. | Woolen Sweaters | 2 in 2 years (in cold regions) |
| 7. | Woolen Shawls | 1 in 2 years (in cold regions) |

**Clothing for Boys**

| | | |
|---|---|---|
| 1. | Shirts | 5 sets per year |
| 2. | Shorts | 5 sets per year for younger boys |

| *Sl. No.* | *Article* | *Quantity to be provided per child* |
|---|---|---|
| 3. | Pants | 5 sets per year for older boys |
| 4. | Vest | 4 sets per year |
| 5. | Underwear | 4 sets per year |
| 6. | Woolen Jerseys | 2 in 2 years (for cold regions) |
| 7. | Scarfs | 2 in 2 years (for cold regions) |
| | **Bedding** | |
| 1. | Towels | 4 per Years |
| 2. | Cotton Bed Sheets | 2 per 2 Years |
| 3. | Pillow (Cotton stuffed) | 1 per 2 Years |
| 4. | Pillow Covers | 2 per 2 Years |
| 5. | Woolen blankets | 2 per 2 Years |
| 6. | Cotton Durry | 2 per 2 Years |
| 7. | Cotton filled quilt | 1 per 2 Years (in cold regions) |
| 8. | Mattress | 1 per 2 Years |
| 9. | Mosquito Net | 1 per 2 Years |
| | **Miscellaneous Articles** | |
| 1. | Slippers | 1 pair per year |
| 2. | Shoes | 1 pair per year |
| 3. | School Uniform | 2 sets per year for children attending outside schools |
| 4. | School Shoes | 1 pair per year for children attending outside schools |
| 5. | School Bag and Stationery | 1 set per year for children attending outside schools |
| 6. | Handkerchiefs | 6 per year |

Table - Frequency of cleanliness

| S. No. | Homes | N | Sunning of bedding and clothing | | | | | Cleanliness in the medical centre | | | | | Cleanliness in the Kitchen | | | | | Cleanliness in the toilets | | | | | Total | | | | |
|---|---|---|---|---|---|---|---|---|---|---|---|---|---|---|---|---|---|---|---|---|---|---|---|---|---|---|---|
| | | | Daily | Weekly | Fortnightly | Once a month | More than a month | Daily | Weekly | Fortnightly | Once a month | More than a month | Daily | Weekly | Fortnightly | Once a month | More than a month | Daily | Weekly | Fortnightly | Once a month | More than a month | Daily | Weekly | Fortnightly | Once a month | More than a month |
| 1 | Observation Home | 195 | 8 | 67 | 10 | 10 | 9 | 26 | 21 | 7 | 13 | 1 | 89 | 12 | 2 | 6 | 1 | 102 | 17 | 2 | 4 | 1 | 225 | 117 | 21 | 10 | 12 |
| 2 | Special Home | 58 | 2 | 18 | 3 | 1 | 3 | 8 | 10 | 2 | 1 | 2 | 28 | 4 | 1 | 0 | 0 | 32 | 4 | 0 | 1 | 0 | 70 | 36 | 6 | 1 | 5 |
| 3 | Children Home | 369 | 44 | 131 | 20 | 28 | 23 | 106 | 77 | 23 | 26 | 13 | 245 | 30 | 11 | 9 | 2 | 277 | 32 | 7 | 6 | 8 | 672 | 270 | 61 | 38 | 46 |
| 4 | Shelter Home | 21 | 5 | 4 | 0 | 2 | 2 | 7 | 3 | 1 | 1 | 0 | 13 | 1 | 1 | 0 | 0 | 13 | 2 | 2 | 0 | 0 | 38 | 10 | 4 | 2 | 2 |
| 5 | Aftercare Home | 26 | 2 | 12 | 1 | 0 | 1 | 4 | 2 | 0 | 2 | 0 | 14 | 3 | 0 | 1 | 0 | 16 | 3 | 0 | 0 | 0 | 36 | 20 | 1 | 55 | 1 |
| 6 | Others | 117 | 23 | 23 | 6 | 4 | 0 | 33 | 21 | 5 | 7 | 1 | 64 | 5 | 2 | 0 | 1 | 77 | 5 | 0 | 0 | 0 | 197 | 54 | 13 | 3 | 2 |
| | All India Total | 786 | 84 | 255 | 40 | 45 | 38 | 184 | 134 | 38 | 50 | 17 | 453 | 55 | 17 | 16 | 4 | 517 | 63 | 11 | 11 | 9 | 1238 | 507 | 106 | 29 | 68 |

## Cleanliness of Homes

Cleanliness maintained at different homes was also observed by the research team and information related to this was obtained which is presented in table on previous page.

Sunning of bedding and clothing, cleanliness in the medical centre, kitchen and toilets were observed by the team members who visited different homes. It was found that these were done on daily, weakly, fortnightly, once in a month and more than a month in different homes. It is evident from table that in majority of the Homes sunning of bedding and clothing were done on weekly basis. Cleanliness in the medical centre was also done on daily and weekly basis in majority of homes and frequency of cleanliness in kitchens and toilets were also observed at the same frequency in the majority of the homes.

## Staff Strength of Institutions

To run the child care institutions smoothly adequate staff strength is required. Keeping this in view, data related to sanction and actual staff strength were obtained and the same is presented in Table 3.6 on next page.

It is evident from Table that in 79.4 percent homes, doctors were in position on contract basis and almost similar percentage (78.9%) para-medical staff were also available. Percentage of cook (84%), were also observed to be less specially in After Care Homes and Children Homes and situation is almost similar in case of availability of Sweepers in the Homes. Art and craft teachers in different Homes were also observed to be grossly adequate (74.6%).

## Conclusion

From the foregoing discussions it can be summarized that a substantial number of children's institutions were having classrooms, dormitories, kitchens, recreation rooms etc. as per the norms laid down in the Rules of JJ Act. However, it has been observed that Shishu Grehs and other

Table - Staff Strength of Institution

| S. No | Staff | Observation Home | | | Special Home | | | Children Home | | | Shelter Home | | | Aftercare Home | | | Other | | | Total | | |
|---|---|---|---|---|---|---|---|---|---|---|---|---|---|---|---|---|---|---|---|---|---|---|
| | | Sanctioned Strength | Actual Strength | In % | Sanctioned Strength | Actual Strength | In % | Sanctioned Strength | Actual Strength | In % | Sanctioned Strength | Actual Strength | In % | Sanctioned Strength | Actual Strength | In % | Sanctioned Strength | Actual Strength | In % | Sanctioned Strength | Actual Strength | In % |
| 1 | Superintendent | 153 | 129 | 84.31 | 67 | 57 | 85.07 | 351 | 307 | 87.46 | 23 | 23 | 100.00 | 118 | 75 | 63.56 | 81 | 79 | 97.53 | 749 | 714 | 95.33 |
| 2 | Counsellor | 218 | 200 | 91.74 | 50 | 43 | 86.00 | 392 | 322 | 82.14 | 31 | 22 | 70.97 | 48 | 23 | 47.92 | 99 | 89 | 89.90 | 788 | 749 | 95.05 |
| 3 | Case worker | 170 | 170 | 100.00 | 30 | 27 | 90.00 | 366 | 271 | 74.04 | 12 | 10 | 83.33 | 22 | 18 | 81.82 | 131 | 125 | 95.42 | 723 | 629 | 87.00 |
| 4 | House Mother | 140 | 121 | 86.43 | 38 | 33 | 86.84 | 251 | 215 | 85.66 | 10 | 9 | 90.00 | 15 | 11 | 73.33 | 70 | 67 | 95.71 | 502 | 478 | 95.22 |
| 5 | Educator | 118 | 112 | 94.92 | 52 | 52 | 100.00 | 274 | 249 | 90.88 | 11 | 10 | 90.91 | 14 | 9 | 64.29 | 53 | 45 | 84.91 | 508 | 491 | 96.65 |
| 6 | Vocational Instructor | 151 | 131 | 86.75 | 40 | 40 | 100.00 | 267 | 241 | 90.26 | 26 | 17 | 65.38 | 15 | 12 | 80.00 | 48 | 48 | 100.00 | 527 | 509 | 96.58 |
| 7 | Doctor | 124 | 110 | 88.71 | 32 | 31 | 96.88 | 220 | 166 | 75.45 | 11 | 10 | 90.91 | 18 | 9 | 50.00 | 62 | 43 | 69.35 | 466 | 370 | 79.40 |
| 8 | Paramedical Staff | 92 | 89 | 96.74 | 30 | 28 | 93.33 | 185 | 122 | 65.95 | 6 | 5 | 83.33 | 9 | 5 | 55.56 | 56 | 46 | 82.14 | 376 | 297 | 78.99 |
| 9 | Store-keeper cum acc. | 101 | 88 | 87.13 | 17 | 16 | 94.12 | 168 | 136 | 80.95 | 8 | 7 | 87.50 | 13 | 8 | 61.54 | 47 | 38 | 80.85 | 340 | 307 | 90.29 |
| 10 | Driver | 70 | 63 | 90.00 | 25 | 24 | 96.00 | 141 | 107 | 75.89 | 4 | 2 | 50.00 | 16 | 15 | 93.75 | 53 | 41 | 77.36 | 301 | 260 | 86.38 |
| 11 | Cook | 55 | 54 | 98.18 | 26 | 21 | 80.77 | 147 | 105 | 71.43 | 1 | 1 | 100.00 | 6 | 4 | 66.67 | 32 | 31 | 96.88 | 262 | 221 | 84.35 |
| 12 | Helper | 57 | 49 | 85.96 | 34 | 22 | 64.71 | 98 | 85 | 86.73 | 6 | 4 | 66.67 | 10 | 6 | 60.00 | 50 | 42 | 84.00 | 236 | 227 | 96.19 |
| 13 | Sweeper | 35 | 30 | 85.71 | 11 | 10 | 90.91 | 73 | 55 | 75.34 | 18 | 15 | 83.33 | 6 | 4 | 66.67 | 26 | 21 | 80.77 | 165 | 139 | 84.24 |
| 14 | Art & craft cum Music teacher | 27 | 24 | 88.89 | 16 | 16 | 100.00 | 78 | 52 | 66.67 | 2 | 2 | 100.00 | 10 | 6 | 60.00 | 16 | 6 | 37.50 | 146 | 109 | 74.66 |
| 15 | Gardner | 21 | 17 | 80.95 | 17 | 15 | 88.24 | 38 | 26 | 68.42 | 2 | 1 | 50.00 | 8 | 7 | 87.50 | 11 | 10 | 90.91 | 91 | 82 | 90.11 |
| 16 | Other | 123 | 120 | 97.56 | 82 | 76 | 92.68 | 286 | 233 | 81.47 | 17 | 26 | 152.94 | 12 | 11 | 91.67 | 69 | 60 | 86.96 | 589 | 526 | 89.30 |

Homes were more crowded in terms of lack of space in dormitories, classrooms, recreation rooms. Number of toilets and bathrooms were found to be inadequate and not as per the norms. Majority of (71%) homes were having indoor and outdoor game facilities. Safe drinking water and water for bathing and washing, proper drainage system, disposal of garbage were available in majority of homes. It was found that sunning of bedding and clothing, cleanliness in the medical centres, kitchen and toilets were done on daily, weekly, fortnightly, once in a month and more than a month in different homes. Most of the Homes engaged medical doctors on part time/contract basis and around 80 per cent homes were having para-medical staff.

Age structure of inmates in different homes was observed to be young as 57 percent children were between age-group 6–14 years and about one-third children were from the age-group 14–18 years. It is disheartening to note that 4 per cent children were between 0–6 years and about 5 per cent above 18 years were found in Observation Homes. This might have happened because of non-austification of their ages or lack of After Care Homes in respective region. Maximum number of children was staying up to 3 years as compared to 3-5 years and more than 5 years. Even those were also staying in homes for more than 5 years. Maximum percentage of children was found to be placed in special home followed by shelter home. Data regarding death of children in their institutions reveals that very few percentages of children died within institutions. About 6 percent were sent to hospital for treatment and died over there only. In the institution only 0.5 percent children were died.

# 4

# Assessment of Standard of Care and Protection of Children

Basic facilities to be provided to the children entrusted to the institutional care and protection as well as psychological and social services. Official data brings out that daily average population of children in NGO run institutions ranges from as low as two children to as large as 745 children. Whereas, on the other hand, daily average population of children and juveniles in government run institutions ranges from 15-106. However, it has also been found that some of these institutions are underutilized. But these institutions have to cater to the basic needs of the children and juveniles under their charge.

Children or juveniles, when admitted to an institution, they are to be provided to living condition or dormitories. In addition, they are supposed to be provided clothes, food, medical facilities, recreation etc. at the institutions. The present chapter exhibits an assessment of standard of care and protection provided to children or juveniles in different Homes.

## Minimum Standards of Care and Protection for Children

*Physical infrastructure:* As per the revised rules, the homes for juveniles in conflict with law and children in need of care and protection should function from separate premises. The accommodation in each institution should be as per the following criteria, namely:

(a) *Observation Home:*

(i) Separate observation homes for girls and boys;

(ii) Classification and segregation of juveniles according to their age group preferably 7–11 years, 2–6 years and 16-18 years, giving due consideration to physical and mental status and the nature of the offence committed.

(b) *Special Home:*

(i) Separate special homes for girls above the age of 10 years and boys in the age groups of 11 to 15 and 16 to 18 years;

(ii) Classification and segregation of juveniles on the basis of age and nature of offences and their mental and physical status.

(c) *Children's Home:*

(i) While children of both sexes below 10 years can be kept in the same home, separate bathing and sleeping facilities shall be maintained for boys and girls in the age group of 0–5 years;

(ii) Separate children's homes for boys and girls in the age group of 7-11 and 12-18 years;

(iii) Separate facilities for children in the age group of 0–5 years with appropriate facilities for infants.

(d) *Shelter Home:*

(i) Separate shelter homes for girls and boys;

(ii) Separate shelter homes for girls above the age of 10 years and boys in the age groups of 11 to 15 and 16 to 18 years.

The norms for building or accommodation for an institution with 50 juveniles or children shall be as under:

| | | |
|---|---|---|
| 1. | 2 Djormitories | Each 1000 sq.ft. for 25 juveniles/children i.e. 2000 sq.ft. |
| 2. | 2 Classrooms | 300 sq.ft. for 25 juveniles/children i.e. 600 sq.ft. |
| 3. | Sickroom/first-aid room | 75 sq.ft. per juvenile/children for 10 i.e. 750 sq.ft. |
| 4. | Kitchen | 250 sq.ft. |
| 5. | Dining hall | 800 sq.ft. |
| 6. | Store | 250 sq.ft. |
| 7. | Recreation room | 300 sq.ft. |
| 8. | Library | 500 sq.ft. |
| 9. | 5 bath rooms | 25 sq.ft. each i.e. 125 sq.ft. |
| 10. | 8 toilets/latrines | 25 sq.ft. each i.e. 200 sq.ft. |
| 11. | Office rooms | (a) 300 sq.ft. (b) Superintendent's room 200 sq. fit |
| 12. | Counseling and guidance room | 120 sq.ft. |
| 13. | Workshop | 1125 sq.ft. for 15 juvenile @ 75 Sq. ft. per trainee |
| 14. | Residence for Superintendent | *(a)* 2 rooms of 150 sq.ft. each *(b)* kitchen 75 sq.ft. *(c)* bathroom-cum-Toilet/latrine 50 sq.ft. |
| 15. | 2 rooms for juvenile justice board/child welfare committee | 300 sq.ft. each *i.e.* 600 sq.ft. |
| 16. | Playground sufficient area according to the total number of juveniles or children | |
| | **Total** | **8495 sq.ft.** |

The standards of accommodation as per the norms laid down in rule 40(2) shall be observed to the extent possible and shall include a minimum of following facilities:

*(a)* Dormitory: 40 sq.ft. per juvenile or child
*(b)* Classroom: 300 sq.ft. for 25 juvenile or child
*(c)* Workshop: 75 sq.ft. per juvenile or child

(*d*) Playground: Sufficient play ground area shall be provided in every institution according to the total number of juveniles in institution.

(*i*) there shall be proper and smooth flooring for preventing accidents.
(*ii*) there shall be adequate lighting, ventilation, heating and cooling arrangements, safe drinking water and clean toilets, in terms of gender, age appropriateness and accessibility.
(*iii*) all institutions under the Act shall make provision of first aid kit, fire extinguishers in kitchen, dormitories, store-rooms, counseling room, periodic review of electrical installations, proper storage and inspection of articles of food stuffs, stand-by arrangements for water storage and emergency lighting.

The observation homes and special homes shall be child-friendly and in no way shall they look like a jail or lock-up.

The Superintendent should stay within the institution and be provided with quarters and in case he is not able to stay in the home for legitimate reason (to be permitted by Director, Child Protection), any other senior staff member of the institution shall stay in the institution and be in a position to supervise the overall care of the children or juveniles and, take decisions in the case of any crisis and emergency.

***Clothing and bedding***: The clothing and bedding shall be as per the scale and climatic conditions. The requirements of each juvenile or child and the minimum standards for clothing and bedding are laid down in Schedule 1 of these rules.

***Sanitation and Hygiene***: Every institution shall have the following facilities, namely:

(*a*) sufficient treated drinking water; water filters shall be installed;
(*b*) sufficient water for bathing and washing clothes, maintenance and cleanliness of the premises;
(*c*) proper drainage system;
(*d*) arrangements for disposal of garbage;
(*e*) protection from mosquitoes by providing mosquito nets;
(*f*) annual pest control;
(*g*) sufficient number of well lit and airy toilets in the proportion of at least one toilet for seven children;
(*h*) sufficient number of well lit and airy bathrooms in the proportion of at least one bath room for ten children;
(*i*) sufficient space for washing;
(*j*) clean and fly-proof kitchen and separate area for washing utensils;
(*k*) sunning of bedding and clothing;
(*l*) maintenance of cleanliness in the Medical Centre.

**Daily Routine**

(1) Every institution shall have a daily routine for the juveniles or children developed in consultation with the Children's Committees, which shall be prominently displayed at various places within the institution.
(2) The daily routine shall provide, *inter alia,* for a regulated and disciplined life, personal hygiene and cleanliness, physical exercise, yoga, educational classes, vocational training, organized recreation and games, moral education group activities, prayer and community singing and special programmes for Sundays and holidays.

*Nutrition and Diet Scale:* The following nutrition and diet scale shall be followed by the institutions, namely:
(*a*) the children shall be provided four meals in a day including breakfast;

(*b*) the menu shall be prepared with the help of a nutritional expert or doctor to ensure balanced diet and variety in taste as per the minimum nutritional standard and diet scale set out in Schedule II of these rules;

(*c*) every institution under this Act shall strictly adhere to the minimum nutritional standard and diet scale specified in Schedule II;

(*d*) juveniles or children may be provided special meals on holidays and festivals;

(*e*) infants and sick juveniles or children shall be provided special diet according to the advise of the doctor on their dietary requirement.

## Assessment of Educational Facilities within the Premises of Homes

Every institution as per the rules should provide education to all juveniles or children according to the age and ability, both inside the institution or outside, as per the requirement. There should be a range of educational opportunities including, mainstream inclusive schools, bridge school, open schooling, non-formal education and learning and input from special educators where needed. Wherever necessary, extra coaching should made available to school going children in the institutions by encouraging volunteer services or tying up with coaching centers.

It is evident from Table 4.1 that majority of the Homes (more than 7%) were having either formal school within the premises, non-formal classes or providing coaching system in their Homes. However, 22 percent Observation Homes, 17 percent Special Homes, 30 percent Children Homes, 14 percent Shelter Homes and about 12 percent After Care Homes were not having schooling facilities within the premises of homes. A substantial number of homes were having pre-primary school, formal school within the premises.

Data regarding availability of educational facilities within the premises of homes is presented in Table 1:

**Table 4.1**

**Availability of Educational Facilities within the Premises of Homes**

(In Percentage)

| Sl. No. | Homes | N | Formal school on premises | | | | Non-Formal | Private coaching | No Schooling facilities |
|---|---|---|---|---|---|---|---|---|---|
| | | | Pre-school | Primary | Secondary | Higher | | | |
| 1. | Observation home | 195 | 16.92 | 24.62 | 12.82 | 10.77 | 34.36 | 16.92 | 21.54 |
| 2. | Special home | 58 | 22.41 | 36.21 | 17.24 | 10.34 | 43.10 | 17.24 | 17.24 |
| 3. | Children home | 369 | 23.04 | 39.30 | 21.95 | 13.28 | 26.56 | 29.00 | 29.81 |
| 4. | Shelter home | 21 | 19.05 | 23.81 | 14.29 | 4.76 | 38.10 | 19.05 | 14.29 |
| 5. | Aftercare home | 26 | 11.54 | 11.54 | 7.69 | 0.00 | 3.85 | 11.54 | 11.54 |
| 6. | Others | 117 | 23.08 | 29.06 | 18.80 | 11.11 | 23.93 | 27.35 | 18.80 |

## School Outside the Premises of Homes

An attempt has also been made to obtain information regarding percentage of children attending school outside the premises of the institution and data in this regard is presented in Table 4.2 and Figure 4.1 on next page.

It can be seen as given in data and figure that a total of 46.38 percent children were attending school outside the premises of the institution. It is interesting to note that 33 percent children of Observation Homes, 41 per cent children of Special Homes and 55 percent children of Children's Homes were attending school outside the premises of the institution. Even in the After Care Homes a little over one-fifth children were attending school outside the premises.

It is also evident from the table that these problems were having mostly in the juveniles of Special Homes. However, 0.96 per cent children were also having HIV/AIDS problems. HIV/AIDS were found maximum in Shelter Homes (45%) followed by Special Homes (18%). In addition to these, severe/chronic diseases were found in 16 percent children of different Homes and few of them were also having minor illness like; skin disease, cold and cough, etc.

*Medical Care*. Every institution shall;

(*a*) maintain a medical record of each juvenile or child on the basis of monthly medical check-up and provide necessary medical facilities;

(*b*) ensure that the medical record includes weight and height record any sickness and treatment, and other physical or mental problem;

(*c*) have arrangement for the medical facilities, including a doctor on call available on all working days for regular medical check-ups and treatment of juveniles or children;

(*d*) have sufficient medical equipments to handle minor health problems including first aid kit with stock of emergency medicines and consumables;

(*e*) train all staff in handling first aid;

(*f*) tie-up with local Primary Health Centre, government

## Table 4.2
## Percentage of Children Attending School Outside the Premises of the Institution

| Sl. No. | Homes | N | Pre-school | Primary | Secondary | Higher | Non-Formal classes | Other | Total |
|---|---|---|---|---|---|---|---|---|---|
| 1. | Observation home | 6925 | 261 (3.77) | 1019 (14.71) | 674 (9.73) | 139 (2.01) | 169 (2.44) | 25 (0.36) | 2287 (33.03) |
| 2. | Special home | 2063 | 45 (2.18) | 335 (16.24) | 218 (10.57) | 104 (5.04) | 75 (3.64) | 65 (3.15) | 842 (40.81) |
| 3. | Children home | 22690 | 924 (4.07) | 4359 (19.21) | 5088 (22.42) | 1638 (7.22) | 189 (0.83) | 277 (1.22) | 12475 (54.98) |
| 4. | Shelter home | 902 | 94 (10.42) | 125 (13.86) | 72 (7.98) | 23 (2.55) | 14 (1.55) | 14 (1.55) | 342 (37.92) |
| 5. | Aftercare home | 962 | 7 (0.73) | 36 (3.74) | 87 (9.04) | 39 (4.05) | 0 (0.00) | 36 (3.74) | 205 (21.31) |
| 6. | Others | 4990 | 168 (3.37) | 813 (16.29) | 371 (7.43) | 210 (4.21) | 104 (2.08) | 55 (1.10) | 1721 (34.49) |
| | **All India Total** | **38532** | **1499 (3.89)** | **6687 (17.35)** | **6510 (16.90)** | **2153 (5.59)** | **551 (1.3)** | **472 (1.22)** | **17872 (46.38)** |

Fig.4.1 : Children attending school outside the premises

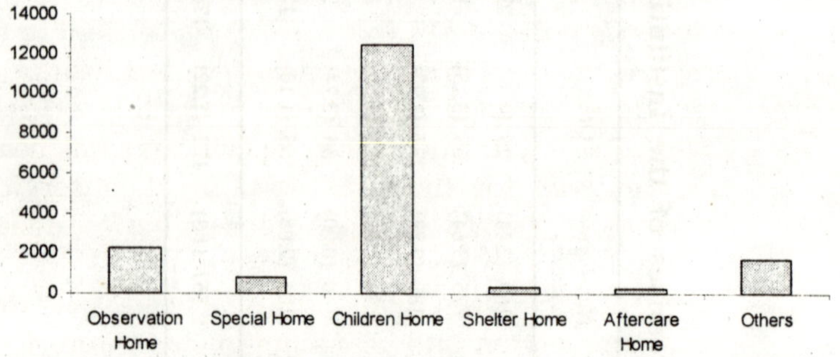


hospital, medical colleges, other hospitals, clinical psychologists and psychiatrists and mental health institutes for regular visits by their doctors and students and for holding periodic health camps within the institutions;

(*g*) make necessary arrangements made for the immunization coverage;

(*h*) take preventive measures in the event of out break of contagious or infectious diseases;

(*i*) keep sick children under constant medical supervision;

(*k*) admit a juvenile or child without insisting on a medical certificate at the time of admission;

(*l*) arrange for a medical examination of each juvenile or child admitted in an institution by the Medical Officer within twenty-four hours and in special cases or medical emergencies immediately;

(*m*) arrange for a medical examination of the juvenile or child by the Medical Officer at the time of transfer within twenty-four hours before transfer;

(*n*) not carry out any surgical treatment on any juvenile or child without the previous consent of his parent or guardian, unless either the parent or guardian cannot be found and the condition of the juvenile or child is such that any delay shall, in the opinion of the medical officer, involve unnecessary suffering or injury to the health of the juvenile or child, or otherwise without obtaining a written consent to this effect from the Officer-in-Charge of the institution;

*(o)* Provide or arrange for regular counseling of every juvenile or child and ensure specific mental health interventions for those in need of such services, including separate rooms for counseling sessions within the premises of the institution;

*(p)* refer such children who require specialized drug abuse prevention and rehabilitation program, to an appropriate center administered by qualified personnel where these programs shall be adopted to the age, gender and other specifications of the concerned child.

**Mental Health**

1. A mental health record of every juvenile or child shall be maintained by the concerned institutions.
2. Both milieu-based interventions that is creating an enabling environment for children and individual therapy are must for every child and shall be provided in all institutions.
   *Explanation.* For the purpose of this sub-rule, milieu-based intervention is a process of recovery, which starts through providing an enabling culture and environment in an institution so as to ensure that each child's abilities are discovered and they have choices and right to take to decisions regarding their life and thus, they develop and identify beyond their negative experiences and such intervention has a critical emotional impact on the child.
3. The environment in an institution shall be free from abuse, allowing juveniles or children to cope with their situation and regain confidence.
4. All persons involved in taking care of the juveniles or children in an institution shall participate in

facilitating an enabling environment and work in collaboration with the therapists.

5. Individual therapy is a specialized process and each institution shall make provisions for it as a critical mental health intervention.
6. Every institution shall have the services of trained counselors or collaboration with external agencies such as child guidance centers, psychology and psychiatric department or similar government and non-governmental agencies, for specialized and regular individual therapy for every juvenile or child in the institution.
7. A mental health care plan shall be developed for every juvenile or child by the child welfare officers in consultation with mental health experts associated with the institution and integrated into the individual care plan of the concerned juvenile or child.
8. The recommendations of mental health experts shall be maintained in very case file and integrated into the care plan for every child.
9. All care plans shall be produced before the Management Committee set-up under rule 55 of these rules every month and before the Child Welfare Committee every quarter.
10. No juvenile or child shall be administered medication for mental health problems without a psychological evaluation and diagnosis by appropriately trained mental health professionals.

For rehabilitation and social reintegration, there are three types of services available for the children *viz.* adoption, foster care and sponsorship program. It is evident from table that 38 percent children were adopted since the different homes were established. About 32 percent children were given for foster care from different homes and 4 percent children were given for sponsorship program. These statistics are since the different homes were established. Children were mostly adopted, given foster care and sponsorship program were from Children's Homes followed by Shelter Homes and Observation Homes respectively. In the other categories, as stated earlier, mostly Shishu Grehs are placed where about 94 percent children were given for adoption and 25 percent children for foster care and 3 percent for sponsorship program.

**Summing-up**

As stated earlier, this Chapter deals with an assessment of standards of care and protection provided to children or juveniles in different homes. In the beginning of the Chapter-4, minimum standards of care and protection of children have been explained as per the JJ Amendment Act, 2006 and subsequent rules on the same released in October, 2007. Norms and standards laid down in the rules are given in the beginning of this Chapter.

It has been found that majority of the Homes (more than 70%) were having either formal school within the premises, non-formal classes or providing some sort of coaching in their homes. A total of 22 percent Observation Homes, 17 percent Special Homes, 30 percent Children Homes, 14 percent Shelter Homes and 12 percent After Care Homes were not having schooling facilities within the premises. However, a total of 46.38 percent children were attending school outside the premises of different homes. Even one-fifth of the total children lodged in After Care Homes were also attending school outside the premises. It is interesting to note that 39 percent homes were having library facilities.

Every institution should provide gainful vocational training to juveniles or children as per the prescribed JJ Rules through networking with the Technical Institutions, Jan Shikshan Sansthan, Government and private organizations. Data from where information related to vocational training was obtained shows that children were imparted vocational training in 14 different trades. The most common among them were electrical trade (1252 children), teaching (1012 children) printing (314 children) and fittering job (279 children). About 11 percent Children

Homes and Shelter Homes were also imparting vocational training under different trades. On the whole, only 10 percent homes were imparting vocational training in different trades and since this percentage is very low, an attempt was made to find out reasons thereof. It was stated by different homes that majority of them were having funds and manpower constraints for offering vocational training. Itwas also pointed out by them that lack of equipments and lack of space were another constraints and thus 62 percent homes had shown their inability to offer vocational training.

In addition to above, 31 percent homes were making efforts to take their children out of the Home for exposure visit. It is interesting to note that 38 percent Children Homes, 33 percent Shelter Homes, 24 percent special homes, 23 percent After Care Homes and about 17 percent Observation Homes were taking their inmates for the exposure visit outside the home. A substantial number of homes (37.4%) were having yoga facilities for their children.

As per the guidelines, medical facilities to the children/ juveniles are supposed to be provided by different homes. Data in this regard shows that 36 percent homes were having medical care unit inside the homes, 43 percent each Special and Children Homes, 33 percent Shelter Homes, 21 percent Observation Homes and 19 percent After Care Homes were having medical care unit inside the premises. However, few of them were calling the doctors from outside. Children staying in different Homes were suffering different type of illnesses. The most common diseases among children were tuberculoses (9%) and sexually transmitted diseases (8%). Very few percentages (0.9%) of children were having HIV/ AIDS problems. In addition to these severe chronic diseases were also found in 16 percent children of different Homes.

The provision of guided recreation has been made in the rules that all juveniles or children in the institution which should include indoor and outdoor games, music, television, picnic, outings, cultural programs etc. Data in this regard show that only one-third homes were having recreation facilities for their inmates. Television and radio facilities were provided in 42 percent homes. The most common Homes which were having television and radio facilities were shelter homes, After Care Homes and Children Homes. Cultural activities were found to be another entertainment effort made by different Homes. About 53 percent Homes were organizing cultural programmes inside the homes and 34 percent were organizing the same outside the homes. The final outcome of the child care institutions are supposed to be social rehabilitation and reintegration of children/juveniles. It is evident that 38 percent children were adopted so far since different Homes were established. About 32 percent children were given for foster care and 4 percent children were given for sponsorship program. Children were mostly given for adoption from Shishu Grehs and Children Homes.

# 5

# Conclusion

With a view to provide for better implementation and administration of the provisions of the Juvenile Justice Act in its true spirit and substance, the Central Government in pursuance to the provisions and in exercise of the powers conferred by the provision to the sub-section (1) and Section 68 of the Juvenile Justice (Care and Protection of Children) Act 2000 (56 of 2000). The need for a comprehensive assessment to assess juvenile justice system at the national level was felt at the advent of the new proposed ICPS program which is on the verge of launching. The Ministry of Women and Child Development, Government of India, the nodal Ministry for the implementation of the program related to juvenile justice, desired to undertake a comprehensive assessment of the entire gamut of juvenile justice system including status of Juvenile Homes created under the Act. The present assessment was accordingly conceived at the national level. Out of 35 States/UTs data was collected from 25 States and one UT. Data could not be collected from the States of Jharkhand, Arunachal Pradesh, Jammu & Kashmir and Nagaland. Data was also not collected from few UTs like Daman & Diu, Lakshadweep, Andaman and Nicobar Islands. But all the major states have been covered for assessment of implementation of JJ Act. A pre-designed questionnaire was developed and the same was used for data collection all over the country. Besides interview, observation method was also used for collecting information. Availability of reports, guidelines, instructions and other documents were found additional source of data.

The following paragraphs carry forth the conclusions and recommendations that have emerged out of the present assessment:

**Children Institutions**

An attempt has been made to find out the latest status of the implementation of the Juvenile Justice (Care and Protection of Children) Act, 2006 in the States/UTs and information regarding number of homes obtained from State Governments/ UTs. A substantial number of different types of homes were visited and details were obtained by the enumerators. A total of 1135 children homes are created under the Juvenile Justice Act out of which 69.25 percent were covered. Although Special and After Care Homes were less in number but 93.55 percent and 49.06 percent respectively were covered for the present assessment. More than two-third (69.25%) Observation Homes were assessed by the team members.

**Physical Infrastructure**

A substantial number of children's institutions were having classrooms, dormitories, kitchens, recreation rooms etc. as per the norms laid down in the Rules of JJ Act. However, it has been observed that *Shishu Grehs* and other Homes were more crowded in terms of lack of space in dormitories, classrooms, recreation rooms. Number of toilets and bathrooms were found to be inadequate and not as per the norms. Majority of (71%) Homes were having indoor and outdoor game facilities. Safe drinking water and water for bathing and washing, proper drainage system, disposal of garbage were available in majority of Homes.

**Sanitation**

It was found that sunning of bedding and clothing, cleanliness in the medical centres, kitchen and toilets were done on daily, weekly, fortnightly, once in a month and more than a month in different Homes. Most of the homes engaged medical doctors on part time/contract basis and around 80 percent homes were having para-medical staff.

**Inmates in Different Homes**

On an average 50 children were actually putting up in different Homes. It is interesting to note that on an average only 35 children were staying in Observation Homes which was less than any other Homes. Maximum number of children (62) is found to be in Children Homes followed by 46 in Shelter Home and 42 in Special Home. An attempt has also been made to assess total capacity of different Homes and present strength. A total of 62 percent homes were occupied as against their total capacity. The percentage of minimum occupancy was found to be 53 in Shishu Grehs and other homes. However, maximum percentage of occupancy was observed (65%) in Children Home followed by Shelter Home (62%). It is evident from the table that a little more over one-third capacity in all the Homes was utilized. In different categories of Homes also boys were more as compared to girls except in Shelter Homes and After Care Homes.

Age structure of inmates in different Homes was observed to be young as 57 percent children were between age-group 6–14 years and about one-third children were from the age-group 14–18 years. It is disheartening to note that 4 percent children were between 0–6 years and about 5 percent above 18 years were found in Observation Homes. This might have happened because of non-austification of their ages or lack of After Care Homes in respective region. Maximum number of children was staying up to 3 years as compared to 3–5 years and more than 5 years. Even those were also staying in Homes for more than 5 years. Maximum percentage of children was found to be placed in special home followed by shelter Home. Data regarding death of children in their institutions reveals that very few percentages of children died within institutions. About 6 percent were sent to hospital for treatment and died over there only. In the institution only 0.5 percent children were died.

**Educational Facilities at Homes**

Majority of the Homes (more than 70%) were having either formal school within the premises, non-formal classes or providing some sort of coaching in their Homes. A total of 22 percent Observation Homes, 17 percent Special Homes, 30 percent Children Homes, 14 per cent Shelter Homes and 12 percent After Care Homes were not having schooling facilities within the premises. However, a total of 46.38 percent children were attending school outside the premises of different Homes. Even one-fifth of the total children lodged in After Care Homes were also attending school outside the premises. It is interesting to note that 39 percent Homes were having library facilities.

**Vocational Training**

It has been found that children were imparted vocational training in 14 different trades at different homes. The most common among them were electrical trade (1252 children), teaching (1012 children) printing (314 children) and fitter job (279 children). About 11 percent Children Homes and Shelter Homes were also imparting vocational training under different trades. On the whole, only 10 percent Homes were imparting vocational training in different trades and since this percentage is very low, an attempt was made to find out reasons thereof. It was stated by different Homes that majority of them were having funds and manpower constraints for offering vocational training. It was also pointed out by them that lack of equipments and lack of space were another constraints and thus 62 percent Homes had shown their inability to offer vocational training.

**Exposure Visit**

A total of 31 percent Homes were making efforts to take their children out of the Home for exposure visit. It is interesting to note that 38 percent Children Homes, 33 percent Shelter Homes, 24 percent Special homes, 23 percent After Care Homes and about 17 percent Observation Homes were taking their inmates for the exposure visit outside the Home. A substantial number of Homes (37.4%) were having yoga facilities for their children.

**Medical Facilities**

About 36 percent Homes were having medical care unit inside the homes, 43 percent each Special and Children Homes, 33 percent Shelter Homes, 21 percent Observation Homes and 19 percent After Care Homes were having medical care unit inside the premises. However, few of them were calling the doctors from outside. Children staying in different Homes were suffering different type of illnesses. The most common diseases among children were tuberculoses (9%) and sexually transmitted diseases (8%). Very few percentages (0.9%) of children were having HIV/AIDS problems. In addition to these severe chronic diseases were also found in 16 percent children of different Homes.

**Recreational Facilities**

The recreational facilities include indoor and outdoor games, music, television, picnic, outings, cultural programs etc. Data in this regard shows that only one-third homes were having recreation facilities for their inmates. Television and radio facilities were provided in 42 percent homes. The most common homes which were having television and radio facilities were Shelter Homes, After Care Homes and Children Homes. Cultural activities were found to be another entertainment effort made by different Homes. About 53 percent homes were organizing cultural programs inside the homes and 34 percent were organinsing the same outside the Homes.

**Social Rehabilitation and Reintegration**

The final outcome of the child care institutions are supposed to be social rehabilitation and reintegration of children/juveniles. It is evident that 38 percent children were adopted so far since different homes were established. About 32 percent children were given for foster care and 4 percent children were given for sponsorship program. Children were mostly given for adoption from Shishu Grehs and Children Homes.

**Recommendations**

In Section 1 of the principal Act, in the marginal heading the words "and commencement", the words "commencement and application" have been substituted meaning thereby Act should come into force and State Rules should be framed within a year of the release of Central Model Rules. But none of the State has framed its rules as yet. Therefore, they should expedite the same at the earliest.

As per Section 4 of 2006 Amendment Act there should be one JJB in each district but the ground reality is none of the State has such provision. One reason could be they do not have observation homes in each district. So they should establish more number of observation and special homes by itself or with the help of Voluntary Organizations.

Almost similar situation has been observed so far as the case of CWCs and children's homes are concerned. Therefore, there is a need to increase the number of CWC and children's homes.

There is a provision of JJ fund as per Section 61 and Rule 95, and few states have created this. All the state governments should create JJ fund.

Need of information and data base of service providers and interested individuals and organizations and their sensitization through advocacy campaign are required.

According to Rule 64, the Central Government or the State Governments should monitor and evaluate the implementation of the Act annually by reviewing matters concerning establishment of the Board or Committee or Special Juvenile Police Unit where required, functioning of Board or Committee or Special Juvenile Police Unit, functioning of institutions and staff, of agencies, child friendly administration of juvenile justice and any other matter concerning effective implementation of the Act in the State. But in none of the States, social auditing or monitoring or any evaluation has been carried out so far. Whereas, it should be annually carried out with support and involvement of organizations working in the field of mental health, child care and protection and autonomous bodies like the National Institute of Public Cooperation and Child Development, Indian Council for Child Welfare, Childline India Foundation, Central and State level Social Welfare Boards, School of Social Work and School of Law.

Involvement of Civil Societies in gathering information and data base, resource mapping, orientation training and sensitization through advocacy campaign etc. is the need of the hour.

In identification of children's need and sensitizing them, Civil Societies can play a positive role and hence, they should be involved.

Any Civil Society/NGO can work for systematic growth of the Institutions provided they are given opportunities.

NGOs can play important role in linking-up community services to be given by children in conflict with law.

NGOs can also play important role in the following areas:

- In counseling services
- Trauma management
- Orientation of parents
- Family conferencing.

In most of the States, State Commission for Children are under process. Therefore, State Governments should expedite the same at the earliest.

In majority of the homes vocational training is the weakest component. So for more than 10 years old children vocational training in the trade like computer tailoring etc. should be imparted.

Educational program like bridge course etc. for the school drop out children should be provided in side the homes.

Minimum standards of care in terms of infrastructure (bathroom, toilets etc.) and in terms of clothing, bedding, diet Rule 44 should strictly be adhered to by each home.

# Annexures

*ANNEXURE I*

## MINIMUM STANDARD OF CARE

SCHEDULE 1

**Clothing, Bedding, Toiletries and Other Articles (Rule 41) (1)**

**1.** Juveniles or children shall be provided with the following articles:

**Bedding**

| S. No. | Article | Quantity to be provided per child |
|---|---|---|
| 1. | Towels | 4 per years |
| 2. | Cotton bed sheets | 2 per 2 years |
| 3. | Pillow (cotton stuffed) | 1 per 2 years |
| 4. | Pillow covers | 2 per 2 years |
| 5. | Woollen blankets | 2 per 2 years |
| 6. | Cotton durry | 2 per 2 years |
| 7. | Cotton filled quilt | 1 per 2 years (in cold regions) |
| 8. | Mattress | 1 per 2 years |
| 9. | Mosquito net | 1 per 2 years |

## Clothing for Girls

| | | |
|---|---|---|
| 1. | Skirts and blouse or salwar kameez or half sari blouses and petticoats | 5 sets per year for girls depending on age and regional preferences |
| 2. | Banyans (1 metre each) | 6 per year for younger girls |
| 3. | Brassieres | 6 per year for older girls |
| 4. | Panties (1 metre cloth each) | 6 per year |
| 5. | Sanitary towels | 12 packs per year for older girls |
| 6. | Woollen sweaters | 2 in 2 years (in cold regions) |
| 7. | Woollen shawls | 1 in 2 years (in cold regions) |

## Clothing for Boys

| | | |
|---|---|---|
| 1. | Shirts | 5 sets per year |
| 2. | Shorts | 5 sets per year for younger boys |
| 3. | Pants | 5 sets per year for older boys |
| 4. | Vest | 4 sets per year |
| 5. | Underwear | 4 sets per year |
| 6. | Woollen jerseys | 2 in 2 years (for cold regions) |
| 7. | Scarfs | 2 in 2 years (for cold regions) |

## Miscellaneous Articles

| | | |
|---|---|---|
| 1. | Slippers | 1 pair per year |
| 2. | Shoes | 1 pair per year |
| 3. | School uniform | 2 sets per year for children attending outside schools |
| 4. | School shoes | 1 pair per year for children attending outside schools |
| 5. | School bag and stationery | 1 set per year for children attending outside schools |
| 6. | Handkerchiefs | 6 per year |

**Note.** In addition to the clothing specified above, each child shall be provided, once in three years, with a suit consisting of one white shirt, one pair of Khaki shorts or pants, one pair of white canvas shoes and one blazer (for cold regions) for use during ceremonial occasions. In the case of girls it shall be one white half sari or one salwar kameez or one white skirt and one white blouse, a pair of white canvas shoes and a blazer (for cold regions).

**2.** In every hospital attached to the institution where there is provision for in-patient cots, the following scale has to be followed:-

| *Night clothing & bedding* | *Scale for supply* |
|---|---|
| 1. Mattress | One per bed per 3 years |
| 2. Cotton bed sheets | Four per bed per year |
| 3. Pillows | One per bed per two years |
| 4. Pillow covers | Four per bed per year |
| 5. Woollen blankets | One per bed per 2 years |
| 6. Pyjamas and loose shirts (Hospital type for boys) | 3 pairs per child per year |
| 7. Skirts and blouses or salwar kameez for girls | 3 pairs per child per year |
| 8. Cotton durry | One per bed per three years |

**Notes.** *(i)* When a child is admitted as an in-patient in the institution Hospital, the Institution Doctor shall issue the in-patient with the hospital clothing, the clothes on body being preserved, duly washed and handed back, at the time of the child's discharge from the hospital.

*(ii)* Each child shall be provided with Kit Box or a Locker, as per convenience and necessity.

*(iii)* The Superintendent shall make arrangements for two-tier bed system in place of conventional cots, as per convenience and necessity.

**3.** *Toiletry:* Every resident of the Home shall be issued with oil, soap and other material for in accordance with the following scales:

| | |
|---|---|
| Hair oil for grooming the hair | 100 mgs per month |
| Toilet soap or carbolic soap | 1 large bar per month |
| Tooth paste and brush | 1 brush per 3 months 50 gins paste per month |
| Comb | 1 per year |

**Notes.** *(a)* For washing of cloth and towels, bed-sheet etc., the following scale may be followed:

| | |
|---|---|
| *(i)* Washing soap | 1 soap for one month (125 gms) |
| *(ii)* Whitening/ bleaching agent | to the extent required only for white clothing |

Provided, however, the hospital clothing is not mixed with other clothing at the time of washing and if necessary, the Superintendent can issue the above items separately for washing of hospital clothing.

*(b)* The children attending school outside the institution may be issued with one additional bar of washing soap (100 gms) per head per month for washing their school uniform.

**4.** The following items shall be provided for maintaining the Homes in a healthy and sanitary condition:

| | *Item* | *Scale of supply* |
|---|---|---|
| 1. | Broom stick | 25 to 40 nos. per month depending on the area of the institution |
| 2. | DDT spray | As per the institution doctor's advice |
| 3. | Effective bugs killing agent | As required |
| 4. | Phenyl and cleaning acid (daily) | Depending on the area of lavatories to be cleaned as per institution doctor's advice |

## SCHEDULE II
## Nutrition and Diet Scale (Rule 44)

| | *Name of the articles of diet* | *Scale per head per day* |
|---|---|---|
| 1. | Rice/wheat/ragi/jowar | 600 cms, (700 cms for 16-18 yrs age) of which atleast 100 gms to be either Wheat or Ragi or Jowar |
| 2. | Dal/rajma/chana | 120 gms |
| 3. | Edible Oil | 25 gms |
| 4. | Onion | 25 gms |
| 5. | Salt | 25 gms |
| 6. | Turmeric | 05 gms |
| 7. | Coriander seed powder | 05 gms |
| 8. | Ginger | 05 gms |
| 9. | Garlic | 05 gms |
| 10. | Tamarind/mango powder | 05 gms |
| 11. | Milk at breakfast) | 150 ml |
| 12. | Dry chillies | 05 gms |
| 13. | Vegetables leafy | 100 gms |
| | Non -leafy | 130 gms |
| 14. | Curd or butter milk | 100 gms/ Ml |
| 15. | Chicken once a week or Eggs 4 days | 115 gms |
| 16. | Jaggery & ground nut Seeds or Paneer (vegetarian only) | 60 gms each (100 gms for paneer) Once in a week |
| 17. | Sugar | 40 gms |

*Following items for 50 Children per day*

| | | |
|---|---|---|
| 18. | Pepper | 25 gms |
| 19. | Jeera seeds | 25 gms |
| 20. | Black gramdal | 50 gms |
| 21. | Mustard seeds | 50 gms |
| 22. | Ajwain seeds | 50 gms |

*On Chicken Day for 10 kg, of Chicken*

| | | |
|---|---|---|
| 23. | Garam masala | 10 gms |
| 24. | Kopra | 150 gms |
| 25. | Khas khas | 150 gms |
| 26. | Groundnut oil | 500 gms |

*For Sick Children*

| | | |
|---|---|---|
| 27. | Bread | 500 gms |
| 28. | Milk | 500 ml |

*Other Items*

29. LP Gas for Cooking only

**Instructions:**

1. Variation in Diet
   - *(a)* Three varieties of dal *i.e.*, toor (tuvari), moong (green gram) and Ghana (Bengal gram) may be issued alternatively.
   - *(b)* The Superintendent may also arrange to substitute chicken with fish at his discretion, provided that there is no extra expenditure to Government.
   - *(c)* On non-vegetarian days, vegetarian children shall be issued with either 60 Gms of Jaggery and 60 gms of groundnut seeds per head in the shape of laddus or any other sweet dish or 100 gms paneer.
   - *(d)* Potatoes shall be issued in lieu of vegetables once in a week.
   - *(e)* Leafy vegetables such as Fenugreek (methi), spinach (palak), sarson (mustard leaves) gongura thotakura or any other saag etc., may also be issued once in a week. If a kitchen garden is attached to any institution leafy vegetables, in addition to drumstick trees, curry leaves trees

and coriander leaves, should be grown and issued and the superintendent should try to issue variety of vegetables and see that the same vegetable is not repeated for at least a period of one week.

(*f*) The Superintendent may make temporary alternations in the scale of diet in individual cases when considered necessary by him, or on the institution Doctor's advice subject to the condition that the scale laid down is not exceeded.

2. **Meal Timing and Menu**

(*a*) Breakfast after 8:00 a.m.

(*i*) Upma or chapattis made of Wheat or Ragi or any other dish.

(*ii*) Chutneys from Gongura or fresh curry leave or fresh coriander or Coconut and Putnadal etc., Dal/vegetable may be issued as a dish.

(*iii*) Milk

(*iv*) Any seasonal fruit in sufficient quantity

(*b*) Lunch at 1:00 P.M. and Dinner After 7:00 P.M. (*i*) Rice/Chapattis or combination of both (*ii*) Vegetable Curry (*iii*) Sambar or Dal (*iv*) Butter Milk or curd

3. **Others**

(*a*) Depending on the season, the Superintendent shall have the discretion to alter the time for distribution of food.

(*b*) On the advise of the Institution Doctor, every sick child who is prevented from taking regular food, on account of his ill-health, may be issued with medical diet, as indicated in diet scale.

(*c*) Extra diet for nourishment like milk, eggs, sugar

and fruits shall be issued to the children on the advice of the Institution Doctor in addition to the regular diet, to pick up weight or for other health reasons and for the purpose of calculation of the daily ration, the sick children shall be excluded from the day's strength.

*(d)* On the following national and festival occasions, sweet dishes may be distributed to all the children at the home at the rate fixed by the Commissioner, from time-to-time.

1. Republic Day (26th January)
2. Ambedkar's Birthday (14th April)
3. Independence Day (15th August)
4. Mahatma Gandhi's Birthday (2nd October)
5. Children's Day (14th November)
6. Child Rights Day (20th November)
7. Dussehra (Vijayadasmi)
8. Deepawali
9. Ramzan (Id-Ul-Fitr)
10. Bakrid (Id-Ul-Zuha)
11. Christmas ($25^{th}$ December).

The States may specify additional festivals depending upon local preferences.

**Form I**

(Rule 13(l)(c)]

**Supervision Order**

When the juvenile is placed under the care of a parent, guardian or other fit person/ fit institution Profile No. of.................20......

Whereas (name of the juvenile/) has this day found to have committed an offence and has been placed under the care of (name)...................(address)..........on executing a bond by he said............and the Board is satisfied that it is expedient to deal with the said juvenile by making an order placing him/her under supervision.

It is hereby ordered that the said juvenile be placed under the supervision of..................probation officer/case worker, for a period of.................... subject to the following conditions:

1. that the juvenile along with the copies of the order and the bond executed by the said......................shall be produced before the probation officer/case worker named therein... .
2. that the juvenile shall be submitted to the supervision of the aforesaid probation officer/case worker.
3. that the juvenile shall reside at............for a period of..... .
4. that the juvenile shall not be allowed to quit the district jurisdiction of.............without the permission of the probation officer/case-worker.
5. that the juvenile shall not be allowed to associate with bad characters.
6. that the juvenile shall live honestly and peacefully; and will go to school regularly/endeavor to earn an honest livelihood.
7. that the juvenile shall attend the attendance centre regularly.
8. that the person under whose care the juvenile is placed shall arrange for the proper care, education and welfare of the juvenile.
9. that the preventive measures will be taken by the person under whose care the juvenile is placed to see that the juvenile does not commit any offence punishable by any law in India.
10. that the juvenile shall be prevented from taking narcotic drugs or psycho-tropic substances or any other intoxicants.
11. That the directions given by the probation officer/case-worker from time-to-time, for the due observance of the conditions mentioned above, shall be carried out. Dated this..................day of.....................20.......

(Signature)

Principal Magistrate, Juvenile Justice Board Additional, conditions, if any may be inserted by the Juvenile Justice Board.

**Form II**

[Rule 13(l)(d)]

Order of detention under sub-section..........of section.........sub-section.......... of section..........and sub-section.........of section........

To

The Officer-in-charge

..................

..................

Whereas on the...........day of.................20....................(name of the juvenile), son/daughter of........... aged.................residing at....................being found in Profile No..................to be juvenile in conflict with law/section..........is ordered by me........Principal Magistrate, Juvenile Justice Board under section...........of Juvenile Justice Act, 2000 to be kept in the Observation Home/Special Home/............for a period of............This is to authorize and require you to receive the said juvenile; into your charge, and to keep him/her in the Observation Home/Special Home/.............for the aforesaid order to be carried into execution according to law.

Given under my hand and the seal of Juvenile Justice Board.

This.................day of.............................. 20.

(Signature)

Principal Magistrate,
Juvenile Justice Board

Encl:

Copy of the judgment, if any, or orders, particulars of home and case-history and individual care plan, if any:

Strike which is not required.

**Form III**

[Rules 13(l)(e) and (5)]

Order of Social Investigation/Inquiry

To

Probation Officer/Case-Worker/Person in-charge of Voluntary Organization/Case-Worker ________Whereas a report/complaint under section...............of the Juvenile Justice (Care and Protection of Children) Act, 2000 has been received from...........in respect of................(name of the juvenile), son/daughter of..........approximate age...............residing at.............who has been produced before the Board.

You are hereby directed to enquire into the social antecedents, family background and circumstances of the alleged offence by the said juvenile and submit your social investigation report on or before..........or within such time allowed to you by the Board.

You are also hereby directed to consult an expert in child psychology, psychiatric treatment or counseling for their expert opinion if necessary and submit such report along with your Social Investigation-Report.

Dated this.............day of........20.............

(Signature)

Principal Magistrate, Juvenile Justice Board

*ANNEXURE II*

## SIR AND OTHER FORMS

### Form IV

[Rules 13(5) and 87(l)(a) land (2)]

### Social Investigation Report

Sl. No.............

Submitted to the Juvenile Justice Board.................. (address).

Probation Department/Concerned State Government Authority/Voluntary Organisation............ (Signature and Stamp)

Profile No.

Under Section:

Title of Profile:

Police Station:

Nature of offence charge:

---

| | |
|---|---|
| Name | Religion |
| Father's Name | Caste |
| Permanent Address | Year of birth |
| Last address before apprehension | Age |
| | Sex |

---

Previous institutional/case history and individual care plan, if any

**Family**

| *Members of family* | *Name* | *Age* | *Health* | *Edu-cation* | *Occu-pation* | *Monthly earnings* | *Disabi-lities* | *Any other e.g social habits* |
|---|---|---|---|---|---|---|---|---|
| Father | | | | | | | | |
| Step-Father | | | | | | | | |
| Mother | | | | | | | | |
| Step mother | | | | | | | | |
| Siblings | | | | | | | | |
| Any other legal guardian/ relative | | | | | | | | |

If married, relevant particulars ..........................................
Other near relatives or agencies Interested ..................
Attitude towards religion normal
And ethical code of the home etc ..................................
Social and economic status ......................................
Delinquency record of members of family ..................
Present living conditions ...........................................
Relationship between parents/
Parents and children especially
With the juvenile under investigation ...........................
Other factors of importance if any ..............................

**Juveniles History**

Mental condition
(Present and past) ............................................................
Physical condition ............................................................
(Present and past) ............................................................
Habits, interests
(moral, recreational etc.) ..................................................
Outstanding characteristics and personality traits.........
Companions and their influence ....................................
Truancy from home, if any ...........................................
School (attitude towards school, teachers, class mates and *vice-versa)* ..........................................................................
..........................................................................................
Work record (jobs held, reasons for leaving, vocational interests, attitude towards job or employers) ....................
Neighbourhood and neighbours report .........................
Parent's attitude towards discipline in the home and child's reaction ..........................................................................
..........................................................................................
Any other remarks

---

**Result of Inquiry**

Emotional factors
Physical condition

Intelligence
Social and economic factors
Religious factors
Suggested causes of the problems
Analysis of the case including reasons for delinquency
Opinion of experts consulted
Recommendation regarding treatment and its Plan by Probation Officer

Signature of the Probation Officer/
Case-Worker

**Form V**

[Rules 15(5) and 79(2)]

**Undertaking/Bond to be Executed by a Parent/Guardian/ Relative/Fit Person in Whose Care a Junvenile is Paced**

Whereas I....................being the parent, guardian, relative or fit person under whose care...............(name of the juvenile) has been ordered to be placed by the Juvenile Justice Board........................have been directed by the said-Board to execute an undertaking/bond with surety in the sum of Rs. ..............(Rupees..................) or without surety. I hereby bind myself on the said........................ being placed under my care. I shall have the said................................properly taken care of and I do further bind myself to be responsible for the good behavior of the said.......and to observe the following conditions for a period of............w.e.f..............

1. that I shall not change my place of residence without giving previous intimation in, writing to the Juvenile Justice Board through the Probation Officer/Case-Worker;
2. that I shall not remove the said juvenile from the limits of the jurisdiction of the Juvenile Justice Board without previously obtaining the written permission of the Board;
3. that I shall send the said juvenile daily to school/ to such vocation as is approved by the Board unless

prevented from so doing by circumstances beyond control;

4. that I shall send the said juvenile to an Attendance Centre regularly unless prevented from doing so by circumstances beyond my control;
5. that I shall report immediately to the Board whenever so required by it;
6. that I shall produce the said juvenile in my care before the Board, if he/she does not follow the orders of Board or his/her behavior is beyond control;
7. that I shall render all necessary assistance to the Probation Officer/Case-Worker to enable him to carry out the duties of supervision;
8. in the event of my making default herein, I undertake to produce myself before the Board for appropriate action or bind myself, as the case may be, to forfeit to Government the sum of Rs.................... (Rupees...........................).

Dated this..........................day of.......................20.

Signature of person executing the Undertaking/ Bond

(Signed before me)

Principal Magistrate, juvenile Justice Board

Additional conditions, if any, by the Juvenile Justice Board may be entered numbering them properly;

(Where a bond with sureties is to executed add)

I/We................of..........(place of residence with full particulars) hereby declare myself/ourselves as surety/ sureties for the aforesaid....... (name of the person executing the undertaking/bond) to adhere to the terms and conditions of this undertaking/bond. In case of .....................(name of the person executing the bond) making fault therein, I/We hereby bind myself/ourselves jointly or severally to forfeit to government the sum of Rs...........(Rupees..........) dated this the.........day of..........20..........in the presence of.............

Signature of Surety(ties)

(Signed before me)
Principal Magistrate, Juvenile Justice Board

**Form VI**

[Rules 15(6) and 79(2)]

**Personal Bond by Junenile/Child**

Personal Bond to be signed by juvenile/child who has been ordered under Clause...........of sub-section.....................of section........of the Act.

Whereas, I.....................inhabitant of.............(give full particulars such as house number, road, village/ town, tehsil, district, state)..........have been ordered to be sent back/restored to my native place by the Juvenile Justice Board/Child Welfare Committee..............under section.............of the Juvenile Justice (Care and Protection of Children) Act, 2000 on my entering into a personal bond under sub-rule...........of rule...........and sub-rule......... of rele........of these Rules to observe the conditions mentioned herein below. Now, therefore, I do solemnly promise to abide by these conditions during the period......

I hereby bind myself as follows:

1. That during the period............I shall not ordinarily leave the village/town/ district to which I am sent and shall not ordinarily return to.............or go any whereelse beyond the said district without the prior permission of the Board/Committee;
2. That during the said period I shall attend school/ vocational training in the village/town or in the said district to which I am sent;
3. That in case of my attending school/vocational training at any other place in the said district I shall keep the Board/Committee informed of my ordinary place of residence.

I hereby acknowledge that I am aware of the above conditions which have been read over/explained to me and that I accept the same.

(Signature or thumb impression of the juvenile/child)

Certified that the conditions specified in the above order have been read over/explained to (Name of juvenile/child).............and that he/she has accepted there as the conditions upon which his/her period of detention/placement in safe custody may be revoked.

Certified accordingly that the said juvenile/child has been released/relived on the.........

Signature and Designation of the
Certifying Authority *i.e.*
Officer-in-Charge of the institution

**Form VII**

[Rule 17(10)]

**Discharge Order**

I..................name and designation of the discharging authority.......State Government/Union Territory Administration, do by this order permit............son/daughter of...............residence.........Profile Number.........who was ordered to be detained/placed in a observation home/special home/after care home by the Juvenile Justice Board..........under section...............of the Juvenile Justice (Care and Protection of Children) Act, 2000, for a term of.......on the.......day of........20.......and who is now in the.....home, at.............to be discharged from the said........home and supervision and the authority of...........during the remaining period of stay.

This order is granted subject to the conditions hereon, upon the breach of any of which it shall be liable to be revoked.

Signature and Designation of Releasing Authority

Dated:

Place:

**Conditions:**

1. The discharged person shall proceed to..........and live

under the supervision and authority of.........until the expiry of the period of his/her detention unless the remission is sooner cancelled.

2. He/she shall not, without the consent of the......remove himself/herself from that place or any other place, which may be named by the said....................
3. He/she shall obey such instruction as he/she may receive from the said...........with regard to punctual and regular attendance at school/vocation or otherwise.
4. He/she shall attend the Attendance Centre located at.....regularly.
5. He/she shall abstain from committing any offense and shall lead a sober and industrious life to the satisfaction of...........
6. In the event of his/her committing a breach of any of the above conditions the remission of the period of detention hereby granted shall be liable to be cancelled and on such cancellation he/she shall be dealt with under sub-section (3) of Section 59 of the Juvenile Justice (Care and Protection of Children) Act, 2000.

I hereby acknowledge that I am aware of the above conditions which have been read over/explained to me and that I accept the same.

(Signature or mark of the released juvenile)

Certified that the conditions specified in the above order have been read over/explained to (Name of juvenile/child)........and that he/she has accepted them as the conditions upon which his/her period of detention may be revoked.

Certified accordingly that the said juvenile/child has been discharged on the.........

Signature and Designation of the certifying authority
*i.e.* Officer-in-Charge of the institution

## Form VIII
[Rule 27(17)]
**Supervision Order**

When the child is placed under the case of a parent/ guardian or other fit person Case No........of.........20... Whereas (name of the child)........... has this day been found to be in need of care and protection, and has been placed under the care and supervision of (name).... (address).....on executing a bond by the said......and the Committee is satisfied that it is expedient to deal with the said child by making an order placing him/her under supervision.

It is hereby ordered that the said child be placed under the supervision of (name)........ (address)..........for a period of..........subject to the following conditions that:

1. the child along with the copies of the order and the bond, if any, executed by the said......shall be produced before the Committee as and when required by the person executing the bond.
2. the child shall be placed under the supervision of the aforesaid parent/guardian/ fit person.
3. the child shall reside at............ for a period of........
4. the child shall not be allowed to quit the district jurisdiction of......... with the permission of the Committee.
5. the child shall go to school regularly/endeavor to earn an honest livelihood.
6. the person under whose care the child is placed shall arrange for the proper care, education and welfare of the child.
7. the child shall not be allowed to associate with undesirable characters and shall be prevented from coming in conflict with law.
8. the child shall be prevented from taking narcotic drugs or psychotropic substances or any other intoxicants.
9. the directions given by the Committee from time to time, for the due observance of the conditions

mentioned above, shall be carried out. Dated this........day of........ 20.........

(Signature)

Chairperson, Child Welfare Committee

• Additional conditions, if any may be interested by the Child Welfare Committee.

**Form IX**

[Rules 27(17) and 79(2)]

**Undertaking by the Parent or 'Fit Person' to Whom Child is Restored**

I.....resident of House No.........Street.......Village/Town...... District....... State....... do hereby declare that I am willing to take charge of (name of the child)..... Aged.........under the orders of the Child Welfare Committee.......subject to the following terms and conditions:

*(i)* If his/her conduct is unsatisfactory I shall at once inform the Committee,

*(ii)* I shall do may best for the welfare and education of the said child as long as he/she remains in my charge and shall make proper provision for his/her maintenance.

*(iii)* In the event of his/her illness, he/she shall have proper medical attention in the nearest hospital,

*(iv)* I undertake to produce him/her before the competent authority as and when required.

1 Dated this...............day of...........

Signature

Signature and address

(Signed before me) of witnesses(es)

Chairperson, Child Welfare Committee

**Form X**

[Rule 27(18)]

**Order of Short-Term Placement Pending Inquiry**

Name of the child

Sex :
Age :
Father's Name :
Mother's Name :
Address :
Date of receiving :
by Organization/Institution
Produced by

This is to authorize and direct you to receive the said child in your charge, and keep her/him in the Shelter Home/ Children's Home for care and protection under Section 33(1) of the Juvenile Justice Act, 2000.

Next Date:

(Signature)

Chairperson/Member
Child Welfare Committee

**Form XI**
[Rule 27(19)]
**Order of Restoration of a Child to an Institution**

To
The Officer-in-Charge

Whereas on the..............day of.........20......(name of the child) ............son/daughter of........aged........residing at.......being in care and protection under Section 33(4) of the Juvenile Justice (Care and Protection) Act, 2000 is ordered by the Child Welfare Committee..................to be kept in the Children's Home/Shelter Home.........for a period of..........

This is to authorize and require you to receive the said child in your charge, and to kept him/her in the Children's Home/Shelter Home...........for the aforesaid order to be carried into execution according to law.

Given under may hand and the seal of Child Welfare Committee.

This.......day of........20.

(Signature)

Chairperson/Member
Child Welfare Committee

Encl:

Copy of the orders, particulars of home and previous record, case-history and individual care plan, whichever is applicable:

**Form XII**
[Rule 28(1)]
**Order form Enquiry**

To

Child Welfare Officer /Person in-charge of Voluntary Organization/Social Worker/ Case-Worker.

Whereas a report under Section......of the Juvenile Justice (Care and Protection of Children) Act, 2000 has been received from.......... in respect of (name of the child)..... aged (approximate)......... son/daughter of.............residing at........ who has been produced before the Committee under section......of the Juvenile Justice (Care and Protection of Children) Act, 2000.

You are hereby directed to enquire into the social and family background of the said child and submit your inquiry report on or before....... or within such time allowed to you by the Committee.

You are also hereby directed to consult an expert in child psychology, psychiatric treatment or counseling for their expert opinion if necessary and submit such report along with your Inquiry Report.

You are hereby directed to enquire into the character and social antecedents of the said juvenile and submit your social investigation report on or before........or within such time allowed to you by the Board/Committee.

Dated this.......day of.... 20.......

(Signature)

Chairperson/Member
Child Welfare Committee

SEAL

## Form XIII
**[Rules 28(3); 33(3)(g)*(ii)* and (4)(f); 87(l)(a) and (2)]**
## Format for Inquiry Report

Sl. No..........

Produced before the Child Welfare Committee ............(address).

Case No.

Concerned Government Department/Voluntary Organization

Category of child in need of care and protection:

---

| | |
|---|---|
| Name | Religion |
| Father's Name | Caste |
| Permanent Address | Year of birth |
| Address of last residence | Age |
| | Sex |

---

Previous institutional/case history and individual care plan, if any

### Family

| *Members of family* | *Name* | *Age* | *Health* | *Edu-cation* | *Occu-pation* | *Monthly earnings* | *Disabi-lities* | *Any other e.g. social habits* |
|---|---|---|---|---|---|---|---|---|
| Father | | | | | | | | |
| Step-Father | | | | | | | | |
| Mother | | | | | | | | |
| Step-mother | | | | | | | | |
| Siblings | | | | | | | | |
| Any other legal guardian/ relative | | | | | | | | |

If married, relevant particulars ........................................

Other near relatives or agencies interested ..................

Attitude towards religion normal
and ethical code of the home etc. ..................................
Social and economic status ..............................................
Delinquency record of members of family ...................
Present living conditions ...................................................
Relationship between parent/
parents and children especially
with the said child ............................................................
Other factors of importance if any .................................

**Child's History**

Mental condition
(Present and past) ..........................................................
Physical condition
(Present and past) ..........................................................
Habits, interests
(moral, recreational, etc.) .................................................
Outstanding characteristics and personality traits .......
Companions and their influence .................................
Truancy from home, if any ...........................................
School (attitude towards school, teachers, class-mates and *vice-verso)* ..........................................................................

..........................................................................................

Work record (jobs held, reasons for leaving, vocational interests, attitude towards job or employers) .....................

Neighborhood and neighbors report ............................

Parent's attitude towards discipline in the home and child's reaction ..............................................................................

..........................................................................................

Any other remarks

---

**Result of Inquiry**

Emotional factors
Physical condition
Intelligence
Social and economic factors
Religious factors

Reasons for child's need for care and protection
Opinion of experts consulted
Recommendation of Child Welfare Officer/Case-Worker/ Social Worker regarding psychological support, rehabilitation and reintegration of the child and suggested plan.

Signature of the Child Welfare Officer/Case-Worker/ Social Worker

**Form XIV**

[Rule 33(3)(c)3

**Order for Declaring Child Legally Free for Adoption**

1. In exercise of the powers vested in the Child Welfare Committee..........constituted under sub-section.........of section........of the Juvenile Justice (Care and Protection of Children) Act, 2000 and sub-rule......of rule......of these rules, minor.......born on (date)........placed in custody of Specialized Adoption Agency (name and address)...... *vide* order......dated.....of the Chairperson, Child Welfare Committee......has been declared legally free for adoption on the basis of details furnished through:

(*a*) Inquiry/home study conducted by Child Welfare Officer/Social Worker/Case-Worker.

(*b*) Document of surrender executed by the parent(s) and surrender deed signed in the presence of the Committee under sub-rules.....of rule......of these rules.

(*c*) Declaration submitted by the Specialized Adoption Agency under sub-rules.......of rule......of these rules.

2. ...........(name of the Specialized Adoption Agency) shall fulfil all conditions specified in Juvenile Justice (Care and Protection of Children) Act, 2000 and the rules relating thereto and furnish a copy of adoption decree/guardianship order in respect of the minor as may be required by Committee and the concerned Department of the State Government of.........

Date: Chairperson/Member Place: Child Welfare Committee

For completion by the Specialized Adoption Agency.

i. I have read and understood Chapters III and IV of Juvenile Justice (Care and Protection of Children) Act, 2000 and the rules thereunder and agree to abide/be bound by the same while placing said minor in adoption.

*(ii)* I further declare that the particulars stated in the declaration submitted by me on..........true and correct. In case they are found to be false or incorrect, the Committee has right to suspend this Release Order for (name of the minor)..................and ask for production of said minor before the Committee.

Date:
Place:

Child Welfare Officer/Social Worker

**Form XV**
[Rule 33(4)(c)]
**Deed of Surrender**

I..................d/o or s/o............residing at............am not in a position due to social reasons/due to being single/ill/ disabled to take care of my child (name, if any)...........approximate age......years. I am explained the consequences of surrendering my child by the Child Welfare Officer/Social Worker (name).............and the Child Welfare Committee...... In full knowledge of all these facts, I am surrendering my child before the Committee today, dated............ Within two months from this stated date if I do not revise my decision to take back my child and do not approach the said Committee for the same, the Committee shall declare my child legally free for adoption and I shall have no further claim on my child.

Signature of parent/guardian
Date

That I.........Child Welfare Officer/Social Worker have

explained the procedure and the consequences of surrendering the child to the concerned parent/guardian on (date).............. .

Signature of Child Welfare Officer/Social Worker
Date

(Signed before me)

Chairperson/Member
Child Welfare Committee

**Form XVI**
[Rule 35(3)]

**A. Foster Carer's Assessment**

**1. Agency Details**

Name of the Agency
Address
Telephone
Fax
E-mail
Name of the Social Worker
Tel
Date...............(Form Completed)

**2. Details of the Applicant**

Surname

Full Name

Date of Birth

Religion

Language(s) spoken at Home

Occupation

(*a*) Nature of Work
(*b*) Hours of Work Address Telephone

**3. Description of a preferred child**

The type of child, the foster-carer would consider
(To be filled after a full discussion with the Foster-carer)

Age Range Under 2 years 3–6 years
7–12 years 13–15 years 16–18 years

| *Sl. No.* | *Type of Placement* | *Duration* |
|---|---|---|
| *(i)* | Pre-adoption | |
| *(ii)* | Emergency | |
| *(iii)* | Short-term | |
| *(iv)* | Assessment | |
| *(v)* | Long-term | |

The Child an applicant can care for
(Please Tick)
A child who is:

1. Neglected
2. Orphaned
3. With Physical impairment
4. Mental impairment
5. Hearing impairment
6. Speech impairment
7. Special Education needs
8. Learning difficulties
9. Physical abuse
10. Sexual abuse
11. Who does not relate easily
12. Who needs control/may defy authority
13. Born of rape/incest
14. Who's parent(s) is suffering from disease
15. Whose parent(s) is HIV positive
16. Whose parent(s) is AIDS patient
17. Whose parent(s) are alcoholic
18. Drug addicts
19. Are in jail
20. Relinquished
21. Belong to another caste
22. Are of different religion

**4. Profile of the Family**

**Brief Family Profile**

| *Name* | *Gender* | *Approx. Age* | *Occu-pation* | *Edu-cation* | *Relationship with the applicant* |
|---|---|---|---|---|---|
| | | | | | |
| | | | | | |

(Give details of personalities, family life, experiences etc. Also highlight specific qualities of the family that can match with a child's needs. The details should facilitate initial identification of a potential match with a specific child.)

Accommodation (House)

(Details of type, size, own/rented space, amenities etc.)

Neighborhood (Details of composition, amenities and facilities, public transport etc.)

**5. Verification of applicant's identity**

Place of residence

Period of stay

Nationality

Marital status date/length of marriage)

Has either of the applicant had a previous marriage? Details

If children from previous marriage? Details

Specify documents seen with date

**6. Career History**

(Details of education, employment, voluntary work, part-time work, leisure activities)

**7. Agency Inquiries**

Medical check

Police check

Employer

8. Personal references (from 2 persons)

This section to be completed after interviews with two references; information gathered through these interviews should include:

- Length of time known
- Relationship to the applicant
- Provide evidence on the applicants ability to perform the tasks involved in......
- Caring for children
- Providing a safe and caring environment
- Applicant as a neighbor
- Interests, talents, personality.

Assessment of the social worker for these references.

**B. Home Study Report**

A Home Study Report of the foster carer(s) being a crucial document being prepared by the social worker of the Specialized Adoption 'Agency based on the information collected by the format given above should broadly include the following information:

- Social status and family background
- Description of the home
- Standard of living as it appears in the home
- Current relations amongst the members in the home
- Status of development of the children already in the home
- Employment and economic status
- Health details
- Details of facilities of education, medical, vocational trainings available in the neighborhood
- Reasons for wanting a child in foster care
- Attitudes of the grandparents and other relatives
- Anticipated plans for the foster child
- Legal status of the foster carer(s)
- Willingness to undergo training.

**C. Details of Applicants(s)**

1. *Background:*

Family structure with details of parents and siblings,

significant details of other family members, childhood experiences, etc.

*2. Relationships*

If couple—Length of married life, what qualities does each applicant bring to the partnership, what makes the relationship positive for each other? Within the relationship how do applicants cope with problems/stress/anger? How do applicants support each other? What is each applicant's assessment of how the foster placement will affect his or her relationship?

*3. Decision-making*

How is decision-making exercised in this relationship and how does each of the applicants view this? Is there wider extended family involvement in the couple's decision-making process? If so, how will this affect the child to be placed?

What are the strengths and vulnerabilities of this partnership?

- Children
- Children and their parent's relationships
- Children's attitude and readiness for a foster placement sibling. Describe each child and their temperament, any special talent and need, how children have been involved in preparation.

*4. Applicants Support Networks*

Give a general picture of support systems currently used by the applicants including extended family, friends, neighbours, religious activities, community groups, etc., include details of the location etc.

*5. Other Significant Members of the Family*

Living in the house or not. Their relationship to the applicants, how much time they spent within the home, their attitude to the proposed placement? How important is their acceptance of placement to the applicant.

*6. Description of the Family Life Style*

Outline what family considers important *e.g.,* how important are religious and cultural practices. How is affection shown in the family? How do the members spend their time? What expectations family members have with regard to personal space? What value is placed on education/ Hobbies and leisure activities that the whole family undertakes?

*7. Parenting Capacities*

Experience of the applicants of caring and working with children. Describe their adjustment to parenthood. What is their understanding of how children develop?

Using their own childhood experiences what patterns of parenting would they repeat and what would they change? What is their understanding of their own parenting strengths/ potentials and about their parenting skills to meet the needs of individual child. To what extent they would expect other family members to be involved in parenting of their children/ placed children.

How will they ensure that a child will be safe from physical sexual abuse in their family and within wider support networks?

*8. Managing Unacceptable Behavior*

What are rules in the household? How do the applicants show approval/disapproval? What are discipline measures they use? Their attitude towards punishment?

What do they anticipate would be the issues and difficulties and themselves for their own children and for their support network? What do they anticipate would be the issues and difficulties for the child? Which changes do they anticipate would need in their lifestyle?

**Social Workers Assessment**

It should provide an analysis of all the information collected through the format and its significance with regard to the capacity of the applicant to carryout fostering task: (What skills do the applicants have in relating to and working with children? How well will the applicant work with the agency, with biological parents? What are the strengths and resources of the applicants and which are the areas where they may experience difficulty? Also the point of disagreement between the social worker and the applicants should be recorded here)

Recommendations of the Child Welfare Officer/Social Worker

(Signature)

**Form XVII**

[Rule 34(1)]

**Order of Foster Care Placement**

The child (name and address)...........approximate age.... d/o or s/o Mr...........and Mrs................or Ms. ............is in need of care and protection of a family. Mr...........and Mrs. ........or Ms.........resident of (complete address and contact numbers)...................is/are declared fit person/persons for foster-care placement of the child based on the home study report of the Child Welfare Officer/ Social Worker Ms./Mr...............of the organization The child (name)............. is placed in foster care for a period of........... (days/months), under the supervision of the aforesaid Child Welfare Officer/Social Worker (name and contact)..........

Chairperson/Member

Child Welfare Committee

**Form XVIII**

[Rule 37(5)]

**Order of Sponsorship Placement**

The juvenile/child (name and address)......................

approximate age..........d/o or s/o Mr............and Mrs........or Ms...............has been identified by the State/District Child Protection Unit as a juvenile /child at risk needing urgent care and protection. On the basis of the Inquiry Report submitted by the State/District Child Protection Unit/Child Welfare Officer/ Social Worker it is established that the said juvenile/child needs sponsorship support for education/ health/nutrition/other developmental needs.........*(please specify)*. The State/District Child Protection Unit is hereby directed to release Rs........per month/Rs.........as one time sponsorship support to the said juvenile/child for a period of........(days/month) and carryout necessary follow-up.

The State/District Child Protection Unit is also directed to clearly lay down the terms and conditions for sponsorship support and follow-up.

Principal Magistrate, Juvenile justice Board/ Chairperson/Member, Child Welfare Committee.

*Copy to:* State/District Child Protection Unit or concerned Department of the State Government.

**Form XIX**

[Rule 38(3)]

**Order of After Care Placement**

The juvenile/child (name).............d/o or s/o........has/will be completing 18 years of age on (date)........ . She/he is still in need of care and protection for the purpose of rehabilitation and reintegration. She/he is placed in (name of organization).....for providing aftercare. The in-charge of the Organization is directed to admit the child and provide all possible opportunities for her/his rehabilitation and reintegration in its truest sense. The person shall be provided all these opportunities maximum till the age of 21 years only or till reintegration in the society, whichever is earlier. The in-charge will send half yearly report on the status of the child/youth to the Child Welfare Committee.

The State/District Child Protection Unit is hereby directed to arrange for aftercare for the said juvenile/child for a period of........(days/month) and carryout necessary follow-up. The State/District Child Protection Unit is also directed to clearly lay down the terms and conditions for aftercare programme and carryout necessary follow-up.

Principal Magistrate, Juvenile Justice Board/ Chairperson/Member, Child Welfare Committee

*Copy to:* State/District Child Protection Unit or concerned Department of the State Government.

**Form XIX**

[Rules 50(9) and 54(l)(t)]

**Case History Form for Children in Need of Care and Protection**

Affix a latest photograph here

Case/Profile No..................

Date and Time......................

**A. Personal Data**

1. Name
2. Male/Female (tick the appropriate category)
3. *(a)* age at the time of admission (b) present age:
4. Category:
   - Separated from family
   - Abandoned/deserted
   - Victim of exploitation and violence (give detail)
   - Run-away
   - Any other

5 Religion Hindu (OC/BC/SC/ST) Muslim/Christian/Other (pl. specify)

6. Location of Residence Urban/Sub-urban/ Rural/Slum/ Industrial/Other (pl. specify)
7. Native District and State:
8. Description of the Housing:
   *(i)* Concrete building Tiled House/Hut/On the street/Others (please specify)
   *(ii)* Three-bed room/two-bed room/one-bed room/ no separate bed-room
   *(iii)* Owned/rental

9. By whom the juvenile was brought before the Child Welfare Committee:
   *(i)* Police-Local Police/Special Juvenile Police Unit/Railway Police/Women Police
   *(ii)* Probation Officers
   *(iii)* Social Welfare Organization
   *(iv)* Social Worker
   *(v)* Parent(s)/Guardian(s) (please specify the relationship)
   *(vi)* Child himself/herself
10. Reasons for leaving the family
    *(i)* Abuse by parent(s)/guardian(s)/step-parents(s)
    *(ii)* In search of employment
    *(iii)* Peer group influence
    *(iv)* Incapacitation of parents
    *(v)* Criminal behavior of parents
    *(vi)* Separation of Parents
    *(vii)* Demise of parents
    *(viii)* Poverty
    *(ix)* Others (please specify)
11. Types of abuse met by the child
    *(i)* Verbal abuse—Parents/siblings/employers/others (please specify)
    *(ii)* Physical abuse
    *(iii)* Sexual abuse parents/siblings/hmployers/othcrs please specify)
    *(iv)* Others—parents/siblings/employers/others (pl. Specify)
12. Types of ill-treatment met by the child.
    *(i)* Denial of food—parents/sib lings employers/other (please specify)
    *(ii)* Beaten mercilessly—parents/siblings/employers/other (please specify)
    *(iii)* Causing injury—parents/siblings/employers/other (please specify)
    *(iv)* Other (please specify)-parents/siblings/employers/others (please specify)

13. Exploitation faced by the child
    (i) Extracted work without payment
    (ii) Little (low) wages with longer duration of work
    (iii) Others (please specify)
14. Health status of the child before admission.
    (i) Respiratory disorders —present/not known/absent
    (ii) Hearing impairment —present/not known/absent
    (iii) Eye diseases —present/not known/absent
    (iv) Dental disease —present/not known/absent
    (v) Cardiac diseases —present/not known/absent
    (vi) Skin disease —present/not known/absent
    (vii) Sexually transmitted diseases —present/not known/absent
    (viii) Neurological disorders —present/not known/absent
    (ix) Mental handicap—present/not known/absent
    (x) Physical handicap —present/not known/absent
    (xi) Others (please specify) —present/not known/absent
15. With whom the child was staying prior to admission
    (i) Parent(s)—Mother/Father/Both
    (ii) Guardian(s)—Relationship
    (iii) Friends
    (iv) On the street
    (v) Night shelter
    (vi) Orphanages/Hostels/Similar Homes
    (vii) Other (please specify)
16. Visit of the parents to meet the child
    (i) Prior to institutionalization—Frequently/Occasionally/Rarely/Never
    (ii) After institutionalization—Frequently/Occasionally/Rarely/Never
17. Visit of the child to his family
    (i) Prior to institutionalization—Frequently/Occasionally/Rarely/During holidays/Whenever fallen sick/never

   (*ii*) After institutionalization–
   Frequently/Occasionally/Rarely/During holidays/Whenever fallen sick/never

18. Correspondence with parents–
   (*i*) Prior to institutionalization –
   Frequently/Occasionally/Rarely/During holidays/Whenever fallen sick/never
   (*ii*) After institutionalization–
   Frequently/Occasionally/Rarely/During festival times/During summer holidays/Whenever fallen sick/never.

**B. Childhood History (up to the Age of 12 Years)**

19. Diet of mother during pregnancy:
   (*i*) Taken nutritious diet
   (*ii*) Ordinary diet
   (*iii*) Inadequate food intake
20. Health during pregnancy
   (*i*) Mother infected with contagious diseases
   (*ii*) Mother consumed/used contraceptives
   (*iii*) Intake of antibiotics
   (*iv*) No such details available
21. Birth details
   (*i*) Normal delivery/prolonged delivery/caesarian
   (*ii*) Under weight/normal weight/over weight
22. Details of immunization provided
23. Details of handicap
   (*i*) Hearing impairment
   By birth/after accident/diseases
   (*ii*) Speech impairment
   By birth/after accident/diseases
   (*iii*) Physical handicap
   By birth/after accident/diseases
   (*iv*) Mental handicap
   By birth/after accident/diseases
   (*v*) Others (please specify)

## C Family Details

24. Household Composition:

| *Sl. No.* | *Name & Relationship* | *Age* | *Sex* | *Education* | *Occupation* | *Income* |
|---|---|---|---|---|---|---|
| 1 | 2 | 3 | 4 | 5 | 6 | 7 |

| *Health* | *History of Mental illness* | *Handicap* | *Habit* | *Socialization* |
|---|---|---|---|---|
| 8 | 9 | 10 | 11 | 12 |

25. Type of family:
    Nuclear family/joint family/broken family
26. Relationship among the family members:
    - *(i)* Father & mother—Cordial/Non-cordial/Not known
    - *(ii)* Father & child—Cordial/Non-cordial/Not known
    - *(iii)* Mother & child—Cordial/Non-cordial/Not known
    - *(iv)* Father & siblings—Cordial/Non-cordial/Not known
    - *(v)* Mother &siblings—Cordial/Non-cordial/Not known
    - *(vi)* Juvenile & siblings—Cordial/Non-cordial/Not known
27. History of crime committed by family members:

| *S. No.* | *Relationship* | *Nature of crime* | *Arrest if any made* | *Period of confinement* | *Punishment awarded* |
|---|---|---|---|---|---|
| 1. | Father | | | | |
| 2. | Step-father | | | | |
| 3. | Mother | | | | |
| 4. | Step-mother | | | | |
| 5. | Brother | | | | |
| | *(a)* | | | | |
| | *(b)* | | | | |
| | *(c)* | | | | |
| | *(d)* | | | | |
| 6. | Sister | | | | |
| | *(a)* | | | | |
| | *(b)* | | | | |
| | *(c)* | | | | |
| | *(d)* | | | | |
| 7. | Child | | | | |
| 8. | Others (uncle/aunty/ grandparents) | | | | |

28. Properties owned by the family:
    - *(i)* Landed properties (pl. specify the area)
    - *(ii)* Household articles—cows/cattle/bull
    - *(iii)* Vehicles—two-wheeler/three-wheeler/four - wheeler (lorry/bus/car/tractor/jeep)
    - *(iv)* Others (please specify)
29. Marriage details of family members:
    - *(i)* Parents Arranged/Special Marriage/Local Union
    - *(ii)* Brothers Arranged/Special Marriage/Local Union
    - *(iii)* Sisters Arranged/Special Marriage/Local Union
30. Social activities of family members:
    - *(i)* Participate in social and religious functions
    - *(ii)* Participate in cultural activities
    - *(iii)* Does not participate in social and religious functions
    - *(iv)* Not known
31. Parental care towards juvenile before admission:
    - *(i)* Over protection
    - *(ii)* Affectionate
    - *(iii)* Attentive
    - *(iv)* Not affectionate
    - *(v)* Not attentive
    - *(vi)* Rejection

**D. Adolescence History (Between 12 and 18 Years)**

32. Puberty
    Early
    Middle age
    Late
33. Details of delinquent behavior if any
    - *(i)* Stealing
    - *(ii)* Pick pocketing
    - *(iii)* Arrack selling
    - *(iv)* Drug pedalling
    - *(v)* Petty offences
    - *(vi)* Violent crime

(vii) Rape
(viii) None of the above
(ix) Others (please specify)

34. Reason for delinquent behavior
(i) Parental neglect
(ii) Parental overprotection
(iii) Parents criminal behavior
(iv) Parents influence (negative)
(v) Peer group influence
(vi) To buy drugs/alcohol
(vii) Others (pl. specify)

35. Habits

| A | B |
|---|---|
| (i) Smoking | (i) Watching TV/movies |
| (ii) Alcohol consumption | (ii) Playing indoor/outdoor games |
| (iii) Drug use (specify) | (iii) Reading books |
| (iv) Gambling | (iv) Religious activities |
| (v) Begging | (v) Drawing/painting/acting/singing |
| (vi) Any other | (vi) Any other |

**E. Employment Details**

Employment details of the juveniles prior to entry into the Home:

| *Sl.No.* | *Details of employment* | *Duration* | *Wages earned* |
|---|---|---|---|
| (i) | Cooly | | |
| (ii) | Rag picking | | |
| (iii) | Mechanic | | |
| (iv) | Hotel work | | |
| (v) | Tea shop work | | |
| (vi) | Shoe polish | | |
| (vii) | Household works | | |
| (viii) | Others (pl. specify) | | |

36. Details of income utilization:
    - *(i)* Sent to family to meet family need
    - *(ii)* For dress materials
    - *(iii)* For gambling
    - *(iv)* For prostitution
    - *(v)* For alcohol
    - *(vi)* For drug
    - *(vii)* For smoking
    - *(viii)* Savings
37. Details of savings
    - *(i)* With employers
    - *(ii)* With friends
    - *(iii)* Bank/Post Office
    - *(iv)* Others (pls. specify)
38. Duration of working hours
    - *(i)* Less than six hours
    - *(ii)* Between six and eight hours
    - *(iii)* More than eight hours

**F. Educational Details**

39. The details of education of the juvenile prior to the admission to Children's home
    - *(i)* Illiterate
    - *(ii)* Studied up to V Standard
    - *(iii)* Studied above V Std but below VIII Standard
    - *(iv)* Studied above VIII Std but below X Standard
    - *(v)* Studied above X Standard
40. The reason for leaving the school
    - *(i)* Failure in the class last studied
    - *(ii)* Lack of interest in the school activities
    - *(iii)* Indifferent attitude of the teachers
    - *(iv)* Peer group influence
    - *(v)* To earn and support the family
    - *(vi)* Sudden demise of parents
    - *(vii)* Rigid school atmosphere
    - *(viii)* Absenteeism followed by running away from school
    - *(ix)* Others (pl. specify)

41. The details of the school in which studied last:
    *(i)* Corporation/Municipal/Panchayat Union
    *(ii)* Government/SC Welfare School/DC Welfare School
    *(iii)* Private management
    *(iv)* Convents
42. Medium of instruction:
    Hindi/English/Urdu/Tamil/Malayalam/Kannada/Telugu and other language (please specify)
43. After admission to Children's Home, the educational attainment from the date of admission till date;
    *No. of years* *Class studied* *Promoted/detained*
44. Vocational training undergone form the date of admission into Children's Home till date.
    No. of years Name of Vocational Trade Proficiency Attained
45. Extra curricular activities developed from the date of admission into the Children's Home till date
    *(i)* Scout
    *(ii)* Sports (please specify)
    *(iii)* Athletics (please specify)
    *(iv)* Drawing
    *(v)* Painting
    *(vi)* Others (please specify)

**G. Medical History**

46. Height and weight at the time of admission:
47. Physical condition:
48. Medical history of child (gist):
49. Medical history of parent/guardian (gist):
50. Present health status of the child:

| *Sl. No.* | *Annual Observation* | *1st Quarter* | *2nd Quarter* | *3rd Quarter* | *4th Quarter* |
|---|---|---|---|---|---|
| 1. | Date of review | | | | |
| 2. | Height | | | | |
| 3. | Weight | | | | |
| 4. | Nutritious diet given | | | | |

| *Sl. No.* | *Annual Observation* | *1st Quarter* | *2nd Quarter* | *3rd Quarter* | *4th Quarter* |
|---|---|---|---|---|---|
| 5. | Stress disease | | | | |
| 6. | Dental | | | | |
| 7. | ENT- Tonsils | | | | |
| 8. | External eye problem: vision | | | | |
| | Left | | | | |
| | Right | | | | |

51. Height and Weight Chart:

| *Date, Month & Year* | *Height* | *Admissible weight* | *Actual weight* |
|---|---|---|---|
| | | | |
| | | | |
| | | | |
| | | | |
| | | | |
| | | | |
| | | | |

**H. Social History**

52. Details of friendship prior to admission into Children's Home:
    - *(i)* Co-workers
    - *(ii)* School/Class-mate
    - *(iii)* Neighbors
    - *(iv)* Others (please specify)
53. Majority of the friends are
    - *(i)* Educated
    - *(ii)* Illiterate
    - *(iii)* The same age group

(*iv*) Older in age
(*v*) Younger in age
(*vi*) Same sex
(*vii*) Opposite sex

54. Details of membership in group (please specify details)
(*i*) Associated with cine fans association
(*ii*) Associated with religious group
(*iii*) Associated with arts and sports club'
(*iv*) Associated with gangs
(*v*) Associated with voluntary social service league
(*vi*) Others (please specify)

55. The position of the child in the groups/league
(*i*) Leader
(*ii*) Second level leader
(*iii*) Middle level functionary
(*iv*) Ordinary member

56. Purpose of taking membership in the group:
(*i*) For social service activities
(*ii*) For leisure time spending
(*iii*) For pleasure seeking activities
(*iv*) For deviant activities
(*v*) Others (please specify)

57. Attitude of the group/league
(*i*) Respect the social norms and follow the rules
(*ii*) Interested in violating the norms
(*iii*) Impulsive in violating the rules

58. The location/meeting point of the groups
(*i*) Usually at fixed place
(*ii*) Places are changed frequently
(*iii*) No specific places
(*iv*) Meeting point is fixed conveniently

59. The reaction of the society when the child first came out of the family
(*i*) Supportive
(*ii*) Rejection
(*iii*) Abuse
(*iv*) Ill-treatment
(*v*) Exploitation

60. The reaction of the police towards children
    (*i*) Passionate
    (*ii*) Cruel
    (*iii*) Abuse
    (*iv*) Exploitation
    (*v*) Ill-treatment
61. The response of the general public towards the child

**I. History of the Child (Gist)**

(*i*) Education
(*ii*) Health
(*iii*) Vocational training
(*iv*) Extra curricular activities
(*v*) Others

Suggestion of Child Welfare Officer/Probation Officer after orientation to juvenile/ child and the response towards orientation.

Follow-up by Child Welfare Officer/Probation Officer/ Case-Worker/Social Worker Quarterly Review of Case History by Management Committee

Superintendent/
Welfare Officer/Probation Officer

**Form XXI**

[Rules 50(12)(a), 54(1)(o) and 87(l)(k)]

**Individual Care Plan**

Individual care plan for each child shall be prepared following the principle of the best interest of the child. In preparing individual care plan the care options in the following order of preferences shall be considered:

(*i*) Preserving the biological family
(*ii*) Kinship Care
(*iii*) In-country adoption
(*iv*) Foster Care
(*v*) Inter-country Adoption
(*vi*) Institutional Care

Case/Profile No. of 20.....(year) of the Board/Committee Admission No. Date of Admission:

**A. Personal Details**

1. Name of the Child:
2. Age:
3. Sex: Male/Female
4. Father's/Mother's name:
5. Nationality:
6. Religion/Caste:
7. Educational Attainment:
8. Summary of Case History:
    - Health needs
    - Emotional and psychological support needed
    - Educational and training needs
    - Leisure, creativity and play
    - Attachments and Relationships
    - Religious beliefs
    - Protection from all kinds of abuse, neglect and maltreatment
    - Social mainstreaming
    - Follow-up post release/restoration

**B. Fortnightly Progress Report of Probationer**

**Part One**

1. Name of the Probation Officer/Case-Worker
2. For the month of
3. Registration No.
4. Competent Authority
5. Profile No.
6. Name of the Child
7. Date of Supervision Order
8. Address of the Child
9. Period of Supervision

**Part Two**

| Places of interview | Dates |
|---|---|
| ........................ | ........................ |
| ........................ | ........................ |
| ........................ | ........................ |

1. Where the child is residing?
2. Progress made in any educational/training course,
3. What work he/she is doing and his/her monthly average earning, if employed.
4. Savings kept in the Post Office.
5. Savings Bank Account in his/her name.
6. Remarks on his/her general conduct and progress.
7. Whether property cared for?

**Part Three**

1. Any proceedings before the competent authority of or
   *(a)* Variation of conditions of bond
   *(b)* Change of residence
   *(c)* Other matters
2. Period of supervision completed on...............
3. Result of supervision with remarks (if any)
4. Name and Addresses of the parent or guardian or fit person under whose care the juvenile is to live after the supervision is over.

Date of report..........Signature of the Probation Officer/ Case-Worker............

**C. Pre-Release Report**

Tick whichever is applicable

Final Release ☐ Transfer ☐

1. Details of place of transfer and concerned authority responsible in the place of transfer/release
2. Details placement of the juvenile/child in different institutions
3. Training undergone and skills acquired
4. Final progress report of the Officer-in-Charge/ probation officer/child welfare officer/case-worker/ social worker (to be attached)
5. Date of release/transfer

6. Date of repatriation
7. Requisition for escort if required
8. Identification of escort
9. Recommended rehabilitation plan including possible placements
10. Sponsorship requirement and report, if applicable
11. Identification of Probation Officer/Case-worker/ social worker/non-governmental organization for post-release follow-up
12. Memorandum of understanding with non-governmental organization identified for post-release follow-up
13. Identification of sponsorship agency/individual sponsor for the child post-release, if any
14. Memorandum of understanding between the sponsoring agency and individual sponsor
15. Details of Savings Account of the child, if any
16. Details of child's earnings and belongings if any
17. Details of awards/rewards due to the child if any
18. Opinion of the child
19. Any other information

**Note:** Pre-release report shall be prepared 6 months prior to the date of release/ transfer of juvenile/child and shall take into account the recommendations of the last review report and all other relevant information.

**D. Post-Release Report**

1. Status of Bank Account: Closed/Transferred
2. Earnings and belongings of the child: handed over to the child or his/her parents /guardiana—Yes/No
3. First interaction report of the probation officer/child welfare officer/case-worker/ social worker/non-gcvernmental organization identified for follow-up with the child post-release
4. Placement of the juvenile/child if any
5. Family's behavior towards the child
6. Social milieu of the child, particularly attitude of neighbors/community

7. How is the child using the skills acquired?
8. Whether the child has been admitted to a school or vocation? Give date and name of the school/ institute/any other agency
9. Report of second and third follow-up interaction with the child after two months and six months respectively.

**FORM XXII**

[Rule 65(2)]

**Escort Order**

Case No...............

In the matter of Boy/Girl Child………..........................................
Aged about.........year taken charge for sole custody under Section 33(3) of the Juvenile Justice Act, 2000

The Parents of the boy/girl child are reported to be residing at:

He/she therefore be sent under supervision of a proper police/non-governmental organization escort to the.............

For handing over to the parents or close relatives of the said Boy Child/Girl Child resident at the aforesaid address or at other Place which may be shown by the Child, if no such parents or relative are traced or if traced but they are unwilling to take charge of the boy/girl be kept in the custody of the Superintendent.......Children's Home and the said Boy/Girl child be produced before the concerned Child Welfare Committee for further orders.

**Orders**

Pending Escort, the said Boy/Girl Child shall remain in Children's Home, residing at present at........The state/District Child Protection Unit, or Police Department or non-governmental organization/Childline shall positively make immediate arrangement not less than 15 days from the date of receipt of this order by him and send the said Boy Child/ Girl Child at his/her aforesaid place of residence.

Dated this..........day of..........20....... Chairperson/Member Child Welfare Committee

CC *to:*

1. The Superintendent Children Home.
2. The State/District Child Protection Unit or non-governmental organization or Childline

*Ref.:* 1. Order of admission of minor.......... Born on..........Profile No.....

*ANNEXURE III*

## United Nations Standard Minimum Rules for the Administration of Juvenile Justice

*("TheBeijing Rules")*

Adopted by General Assembly resolution 40/33 of 29 November, 1985

**Part One**

General Principles

### 1. Fundamental Perspectives

1.1 Member States shall seek, in conformity with their respective general interests, to further the well-being of the juvenile and her or his family.

1.2 Member States shall endeavor to develop conditions that will ensure for the juvenile a meaningful life in the community, which, during that period in life when she or he is most susceptible to deviant behavior, will foster a process of personal development and education that is as free from crime and delinquency as possible.

1.3 Sufficient attention shall be given to positive measures that involve the full mobilization of all possible resources, including the family, volunteers and other community groups, as well as schools and other community institutions, for the purpose of promoting the well-being of the juvenile, with a view to reducing the need for intervention under the law, and of effectively, fairly and humanely dealing with the juvenile in conflict with the law.

1.4 Juvenile justice shall be conceived as an integral part of the national development process of each country, within a comprehensive framework of social justice for all juveniles, thus, at the same time, contributing to the protection of the young and the maintenance of a peaceful order in society.

1.5 These Rules shall be implemented in the context of economic, social arid cultural conditions prevailing in each Member State.

1.6 Juvenile justice services shall be systematically developed and coordinated with a view to improving and sustaining the competence of personnel involved in the services, including their methods, approaches and attitudes.

**Commentary**

These broad fundamental perspectives refer to comprehensive social policy in general and aim at promoting juvenile welfare to the greatest possible extent, which will minimize the necessity of intervention by the juvenile justice system, and in turn, will reduce the harm that may be caused by any intervention. Such care measures for the young, before the onset of delinquency, are basic policy requisites designed to obviate the need for the application of the Rules.

Rules 1.1 to 1.3 point to the important role that a constructive social policy for juveniles will play, inter alia, in the prevention of juvenile crime and delinquency. Rule 1.4 defines juvenile justice as an integral part of social justice for juveniles, while Rule 1.6 refers to the necessity of constantly improving juvenile justice, without falling behind the development of progressive social policy for juveniles in general and bearing in mind the need for consistent improvement of staff services.

Rule 1.5 seeks to take account of existing conditions in Member States which would cause the manner of implementation of particular rules necessarily to be different from the manner adopted in other States.

**2. Scope of the Rules and Definitions Used**

2.1 The following Standard Minimum Rules shall be applied to juvenile offenders impartially, without distinction of any kind, for example as to race, colour, sex, language, religion, political or other opinions, national or social origin, property, birth or other status.

2.2 For purposes of these Rules, the following definitions shall be applied by Member States in a manner which is compatible with their respective legal systems and concepts:

(*a*) A juvenile is a child or young person who, under the respective legal systems, may be dealt with for an offence in a manner which is different from an adult;

(*b*) An offence is any behaviour (act or omission) that is punishable by law under the respective legal systems;

(*c*) A juvenile offender is a child or young person who is alleged to have committed or who has been found to have committed an offence.

2.3 Efforts shall be made to establish, in each national jurisdiction, a set of laws, rules and provisions specifically applicable to juvenile offenders and institutions and bodies entrusted with the functions of the administration of juvenile justice and designed:

(*a*) To meet the varying needs of juvenile offenders, while protecting their basic rights;

(*b*) To meet the needs of society;

(*c*) To implement the following rules thoroughly and fairly.

**Commentary**

The Standard Minimum Rules are deliberately formulated so as to be applicable within different legal systems and, at the same time, to set some minimum standards for the handling of juvenile offenders under any definition of a juvenile and under any system of dealing with juvenile offenders. The Rules are always to be applied impartially and without distinction of any kind.

Rule 2.1 therefore stresses the importance of the Rules always being applied impartially and without distinction of any kind. The rule follows the formulation of principle 2 of the Declaration of the Rights of the Child.

Rule 2.2 defines "juvenile" and "offence" as the components of the notion of the "juvenile offender", who is the main subject of these Standard Minimum Rules (see, however, also Rules 3 and 4). It should be noted that age limits will depend on, and are explicitly made dependent on, each respective legal system, thus fully respecting the economic, social, political, cultural and legal systems of Member States. This makes for a wide variety of ages coming under the definition of "juvenile", ranging from 7 years to 18 years or above. Such a variety seems inevitable in view of the different national legal systems and does not diminish the impact of these Standard Minimum Rules.

Rule 2.3 is addressed to the necessity of specific national legislation for the optimal implementation of these Standard Minimum Rules, both legally and practically.

**3. Extension of the Rules**

3.1 The relevant provisions of the Rules shall be applied not only to juvenile, offenders but also to juveniles who may be proceeded against for any specific behavior that would not be punishable if committed by an adult.

3.2 Efforts shall be made to extend the principles embodied in the Rules to all juveniles who are dealt with in welfare and care proceedings.

3.3 Efforts shall also be made to extend the principles embodied in the Rules to young adult offenders.

**Commentary**

Rule 3 extends the protection afforded by the Standard Minimum Rules (or the Administration of Juvenile Justice to cover:

- *(a)* The so-called "status offences" prescribed in various national legal systems where the range of behavior considered to be an offence is wider for juveniles than it is for adults (for example, truancy, school and family disobedience, public drunkenness, etc.) (rule 3.1);
- *(b)* Juvenile welfare and care proceedings (Rule 3.2);
- *(c)* Proceedings dealing with young adult offenders, depending of course on each given age limit (Rule 3.3).

The extension of the Rules to cover these three areas seems to be justified. Rule 3.1 provides minimum guarantees in those fields, and Rule 3.2 is considered a desirable step in the direction of more fair, equitable and humane justice for all juveniles in conflict with the law.

**4. Age of Criminal Responsibility**

4.1 In those legal systems recognizing the concept of the age of criminal responsibility for juveniles, the beginning of that age shall not be fixed at too low an age level, bearing in mind the facts of emotional, mental and intellectual maturity.

**Commentary**

The minimum age of criminal responsibility differs widely owing to history and culture. The modem approach would be to consider whether a child can live up to the moral and psychological components of criminal responsibility; that is, whether a child, by virtue of her or his individual discernment and understanding, can be held responsible for essentially antisocial behavior. If the age of criminal responsibility is fixed too low or if there is no lower age limit at all, the notion of responsibility would become meaningless. In general, there is a close relationship between the notion of responsibility for delinquent or criminal behavior and other social rights and responsibilities (such as marital status, civil majority, etc.).

Efforts should therefore be made to agree on a reasonable lowest age limit that is applicable internationally.

**5. Aims of Juvenile Justice**

5.1 The juvenile justice system shall emphasize the well-being of the juvenile and shall ensure that any reaction to juvenile offenders shall always be in proportion to the circumstances of both the offenders and the offence.

**Commentary**

Rule 5 refers to two of the most important objectives of juvenile justice. The first objective is the promotion of the well-being of the juvenile. This is the main focus of those legal systems in which juvenile offenders are dealt with by family courts or administrative authorities, but the well-being of the juvenile should also be emphasized in legal systems that follow the criminal court model, thus contributing to the avoidance of merely punitive sanctions. (See also Rule 14.)

The second objective is "the principle of proportionality". This principle is well-known as an instrument for curbing punitive sanctions, mostly expressed in terms of just deserts in relation to the gravity of the offence. The response to young offenders should be based on the consideration not only of the gravity of the offence but also of personal circumstances. The individual circumstances of the offender (for example social status, family situation, the harm caused by the offence or other factors affecting personal circumstances) should influence the proportionality of the reactions (for example by having regard to the offender's endeavor to indemnify the victim or to her or his willingness to turn to wholesome and useful life).

By the same token, reactions aiming to ensure the welfare of the young offender may go beyond necessity and therefore infringe upon the fundamental rights of fhe young individual, as has been observed in some juvenile justice systems. Here, too, the proportionality of the reaction to the circumstances of both the offender and the offence, including the victim, should be safeguarded.

In essence, Rule 5 calls for no less and no more than a fair reaction in any given cases of juvenile delinquency and crime. The issues combined in the rule may-help to stimulate development in both regards; new and innovative types of reactions are as desirable as precautions against any undue widening of the net of formal social control over juveniles.

**6. Scope of Discretion**

6.1 In view of the varying special needs of juveniles as well as the variety of measures available, appropriate scope for discretion shall be allowed at all stages of proceedings and at the different levels 67 juvenile justice administration, including investigation, prosecution, adjudication and the follow-up of dispositions.

6.2 Efforts shall be made, however, to ensure sufficient accountability at all stages and levels in the exercise of any such discretion.

6.3 Those who exercise discretion shall be specially qualified or trained to exercise it judiciously and in accordance with their functions and mandates.

**Commentary**

Rules 6.1, 6.2 and 6.3 combine several important features of effective, fair and humane juvenile justice administration: the need to permit the exercise of discretionary power at all significant levels of processing so that those who make determinations can take the actions deemed to be most appropriate in each individual case; and the need to provide checks and balances in order to curb any abuses of discretionary power and to safeguard the rights of the young offender. Accountability and professionalism are instruments best apt to curb broad discretion. Thus, professional qualifications and expert training are emphasized here as a valuable means of ensuring the judicious exercise of discretion in matters of juvenile offenders. (See also Rules 1.6 and 2.2.) The formulation of specific guidelines on the exercise of discretion and the provision of systems of review, appeal and the like in order to permit scrutiny of decisions and accountability are emphasized in this context. Such mechanisms are not specified here, as they do not easily lend themselves to incorporation into international standard minimum rules, which cannot possibly cover all differences in justice systems,

**7. Rights of Juveniles**

7.1 Basic procedural safeguards such as the presumption of innocence, the right to be notified of the charges, the right to remain silent, the right to counsel, the right to the presence of a parent or guardian, the right to confront and cross-examine witnesses and the right to appeal to a higher authority shall be guaranteed at all stages of proceedings.

**Commentary**

Rule 7.1 emphasizes some important points that represent essential elements for a fair and just trial and that are internationally recognized in existing human rights instruments (See also Rule 14.). The presumption of innocence, for instance, is also to be found in Article 11 of the Universal Declaration of Human rights and in Article 14, Paragraph 2, of the International Covenant on Civil and Political Rights. Rules 14 seq. of these Standard Minimum Rules specify issues that are important for proceedings in juvenile cases, in particular, while Rule 7.1 affirms the most basic procedural safeguards in a general way.

**8. Protection of Privacy**

8.1 The juvenile's right to privacy shall be respected at all stages in order to avoid harm being caused to her or him by undue publicity or by the process of labelling.

8.2 In principle, no information that may lead to the identification of a juvenile offender shall be published.

**Commentary**

Rule 8 stresses the importance of the protection of the juvenile's right to privacy. Young persons are particularly susceptible to stigmatization. Criminological research into labelling processes has provided evidence of the detrimental effects (of different kinds) resulting from the permanent identification of young persons as "delinquent" or "criminal".

Rule 8 stresses the importance of protecting the juvenile from the adverse effects that may result from the publication in the mass media of information about the case (for example the names of young offenders, alleged or convicted). The interest of the individual should be protected and upheld, at least in principle (The general contents of Rule 8 are further specified in Rule 21).

**9. Saving Clause**

9.1 Nothing in these Rules shall be interpreted as precluding the application of the Standard Minimum Rules for the Treatment of Prisoners adopted by the United Nations and other human rights instruments and standards recognized by the international community that relate to the care and protection of the young.

**Commentary**

Rule 9 is meant to avoid any misunderstanding in interpreting and implementing the present Rules in conformity with principles contained in relevant existing or emerging international human rights instruments and standards—such as the Universal Declaration of Human Rights, the International Covenant on Economic, Social and Cultural Rights and the International Covenant on Civil and Political Rights, and the Declaration of the Rights of the Child and the draft convention on the rights of the child. It should be understood that the application of the present Rules is without prejudice to any such international instruments which may contain provisions of wider application (See also Rule 27.).

## Part Two

## INVESTIGATION AND PROSECUTION

**10. Initial Contact**

10.1 Upon the apprehension of a juvenile, her or his parents or guardian shall be immediately notified of such apprehension, and, where such immediate notification is not possible, the parents or guardian shall be notified within the shortest possible time thereafter.

10.2 A judge or other competent official or body shall, without delay, consider the issue of release.

10.3 Contacts between the law enforcement agencies and a juvenile offender shall be managed in such a way as to respect the legal status of the juvenile, promote the well-being of the juvenile and avoid harm to her or him, with due regard to the circumstances of the case.

**Commentary**

Rule 10.1 is in principle contained in Rule 92 of the Standard Minimum Rules for the Treatment of Prisoners.

The question of release (Rule 10.2) shall be considered without delay by a judge or other competent official. The latter refers to any person or institution in the broadest sense of the term, including community boards or police authorities having power to release an arrested person. (See also the International Covenant on Civil and Political Rights, Article 9, Paragraph 3.)

Rule 10.3 deals with some fundamental aspects of the procedures and behavior on the part of the police and other law enforcement officials in cases of juvenile crime. To "avoid harm" admittedly is flexible wording and covers many features of possible interaction (for example the use of harsh language, physical violence or exposure to the environment). Involvement in juvenile justice processes in itself can be "harmful" to juveniles; the term "avoid harm" should be broadly interpreted, therefore, as doing the least harm possible to the juvenile in the first instance, as well as any additional or undue harm. This is especially important in the initial contact with law enforcement agencies, which might profoundly influence the juvenile's attitude towards the State and society. Moreover, the success of any further intervention is largely dependent on such initial contacts. Compassion and kind firmness are important in these situations.

**11. Diversion**

11.1 Consideration shall be given, wherever appropriate, to dealing with juvenile offenders without resorting to formal trial by the competent authority, referred to in rule 14.1 below.

11.2 The police, the prosecution or other agencies dealing with juvenile cases shall be empowered to dispose of such cases, at their discretion, without recourse to formal hearings, in accordance with the criteria laid down for that purpose in the respective legal system and also in accordance with the principles contained in these Rules.

11.3 Any diversion involving referral to appropriate community or other services shall require the consent of the juvenile, or her or his parents or guardian provided that such decision to refer a case shall be subject to review by a competent authority, upon application.

11.4 In order to facilitate the discretionary disposition of juvenile cases, efforts shall be made to provide for community programs, such as temporary supervision and guidance, restitution, and compensation of victims.

**Commentary**

Diversion, involving removal from criminal justice processing and, frequently, redirection to community support services, is commonly practised on a formal and informal basis in many legal systems. This practice serves to hinder the negative effects of subsequent proceedings in juvenile justice administration (for example the stigma of conviction and sentence). In many cases, non-intervention would be the best response. Thus, diversion at the outset and without referral to alternative (social) services may be the optimal response. This is especially the case where the offence is of a non-serious nature and where the family, the school or other informal social control institutions have already reacted, or are likely to react, in an appropriate and constructive manner.

As stated in Rule 11.2, diversion may be used at any point of decision-making-by the police, the prosecution or other agencies such as the courts, tribunals, boards or councils. It may be exercised by one authority or several or all authorities, according to the rules and policies of the respective systems and in line with the present Rules. It need not necessarily be limited to petty cases, thus rendering diversion an important instrument.

Rule 11.3 stresses the important requirement of securing

the consent of the young offender (or the parent or guardian) to the recommended diversionary measure(s). (Diversion to community service without such consent would contradict the Abolition of Forced Labour Convention.) However, this consent should not be left unchallengeable, since it might sometimes be given out of sheer desperation on the part of the juvenile. The rule underlines that care should be taken to minimize the potential for coercion and intimidation at all levels in the diversion process. Juveniles should not pressured (for example in order to avoid court appearance) or be pressured into consenting to diversion programs. Thus, it is advocated that provision should be made for an objective appraisal of the appropriateness of dispositions involving young offenders by a "competent authority upon application". (The "competent authority/may be different from that referred to in Rule 14.)

Rule 11.4 recommends the provision of viable alternatives to juvenile justice processing in the form of community-based diversion. Programs that involve settlement by victim restitution and those that seek to avoid future conflict with the law through temporary supervision and guidance are especially commended. The merits of individual cases would make diversion appropriate, even when more serious offences have been committed (for example first offence, the act having been committed under peer pressure, etc.).

**12. Specialization Within the Police**

12.1 In order to best fulfil their functions, police officers who frequently or exclusively deal with juveniles or who are primarily engaged in the prevention of juvenile crime shall be specially instructed and trained. In large cities, special police units should be established for that purpose.

**Commentary**

Rule 12 draws attention to the need for specialized training for all law enforcement officials who are involved in the administration of juvenile justice. As police are the first point of contact with the juvenile justice system, it is most important that they act in an informed and appropriate manner.

While the relationship between urbanization and crime is clearly complex, an increase in juvenile crime has been associated with the growth of large cities, particularly with rapid and unplanned growth. Specialized police units would therefore be indispensable, not only in the interest of implementing specific principles contained in the present instrument (such as Rule 1.6) but more generally for improving the prevention and control of juvenile crime and the handling of juvenile offenders.

### 13. Detention Pending Trial

13.1 Detention pending trial shall be used only as a measure of last resort and for the shortest possible period of time.

13.2 Whenever possible, detention pending trial shall be replaced by alternative measures, such as close supervision, intensive care or placement with a family or in an educational setting or home.

13.3 Juveniles under detention pending trial shall be entitled to all rights and guarantees of the Standard Minimum Rules for the Treatment of Prisoners adopted by the United Nations.

13.4 Juveniles under detention pending trial shall be kept separate from adults and shall be detained in a separate institution or in a separate part of an institution also holding adults.

13.5 While in custody, juveniles shall receive care, protection and all necessary individual assistance social, educational, vocational, psychological, medical and physical that they may require in view of their age, sex and personality.

**Commentary**

The danger to juveniles of "criminal contamination" while in detention pending trial must not be underestimated, it is therefore important to stress the need for alternative measures. By doing so, Rule 13.1 encourages the devising of new and innovative measures to avoid such detention in the interest of the well-being of the juvenile. Juveniles under detention pending trial are entitled to all the rights and guarantees of the Standard Minimum Rules for the Treatment of Prisoners as well as the International Covenant on Civil and Political Rights, especially Article 9 and Article 10, Paragraphs 2 *(b)* and 3.

Rule 13.4 does not prevent States from taking other measures against the negative influences of adult offenders which are at least as effective as the measures mentioned in the rule.

Different forms of assistance that may become necessary have been enumerated to draw attention to the broad range of particular needs of young detainees to be addressed (for example females or males, drug addicts, alcoholics, mentally ill juveniles, young persons suffering from the trauma, for example, of arrest, etc.).

Varying physical and psychological characteristics of young detainees may warrant classification measures by which some are kept separate while in detention pending trial, thus contributing to the avoidance of victimization and rendering more appropriate assistance.

The Sixth United Nations Congress on the Prevention of Crime and the Treatment of Offenders, in its resolution 4 on juvenile justice standards, specified that the Rules, inter alia, should reflect the basic principle that pre-trial detention should be used only as a last resort, that no minors should be held in a facility where they are vulnerable to the negative influences of adult detainees and that account should always be taken of the needs particular to their stage of development.

## Part Three
## ADJUDICATION AND DISPOSITION

### 14. Competent Authority to Adjudicate

14.1 Where the case of a juvenile offender has not been diverted (under Rule 11), she or he shall be dealt with by the competent authority (court, tribunal, board, council, etc.) according to the principles of a fair and just trial.

14.2 The proceedings shall be conducive to the best interests of the juvenile arid shall be conducted in an atmosphere of understanding, which shall allow the juvenile to participate therein and to express herself or himself freely.

**Commentary**

It is difficult to formulate a definition of the competent body or person that would universally describe an adjudicating authority. "Competent authority" is meant to include those who preside over courts or tribunals (composed of a single judge or of several members), including professional and lay magistrates as well as administrative boards (for example the Scottish and Scandinavian systems) or other more informal community and conflict resolution agencies of an adjudicatory nature.

The procedure for dealing with juvenile offenders shall in any case follow the minimum standards that are applied almost universally for any criminal defendant under the procedure known as "due process of law". In accordance with due process, a "fair and just trial" includes such basic safeguards as the presumption of innocence, the presentation and examination of witnesses, the common legal defences, the right to remain silent, the right to have the last word in a hearing, the right to appeal, etc. (See also Rule 7.1.)

**15. Legal Counsel, Parents and Guardians**

15.1 Throughout the proceedings the juvenile shall have the right to be represented by a legal adviser or to apply for free legal aid where there is provision for such aid in the country.

15.2 The parents or the guardian shall be entitled to participate in the proceedings and may be required by the competent authority to attend them in the interest of the juvenile. They may, however, be denied participation by the competent authority if there are reasons to assume that such exclusion is necessary in the interest of the juvenile.

**Commentary**

Rule 15.1 uses terminology similar to that found in Rule 93 of the Standard Minimum Rules for the Treatment of Prisoners. Whereas legal counsel and free legal aid are needed to assure the juvenile legal assistance, the right of the parents or guardian to participate as stated in Rule 15.2 should be viewed as general psychological and emotional assistance to the juvenile a function extending throughout the procedure.

The competent authority's search for an adequate disposition of the case may profit, in particular, from the co-operation of the legal representatives of the juvenile (or, for that matter, some other personal assistant who the juvenile can and does really trust). Such concern can be thwarted if the presence of parents or guardians at the hearings plays a negative role, for instance, if they display a hostile attitude towards the juvenile, hence, the possibility of their exclusion must be provided for.

**16. Social Inquiry Reports**

16.1 In all cases except those involving minor offences, before the competent authority renders a final disposition prior to sentencing, the background and circumstances in which the juvenile is living or the conditions under which the offence has been committed shall be properly investigated so as to facilitate judicious adjudication of the case by the competent authority.

**Commentary**

Social inquiry reports (social reports or pre-sentence reports) are an indispensable aid in most legal proceedings involving juveniles. The competent authority should be informed of relevant facts about the juvenile, such as social and family background, school career, educational experiences, etc. For this purpose, some jurisdictions use special social services or personnel attached to the court or board. Other personnel, including probation officers, may serve the same function. The rule therefore requires that adequate social services should be available to deliver social inquiry reports of a qualified nature.

**17. Guiding Principles in Adjudication and Disposition**

17.1 The disposition of the competent authority shall be guided by the following principles:

(*a*) The reaction taken shall always be in proportion not only to the circumstances and the gravity of the offence but also to the circumstances and the needs of the juvenile as well as to the needs of the society;

(*b*) Restrictions on the personal liberty of the juvenile shall be imposed only after careful consideration and shall be limited to the possible minimum;

(*c*) Deprivation of personal liberty shall not be imposed unless the juvenile is adjudicated of a serious act involving violence against another person or of persistence in committing other serious offences and unless there is no other appropriate response;

(*d*) The well-being of the juvenile shall be the guiding factor in the consideration of her or his case.

17.2 Capital punishment shall not be imposed for any crime committed by juveniles.

17.3 Juveniles shall not be subject to corporal punishment.

17.4 The competent authority shall have the power to discontinue the proceedings at any time.

**Commentary**

The main difficulty in formulating guidelines for the adjudication of young persons stems from the fact that there are unresolved conflicts of a philosophical nature, such as the following:

(*a*) Rehabilitation *versus* just desert;

(*b*) Assistance versus repression and punishment;

(*c*) Reaction according to the singular merits of an individual case versus reaction—according to the protection of society in general;

(*d*) General deterrence *versus* individual incapacitation.

The conflict between these approaches is more

pronounced in juvenile cases than in adult cases. With the variety of causes and reactions characterizing juvenile cases, these alternatives become intricately interwoven.

It is not the function of the Standard Minimum Rules for the Administration of Juvenile Justice to prescribe which approach is to be followed but rather to identify one that is most closely in consonance with internationally accepted principles. Therefore, the essential elements as laid down in Rule 17.1, in particular in subparagraphs *(a)* and *(c)*, are mainly to be understood as practical guidelines that should ensure a common starting point; if heeded by the concerned authorities (see also Rule 5), they could contribute considerably to ensuring that the fundamental rights of juvenile offenders are protected, especially the fundamental rights of personal development and education.

Rule 17.1 (b) implies that strictly punitive approaches are not appropriate, Whereas in adult cases, and possibly also in cases of severe offences by juveniles, just desert and retributive sanctions might be considered to have some merit, in juvenile cases such considerations should always be outweighed by the interest of safeguarding the well-being and the future of the young person.

In line with resolution 8 of the Sixth United Nations Congress, Rule 17.1 *(b)* encourages the use of alternatives to institutionalization to the maximum extent possible, bearing in mind the need to respond to the specific requirements of the young, thus, full use should be made of the range of existing alternative sanctions and new alternative sanctions should be developed, bearing the public safety in mind. Probation should be granted to the greatest possible extent via suspended sentences, conditional sentences, board orders and other dispositions.

Rule 17.1 *(c)* corresponds to one of the guiding principles in resolution 4 of the Sixth Congress which aims at avoiding incarceration in the case of juveniles unless there is no other appropriate response that will protect the public safety. The provision prohibiting capital punishment in Rule 17.2 is in accordance with Article 6, Paragraph 5, of the International Covenant on Civil and Political Rights.

The provision against corporal punishment is in line with Article 7 of the International Covenant on Civil and Political Rights and the Declaration on the Protection of All Persons from Being Subjected to Torture and Other Cruel, Inhuman or Degrading Treatment or Punishment, as well as the Convention against Torture and Other Cruel, Inhuman or Degrading Treatment or Punishment and the draft convention on the rights of the child.

The power to discontinue the proceedings at any time (Rule 17.4) is a characteristic inherent in the handling of juvenile offenders as opposed to adults. At any time, circumstances may become known to the competent authority which would make a complete cessation of the intervention appear to be the best disposition of the case.

**18. Various Disposition Measures**

18.1 A large variety of disposition measures shall be made available to the competent authority, allowing for flexibility so as to avoid institutionalization in the greatest extent possible. Such measures, some of which may be combined, include:

*(a)* Care, guidance and supervision orders;
*(b)* Probation;
*(c)* Community service orders;
*(d)* Financial penalties, compensation and restitution;
*(e)* Intermediate treatment and other treatment orders;
*(f)* Orders to participate in group counseling and similar activities;
*(g)* Orders concerning foster care, living communities or other educational settings;
*(h)* Other relevant orders.

18.2 No juvenile shall be removed from parental supervision, whether partly or entirely, unless the circumstances of her or his case make this necessary.

**Commentary**

Rule 18.1 attempts to enumerate some of the important reactions and sanctions that have been practised and proved successful thus far, in different legal systems. On the whole they represent promising opinions that deserve replication and further development. The rule does not enumerate staffing requirements because of possible shortages of adequate staff in some regions. In those regions measures requiring less staff may be tried or developed.

The examples given in Rule 18.1 have in common, above all, a reliance on and an appeal to the community for the effective implementation of alternative dispositions. Community based correction is a traditional measure that has taken on many aspects. On that basis, relevant authorities should be encouraged to offer community-based services.

Rule 18.2 points to the importance of the family which, according to Article 10, Paragraph I, of the International Covenant on Economic, Social and Cultural Rights, is "the natural and fundamental group unit of society." Within the family, the parents have not only the right but also the responsibility to care for and supervise their children. Rule 18.2, therefore, requires that the separation of children from their parents is a measure of last resort. It may be resorted to only when the facts of the case clearly warrant this grave step (for example child abuse).

**19. Least Possible Use of Institutionalization**

19.1 The placement of a juvenile in an institution shall always be a disposition of last resort and for the minimum necessary period.

**Commentary**

Progressive criminology advocates the use of non-institutional over institutional treatment. Little or no difference has been found in terms of the success of institutionalization as compared to non-institutionalization. The many adverse influences on an individual that seem unavoidable within any institutional setting evidently cannot be outbalanced by treatment efforts. This is especially the case for juveniles, who are vulnerable to negative influences.

Moreover, the negative effects, not only of loss of liberty but also of separation from the usual social environment, are certainly more acute for juveniles than for adults because of their early stage of development.

Rule 19 aims at restricting institutionalization in two regards: in quantity ("last resort",) and in time ("minimum necessary period"). Rule 19 reflects one of the basic guiding principles of resolution 4 of the Sixth United Nations Congress: a juvenile offender should not be incarcerated unless there is no other appropriate response. The rule, therefore, makes the appeal that if a juvenile must be institutionalized, the loss of liberty should be restricted to the least possible degree, with special institutional arrangements for confinement and bearing in mind the differences in kinds of offenders, offences and institutions. In fact, priority should be given to "open" over "closed" institutions. Furthermore, any facility should be of a correctional or educational rather than of a prison type.

**20. Avoidance of Unnecessary Delay**

20.1 Each case shall from the outset be handled expeditiously, without any unnecessary delay.

**Commentary**

The speedy conduct of formal procedures in juvenile cases is a paramount concern. Otherwise whatever good may be achieved by the procedure and the disposition is at risk. As time passes, the juvenile will find it increasingly difficult, if not impossible, to relate the procedure and disposition to the offence, both intellectually and psychologically.

**21. Records**

21.1 Records of juvenile offenders shall be kept strictly confidential and closer in third parties. Access to such records shall be limited to persons directly concerned with the disposition of the case at hand or other duly authorized persons.

21.2 Records of juvenile offenders shall not be used in adult proceedings in subsequent cases involving the same offender.

**Commentary**

The rule attempts to achieve a balance between conflicting interests connected with records or files: those of the police, prosecution and other authorities in improving control versus the interests of the juvenile offender. (See also Rule 8.). "Other duly authorized persons" would generally include among others, researchers.

**22. Need for Professionalism and Training**

22.1 Professional education, in-service training, refresher courses and other appropriate modes of instruction shall be utilized to establish and maintain the necessary professional competence of all personnel dealing with juvenile cases.

22.2 Juvenile justice personnel shall reflect the diversity of juveniles who come into contact with the juvenile justice system. Efforts shall be made to ensure the fair representation of women and minorities in juvenile justice agencies.

**Commentary**

The authorities competent for disposition may be persons with very different backgrounds (magistrates in the United Kingdom of Great Britain and Northern Ireland and in regions influenced by the common law system; legally trained judges in countries using Roman law and in regions influenced by them; and elsewhere elected or appointed laymen or jurists, members of community-based boards, etc.). For all these authorities, a minimum training in law, sociology, psychology, criminology and behavioral sciences would be required. This is considered as important as the organizational specialization and independence of the competent authority.

For social workers and probation officers, it might not be feasible to require professional specialization as a prerequisite for taking over any function dealing with juvenile offenders. Thus, professional on-the job instruction would be minimum qualifications.

Professional qualifications are an essential element in ensuring the impartial and effective administration of juvenile justice. Accordingly, it is necessary to improve the recruitment, advancement and professional training of personnel and to provide them with the necessary means to enable them to properly fulfil their functions.

All political, social, sexual, racial, religious, cultural or any other kind of discrimination in the selection, appointment and advancement of juvenile justice personnel should be avoided in order to achieve impartiality in the administration of juvenile justice. This was recommended by the Sixth Congress. Furthermore, the Sixth Congress called on Member States to ensure the fair and equal treatment of women as criminal justice personnel and recommended that special measures should be taken to recruit, train and facilitate the advancement of female personnel in juvenile justice administration.

## Part Four
## NON-INSTITUTIONAL TREATMENT

### 23. Effective Implementation of Disposition

23.1 Appropriate provisions shall be made for the implementation of orders of the competent authority, as referred to in Rule 14.1 above, by that authority itself or by some other authority as circumstances may require.

23.2 Such provisions shall include the power to modify the orders as the competent authority may deem necessary from time-to-time, provided that such modification shall be determined in accordance with the principles contained in these Rules.

**Commentary**

Disposition in juvenile cases, more so than in adult cases, tends to influence the offender's life for a long period of time. Thus, it is important that the competent authority or an independent body (parole board, probation office, youth welfare institutions or others) with qualifications equal to those of the competent authority that originally disposed of the case should monitor the implementation of the disposition. In some countries, a juge de l' execution des peines has been installed for this purpose.

The composition, powers and functions of the authority must be flexible; they are described in general terms in rule 23 in order to ensure wide acceptability.

### 24. Provision of Needed Assistance

24.1 Efforts\shall be made to provide juveniles, at all stages of the proceedings, with necessary assistance such as lodging, education or vocational training, employment or any other assistance, helpful and practical, in order to facilitate the rehabilitative process.

#### Commentary

The promotion of the well-being of the juvenile is of paramount consideration. Thus, Rule 24 emphasizes the importance of providing requisite facilities, services and other necessary assistance as may further the best interests of the juvenile throughout the rehabilitative process.

### 25. Mobilization of Volunteers and Other Community Services

25.1 Volunteers, voluntary organizations, local institutions and other community resources shall be called upon to contribute effectively to the rehabilitation of the juvenile in a community setting and, as far as possible, within the family unit.

#### Commentary

This rule reflects the need for a rehabilitative orientation of all work with juvenile offenders. Co-operation with the community is indispensable if the directives of the competent authority are to be carried out effectively. Volunteers and voluntary services, in particular, have proved to be valuable resources but are at present underutilized. In some instances, the co-operation of ex-offenders (including ex-addicts) can be of considerable assistance.

Rule 25 emanates from the principles laid down in Rules 1.1 to 1.6 and follows the relevant provisions of the International Covenant on Civil and Political Rights.

## Part Five

## INSTITUTIONAL TREATMENT

### 26. Objectives of Institutional Treatment

26.1 The objective of training and treatment of juveniles placed in institutions is to provide care, protection, education and vocational skills, with a view to assisting them to assume socially constructive and productive roles in society.

26.2 Juveniles in institutions shall receive care, protection and all necessary assistance—social, educational, vocational, psychological, medical and physical—that they may require because of their age, sex, and personality and in the interest of their wholesome development.

26.3 Juveniles in institutions shall be kept separate from adults and shall be detained in a separate institution or in a separate part of an institution also holding adults.

26.4 Young female offenders placed in an institution deserve special attention as to their personal needs and problems. They shall by no means receive less care, protection, assistance, treatment and training than young male offenders. Their fair treatment shall be ensured.

26.5 In the interest and well-being of the institutionalized juvenile, the parents or guardians shall have a right of access.

26.6 Inter-ministerial and inter-departmental co-operation shall be fostered for the' purpose of providing adequate academic or, as appropriate, vocational training to institutionalized juveniles, with a view to ensuring that they do no leave the institution at an educational disadvantage.

**Commentary**

The objectives of institutional treatment as stipulated in Rules 26.1 and 26.2 would be acceptable to any system and culture. However, they have not yet been attained everywhere and much more has to be done in this respect.

Medical and psychological assistance, in particular, are extremely important for institutionalized drug addicts, violent and mentally ill young persons.

The avoidance of negative influences through adult offenders and the safeguarding of the well-being of juveniles in an institutional setting, as stipulated in Rule 26.3, are in line with one of the basic guiding principles of the Rules, as set out by the Sixth Congress in its resolution 4. The rule does not prevent States from taking other measures against the negative influences of adult offenders, which are at least as effective as the measures mentioned in the rule. (See also Rule 13.4)

Rule 26.4 addresses the fact that female offenders normally receive less attention than their male counterparts, as pointed out by the Sixth Congress. In particular, resolution 9 of the Sixth Congress calls for the fair treatment of female offenders at every stage of criminal justice processes and for special attention to their particular problems and needs while in custody. Moreover, this rule should also be considered in the light of the Caracas Declaration of the Sixth Congress, which, inter alia, calls for equal treatment in criminal justice administration, and against the background of the Declaration on the Elimination of Discrimination against Women and the Convention on the Elimination of All Forms of Discrimination against Women.

The right of access (Rule 26.5) follows from the provisions of Rules 7.1, 10.1, 15.2 and 18.2. Inter-ministerial and inter-departmental co-operation (Rule 26.6) are of particular importance in the interest of generally enhancing the quality of institutional treatment and training.

**27. Application of the Standard Minimum Rules for the Treatment of Prisoners adopted by the United Nations**

27.1 The Standard Minimum Rules for the Treatment of Prisoners and related recommendations shall be applicable as far as relevant to the treatment of juvenile offenders in institutions, including those in detention pending adjudication.

27.2 Efforts shall be made to implement the relevant principles laid down in the Standard Minimum Rules for the Treatment of Prisoners to the largest possible extent so as to meet the varying needs of juveniles specific to their age, sex and personality.

**Commentary**

The Standard Minimum Rules for the Treatment of Prisoners were among the first instruments of this kind to be promulgated by the United Nations, it is generally agreed that they have had a world-wide impact. Although there are still countries where implementation is more an aspiration than a fact, those Standard Minimum Rules continue to be an important influence in the humane and equitable administration of correctional institutions.

Some essential protections covering juvenile offenders in institutions are contained in the Standard Minimum Rules for the Treatment of Prisoners (accommodation, architecture, bedding, clothing, complaints and requests, contact with the outside world, food, medical care, religious service, separation of ages, staffing, work, etc.) as are provisions concerning punishment and discipline, and restraint for dangerous offenders. It would not be appropriate to modify those Standard Minimum Rules according to the particular characteristics of institutions for juvenile offenders within the scope of the Standard Minimum Rules for the Administration of Juvenile Justice.

Rule 27 focuses on the necessary requirements for juveniles in institutions (Rule 27.1) as well as on the varying needs specific to their age, sex and personality (Rule 27.2). Thus, the objectives and content of the rule interrelate to the relevant provisions of the Standard Minimum Rules for the Treatment of Prisoners.

**28. Frequent and Early Recourse to Conditional Release**

28.1 Conditional release from an institution shall be used by the appropriate authority to the greatest possible extent, and shall be granted at the earliest possible time.

28.2 Juveniles released conditionally from an institution shall be assisted and supervised by an appropriate authority and shall receive full support by the community.

**Commentary**

The power to order conditional release may rest with the competent authority, as mentioned in Rule 14.1 or with some other authority. In view of this, it is adequate to refer here to the "appropriate," rather than to the "competent" authority.

Circumstances permitting, conditional release shall be preferred to serving a full sentence. Upon evidence of satisfactory progress towards rehabilitation, even offenders who had been deemed dangerous at the time of their institutionalization can be conditionally released whenever feasible. Like probation, such release may be conditional on the satisfactory fulfilment of the requirements specified by the relevant authorities for a period of time established in the decision, for example relating to "good behavior of the offender, attendance in community programs, residence in half-way houses, etc.

In the case of offenders conditionally released from an institution, assistance and supervision by a probation or other officer (particularly where probation has not yet been adopted) should be provided and community support should be encouraged.

**29. Semi-Institutional Arrangements**

29.1 Efforts shall be made to provide semi-institutional

arrangements, such as half-way houses, educational homes, day-time training centres and other such appropriate arrangements that may assist juveniles in their proper reintegration into society.

**Commentary**

The importance of care following a period of institutionalization should not be underestimated. This rule emphasizes the necessity of forming a net of semi-institutional arrangements.

This rule also emphasizes the need for a diverse range of facilities and services designed to meet the different needs of young offenders re-entering the community and to provide guidance and structural support as an important step towards successful reintegration into society.

## Part Six

## RESEARCH, PLANNING, POLICY FORMULATION AND EVALUATION

### 30. Research as a Basis for Planning, Policy Formulation and Evaluation

30.1 Efforts shall be made to organize and promote necessary research as a basis for effective planning and policy formulation.

30.2 Efforts shall be made to review and appraise periodically the trends problems and causes of juvenile delinquency and crime as well as the varying particular needs of juveniles in custody.

30.3 Efforts shall be made to establish a regular evaluative research mechanism built into the system of juvenile justice administration and to collect and analyze relevant data and information for appropriate assessment arid future improvement and reform of the administration.

30.4 The delivery of services in juvenile justice administration shall be systematically planned and implemented as an integral part of national development efforts.

The utilization of research as a basis for an informed juvenile justice policy is widely acknowledged as an important mechanism for keeping practices abreast of advances in knowledge and the continuing development and improvement of the juvenile justice system. The mutual feedback between research and policy is especially important in juvenile justice. With rapid arid often drastic changes in the life-styles of the young and in the forms and dimensions of juvenile crime, the societal and justice responses to juvenile crime and delinquency quickly become outmoded and inadequate.

Rule 30 thus establishes standards for integrating research into the process of policy formulation and application in juvenile justice administration. The rule particular attention to the need for regular review and evaluation of existing programs and measures and for planning within the broader context of overall development objectives.

A constant appraisal of the needs of juveniles, as well as the trends and problems of delinquency, is a prerequisite for improving the methods of formulating appropriate policies and establishing adequate interventions, at both formal and informal levels. In this context, research by independent persons and bodies should be facilitated by responsible agencies, and it may be valuable to obtain and to take into account the views of juveniles themselves, not only those who come into contact with the system.

The process of planning must particularly emphasize a more effective and equitable system for the delivery of necessary services. Towards that end, there should be a comprehensive and regular assessment of the wide-ranging, particular needs and problems of juveniles and an identification of clear-cut priorities. In that connection, there should also be a co-ordination in the use of existing resources, including alternatives and community support that would be suitable in setting up specific procedures designed to implement and monitor established programs.

*ANNEXURE IV*

## Convention on the Rights of the Child History, Content, Impact

The Convention on the Rights of the Child is a universal international agreement relating to human rights fundamental freedoms. It is one of those international instruments in the field of human rights, whose aim is to promote and protect rights of people who are particularly vulnerable to have their rights disrespected, namely elderly people, the disabled, those belonging to national, ethnic, religious or linguistic minorities, indigenous people, refugees, migrant-employees and their families, etc.

The Convention's objective is a continuous improvement of the situation of children all over the world, as well as their development and education conditions of peace and security. According to the UN General Assembly's estimate, the situation of children in many parts of the world remains critical as a result of inadequate social conditions, natural disasters, armed conflict exploitation, illiteracy, famine and disability. Drawing up the Convention, the UN General Assembly was convinced chat urgent and effective national and international action needed to be called for.

The decision regarding the very title of the Convention was not easy here were proposals to call it a convention on protection of the child not on the rights of the child. There was also an opinion to speak about the group "children" – instead of an individual – "the child" – in order to avoid even the slightest colour of discrimination on the background of sex differences. There were voices to include into the Convention not only rights but also duties of the child. In the course of discussions the final point was made that the Convention would focus on the rights of the child. This does not mean, however, that duties of the child should be disregarded.

The above mentioned vulnerability of the child, as stated in the Declaration of the Rights of the Child of November 20, 1959, has its source in the fact that "the Child by reason of his physical and mental immaturity needs special safeguard and care, including appropriate legal protection before as well as after birth". The Convention on the Rights of the Child deals with what is appropriate for the child after his or her birth. The decision as the form and scope and appropriatcs of legal protection of die cluld before birth has basically been left to individual stares. The Convention provides protection of the rights of the child at the minimal level. In protecting the rights of the child individual states should not go below this level. Yet, the Convention admits a higher level of protection of the rights of the child and strongly encourages the states to follow this encouragement.

Poland was the initiator of the adoption of the Convention. At the beginning of the year 1978 the Polish government submitted the convention draft to the UN Commission on Human Rights with a request of including the issue of working out of the Convention into the Commission's agenda. So far it has been the most significant initiative of Poland in the field of human rights. Yet is was not the only initiative. Almost the same time, on December 15, 1978, the Polish initiative the General Assembly adopted the Declaration on the Preparation of Societies lot Life in Peace. It is also worth mentioning here that following the initiative of a Pole-Ludwik Rajchman – in 1946 the UN General Assembly created UNICEF. The delegates of Poland actively participated in the process of working out of the draft of the Declaration of the Rights of the Child. There existed a specific international tradition of Polish engagement for the improvement, of the situation of the child all over the world. It has its foundation in a particular sensitiveness the Polish society has to misery of children. During both World War I and particularly World War II children in Poland experienced suffering that is hard to describe. It was caused by the wartime operations taking placeon the territory of Poland; children starved, they were deprived of basic health care, of access to education, they were forced to excessive work. During World War II children and their parents were massively displaced from their places of living, they were kidnapped from their Polish families in order to be Germanized. Children of Jewish and Gypsy origin were victims of physical extermination. Few remember today that in Lodz Nazi authorities set up a concentration camp for children. Thousands of children lost their lives there. These past events were a stimulus for the Polish authorities to undertake actions in favour of improvement of fate of children which—as we know—very often was and still is tragic.

As early as between the years 1918 and 1939 a contemporary concept of childhood was developed. Its core is constituted of a conviction that the child is an autonomous person who has his/her own needs, interests and rights, that he/she is not only an object of care and concern but also a subject whose interests and rights should be respected. According to the above concept the child, at a certain stage of his/her development, is capable to formulate and express his/her own opinions that ought to be taken into consideration. The main exponent of this new concept of childhood was Dr. Janusz Korczak—a doctor of medicine, a writer, a philosopher and an educator. He confirmed the loyalty to this vision of childhood with his own life. Having the possibility to save his life he decided to stay with the children lie was taking care of until the very end—and died with them in a gas chamber in Treblinka, a Nazi concentration camp, in 1942. When putting forward the draft Convention on the Rights of the Child the Polish government wished to popularize the above concept of childhood in the world.

Poland wanted to prove, as well, that—as a country at that time belonging to the system of socialist states—it was able to come out with a constructive and very needed initiative in the Field of human rights. It was a good opportunity to show that this type of initiative did not have to be a monopoly of western states.

It should be noted here that in the 1970s the level of implementation of needs and rights of the child, especially social and economic ones, was relatively high. Also legal regulations represented a high level at that time. A confirmation of this opinion may be the fact that when in 1991 Poland ratified the Convention on the Rights of the

Child there was no need to adjust Polish legislature to the standards of the Convention.

Poland was a trustworthy initiator and promoter of the Convention to the world. A historical pretext for Poland's initiative to draft a convention on the rights of the child in 1978 was the 20th anniversary of adoption of the Declaration of the Rights of the Child coming in the year 1979 and this very year-1979—that was proclaimed by the UN General Assembly to be the International Children's Year.

International interest in improvement of the lot of the children began in 1924, when the Fifth Assembly of the League of Nations adopted the Declaration of the Rights of the Child, commonly known as the Declaration of Geneva. This Declaration was the first one ever to acknowledge that mankind should give the child everything the best it can offer. The Declaration, although called the Declaration of the Rights of the Child, was principally concerned with the provision of children's economic, psychological and social needs. It regarded children as recipients of a treatment rather than as holders of specific rights.

The United Nations took care of the situation of the child soon after establishing its organs. In 1946, the Temporary Social Commission of the Economic and Social Council stated, that the terms of the Declaration of Geneva should be as binding on the nations of the world as they had been in 1924. Soon the necessary works were begun to formulate and draft the project of a new declaration of the rights of the child. On November 20, 1959 the General Assembly proclaimed the UN Declaration on the Rights of the Child and called upon parents, men and women as individuals, voluntary organizations, local authorities and national governments—to recognize the rights set out in the Declaration and to strive for their observance by legislative and other measures.

The Declaration comprised ten principles constituting a code for the well-being of every child. The Declaration had a moral and political character; it did not bind the states legally. This is why some countries, including Poland, instantly attempted to create international rules and regulations exposing the rights of the child that would legally bind particular states. In general such assumptions were applied in the both Covenants of Human Rights. International Covenant of Civil and Political Rights stares (Art. 24) that every child shall have, without any discrimination as to race, colour, sex, language, religion, national or social origin, property or birth, the right to such measures of protection as are required by his/her status, as a minor. This protection shall be guaranteed by the child's family, society and state. The Covenant also claims that every child shall be registered immediately after birth and shall have the name, and also that every child shall have the right to require a nationality. In turn, die International Covenant on Economic, Social and Cultural Rights formulates the rights of the child (Art. 10) in the family context. It stipulates that the states-parties to the Covenant should recognize that the widest possible protection and assistance should be accorded to the family, which is the natural and fundamental group unit of society, particularly while it is responsible for the care and education of dependent children. The Covenant specifics that special measures of protection and assistance should be taken on behalf of all children without any discrimination for reasons of parentage or other conditions. Children should be protected from economic and social exploitation. Their employment in work harmful to their health or morality, threatening their life or likely to hamper their normal development should be punishable by law. The Covenant requires that all states should also see age limits below which the paid employment of child labour should be prohibited and punishable by law.

In 1976, the UN's General Assembly proclaimed the year 1979 the International Year of the Child. One of the general objectives of this year-long event was to provide a framework for advocacy on behalf of children and for enhancing the awareness of the special needs for children on the part of decision makers and the public. The International Year of the Child was essentially to be the year of action at the national level to improve the situation of children. It was also supposed to lead to the general recognition of the fact that programs for children should be an integral part of economic and social development plan. A significant contribution to the shape of the universal concept of the rights of the child was the Declaration on Social and Legal Principles, relating to the protection and welfare of children, with special reference to foster placement and adoption at national and international level, adopted by the General Assembly on December 3, 1985. The Declaration states, among others, that in all foster placement and adoption procedures the best interest of the child should be the paramount consideration.

Societies all over the world gradually came to acknowledge the needs and rights of the child and recognized the necessity to have them listed. Major steps forward in this area were also made by declarations and conventions dealing with racial discrimination and discrimination against women.

The Polish government expected the Convention to be adopted within a short period of time. It was considered to be possible since the original draft was to a large extent based on the text of the university accepted Declaration of the Rights of the Child. It was also presumed that the project of the Convention would win broad interest and support from the states being in the process of development In Poland the draft was worked out at the Ministry of Foreign Affairs with assistance of a group of academicians—specialists in the field of law on family and guardianship relations. Before Poland officially submitted the Convention draft, preliminary consultations with some members of the Commission on Human Rights had been held via diplomatic protocol. The support of the initiative had also been sought with states belonging to the socialist bloc.

The Commission approved Poland's motion requesting the inclusion of works on the drafts-convention into its agenda. Following preliminary discussion the Commission decided to send the draft to the UN member-states for their consideration as well as international and non-government organizations who expressed their interest in the matter with a request for their comments. The response was not always enthusiastic. Numerous comments and opinions arrived both from individual states and international and non-government organizations. The majority of respondents took a stand in favour of undertaking workings on the convention draft. It was suggested that the works should proceed at a considerable pace in order to include achievements coming from the International Children's Year in the draft's content. There were voices proposing that the Convention should include the total of the rights of the child-civil and political rights, economic rights, social and cultural rights, while maintaining appropriate balance between them. Those who expressed this type of opinion claimed that the Polish draft excessively exposed economic, social and cultural rights of the child. They suggested increasing the value of political and civil rights in the draft. They also advised that the Convention should refer to specific rights of children in difficult situation, such as disabled children, children of refugees, children who had infringed the penal law, orphans etc. The necessity to guarantee equal rights to girls and boys was also strongly emphasized.

The Polish government followed a large amount of voiced suggestions and recommendations while preparing the second-amended—version of the convention draft. The draft was submitted to the UN Commission on Human Rights in 1979 and became the foundation for further works on the Convention.

The Commission appointed a session Working Croup open to all states that showed interest in the matter, to carry on works on the draft Convention. In the years 1979 and 1980 the Working Group had only several hours for discussions. Its sittings took place simultaneously with the meetings of the Commission and other Open-ended Working Groups called up by the Commission. This fact itself did not allow for great progress in the works on the Convention. The cold war between the West and the East adversely affected the pace at which the draft was taking its shape. Within die Commission on Human Rights itself there was a tough competition going on between the United States and the Soviet Union. The delegates of certain western countries used a tactics of obstruction. For example, they submitted controversial proposals and after a consensus was finally reached following long and tedious discussions—they withdrew them. The western representatives also used to turn in large rounds of proposals at a time which—as known from the very beginning—could not be leaked through and considered in due time because there was too many of them. Although the proposals were as much appropriate as possible, there was need to find the right time to consider them. Part of the submitted proposals were adopted later. Much time was wasted on political arguments which had little in common with the draft of the Convention. During the first years or works on the draft convention even such organizations as UNICEF showed ignorance of the project. The attitude of some delegates of non-government organizations was not conducive to the progress in the works on the draft, either. Activities performed by the late Ms. Evi Underhill constituted a very positive exception to the above. Delegaters of the Holy See, as well, adopted a rather positive attitude towards the idea of the Convention. The progress of works on the draft were made dependent on advancements in arrangements regarding other projects that were of particular importance to some western states. This refers to the draft of Declaration on the Elimination of all Forms of Intolerance and Discrimination Based on Religion or Belief adopted in 1981 and works on the Convention against Torture and oilier Cruel, Inhuman of Degrading Treatment or Punishment: adopted in 1984.

In 1981, the Commission allowed the Working Croup to have sittings a few days before the Commission's session and approved of the Groups works during the session. Later the Working Group was granted the Commissions consent to hold one-week or—in the final stage of the works on the draft—even two-week meetings before the Commissions session. This remarkably increased the pace of proceedings. In the last stage of works on the draft convention the Executive Director of UNICEF—James Grant—involved the organization, both physically and financially, in the process of completion of the draft in order to finalize the whole project before the thirtieth anniversary of adoption of the Declaration on the Rights of the Child and the tenth anniversary of the International Year of the Child. The engagement of such international organizations as the International Labour Organization, UNESCO. WHO and International Red Cross was becoming more and more conspicuous. Non-government organizations cooperated and each year were ready to submit a number of valuable proposals of which part were adopted by the Working Group. It should be pointed our here that non-government organizations led an active international action in favour of the Convention organizing seminars and conferences. Several events of this type rook place in Erevan in the Soviet Union, in Italy, Spain, Jordan and some other countries including Poland. Such meetings provided a good opportunity to evaluate the progress in the works on the draft, share opinions and consider suggestions, for example, a conference in Amman, Jordan, resulted in working out of the concept of international monitoring of the observance of the Convention. It was suggested that for that purpose a Committee on the Rights of the Child should be appointed. The idea found its place in the content of the Convention. It was also agreed that the activity of the Committee would be financed from the regular budget of the United Nations.

From the very beginning of its activities the Working Group followed a principle of adopting all resolutions of the Convention on the way of consensus. It meant that each proposal would be discussed and amended as long as there was no veto voiced from any side in the discussion. Much assistance came from small draft groups whose task was to thoroughly consider a controversial proposal and form a version that the Working Group would accept.

The Working Group decided that the draft, when

completed, would need to undergo the second reading. Following this decision the Convention's draft, after the first reading, was presented to the governments, of the UN member-states and international organizations for their evaluation and comments. The Working Group turned also to the UN Secretary General with a request of that Secretariat's law agents' opinion regarding the technical and legal correctness of the draft. UNICEF appointed its own special expert whose task was to express his opinion on die version of the draft agreed on the first reading. A group of UNICEF employers, very effectively and discreetly headed by Victor Soler Sala-Deputy Director of UNICEF's European office, constructively contributed to the development of works on the draft at that time.

The evaluation of the draft by various bodies resulted with another inflow of new proposals and recommendations aiming at bringing the draft to the finest shape possible. Another two-week session of the Working Group ended with adopting some of the submitted suggestions what positively influenced the quality of the draft. The only matter that the Group did not manage to settle referred to the means of financing the activity of the Committee on the Rights of the Child. The decision on the very issue was taken later by the Third Committee of the UN General Assembly-several days before the Convention was adopted by the General Assembly.

The standpoints represented by delegates of particular states were definitely determined by instructions given by their governments. Nevertheless, personality and attitudes of individual delegates played its role in the discussions. Some states changed their delegates to the Working Group quire often. These changes were rather positive for the development of the work on the draft; this refers, for instance, to the rotation of delegates from the US or Australia. Some changes, in turn, had no influence on the status quo of the work of the Working Group. Others could adversely affect the final appearance of the draft; for example, the government of one of the states sent in a delegate who submitted a set of proposals which, if adopted, could deteriorate the quality of the Convention and could postpone the date of its adoption. Fortunately the delegates proposals met with joint critique from the side of other delegates and were almost entirely rejected. It looked as if the standpoint of the said delegate was based on his personal beliefs rather than on the guidelines of the government of the state he represented.

Generally speaking, throughout the whole period the Working Group worked in the atmosphere of mutual understanding and respect for different opinions. This atmosphere was impermeable for arguments existing in the world of politics.

The Convention draft, likewise all other documents of the UN, was prepared in six official languages. In reality it was English that played the main role there, hence there sometimes occurred misunderstandings resulting from difficulties with translations of certain texts into other languages. In this context it is apt to mention a valuable role played by the delegates from the United Kingdom, the USA and Canada, who eagerly served as linguistic experts as well. A delegate from the United Kingdom, Michael Longford enjoyed great respect also as such an expert.

The UN Secretariat played an important role in documenting the works on the draft. At the beginning of works the Secretariat employee appointed to serve the Working Group turned out to be on inadequate person to do the job. When the post or a director of the Centre for Human Rights in Geneva was taken by a Swedish diplomat-lan Marterson—and after a competent employee of the Secretariat Tom McCarthy came in charge of technical service of the Working Group—the situation changed radically. The Secretariat showed valuable initiatives and provided perfect service to the Working Group. It is worth adding here that significant expert help in the final editing or the Convention articles was rendered by officers of the Vienna section of the UN Secretariat.

Sometimes I was asked half-seriously and half-derisively whether children—the beneficiaries of the Convention-participated in the coordinating works on the Convention draft and if so what were their postulates. It is obvious that the Convention on the Rights of the Child, as any other multilateral international agreement referring to human rights is an accomplishment of all states concerned represented by their governments. The same procedure was followed in case of the Convention on the Rights of the Child. When submitting proposals to the draft delegates of few states referred to opinions held by children and youth organizations active in the countries they represented. Sweden was one of such countries. When the works on the draft were about to be completed a group of Swedish children entered the session hall where the Working Group was holding its meeting and submitted a petition written on a poster one meter wide and several meters long signed by approximately twelve thousand children. The petition contained support for the Convention and especially for Sweden's postulate stating that children should not be called up to armed forces and involved in armed conflicts. A few times school children from Canada listened to debates in the Working Group. Also, representatives of several French children and youth organizations showed active interest in the works on the Convention draft.

An hour after the Convention was adopted by the UN general Assembly thousands of children from all over the world gathered at the UN headquarters in New York celebrating the resolution of the Convention. Such officials as the UN Secretary General, Executive Director of UNICEF, Ambassadors of some states accredited to the United Nations and other representatives of culture and science- they all participated in the manifestation in New York UN headquarters. I believe that a TV recording made of the manifestation could serve as an excellent didactic material. The gathered children received information on the Conventions resolutions with utmost delight.

Working out of some articlesof the Convention proceeded relatively harmoniously. In several other cases, however, die Convention's resolutions were discussed many times, often in a strained atmosphere. When it seemed that finally consensus was reached on certain matters, suddenly delegates of some states or international organizations reverted to its controversial points again. The notion of the child was the most contentious of all—it caused a lot of disagreement and argument and was discussed at length (Article 1). The adherents of the view chat the child begins at the moment of conception insisted on including this view into the Convention's content. Others claimed that the Convention's objective was to protect the child after birch. Finally agreement was reached in a result of which the preamble to the Convention included a sentence from the Declaration of the Rights of the Child saying chat the child needs "appropriate legal protection before as well as after birth". In consequence there is an imprecise statement saying chat "for the purpose of the present Convention a child means every human being below the age of 18 years".

Much time was spaned on formulating article on the right of the child express his or her views (Article 12), the right of the child to freedom of expression (Article 13), the right of the child to freedom of thought, conscience and religion (Article 14). Discussions over Article 17 regarding the function performed by mass-media were instigated by a clash of two conceptions; one of them supported free flow of information whereas the other one favored protection of the child from information and materials injurious to his or her well-being. In the end the first view prevailed.

Unexpectedly for some members of the Working Group there occurred serious difficulties with reaching common agreement on the content of Article 21 concerning adoption. Delegates of states with Islamic culture had problems with accepting the proposed resolutions. In turn, a delegate of one of the Latin America states kept blocking reaching of consensus due to a statement on financial gain for persons or institutions that act as brokers in inter-country adoptions.

The Working Group encountered another controversy when discussing the content of the right of the child to education, especially its pare referring to mandatory primary education that should be available free to all. Delegates of some states claimed that their countries for long would not be able to meet this requirement. A note of pessimism was also struck during formulation of some other social rights of the child.

After long and exhaustive negotiations delegates from Sweden and some other states as well as the representative of the International Red Cross finally agreed to approve the content of Article 38 which admits recruitment of children of 15 years of age to armed forces as well as direct part in hostilities. However, Swedish delegate Anders Ronquist emphasized that Sweden could not reconcile to this resolution.

One of the specific rights for the child is his/her right to live in a family. The Convention assumes that for the full and harmonious development of the child's personality, he/she should grow up in a family environment, in an atmosphere of happiness, love and understanding. Hence the state shall ensure that a child shall not be separated from his/her parents against their will, except for cases in which the competent authorities decide that for the best interest of the child, he/she should be separated from the parents. Nevertheless, in cases like these, the state shall respect the right of the child to maintain personal relations and direct contact with both parents on a regular basis, except if it is contrary to the child's best interest. The state shall take measures to combat the illicit transfer and non-return of child abroad, even if the person carrying out the transfer is one of the parents. Emphasizing the right of the child to live in a family environment, the Convention regards it as the parents' duty to provide the child appropriate direction and guidance in the process of exercising by the child of the rights recognized in the Convention, in a manner consistent with the evolving capacities of the child. It refers also to the possibility given to the child to exercise the right to freedom of thought, conscience and religion. The Convention does not use the term "parental power" or "parental authority". It does not acknowledge total subordination of the child to his/her parents; it introduces partnership relations within the family and assumes that parental love for the child and child's love for the parents will constitute main and the most natural factors of appropriate relations between parents and their children. However, the Convention realizes that sometimes parents' conduct does not necessarily take into consideration interests of the child. Then, the final arbiter between the interests of parents and the best interests of a child is a competent state organ, usually the court of law, that acts according to set procedures.

All children, including those from broken homes—said H.M. Paola, Queen of Belgium—are entitled to grow up in a climate where they are blessed with security, attention, respect and the love of caring parents. No Convention or lofty international conference can guarantee what only a family can provide. I firmly believe in the family as the "inner sanctuary" of society, as the fundamental community of love, as the primary school of humanity in which children's characters are shaped and prepared to assume their responsibilities towards their fellow human beings.

Another specific right of the child is his/her right to rest and leisure, to engage in play and recreational activities appropriate to the age of the child, and to participate freely in cultural life and the arts. The Convention does not establish the right of the child to work. It assumes that the child should learn and play, and indicates only what kind of work the child should not perform and how the child should be protected against deleterious effects of such a work.

Regarding numerous human rights as the rights of the child, the Convention adjusts the core of these rights to the nature and situation of the child; for example, the Convention says that every child has the inherent right to life, and imposes a duty on the state to ensure the survival of and development of the child to the maximum extent possible. Thus the Convention approaches this right in quite a different manner from the way it was formed by the International Covenant on Civil and Political Rights where the main emphasis was that no one shall be arbitrary deprived of his/her life. Another example: the Convention states that the state shall respect the right of the child to freedom of thought, conscience and religion. However, at the same time it says that the parents have the right and duty to provide direction to the child in the exercise of this right in a manner consistent with the evolving capacities of the child. Similarly, while setting the guarantees for the child who is alleged, accused or recognized as having infringed the penal law, the Convention also clearly states that the child should be treated in a manner consistent with the promotion of his/her sense of dignity and worth, which takes into account the child's age and desirability of promoting the child's reintegration and assumption of a constructive role in the society. Other commonly recognized human rights are also suitable adjusted to the child's conditions.

There were opinions voiced during the sittings of the Commission on Human Rights whore the Commission listened to the Working Groups reports on the progress in works on the draft convention achieved in a given year, that standards set in some articles of the Convention were too low and hence did not sufficiently mobilize states-parties to the Convention. Yet, this feature was considered by some other delegates not as a weakness but as an advantage of the Convention; they claimed that such standards of the formulated rights made it possible for less resourceful states to ratify the Convention. They speculated chat this would imply broadening of the Convention's range of influence and in this context referred to Article 41 which provides that "nothing in the Convention shall affect any provisions which are more conducive to the realization of the rights of the child and which may be contained in the law of the state-party or international law in force for that state".

Undoubtedly, the Working Group participants did not even expect that in a relatively short period of time as many as 191 states would become parties to the Convention. Moderately ambitious standards of some articles certainly encouraged the states to consider and then to ratify the Convention. Nevertheless, the matter of the level of requirements laid down by some articles of the Convention remains very lively. Those states that favored more ambitious standards found their own way to realize their ideas. They submitted two facultative protocol drafts to the Convention, namely one that accompanied Article 34 on the protection of the child from all forms of sexual exploitation and sexual abuse, and another one that accompanied Article 38 permitting participation of children in armed conflicts. However, the work on both these protocols proceeds rather slowly and with great difficulty.

During the ten years of the Convention's existence only one amendment has been voiced, what definitely proves the quality of the Convention. The amendment provides for the substitution of-the word "ten" with the word "eighteen" in Article 43. The said "ten" is the number of experts elected to the Committee on the Rights of the Child established for the purpose of examining the progress made by states-parties in achieving the realization of the obligations undertaken in the Convention. The ten-person Committee is no longer capable of considering large numbers of reports from the state-parties. Hence the requirement for an increase in the number of experts in the Committee. The amendment will most probably enter into force shortly The Convention seems to well stand the test of time.

When ratifying the Convention a great number of states voiced significant reservations. Some of the reservations are evidently incompatible with the object and purpose of the Convention, which makes the importance of a given ratification weaker. Some states have also turned in declarations expressing this way a specific understanding of certain provisions of the Convention. The above mentioned reservations as well as declarations can be withdrawn by the state-party at any time. Unfortunately, up to date, appeals for withdrawals of these reservations have not been very successful. Both reservations and-to some less extent-declarations impair the efficiency of the Convention.

Under the influence of the Convention many states have changed their legislation system adjusting it to the requirements of the Convention. The Convention became a framework for the activity of UNICEF Provisions included in the Convention are referred to by such international organizations as UNESCO, WHO, ILO. Through the Convention the matter of improvement of well-being of the child was given political priority in the activities of the United Nations and international organizations concerned. Workings on the Convention draft and its binding force considerably influenced the increase in activities of both international and national non-government organizations moved by concern for well-being of children. In many countries the Convention was a stimulus for development of research on conditions of children and their rights. It is not a secret that the Convention on the Rights of the Child became a stimulus for adoption of regional conventions aiming at improvement of well-being of children. I mean here the African Charter in the Rights and Welfare of the Child of 1990 and the European Convention on the Exercise of Children's Rights of 1996. Unfortunately both these international agreements have not entered into force yet due to insufficient number of individual ratifications.

At present the Convention is a guide to the activity of the Interamerican Institute of the Child, existing since 1927, which is a specialized unit within the Organization of American States.

The Convention on the Rights of the Child has also become a reference base for the process of regulation of certain aspects of selected children's rights. A good example is the Hague Convention on International Cooperation and Protection of Children in Respect of Inter country Adoption, signed in 1993.

The World Conference on Human Rights stated in its Vienna Declaration and Program of Action, that in all actions concerning children—non-discrimination and the best interests of the child should be of the primary consideration, and the views of the child should be given due weight. The Conference also stressed that "International cooperation and solidarity should be promoted to support the implementation of the Convention on the Rights of the Child, should be a priority in the United Nations System-wise action on Human Rights". The World Conference on Human Rights reiterated the principle of "First Call for Children" and in this respect underlined the importance of major national and international efforts for promoting respect for the rights of the child to survival, protection, development and participation. This way the Conference articulated the world-wide significance and topicality of the contents of the Convention on the Rights of the Child.

A special role in the realization of the provisions of the Convention was assigned to UNICEF (Art. 45). Now it is the major organ contributing to the popularization and implementation of the Convention. Owing to UNICEF's efforts. The World Summit for Children rook place on "September 29-30, 1990, in New York. In its declaration the Summit states that the Convention on 'the Rights of the Child is an excellent reflection of the international community's care for the child's welfare. The Summit participants adopted the Plan of Action on behalf of children until the year 2000. They called upon all states to draft and implement a national plan of action, which unfortunately was not followed by many of the states. Ms. Carol Bellamy, UNICEFs Executive Director, said in her Preface to the State of the worlds Children in 1996: "With renewed commitment, we shall work for the day, when the Declaration and the Convention are transformed from articles of faith into expressions of reality for the lives and hopes of the worlds children". The International Symposium organized in May 1996 in Salamanca to celebrate the fiftieth anniversary of UNICEF, in its Salamanca Declaration on the Convention on the Rights of the Child also recognized the significance of the Convention on the Rights of the Child, which embodies ethical values and is based on international human rights law and therefore underscores its usefulness, universality and particularly its idealism, vision and commitment which guide the way towards the future, taking into account the need to promote better understanding of its, principles and its implementation by all educational, political and religious sectors".

The examples presented above prove that the content of the Convention is the outcome of a mature consideration and concordant will of the international community.

The Convention expresses the trend and eagerness to recognize and respect universal values. It takes into consideration fundamental needs of children all over the world, in developed and developing countries, in rich and poor states.

The above mentioned values are the following:

- respect of dignity, personality and subjectivity of the child, and (if possible) the child's participation in exercising of his/her rights;
- elimination of any type of discrimination due to the child's or his/her family's features;
- elimination of all kinds of exploitation and child abuse;
- recognition of the family as the fundamental unit of the society and the natural environment for the growth and well-being of the child;
- acceptation of the fact that in all matters regarding the child—his/her best interest should be treated as the priority;
- admission of the fact that the child is entitled to exercise all human rights and fundamental freedoms that are enjoyed by the adults, and also are entitled to exercise additional rights resulting from specific needs and situation of the child;
- recognition of the idea that the care for implementation and observance of the rights of the child in a national scale should be completed with efforts in this area of international community.

The Convention has created an effective mechanism of international control of observance of the rights of the child by individual states.

Despite the above mentioned beneficial effects of the Convention on the Rights of the Child and also other conspicuous positive outcomes of its functioning, we cannot claim that the Convention has already brought about considerable improvement of well-being of children all over the world. As before "situation of children in many parts of the world remains critical as a result of inadequate social conditions, natural disasters, armed conflict:;, exploitation, illiteracy, hunger and disability" (A/44/736). That is why the statement made by the UN General Assembly chat "children's rights require special protection and call for continuous improvement of the situation of children all over the: world as well as their development and education in conditions of peace and security". This is why "urgent and effective national and international action is called for" (A/44/736).

Certainly, even the greatest optimists could not expect chat in the coming ten years from the adoption of the Convention all children in the world would smile ail the nine. The Convention is an international agreement meant for long-term effect. It has an ability to make states direct their activities in favour of improvement of the situation of children in the 21st century. This may constitute a source of satisfaction for all those who in someway contributed to its origination and providing it with deeply humanistic content. We can say that these people suitably took the chance the fortune granted them.

At present there are several strategic tasks regarding the promotion and protection of the rights of the child by means of the Convention; they are as follows: making all the countries of the world ratify the Convention, making the countries who voiced reservations withdraw them (this refers especially to the countries whose reservations do not fall in line with the object and purpose of the Convention), adjusting national legislation of each country to the Conventions standards, developing international cooperation aiming at full realization of the Conventions provisions, ensuring greater effectiveness of monitoring activity of the Committee on the Rights of the Child, spreading information concerning the contents of the Convention among children and adults of all countries of the world.

***ANNEXURE V***

# UN CONVENTION ON THE RIGHTS OF THE CHILD

## Adopted by the General Assembly of the United Nations by Resolution 44/25 on 20 November, 1989 at the Forty-Fourth Session of the General Assembly of the United Nations

Entry into Force: 2 September, 1990.

Ratified by all countries except USA and Somalia as of August 1997.

**Preamble**

*The States Parties to the Present Convention,*

*Considering* that, in accordance with the principles proclaimed in the Charter of the United Nations, recognition of the inherent dignity and of the equal and inalienable rights of all members of the human family is the foundation of freedom, justice and peace in the world.

*Bearing in mind* that the peoples of the United Nations have, in the Charter, reaffirmed their faith in fundamental human rights and in the dignity and worth of the human person, and have determined to promote social progress and better standards of life in larger freedom.

*Recognizing* that the United Nations has, in the Universal Declaration of Human Rights and in the International Covenants on Human Rights, proclaimed and agreed that everyone is entitled to all the rights and freedoms set forth therein, without distinction of any kind, such as race, colour, sex, language, religion, political or other opinion, national or social origin, property, birth or other status.

*Recalling* that, in the Universal Declaration of Human Rights, the United Nations has proclaimed that childhood is entitled to special care and assistance,

*Convinced* that the family, as the fundamental group of

society and the natural environment for the growth and well-being of all its members and particularly children, should be afforded the necessary protection and assistance so that it can fully assume its responsibilities within the community.

*Recognizing* that the child, for the full and harmonious development of his or her personality, should grow up in a family environment, in an atmosphere of happiness, love and understanding.

*Considering* that the child should be fully prepared to live an individual life, in society, and brought up in the spirit of the ideals proclaimed in the Charter of the United Nations, and in particular in the spirit of peace, dignity, tolerance, freedom, equality and solidarity.

*Bearing in mind* that the need to extend particular care to the child has been stated in the Geneva Declaration of the Rights of the Child of 1924 and in the Declaration of the Rights of the Child adopted by the General Assembly on 20 November, 1959 and recognized in the Universal Declaration of Human Rights, in the International Covenant on Civil and Political Rights (in particular in Articles 23 and 24), in the International Covenant of Economic, Social and Cultural Rights (in particular in Article 10) and in the statutes and relevant instruments of specialized agencies and international organizations concerned with the welfare of children.

*Bearing in mind* that, as indicated in the Declaration of the Rights of the Child, 'the child, by reason of his physical and mental immaturity, needs special safeguards and care, including appropriate legal protection, before as well as after birth.

*Recalling* the provisions of the Declaration on Social and Legal Principles relating to the Protection and Welfare of Children, with Special Reference to Foster Placement and Adoption Nationally and Internationally; the United Nations Standard Minimum Rules for the Administration of Juvenile Justice (The Beijing Rules); and the Declaration on the Protection of Women and Children in Emergency and Armed Conflict.

*Recognizing* that, in all countries in the world, there are children living in exceptionally difficult conditions, and that such children need special consideration.

*Taking due account* of the importance of the traditions and cultural values of each people for the protection and harmonious development of the child.

*Recognizing* the importance of international co-operation for improving the living conditions of children in every country, in particular in the developing countries.

*Have agreed* as follows:

## Part I

### Article 1

For the purposes of the present Convention, a child means every human being below the age of 18 years unless, under the law applicable to the child, majority is attained earlier.

### Article 2

1. States Parties shall respect and ensure the rights set forth in the present Convention to each child within their jurisdiction without discrimination of any kind, irrespective of the child's or his or her parent's or legal guardian's race, colour, sex, language, religion, political or other opinion, national, ethnic or social origin, property, disability, birth or other status.

2. States Parties shall take all appropriate measures to ensure that the child is protected against all forms of discrimination or punishment on the basis of the status, activities, expressed opinions, or beliefs of the child's parents, legal guardians, or family members.

### Article 3

1. In all actions concerning children, whether undertaken by public or private social welfare institutions, courts of law, administrative authorities or legislative bodies, the best interests of the child shall be a primary consideration.

2. States Parties undertake to ensure the child such protection and care as is necessary for his or her well-being, taking into account the rights and duties of his or her parents, legal guardians, or other individuals legally responsible for him or her, and, to this end, shall take all appropriate legislative and administrative measures.

3. States Parties shall ensure that the institutions, services and facilities responsible for the care or protection of children shall conform with the standards established by competent authorities, particularly in the areas of safety, health, in the number and suitability of their staff, as well as competent supervision.

**Article 4**

States Parties shall undertake all appropriate legislative, administrative, and other measures for the implementation of the rights recognized in the present Convention. With regard to economic, social and cultural rights, States Parties shall undertake such measures to the maximum extent of their available resources and, where needed, within the framework of international cooperation.

**Article 5**

States Parties shall respect the responsibilities, rights and duties of parents or, where applicable, the members of the extended family or community as provided for by local custom, legal guardians or other persons legally responsible for the child, to provide, in a manner consistent with the evolving capacities of the child, appropriate direction and guidance in the exercise by the child of the rights recognized in the present Convention.

**Article 6**

1. States Parties recognize that every child has the inherent right to life.

2. States Parties shall ensure to the maximum extent possible the survival and development of the child.

**Article 7**

1. The child shall be registered immediately after birth and shall have the right from birth to a name, the right to acquire a nationality and, as far as possible, the right to know and be cared for by his or her parents.

2. States Parties shall ensure the implementation of these rights in accordance with their national law and their obligations under the relevant international instruments in this field, in particular where the child would otherwise be stateless.

**Article 8**

1. States Parties undertake to respect the right of the child to preserve his or her identity, including nationality, name and family relations as recognized by law without unlawful interference.

2. Where a child is illegally deprived of some or all of the elements of his or her identity, States Parties shall provide appropriate assistance and protection, with a view to speedily re-establishing his or her identity.

**Article 9**

1. States Parties shall ensure that a child shall not be separated from his or her parents against their will, except when competent authorities subject to judicial review determine, in accordance with applicable law and procedures, that such separation is necessary for the best interests of the child. Such determination may be necessary in a particular case such as one involving abuse or neglect of the child by the parents, or one where the parents are living separately and a decision must be made as to the child's place of residence.

2. In any proceedings pursuant to paragraph 1 of the present article, all interested parties shall be given an opportunity to participate in the proceedings and make their views known.

3. States Parties shall respect the right of the child who is separated from one or both parents to maintain personal relations and direct contact with both parents on a regular basis, except if it is contrary to the child's best interests.

4. Where such separation results from any action initiated by a State Party, such as the detention, imprisonment, exile, deportation or death (including death arising from any cause while the person is in the custody of the State) of one or both parents or of the child, that State Party shall, upon request, provide the parents, the child or, if appropriate, another member of the family with the essential information concerning the whereabouts of the absent member(s) of the family unless the provision of the information would be detrimental to the well-being of the child. States Parties shall further ensure that the submission of such a request shall of itself entail no adverse consequences for the person(s) concerned.

**Article 10**

1. In accordance with the obligation of States Parties under article 9, paragraph 1, applications by a child or his or her parents to enter or leave a State Party for the purpose of family reunification shall be dealt with by States Parties in a positive, humane and expeditious manner. States Parties shall further ensure that the submission of such a request shall entail no adverse consequences for the applicants and for the members of their family.

2. A child whose parents reside in different States shall have the right to maintain on a regular basis, save in exceptional circumstances, personal relations and direct contacts with both parents. Towards that end and in accordance with the obligation of States Parties under Article 9, Paragraph 1, States Parties shall respect the right of the child and his or her parents to leave any country, including their own, and to enter their own country. The right to leave any country shall be subject only to such restriction as are prescribed by law and which are necessary to protect the

national security, public order *(ordre public)*, public health or morals or the rights and freedoms of others and are consistent with the other rights recognized in the present Convention.

**Article 11**

1. States Parties shall take measures to combat the illicit transfer and non-return of children abroad.

2. To this end, States Parties shall promote the conclusion of bilateral or multilateral agreements or accession to existing agreements.

**Article 12**

1. States Parties shall assure to the child who is capable of forming his or her own views the right to express those views freely in all matters affecting the child, the views of the child being given due weight in accordance with the age and maturity of the child.

2. For this purpose, the child shall in particular be provided the opportunity to be heard in any judicial and administrative proceedings affecting the child, either directly, or through a representative or an appropriate body, in a manner consistent with the procedural rules of national law.

**Article 13**

1. The child shall have the right to freedom of expression; this right shall include freedom to seek, receive and impart information and ideas of all kinds, regardless of frontiers, either orally, in writing or in print, in the form of art, or through any other media of the child's choice.

2. The exercise of this right may be subject to certain restrictions, but these shall only be such as are provided by law and are necessary:

*(a)* For respect of the rights or reputations of others; or

*(b)* For the protection of national security or of public order *(ordre public)*, or of public health or morals.

**Article 14**

1. States Parties shall respect the right of the child to freedom of thought, conscience and religion.

2. States Parties shall respect the rights and duties of the parents and, when applicable, legal guardians, to provide direction to the child in the exercise of his or her right in a manner consistent with the evolving capacities of the child.

3. Freedom to manifest one's religion or beliefs may be subject only to such limitations as are prescribed by law and are necessary to protect public safety, order, health or morals, or the fundamental rights and freedoms of others.

**Article 15**

1. States Parties recognize the rights of the child to freedom of association and to freedom of peaceful assembly.

2. No restrictions may be placed on the exercise of these rights other than those imposed in conformity with the law and which are necessary in a democratic society in the interests of national security or public safety, public order *(ordre public),* the protection of public health or morals or the protection of the rights and freedoms of others.

**Article 16**

1. No child shall be subjected to arbitrary or unlawful interference with his or her privacy, family, home or correspondence, nor to unlawful attacks on his or her honour and reputation.

2. The child has the right to the protection of the law against such interference or attacks.

**Article 17**

States Parties recognize the important function performed by the mass media and shall ensure that the child has access to information and material from a diversity of national and international sources, especially those aimed at the promotion of his or her social, spiritual and moral well-being and physical and mental health. To this end, States Parties shall:

1. Encourage the mass media to disseminate information and material of social and cultural benefit to the child and in accordance with the spirit of Article 29.

2. Encourage international cooperation in the production, exchange and dissemination of such information and material from a diversity of cultural, national and international sources;

3. Encourage the production and dissemination of children's books.

4. Encourage the mass media to have particular regard to the linguistic needs of the child who belongs 10 a minority group or who is indigenous.

5. Encourage the development of appropriate guidelines for the protection of the child from information and material injurious to his or her well-being, bearing in mind the provisions of articles 13 and 18.

**Article 18**

1. States Parties shall use their best efforts to ensure recognition of the principle that both parents have common responsibilities for the upbringing and development of the child. Parents or, as the case may be, legal guardians, have the primary responsibility for the upbringing and development of the child. The best interests of the child will be their basic concern.

2. For the purpose of guaranteeing and promoting the rights set forth in the present Convention, States Parties shall render appropriate assistance to parents and legal guardians in the performance of their child-rearing responsibilities and shall ensure the development of institutions, facilities and services for the care of children.

3. States Parties shall take all appropriate measures to ensure that children of working parents have the right to benefit from child-care services and facilities for which they are eligible.

**Article 19**

1. States Parties shall take all appropriate legislative, administrative, social and educational measures to protect

the child from all forms of physical or mental violence, injury or abuse, neglect or negligent treatment, maltreatment or exploitation, including sexual abuse, while in the care of parent(s), legal guardian(s) or any other person who has the care of the child.

2. Such protective measures should, as appropriate, include effective procedures for the establishment of social programmes to provide necessary support for the child and for those who have the care of the child, as well as for other forms of prevention and for identification, reporting, referral, investigation, treatment and follow-up of instances of child maltreatment described heretofore, and, as appropriate, for judicial involvement.

**Article 20**

1. A child temporarily or permanently deprived of his or her family environment, or in whose own best interests cannot be allowed to remain in that environment, shall be entitled to special protection and assistance provided by the State.

2. States Parties shall in accordance with their national laws ensure alternative care for such a child.

3. Such care could include, *inter alia,* foster placement, *kafala* of Islamic law, adoption or if necessary placement in suitable institutions for the care of children. When considering solutions, due regard shall be paid to the desirability of continuity in a child's upbringing and to the child's ethnic, religious, cultural and linguistic background.

**Article 21**

States Parties that recognize and/or permit the system of adoption shall ensure that the best interests of the child shall be the paramount consideration and they shall:

1. Ensure that the adoption of a child is authorized only by competent authorities who determine, in accordance with applicable law and procedures and on the basis of all pertinent and reliable information, that the adoption is—

permissible in view of the child's status concerning parents, relatives and legal guardians and that, if required, the persons concerned have given their informed consent to the adoption on the basis of such counselling as may be necessary.

2. Recognize that inter-country adoption may be considered as an alternative means of child's care, if the child cannot be placed in a foster or an adoptive family or cannot in any suitable manner be cared for in the child's country of origin.

3. Ensure that the child concerned by inter-country adoption enjoys safeguards and standards equivalent to those existing in the case of national adoption.

4. Take all appropriate measures to ensure that, in intercountry adoption, the placement does not result in improper financial gain for those involved in it.

5. Promote, where appropriate, the objectives of the present article by concluding bilateral or multilateral arrangements or agreements, and endeavour, within this framework, to ensure that the placement of the child in another country is carried out by competent authorities or organs.

**Article 22**

1. States Parties shall take appropriate measures to ensure that a child who is seeking refugee status or who is considered a refugee in accordance with applicable international or domestic law and procedures shall, whether unaccompanied or accompanied by his or her parents or by any other person, receive appropriate protection and humanitarian assistance in the enjoyment of applicable rights set forth in the present Convention and in other international human rights or humanitarian instruments to which the said States are Parties.

2. For this purpose, States Parties shall provide, as they consider appropriate, cooperation in any efforts by the United Nations and other competent intergovernmental organizations or non-governmental organizations co-operating with the United Nations to protect and assist such a child and to trace the parents or other members of the

family of any refugee child in order to obtain information necessary for reunification with his or her family. In cases where no parents or other members of the family can be found, the child shall be accorded the same protection as any other child permanently or temporarily deprived of his or her family environment for any reason, as set forth in the present Convention.

**Article 23**

1. States Parties recognize that a mentally or physically disabled child should enjoy a full and decent life, in conditions which ensure dignity, promote self-reliance and facilitate the child's active participation in the community.

2. States Parties recognize the right of the disabled child to special care and shall encourage and ensure the extension, subject to available resources, to the eligible child and those responsible for his or her care, of assistance for which application is made and which is appropriate to the child's condition and to the circumstances of the parents or others caring for the child.

3. Recognizing the special needs of a disabled child, assistance extended in accordance with paragraph 2 of the present article shall be provided free of charge, whenever possible, taking into account the financial resources of the parents or others coring for the child, and shall be designed to ensure that the disabled child has effective access to and receives education, training, health care services, rehabilitation services, preparation for employment and recreation opportunities in a manner conducive to the child's achieving the fullest possible social integration and individual development, including his or her cultural and spiritual development.

4. States Parties shall promote, in the spirit in international cooperation, the exchange of appropriate information in the field of preventive health care and of medical, psychological and functional treatment of disabled children, including dissemination of and access to information concerning methods of rehabilitation, education and vocational services,

with the aim of enabling States Parties to improve their capabilities and skills and to widen their experience in these areas. In this regard, particular account shall be taken of the needs of developing countries.

**Article 24**

1. States Parties recognize the right of the child to the enjoyment of the highest attainable standard of health and to facilities for the treatment of illness and rehabilitation of health. States Parties shall strive to ensure that no child is deprived of his or her right of access to such health care services.

2. States Parties shall pursue full implementation of this right and, in particular, shall take appropriate measures:

*(a)* To diminish infant and child mortality;

*(b)* To ensure the provision of necessary medical assistance and health care to all children with emphasis on the development of primary health care;

*(c)* To combat disease and malnutrition, including within the framework of primary health care, through, *inter alia,* the application of readily available technology and through the provision of adequate nutritious foods and clean drinking-water, taking into consideration the dangers and risks of environmental pollution;

*(d)* To ensure appropriate pre-natal and post-natal health care for mothers;

*(e)* To ensure that all segments of society, in particular parents and children, are informed, have access to education and are supported in the use of basic knowledge of child health and nutrition, the advantages of breast-feeding, hygiene and environmental sanitation and the prevention of accidents;

*(f)* To develop preventive health care, guidance for parents and family planning education and services.

3. States Parties shall take all effective and appropriate measures with a view to abolishing traditional practices prejudicial to the health of children.

4. States Parties undertake to promote and encourage international co-operation with a view to achieving progressively the full realization of the right recognized in the present article. In this regard, particular account shall be taken of the needs of developing countries.

**Article 25**

States Parties recognize the right of a child who has been placed by the competent authorities for the purposes of care, protection or treatment of his or her physical or mental health, to a periodic review of the treatment provided to the child and all other circumstances relevant to his or her placement.

**Article 26**

1. States Parties shall recognize for every child the right to benefit from social security, including social insurance, and shall take the necessary measures to achieve the full realization of this right in accordance with their national law.

2. The benefits should, where appropriate, be granted, taking into account the resources and the circumstances of the child and persons having responsibility for the maintenance of the child, as well as any other consideration relevant to an application for benefits made by or on behalf of the child.

**Article 27**

1. States Parties recognize the right of every child to a standard of living adequate for the child's physical, mental, spiritual, moral and social development.

2. The parent(s) or others responsible for the child have the primary responsibility to secure, within their abilities and financial capacities, the conditions of living necessary for the child's development.

3. States Parties, in accordance with national conditions and within their means, shall take appropriate measures to assist parents and others responsible for the child to implement this right and shall in case of need provide material assistance and support programmes, particularly with regard to nutrition, clothing and housing.

4. States Parties shall lake all appropriate measures to secure the recovery of maintenance for the child from the parents or other persons having financial responsibility for the child, both within the State Party and from abroad. In particular, where the person having financial responsibility for the child lives in a State different from that of the child, States Parties shall promote the accession to international agreements or the conclusion of such agreements, as well as the making of other appropriate arrangements.

**Article 28**

1. States Parties recognize the right of the child to education, and with a view to achieving this right progressively and on the basis of equal opportunity, they shall, in particular:

(*a*) Make primary education compulsory and available free to all;

(*b*) Encourage the development of different forms of secondary education, including general and vocational education, make them available and accessible to every child, and lake appropriate measures such as the introduction of free education and offering financial assistance in case of need;

(*c*) Make higher education accessible to all on the basis of capacity by every appropriate means;

(*d*) Make educational and vocational information and guidance available and accessible to all children;

(*e*) Take measures to encourage regular attendance at schools and the reduction of drop-out rates.

2. States Parties shall take all appropriate measures to ensure that school discipline is administered in a manner consistent with the child's human dignity and in conformity with the present Convention.

3. States Parties shall promote and encourage international cooperation in matters relating to education, in particular with a view to contributing to the elimination of ignorance and illiteracy throughout the world and facilitating access to scientific and technical knowledge and modem teaching methods. In this regard, particular account shall be taken of the needs of developing countries.

**Article 29**

1. States Parties agree that the education of the child shall be directed to

*(a)* the development of the child's personality, talents and mental and physical abilities to their fullest potential;

*(b)* the development of respect for human rights and fundamental freedoms, and for the principles enshrined in the Charter of the United Nations;

*(c)* the development of respect for the child's parents, his or her own cultural identity, language and values, for the national values of the country in which the child is living, the country from which he or she may originate and for civilizations different from his or her own;

*(d)* the preparation of the child for responsible life in a free society, in the spirit of understanding, peace, tolerance, equality of sexes, and friendship among all peoples, ethnic, national and religious groups and persons of indigenous origin;

*(e)* the development of respect for the natural environment.

2. No part of the present Article or Article 28 shall be construed so as to interfere with the liberty of individuals and bodies to establish and direct educational institutions, subject always to the observance of the principles set forth in paragraph 1 of the present article and to the requirements that the education given in such institutions shall conform to such minimum standards as may be laid down by the State.

**Article 30**

In those States in which ethnic, religious or linguistic minorities or persons of indigenous origin exist, a child belonging to such a minority or who is indigenous shall not be denied the right, in community with other members of his or her group, to enjoy his or her own culture, to profess and practise his or her own religion, or to use his or her own language.

**Article 31**

1. States Parties recognize the right of the child to rest and leisure, to engage in play and recreational activities appropriate to the age of the child and to participate freely in cultural life and the arts.

2. States Parties shall respect and promote the right of the child to participate fully in cultural and artistic life and shall encourage the provision of appropriate and equal opportunities for cultural, artistic, recreational and leisure activity.

**Article 32**

1. States Parties recognize the right of the child to be protected from economic exploitation and from performing any work that is likely to be hazardous or to interfere with the child's education, or to be harmful to the child's health or physical, mental, spiritual, moral or social development.

2. States Parties shall take legislative, administrative, social and educational measures to ensure the implementation of the present article. To this end, and having regard to the relevant provisions of other international instruments, States Parties shall in particular;

(*a*) Provide for a minimum age or minimum ages for admission to employment;

(*b*) Provide for appropriate regulation of the hours and conditions of employment;

(c) Provide for appropriate penalties or other sanctions to ensure the effective enforcement of the present article.

**Article 33**

States Parties shall take all appropriate measures, including legislative, administrative, social and educational measures, to protect children from the illicit use of narcotic drugs and psychotropic substances as defined in the relevant international treaties, and to prevent the use of children in the illicit production and trafficking of such substances.

**Article 34**

States Parties undertake to protect the child from all forms of sexual exploitation and sexual abuse. For these purposes, States Parties shall in particular take all appropriate national, bilateral and multilateral measures to prevent:

*(a)* The inducement or coercion of a child to engage in any unlawful sexual activity;

*(b)* The exploitative use of children in prostitution or other unlawful sexual practices;

*(c)* The exploitative use of children in pornographic performances and materials.

**Article 35**

States Parties shall take all appropriate national, bilateral and multilateral measures to prevent the abduction of, the sale of or traffic in children for any purpose or in any form.

**Article 36**

States Parties shall protect the child against all other forms of exploitation prejudicial to any aspects of the child's welfare.

**Article 37**

States Parties shall ensure that:

(a) no child shall be subjected to torture or other cruel, inhuman or degrading treatment or punishment. Neither capital punishment nor life imprisonment without possibility of release shall be imposed for offences committed by persons below eighteen years of age;

(b) no child shall be deprived of his or her liberty unlawfully or arbitrarily. The arrest, detention or imprisonment of a child shall be in conformity with the law and shall be used only as a measure of last resort and for the shortest appropriate period of time;

(c) every child deprived of liberty shall be treated with humanity and respect for the inherent dignity of the human person, and in a manner which takes into account the needs of persons of his or her age. In particular, every child deprived of liberty shall be separated from adults unless it is considered in the child's best interest not to do so and shall have the right to maintain contact with his or her family through correspondence and visits, save in exceptional circumstances;

(d) every child deprived of his or her liberty shall have the right to prompt access to legal and other appropriate assistance, as well as the right to challenge the legality of the deprivation of his or her liberty before a court or other competent, independent and impartial authority, and to a prompt decision on any such action.

**Article 38**

1. States Parties undertake to respect and to ensure respect for rules of international humanitarian law applicable to them in armed conflicts which are relevant to the child.

2. States Parties shall take all feasible measures to ensure that persons who have not attained the age of fifteen years do not take a direct part in hostilities.

3. States Parties shall refrain from recruiting any person

who has not attained the age of fifteen years into their armed forces. In recruiting among those persons who have attained the age of fifteen years but who have not attained the age- of eighteen years, States Parties shall endeavour to give priority to those who are oldest.

4. In accordance with their obligations under international humanitarian law to protect the civilian population in armed conflicts, States Parties shall take all feasible measures to ensure protection and care of children who are affected by an armed conflict,

**Article 39**

States Parties shall take all appropriate measures to promote physical and psychological recovery and social reintegration of a child victim of any form of neglect, exploitation, or abuse torture or any other form of cruel, inhuman or degrading treatment or punishment; or armed conflicts. Such recovery and reintegration shall take place in an environment which fosters the health, self-respect and dignity of the child.

**Article 40**

1. States Parties recognize the right of every child alleged as, accused of, or recognized as having infringed the penal law to be treated in a manner consistent with the promotion of the child's sense of dignity and worth, which reinforces the child's respect for the human rights and fundamental freedoms of others and which takes into account the child's age and the desirability of promoting the child's reintegration and the child's assuming a constructive role in society.

2. To this end, and having regard to the relevant provisions of international instruments, States Parties shall, in particular, ensure that:

*(a)* no child shall be alleged as, be accused of, or recognized as having infringed the penal law by reason of acts or omissions that were not prohibited by national or international law at the time they were committed;

(b) Every child alleged as or accused of having infringed the penal law has at least the following guarantees:

*(i)* To be presumed innocent until proven guilty according to law;

*(ii)* To be informed promptly and directly of the charges against him or her, and, if appropriate, through his or her parents or legal guardians, and to have legal or other appropriate assistance in the preparation and presentation of his or her defence;

*(iii)* To have the matter determined without delay by a competent, independent and impartial authority or judicial body in a fair hearing according to Jaw, in the presence of legal or other appropriate assistance and, unless it is considered not to be in the best interest of the child, in particular, taking into account his or her age or situation, his or her parents or legal guardians;

*(iv)* Not to be compelled to give testimony or to confess guilt; to examine or have examined adverse witnesses and to obtain the participation and examination of witnesses on his or her behalf under conditions of equality;

*(v)* If considered to have infringed the penal law, to have this decision and any measures imposed in consequence thereof reviewed by a higher competent, independent and impartial authority or judicial body according to law;

*(vi)* To have the free assistance of an interpreter if the child cannot understand or speak the language used;

*(vii)* To have his or her privacy fully respected at all stages of the proceedings.

3. States Parties shall seek to promote the establishment of laws, procedures, authorities and institutions specifically applicable to children alleged as, accused of, or recognized as having infringed the penal law, and, in particular:

(*a*) the establishment of a minimum age below which children shall be presumed not to have the capacity to infringe the penal law;

(*b*) whenever appropriate and desirable, measures for dealing with such children without resorting to judicial proceedings, providing that human rights and legal safeguards are fully respected.

4. A variety of dispositions, such as care, guidance and supervision orders; counseling; probation; foster care; education and vocational training programs and other alternatives to institutional care shall be available to ensure that children are dealt with in a manner appropriate to their well-being and proportionate both to their circumstances and the offence.

**Article 41**

Nothing in the present Convention shall affect any provisions which are more conducive to the realization of the rights of the child and which may be contained in:

(*a*) The law of a State Party; or

(*b*) International law in force for that State.

## Part II

**Article 42**

States Parties undertake to make the principles and provisions of the Convention widely known, by appropriate and active means, to adults and children alike.

**Article 43**

1. For the purpose of examining the progress made by States Parties in achieving the realization of the obligations undertaken in the present Convention, there shall be established a Committee on the Rights of the Child, which shall carry out the functions hereinafter provided.

2. The Committee shall consist of ten experts of high moral standing and recognized competence in the field

covered by this Convention. The members of the Committee shall be elected by States Parties from among their nationals and shall serve in their personal capacity, consideration being given to equitable geographical distribution, as well as to the principal legal systems.

3. The members of the Committee shall be elected by secret ballot from a list of persons nominated by States Parties. Each State Party may nominate one person from among its own nationals.

4. The initial election to the Committee shall be held no later than six months after the dale of the entry into force of the present Convention and thereafter every second year. At least four months before the date of each election, the Secretary-General of the United Nations shall address a letter to States Parties inviting them to submit their nominations within two months. The Secretary-General shall subsequently prepare a list in alphabetical order of all persons thus nominated, indicating States Parties which have nominated them, and shall submit it to the States Parties to the present Convention.

5. The elections shall be held at meetings of States Parties convened by the Secretary-General at United Nations Headquarters, At those meetings, for which two-thirds of States Parties shall constitute a quorum, the persons elected to the Committee shall be those who obtain the largest number of votes and an absolute majority of the votes of the representatives of States Parties present and voting.

6. The members of the Committee shall be elected for a term of four years. They shall be eligible for re-election if denominated. The term of five of the members elected at the first election shall expire at the end of two years; immediately after the first election, the names of these five members shall be chosen by lot by the Chairman of the meeting.

7. If a member of the Committee dies or resigns or declares that for any other cause he or she can no longer perform the duties of the Committee, the State Party which nominated the member shall appoint another expert from among its

nationals to serve for the remainder of the term, subject to the approval of the Committee.

8. The Committee shall establish its own rules of procedure.

9. The Committee shall elect its officers for a period of two years.

10. The meetings of the Committee shall normally be held at United Nations Headquarters or at any other convenient place as determined by the Committee. The Committee shall normally meet annually. The duration of the meetings of the Committee shall be determined, and reviewed, if necessary, by a meeting of the States Parties to the present Convention, subject to the approval of the General Assembly.

11. The Secretary-General of the United Nations shall provide the necessary staff and facilities for the effective performance of the functions of the Committee under the present Convention.

12. With the approval of the General Assembly, the members of the Committee established under the present Convention shall receive emoluments from the United Nations resources on such terms and conditions as the Assembly may decide.

**Article 44**

1. States Parties undertake to submit to the Committee, through the Secretary-General of the United Nations, reports on the measures they have adopted which give effect to the rights recognized herein and on the progress made on the enjoyment of those rights:

(*a*) Within two years of the entry into force of the Convention for the State Party concerned;

(*b*) Thereafter every five years.

2. Reports made under the present article shall indicate factors and difficulties, if any, affecting the degree of fulfilment of the obligations under the present Convention. Reports shall also contain sufficient information to provide the Committee with a comprehensive understanding of the

implementation of the Convention in the country concerned.

3. A State Party which has submitted a comprehensive initial report to the Committee need not, in its subsequent reports submitted in accordance with paragraph *(b)* of the present article, repeat basic information previously provided.

4. The Committee may request from States Parties further information relevant to the implementation of the Convention.

5. The Committee shall submit to the General Assembly, through the Economic and Social Council, every two years, reports on its activities.

6. States Parties shall make their reports widely available to the public in their own countries.

**Article 45**

In order to foster the effective implementation of the Convention and to encourage international co-operation in the field covered by the Convention:

1. The specialized agencies, the United Nations Children's Fund, and other United Nations organs shall be entitled to be represented at the consideration of the implementation of such provisions of the present Convention as fall within the scope of their mandate. The Committee may invite the, specialized agencies, the United Nations Children's Fund and other competent bodies as it may consider appropriate to provide expert advice on the implementation of the Convention in areas falling within the scope of their respective mandates. The Committee may invite the specialized agencies, the United Nations Children's Fund, and other United Nations organs to submit reports on the implementation of the Convention in areas falling within the scope of their activities;

2. The Committee shall transmit, as it may consider appropriate, to the specialized agencies, the United Nations Children's Fund and other competent bodies, any reports from States Parties that contain a request, or indicate a need, for technical advice or assistance, along with the Committee's observations and suggestions, if any, on these requests or indications;

3. The Committee may recommend to the General Assembly to request the Secretary-General to undertake on its behalf studies on specific issues relating to the rights of the child;

4. The Committee may make suggestions and general recommendations based on information received pursuant to Articles 44 and 45 of the present Convention. Such suggestions and general recommendations shall be transmitted to any State Party concerned and reported to the General Assembly, together with comments, if any, from States Parties.

## Part III

### Article 46

The present Convention shall he open for signature by all States.

### Article 47

The present Convention is subject to ratification. Instruments of ratification shall be deposited with the Secretary-General of the United Nations.

### Article 48

The present Convention shall remain open for accession by any State. The instruments of accession shall be deposited with the Secretary-General of the United Nations.

### Article 49

1. The present Convention shall enter into force on the thirtieth day following the date of deposit with the Secretary-General of the United Nations of the twentieth instrument of ratification or accession.

2. For each State ratifying or acceding to the Convention after the deposit of the twentieth instrument of ratification or accession, the Convention shall enter into force on the

thirtieth day after the deposit by such State of its instrument of ratification or accession.

**Article 50**

1. Any State Party may propose an amendment and file it with the Secretary-General of the United Nations. The Secretary-General shall thereupon communicate the proposed amendment to States Parties, with a request that they indicate whether they favour a conference of States Parties for the purpose of considering and voting upon the proposals. In the event that, within four months from the date of such communication, at least one-third of the States Parties favor such a conference, the Secretary-General shall convene the conference under the auspices of the United Nations. Any amendment adopted by a majority of States Parties present and voting at the conference shall be submitted to the General Assembly for approval.

2. An amendment adopted in accordance with Paragraph 1 of the present article shall enter into force when it has been approved by the General Assembly of the United Nations and accepted by a two-thirds majority of States Parties.

3. When an amendment enters into force, it shall be binding on those States Parties which have accepted it, other States Parries still being bound by the provisions of the present Convention and any earlier amendments which they have accepted.

**Article 51**

1. The Secretary-General of the United Nations shall receive and circulate to all States the text of reservations made by States at the time of ratification or accession.

2. A reservation incompatible with the object and purpose of the present Convention shall not be permitted.

3. Reservations may be withdrawn at any time by notification to that effect addressed to the Secretary-General of the United Nations, who shall then inform all States. Such

notification shall take effect on the date on which it is received by the Secretary-General.

**Article 52**

A State Party may denounce the present Convention by written notification to the Secretary-General of the United Nations. Denunciation becomes effective one year after the date of receipt of the notification by the Secretary-General.

**Article 53**

The Secretary-General of the United Nations is designated as the depositary of the present Convention.

**Article 54**

The original of the present Convention, of which the Arabic, Chinese, English, French, Russian and Spanish texts are equally authentic, shall be deposited with the Secretary-General of the United Nations.

In witness thereof the undersigned plenipotentiaries, being duly authorized thereto by their respective Governments, have signed the present Convention.

| *Country (South Asia)* | *Ratification on* |
|---|---|
| Bangladesh | 3 August, 1990 |
| Bhutan | 1 August, 1990 |
| India | 11 December, 1992 |
| Maldives | 11 February, 1991 |
| Nepal | 14 September, 1990 |
| Pakistan | 12 November, 1990 |
| Sri Lanka | 12 July, 1991 |

**Reservations**

*Bangladesh*

"[The Government of Bangladesh] ratifies the Convention with a reservation to Article 14, Paragraph 1."

"Also Article 21 would apply subject to the existing Jaws and practices in Bangladesh."

Objections to reservation recorded by Ireland and Portugal.

*India*

Declarations:

"While fully subscribing lo the objectives and purposes of the Convention, realizing that certain of the rights of the child, namely those pertaining to the economic, social and cultural rights can only be progressively implemented in the developing countries, subject to the extent of available resources and within the framework of international co-operation; recognizing that the child has to be protected from exploitation of all forms including economic exploitation, noting that for several reasons children of different ages do work in India; having prescribed minimum ages for employment in hazardous occupations and in certain other areas; having made regulatory provisions regarding hours and conditions of employment; and being aware that it is not practical immediately to prescribe minimum ages for admission to each and every area of employment in India- the Government of India undertakes to take measures to progressively implement the provisions of Article 32, particularly Paragraph 2(a) in accordance with its national legislation and relevant international instruments to which it is a State Party.'

*Pakistan*

Reservation made upon signature and confirmed upon ratification: 'Provisions of the Convention shall be interpreted in the light of the principles of Islamic laws and values.'

Objections to reservation recorded by Finland, Ireland, Norway, Portugal and Sweden.

The reservation by Pakistan was withdrawn on 23 July 1997.

*APPENDIX VI*

# LIST OF CONSTITUTION ARTICLES, ACTS AND CASES COUNTRY-WISE, AND MAJOR INTERNATIONAL AND REGIONAL CONVENTIONS

## Constitutions

***Bangladesh***

*Directive Principles of State Policy* Arts. 15, 17 and 25(1)

*Fundamental Rights*

Arts. 27, 28(1), 28(2), 28(3), 28(4), 32, 34, 39(1) and 39(2)

*Power of Judicial Review* Arts. 26(1) and 26(2)

***India***

*Directive Principles of State Policy*

Arts. 39, 45, 47 and 51

*Principles on Treaties*

Arts. 51 and 253

*Citizenship*

Art. 5

*Power of Judicial Review*

Art. 13

*Fundamental Rights*

Arts. 14, 15(1), 15(3), 19, 21, 23, 24 and 25

***Nepal***

*Fundamental Rights*

Arts. 11(1), 11(2), 11(3), 12(1), 12(2)(a), 13, 14(4), 16, 18, 19, 20 and 23

*Power of Judicial Review* Art 88

***Pakistan***

*Fundamental Rights*

Arts. 9, 11(1), 11(2), 11(3), 19, 20, 25(1), 25(2) and 25(3)

*Power of Judicial Review*

Arts. 184(3), 8(1), 8(2) and 8(3)

***Sri Lanka***

*Directive Principles of State Policy*

Arts. 27(12) and 27(13)

*Principles on Treaties*

Arts. 33, 27(15) and 157

*Fundamental Rights*
Arts. 10, 11, 12(1), 12(2), 12(4), *14*, 15, 17 and 27(2)
*Power of Judicial Review*
Arts 16(1), 120 and 126
Legislation
***Bangladesh***
Abandoned Children's (Special Provision) Order (1972)
Child Marriage Restraint Act (1929), as amended (1984)
Children's Act (1974)
Citizenship Act (1951)
Criminal Procedure Code (1898)
Cruelty to Women Ordinance (1983)
Dowry Prohibition Amendment Act (1984)
Family Court Act (1964)
Guardians and Wards Act (1890)
Maternity Benefits Ordinance (1939)
Muslim Family Law Ordinance (1961)
Oppression Against Women and Children Ordinance (1995)
Penal Code (1860)
Railways Act (1890)
Suppression of Immoral Traffic Act (1933)
***India***
Bonded Labour System Abolition Act (1976)
Child Labour Prohibition and Regulation Act (1986)
Child Marriage Restraint Act (1929), as amended (1978)
Citizenship (Amendment) Act (1992)
Citizenship Act (1955)
Criminal Procedure Code (1862), as amended (1973)
Divorce Act (1869)
Dowry Prohibition Act (1961), as amended (1986)
Employee State Insurance Act (1948)
Equal Remuneration Act (1976)
Evidence Act (1872)
Family Court Act (1984)
Guardians and Wards Act (1890)
Hindu Adoption and Maintenance Act (1956)
Hindu Marriage Act (1955)

Hindu Minority and Guardianship Act (1956)
Hindu Succession Act (1956)
Immoral Traffic Prevention Act (1956), as amended (1986)
Juvenile Justice Act (1986)
Majority Act (1875)
Maternity Benefits Act (1961)
Medical Termination of Pregnancy Act (1971)
Muslim Women (Protection of Rights on Divorce) Act (1986)
Penal Code (1860), as amended (1983)
Shariat Act (1937)
Special Marriage Act (1954)
Succession Act (1925)
***The Equal Remuneration Act (1976)***

***Nepal***

Children's Act (1992)
Civil Code Mutuki Ain (1963), as amended (1975)
Civil Rights Act (1957)
Factories Act (1959)
Human Traffic Control Act (1987)

***Norway***

Parents and Children Act (1981)
The Ombudsman for Children Act (1981)

***New Zealand***

Children and Young Persons and Families Act (1989)

***Pakistan***

Child Marriage Restraint Act(1929) Citizenship Act (1951)
Criminal Procedure Code (1898) Dowry Prohibition Act (1976) Employment of Children Act (1991) Family Court Act (1964)
Guardians and Wards Act (1890), Hudood (Zina) Ordinance (1979) Muslim Family Law Ordinance (1961)
Penal Code (1860)
Punjab Children's Ordinance (1983) Shariat Act (1991)

***Sri Lanka***

Adoption of Children Ordinance (1941), as amended (1964) (1977) (1992)
Age of Majority Ordinance (1865), as amended (1989)

Children and Young Persons Ordinance (1939)
Citizenship Act (1948)
Code of Criminal Procedure (1979)
Corporal Punishment Ordinance (1889)
Education Ordinancc (1939)
Employment of Women, Young Persons and Children Act (1956)
Evidence Ordinance (1895)
General Marriage Ordinance (1907)
Jaffna Matrimonial Rights and Inheritance Ordinance (1911)
Judicature Act (1978)
Juvenile Justice Act (1968)
Kandyan Law Ordinance (1938) Kandyan Marriage and Divorce Act (1952)
Maintenance Ordinance (1889), as amended (1972)
Marriage Registration Ordinance (1907)
Married Woman's Property Ordinance (1923)
Maternity Benefits Ordinance (1939), as amended 1978 and 1985 Matrimonial Rights and Inheritance Ordinance (1876)
Mediation Boards Act (1988) Minimum Wages Ordinance (1927) Muslim Marriage and Divorce Act (1951)
National Environmental Act (1980) Nitinighanduwa (1880)
Orphanages Ordinance (1941)
Penal Code (1883)
Penal Code Amendment Act (1995) Poor Law Ordinance (1939) Registration of Births Ordinance (1895)
Shop and Office Employees Act (1954) as amended (1985)
Vagrants Ordinance (1841) Widowers and Orphans Pension Act (1983)
Widows and Orphan's Pension Fund Ordinance (1898)
Wills Ordinance (1844)
Workmen's Compensation Amendment Act (1990)

***United Kingdom***

Children Act, England (1989)
Children and Young Person's Act (1933)

Congenital Disabilities (Civil Liability) Act (1976)
English Bastardy Act (1862)
Family Law Reform Act (1969)
Family Law Reform Act (1987)
Guardianship of Infants Act (4925)
Poor Relief Act (1601);
***United States of America***
Adoption Act (1926)
Child Labour Deterrence Act (1993) Stubborn Child Law (1646)

**Cases**

***Botswana***
Attorney General *v.* Unity Dow Court of Appeal Botswana (1991) Civil Appeal No. 4/91 (unreported).
India
Adam *v.* Gopalakrishnan AIR 1974 Mad. 232
Aiminisa *v.* Muktar Ahmed AIR 1975 All 67
Air India *v.* Nargesh Meerza AIR 1981 SC 1829
Ali Khan *v.* State of Uttar Pradesh AIR 1960 All 637
Amol Singh *v.* Kaur AIR 1961 Punj, 51
Ashish *v.* Tiwari AIR 1970 Del. 98
Bandua Mukti Morcha *v.* Union of India AIR 1984 SC 802
Batra *v.* Batra AIR 1986 Del. 149
Begum *v.* Begum AIR 1939 All 15
Besant *v.* Narayaniah 1914 ICR 38 Mad. 807
Bhat *v.* Bhat AIR 1961 Jammu & Kashmir 5
Chandran *v.* Venkatalakshmi AIR 1981 AP I
Choteylal *v.* Gajadhar Prasad AIR 1954 All. 717
Civil Rights Vigilance Committee, College of Law, Bangalore *v.* Union of India AIR 1983 Kant. 85
Devi v, Singh AIR I960 Punj. 326 Gandi Kota *v.* P.S. Sauta AIR 1967 AP 294
Ganguli *v.* State of West Bengal AIR 1958 SC 143
Gaurav Jain *v.* Union of India AIR 1990 SC 292:
Gajraj Singh *v.* Deohlu AIR 1952 All. 331

Golak Nath *v.* Punjab 1967 2 SCR 762

Inderjit *v.* State of Uttar Pradesh AIR 1979 SC 1867

Indira Jaisingh *v.* Union of India AIR 1989 Bom.

25 Jage Ram *v.* State of Haryana 1987 Ch Cr C 171

Jain *v.* The State AIR 1983 Del. 120 Kalla Maistry *v.* Kanniammal AIR 1963 Mad. 210

Keshavananda Bharati *v.* State of Kerala AIR 1973 SC 1461

Labourers Salal Hydro Project *v.* State of Jammu and Kashmir AIR 1984 SC 177

Lakshmi Kant Pandey *v.* Union of India AIR 1984 SC 469, AIR 1986 SC 276, AIR 1987 SC 232

Lakshmi *v.* Rao AIR 1983 Mad. 9 Latif Tawaif *v.* Prasad AIR 1940 All. 329

Mackinnon Mackenzie & Co. Ltd *v.* Audrey D'Cost, Labour Law Journal (1987) 536

Margahandhu *v.* Kothandarama AIR 1984 Mad. 270

Mehta *v.* State of Tamil Nadu JT 1990 SC 263

Mohamed Ahmed Khan *v.* Shah Bano AIR 1985 SC 945

Mohini Jain *v.* State of Karnataka, Judgements Today 1992 4 SC 292 Mohini *v.* Virendra Kumar 1977 3 SCC 513

Nallathampy *v.* Union of India 1983 4 SCC 598

Narayan *v.* State of Bihar 1988 2 SCALE 965

Nazeranbai *v.* State AIR 1957 Madhya Bharat 1

Olga Tellis *v.* Bombay Municipal Corporation AIR 1986 SC 180

Paras Ram *v.* State AIR I960 All. 479

Parikulangara *v.* Union of India 19S7 2 SCC 165

PUDR *v.* Union of India AIR 1982 SC 1473

Punjab and Puran Sinph *v.* State of Rajasthan 1984 Raj. LW 357 Rahimurissa *v.* Ismail AIR 1956 Hyd. 14

Rai Chand *v.* Bai AIR (1966) Mad. 173

Rajamma *v.* State of Kerala (1983) Labour and Industrial Cases 1400

Ramzan *v.* Taja AIR 3983 J & K 70

Ratlam Municipality *v.* Vardichand AIR 1980 SC 1622

Reddy *v.* Reddy AIR 1975 Kant 138

Santi Devi *v.* Gian Chand AIR 1956 Pun. 234

Saraswatibai *v.* Shripad (1941) Bom. 103

Sheela *v.* Jeevanlal AIR 1988 All. 275

Shiela Barse *v.* Secretary, Children Aid Society AIR 1987 SC 656

Shiela Barse *v.* Union of India AIR 1986 SC 1773, AIR 1988 SC 2211

Shrivas Kumar *v.* Chairman Selection Committee AIR 1987 Guj. 1987.

Singh *v.* Kaur AIR 1974 P & H 124

Singh *v.* Savitri Devi AIR 1982 Del. 458

Sodan Singh *v.* N. Delhi Municipal Committee AIR 1989 SC 1988

Sonia Zacheriah *v.* Union of India (1990) 1 KLT 130

State of Rajasthan *v.* Union of India 1977 3 SCC 334

State of Himachal Pradesh *v.* Ram Sharma 1986 2 SCC 68

Sukia *v.* Makha AIR 1919 All. 49

Sumitra Devi *v.* Chaudhary AIR 1988 SC 765

Thomas *v.* Thomas AIR 1990 Mad. 100

Tukaram and Another *v.* State of Maharashtra AIR 1979 SC 185

Unni Krishnan *v.* State of Andhra Pradesh 1993 1 SC 645

Virendra Singh *v.* State of Uttar Pradesh Int. LR 22 (1955)

Vishal Jeet *v.* Union of India AIR 1990 SC 1412

Ireland

In re M. An Infant 1946 IR 334 Byrne *v.* Ireland 1972 IR 241.

***Pakistan***

Atia Waris *v.* Sultan Khan (1959) PLD WP Lah. 205

Begum *v.* Ahmed 1968 PLD Lah 1112

Begum Rashida Patel and Others *v.* Federation of Pakistan Petition No. 515 of 1987

Constitutional Writ Petition No. 1 of 1988, Pakistan

Jehan Mina *v.* State Pakistan Journ. 1983 FSC

Rashida Begum *v.* Shahab Din 1960 2 PLD Lah 695

Warris Meah *v.* State PLD (1957) SC Pak. 157

Zohra Begum *v.* Latif Ahmed 1965 PLD WP Lah 695

South Africa

Calitz *v.* Calitz (1939) A D 56

Coatzee *v.* Meintjies 1976 (1) SALR 257

Meyer *v.* Van Niekerk 1976 (1) SALR 2525

Pinchin & Another *v.* Santam Insurance Co. Ltd 1963 (2) SA 254.

***Sri Lanka***

Abdul Cader *v.* Razik (1952) 54 NLR 201

Abdul Hameed *v.* Peer Cando (1911) 15 NLR 91

Ariyapala *v.* People's Bank 1986 1 Sri LR 338

Athukorale *v.* Alhukorale (1987) 1 Sri LR 388

Attorney General *v.* Reid (1964) 67 NLR 25

Blanche Anley *v.* Herbert Bois (1945) 46 NLR 466

Burhan *v.* Ismail 1978-1979 2 Sri LR 218

De Silva *v.* de Silva (1947) 49 NLR 73

De Silva *v.* Chairman Ceylon Fertiliser Corporation 1989 2 Sri LR 393

De Silva *v.* Juan Appu (1928) 29 NLR 417

Dissanayaka *v.* Sri Jayawardenapura University (1986) 2 Sri LR 256

Fernando *v.* Fernando (1968) 70 NLR 534

Ghouse *v.* Ghouse (1988) 1 Sri LR 25

Hameen *v.* Maliha Baby (1967) 70 NLR 405

In Re Evelyn Warnakulasuriya (1955) 56 NLR 525

Ivaldy *v.* Ivaldy (1956) 57 NLR 568

Kamalawathie *v.* de Silva (1961) 64 NLR 252

Karunawathie *v.* Wijesuriya (1980) 2 Sri LR 14

Kumari Menike *v.* Aluvihare (1989) 2 Sri LR 91

Leelawathie *v.* Minister of Defence and External Affairs (1965) 68 NLR 487

Lemesurier *v.* Lemesurier (1895) 1 NLR 160.

Madulawathie *v.* Wilpus (1967) 70 NLR 90

Mafthootha *v.* Thassim (1963) 65 NLR 547

Milton *v.* Baby Nona (1984) 1 Sri LR 61, (1985) 1 Sri LR 212

Pallitamby *v.* Saviriathumma (1969) 73 NLR 572

Perera *v.* University Grants Commission 1980 FRD (1) 103

Perumal *v.* Karumegam (1969) 74 NLR 334

Punchi Banda *v.* Seelawathie (1986) 2 Sri LR 414

Rajaratna *v.* Air Lanka Ltd 1987 2 Sri LR 128

Ramupillai *v.* Festus Perera (1991) 1 Sri LR 11

Re Sharmila Begum (1989) 2 Sri LR 239

Seneviratne *v.* University Grants Commission (1978-79-80) 1 Sri LR 182

Sepala Ekanayake *v.* Attorney General (1987) 1 Sri LR 107

Shanmugam *v.* Annamuttu (1964) 69 NLR 63

Silva *v.* Kainerishamy (1955) 57 NLR 567

Subair *v.* Isthika (1974) 77 NLR 397

Ummul Marzoona *v.* Samad (1977) 79 NLR 209

Vaithialingam *v.* Gnanapathipillai (1944) 46 NLR 235

Weragoda *v.* Weragoda (1961) 68 NLR 83

Wijesiriwardene *v.* Kumara (1989) 2 Sri LR 312

United Kingdom

Gillick *v.* West Norfolk and Wisbech Area Health Authority 1986 1 AC 112

R. *v.* Bourne (1930) I KB 687

Re D 1976 Fam. 185

Newton *v.* Edgerly (1959) 1 WLR 1031

Hewer *v.* Bryant 1970 QB 357

United States of America

Belotti *v.* Baird 443 US 622 (1979)

Brown *v.* Board of Education (1954) 347 US 483

Carey *v.* Population Services International 431 US 678 (1977) Goss *v.* Lopez (1975) 419 US 565 Hart *v.* Brown 289 A 2nd 386 (1982) In Re Green 292 A 2nd 387 (1972)

Planned Parenthood of Missouri *v.* Danforth 428 US 52 (1976)

Prince *v.* Massachusetts 1944 321 US 158

Re Gaull 387 US 1 (1967) Roe *v.* Wade 410 US 113 (1973)

Stone *v.* Grahame 449 US 39 (1980)

Tinker *v.* Des Moines Independent School District 393 US 503 (1969). Tremble *v.* Gordon 430 US 762 (1977)

Wallace *v.* Jaffree 472 US 38 (1985) Wisconsin *v.* Yoder 406 US 205 (1972)

International And Regional Conventions And Instruments

Convention on Night Work (1919)

Convention for the Suppression of the Traffic in Women and Children (1921)

Declaration on Children's Rights (1924)

Geneva Protocols (1925) (1977) Slavery Convention (1926)

Universal Declaration of Human Rights (1948)

Convention on the Suppression of Traffic in Persons and of the Exploitation of the Prostitution of Others (1949)

Geneva Conventions (1949) European Convention for the Protection of Human Rights and Fundamental Freedoms (1950)

ILO Convention No. 103 (1952), supplemented by Recommendation No. 95 (1952)

UN Convention on the Nationality of Married Women (1957)

UN Declaration on the Rights of the Child (1959)

Convention on Consent to Marriage, Minimum Age of Marriage and Registration of Marriage (1962)

Convention on the Elimination of All Forms of Racial Discrimination (1965)

International Covenant on Economic, Social and Cultural Rights (1966) International Covenant on Civil and Political Rights (1966)

ILO Convention No. 138 (1973) Convention on the Elimination of All Forms of Discrimination Against Women (1979)

UN Convention against Torture (1984)

Vienna Convention on the Law of Treaties (1986)

UN Convention on the Rights of the Child (1989)

African Charter on the Rights and Welfare of the Child (1990)

World Declaration on the Survival, Protection and Development of Children (1990)

World Summit on Children (1990).

*ANNEXURE VII*

## THE CONVENTION ON THE RIGHTS OF THE CHILD

The Convention on the Rights of the Child was adopted without a vote by the UN General Assembly on November 20th, 1989, exactly 30 years after the adoption of the Declaration of the Rights of the Child, and 10 years after the International Year of the Child. This anchored the moral obligation, enshrined in the 1924 Geneva Declaration and the 1959 Declaration on the Rights of the Child, in so-called hard law. The protection rights in these declarations were rephrased in much more practical terms, and children were no longer regarded as beings who are "not yet" (adults), but as fully-fledged individuals with their own meaning-making. The Convention led to the first faltering steps towards recognizing children "as human beings."[1]

Less than one year later, it intered into force on September 2nd, 1990. At the moment 191 states have already ratified it. Almost a universal ratification, since only Somalia and the USA are lacking. The Convention can be regarded as a historic milestone. On the one hand, it is the culmination of a difficult struggle over a decade, aiming at improving children's situation in society, on the other, it is the beginning of a new way of dealing with children. Hence a new child-image gains in strength an image which assumes that children are to be regarded as individuals with fundamental human tights, and is reflected clearly in recent (draft) legislation and case law. Human rights have now formally been granted to children. Enshrining these rights in positive law is however not the end of the matter. Central to the debate is the relationship between the law and education. Educational science, teaching us how to deal with children, is all about human (children's) rights.

The Convention did not appear out of the blue, however. For some considerable time there had been a great deal of controversy about our relationship with children. Why? There are many explanations. In the brief space of this Article I shall attempt to describe two fundamental developments: on the one hand, our *child-image* which has been undergoing change over the last decade and, on the other, the development of a more global *human rights project* since World War Two. Finally, I shall run over the main issues dealt with in the Convention.

**Our Changing Child-Image[2]**

In essence one can say that until about the end of the Middle Ages there was little or no social awareness of children as a social group. As a separate social category they did not exist at all. Given very high mortality, until they were six or seven their main task was to try to survive. After this age, they disappeared into the world of adults.

This was reflected in the law children simply did not exist, and where they did, they were regarded as their father's private property and... treated like any other goods.

We had to wait until the Enlightenment (18th century), with its belief in the supremacy of Reason, before children were discovered as a social group. Since then, they have been considered the "future makers" of the Enlightened Society. They became "tomorrow's prosperity". This stress on "the future" and "progress" turned children into "not yet" human beings: they do not yet know, are not yet able to, are not yet. Their master status became one of not-yet-being and as such they came to be regarded as a separate social category. Or as Janusz KORCZAK, the great Polish-Jewish Pediatrician, put it at the beginning of the century, because of this dictate of the "future" children gradually lose their "right to the present"[3]

Specific laws and institutions were invented to force the new enlightened moral tasks on children and those responsible for them (parents, teachers,..).

At the beginning or the 20th century, practically simultaneously, in almost all Western countries "child protection laws" (social control) and "compulsory education" (socialization) were introduced. This far-reaching macro-social definition had numerous consequences for children·

- These specific laws and institutions at the same time excluded children from the world and locked them up in a world of their own. They ended up in a kind of limbo, where they had to wait, learn and prepare themselves for "real" life;
- Children became more and more the property of the state and less and less the private property of their father/parents. They were turned into objects by a macro-social process designed to achieve the ideal society of the future.

This is the child-image with which we enter the twentieth century. In fact, it has been further reinforced, and children's stay in limbo (the period of their not-yet-being) extended. In some European countries this period of not-yet-being has even been extended beyond the age of majority.

National legislation reflects this status of the child as object, also found in international rules. The 1924 Geneva Declaration particularly, and, to a lesser extent, also the'1959 Declaration on the Rights of the Child regard the child not as subject but as object. This is clearly demonstrated by the terminology used: "The child shall be given ..."

However over the last few decades, things have changed. The year 1962, when H. Kempe launched the notion of the battered child syndrome, can be considered a turning point. The status of not-yet-being was finally challenged for a variety of reasons by different people from various sectors and levels of society.[4]

The main aim of the school of thought which became known as the Children's Rights Movement was to have children considered as fully-fledged citizens. They argued for children to be regarded as individuals with their own human rights and as competent to exercise them independently. This was new. Indeed we must not forget that the Universal Declaration of Human Rights (1948) does not regard age as a criterion for non-discrimination. In fact over the last few years there has been a growing consensus that children should to be regarded as independent individuals, as bearers of rights. There is, however, still a lot of controversy about their (legal) capacity to exercise their rights independently. The most fundamental, recurring argument against autonomous rights for children is their supposed incompetence to take well-founded decisions. According to this view children are not sufficiently mature physically, intellectively and emotionally and they lack the necessary experience to make a rationed judgement on what is and is not in their interest. In the debate on children's lights, a central role is in fact played by this competence argument. Its validity, soundness and relevance are disputed. However, even among advocates of increased competence for children there are a variety of trends, deriving from the position taken in this debate.

## SECTION 1. A Reformist Trend

First of all there is a trend which regards the arguments in favor of incompetence as valid, but is of the opinion that our society seriously underestimates children's capacity to take well-founded, rational decisions. The supporters of this view feel children acquire this capacity much younger than is generally assumed, and that this capacity is gradually acquired. Hence, they argue in favor of lowering the age of majority and of the gradual acquisition of rights by children.[5]

## SECTION 2. A Radical Trend

The children's liberationists, on the other hand, dispute the validity of die incompetence arguments on moral grounds; their basic principle (the highest moral standard) is equality of all people. Any form of discrimination, including therefore discrimination on the basis of age, is considered morally wrong. To them granting children all human rights is the only solution.[6]

## SECTION 3. A Pragmatic Trend

A third trend is increasing importance. Supporters of

this trend wonder why it would not be possible, in practice, to grant children all civil rights, including the right to exercise them autonomously, unless it can be proven they are incompetent co exercise certain rights, and there is general agreement on this ("children have ail rights unless...").[7] Experience with adults shows this is perfectly possible. The main advantage compared to the present situation would be that the burden of proof is reversed. At the moment children are in a much weaker position because the burden of proof lies with them. They have to demonstrate they are entitled to self-determination (children have no rights unless...).

The outcome of the debate on competence ought to be that it is essential that children's right to self-determination be recognized *in order to* make them more competent and not the other way around: that their right to self-determination be (gradually) recognized because (step-by-step) they have gained more competence.

Therefore, the present situation has become somewhat confused and, at times, even paradoxical. Indeed our relationship with children is still based on the dominant child-image, while, simultaneously, the new one is gaining ground. The Convention on the Rights of the Child reflects this situation. "The child shall have the right to..." is a new form of words, referring directly to the child as subject. The Convention also grants general human rights in its Articles 12–16, 12 being a key article, recognizing the child as a fully-fledged participant in society.

**CHAPTER 2: The Human Rights Project**

The right to participate in democratic decision-making, to self-determination and to exercise rights independently are important human rights. The onthological view is that children as human beings are entitled to all human rights. Human rights have therefore become a point of reference in the debate on children's situation in society.

From this point of view, granting children's rights to

children too forms part of much wider changes which began to take effect internationally especially after World War Two.

**SECTION 1. Internationalization**

At first human rights were to be found in the legislation and constitutions of most Western countries. Although the ideas had gained international acceptance, human rights remained a matter for national concern. The League of Nations (1920) was the first real attempt at internationalization. Its major concern, avoiding the recurrence of war, is characteristic of a mainly re-active (defensive) approach: avoiding human rights abuses. This is exemplified by the Geneva Declaration adopted by the League of Nations m 1924. It would take until after the Second World War for the internationalization of the human rights project really to take off, with the setting up of the UN (1945). This also involved a change of course, since as of now a pro-active (offensive) approach predominated. In fact, the UN Charter (the international community's constitution) not only mentions human rights explicitly, but emphasizes that respect for human rights is the best guarantee for peace and democracy. In other words, people had started dreaming of a more democratic world order. This meant not only fighting human rights abuses, but making efforts to improve people's living conditions to promote human dignity. In this way for the first time human, lights were tackled pro-actively and received an international base in law, as in the Universal Declaration of Human Rights, approved on December 10th, 1948. In 1966, the Universal Declaration was further elaborated in two separate treaties: the international Covenant on Economic, Social and Cultural Rights and the International Covenant on Civil and Political Rights. These three instruments together are called *The International Bill of Human Rights.*

Subsequently more and more declarations and treaties have been adopted which concern on the one hand *specific groups* (children, women, refugees, the stateless, workers...)

and on the other *specific problems* (genocide, war crimes, torture, racial discrimination' ...).

Besides universal instruments there are also *regional human rights instruments.* They are adopted by and on behalf of extensive areas (Europe, Africa, America) where there is, theoretically at least, a greater degree or cultural identity. In fact, the ambition of achieving universal human rights, assuming this to be possible, often leads to vague and imprecise wording (in order to achieve a consensus), making it difficult to turn these rights into positive rules, precisely-defined (for the purposes of the law). The best-known and most influential instrument in Europe is the European Convention on die Protection of Human Rights and Fundamental Freedoms, in force in the 41 members states of the Council of Europe.

## SECTION 2. Three Generations of Human Rights

Modern ideas on human rights gradually evolved as of the eighteenth century. *The first generation* of human rights came about mainly through the American (1776) and French (1789) revolutions. We are thinking fee mainly of the Declaration of the Rights of Man and of the Citizen (1789), which contained *traditional civil and political rights,* such as the right to freedom of opinion, freedom of the press, the right of assembly, the right to life, etc ... They could be described as the first defensive weapons against sovereign rulers. The state is to abstain from interference in the (private) life of its citizens.

The *second generation* of human rights displays a far more offensive attitude to the state. Abstention from exaggerated interference (first generation) is now complemented by an urgent appeal to a sense of social responsibility on the part of the state. Recognizing *economic, social and cultural human rights* (right to a minimum income, work, health care, education, leisure….) means the state has to act. The second generation, dealing in essence with *social justice,* was enshrined in legally binding texts for the first time in the Russian Constitution (1918).

In the last few years, there has been more and more talk of *peoples' rights,* a third generation of human rights. Here we are dealing with so-called *solidarity rights,* such as the right to peace, a healthy environment, cultural integrity, self-government, etc. Debate about the actual shape and content of these new rights is still going on. For instance, in the summer of 1992, under the auspices of the UN, a world conference on the environment and development (UNCED) took place in Rio, resulting, inter alia, in international texts containing rules on to third generation human rights.

**SECTION 3. From a Moral Code to a Legally Binding Instrument**

Rapid translation of *declarations* into legally binding *treaties* (sometimes called "hard law") is also extremely important.

The first far-reaching international treaty was adopted as early as November 4th, 1950 in Rome: the "European Convention on the Protection of Human Rights and Fundamental Freedoms" (the ECHR for short). It entered into force on September 3rd, 1953- All 41 member states of the Council of Europe have signed and ratified it.

The ECHR deals mainly with the political rights of freedom and equality contained in the Universal Declaration, Implementation of the ECHR is monitored by the European Court of Human Rights, based in Strasbourg. Proceedings can only be instituted at the European Court provided alternatives offered by national legal systems have been exhausted.

The Court's rulings are binding on member states (*e.g.* the Bouamar and Marckx rulings on minors). In this sense the ECHR is the very first binding human rights instrument.

Besides the ECHR and the European Social Charter, in this context we also have to mention the extremely important treaties adopted by the UN in1966: the International Covenant on Economic, Social and Cultural Rights , and the Covenant on Civil and Political Rights. This treaty provided an interstate right to complain against infringements of the Treaty: an additional, optional protocol establishes an individual right to complain. The UN Committee on Human Rights is in-charge of international monitoring of this treaty. The Committee is made up of 18 independent experts, who deal with reports submitted by states on steps taken to implement the treaty, and with notification of infringements under the terms of the Optional Protocol. These Covenants round off translation of the content of the Universal Declaration into legally binding rules. They can therefore be considered the most important human rights instruments.

Although in principle the ECHR and the UN Covenants should also apply to children (and practical application of the Covenants to children has only just begun), in 1989, the international community decided to draw up a separate Convention on the Rights of the Child to be approved and ratified by the member states of the UN. Again a legally binding instrument.

### CHAPTER 3: The Unconvention on the Rights of the Child[8]

Events surrounding the UN Convention on the Rights of the Child reflect wider changes in society. In fact, in the last few decades there has been growing support for giving children a fully-fledged position in society. Moreover, the concept of *human rights* was introduced in the debate surrounding this issue: "Children are human beings, therefore they are entitled to all human rights". However, the debate on their (legal) competence to exercise these rights independently is not yet over and questions often are raised as to the usefulness and/or necessity of a separate convention on the rights of the child.

The consequence of all of this is that the present situation is rather confused. On the one hand our old child-image is as forceful and dominant as ever, while on the other children are regarded as entitled to human rights.

It is therefore not surprising that in the new Convention on the Rights of the Child, adopted in 1989, we find both (opposing) child-images. The reader will notice how this essential question (do human rights apply to children as well?) hovered in the background throughout the whole genesis of the UN Convention on the Rights of the Child.[9]

## SECTION 1. Content of the Convention

The text evolved from a declaration (1924) made up of a preamble and five points, to a declaration (1959) with a preamble and 10 principles, to a convention (1989) with an extensive preamble (13 paragraphs) and no less than 54 (!) separate articles.

The preamble contains the main principles of the Convention. The articles can be subdivided into three main parts:

(1) Arts. 1-41: the substantive articles, defining the rights of the child and obligations on states parties ratifying the convention.

(2) Arts. 42-45: procedures for monitoring implementation of the Convention.

(3) Arts. 46-54: formal provisions governing entry into force of the Convention.

Below we shall briefly examine the content of the preamble and the three parts of the Convention.

### 1. Preamble

A preamble explains the background to, and the reasons for, the convention. Hence the preamble does not contain binding principles, but gives a frame of reference, in the light of which the articles are to be interpreted.

The preamble co the Convention on the Rights of the Child refers to:

- the principles of the UN Charter (1945), the Universal Declaration of Human Rights (1948) and the international Covenants on Human Rights (1966);
- the conviction that families should be afforded special protection, and that children should grow up in a family environment, in an atmosphere of happiness, love and understanding;
- the conviction that the child should be brought up in the spirit of the ideals proclaimed in the UN Charter, and in particular in the spirit of peace, dignity, tolerance, freedom, equality and solidarity;

- bearing in mind the need to extend particular care to children, as stated in the Geneva Declaration on the Rights of the Child (1924), and the Declaration of the Rights of the Child (1959), as recognized in the Universal Declaration of Human Rights (1948), International Covenants on Human Rights (1966), several other conventions and the statutes of specialized agencies and other declarations (such as the 1985 Beijing Rules on the Administration of Juvenile Justice);
- recognition that there are children living in exceptionally difficult conditions, and that such children need special consideration;
- the importance of tradition and peoples' cultural values in protecting children and ensuring their harmonious development;
- the importance of international cooperation.

## 2. Rights Guaranteed by the Convention

The rights guaranteed by the convention are covered by Articles 1 to 41. Here we find all those individual or operational articles dealing with the rights of children or others' obligations to them. Considering each article separately would be too much. Furthermore, a subdivision of rights into different categories would be in breach of the spirit of the Convention, which makes no distinction between the different rights, and establishes no hierarchy. Indeed, the intention of bringing them all together in one comprehensive instrument was precisely to indicate that they were all equally important and even interdependent. In other words no one of these rights can stand alone.

### A. General Provisions

First of all, in article one we find the definition of the child: "For the purposes of the present Convention a child means every human being below the age of 18 years". This text also contains the extremely complex and delicate procedure, for reconciling opposing views on protection of the child before birth (explained in the preamble with a text between inverted commas). It is debatable, of course, whether an international convention, involving 191 countries, is a suitable instrument for attempting to agree on an issue - which still causes division within many countries.

We must also mention Article 3, which states that the *best interests of the child* must be the primary consideration in all decisions concerning the child, and that the state must provide appropriate assistance if parents, or others legally if responsible, fail in their duties.

In this context, Articles 5 and 18 are also extremely important. Article 5 stipulates that states undertake to respect the right arid responsibility of parents to provide direction and guidance in the exercise by the child of the rights recognized in the Convention. In addition, Article 18 states that both parents are jointly responsible for the upbringing and development of the child. The state undertakes to render appropriate assistance where necessary. Additional to this it is of importance that the Committee on the Rights of the Child, the treaty-based monitoring body, underlines four fundamental provisions, which are to be the guiding principles for examining other articles: non-discrimination (article 2), the best interest of the child (Article 3), the right to life , survival and development (Article 6), respect for the views of the child (Article 12).

## B. Possible Subdivisions

### I. Traditional Subdivision of Human Rights

The rights of the child, recognized by the Convention, can be subdivided in five headings in line with the traditional classification of human rights:

(a) *Civil rights:* In general, these correspond to the rights recognized by the first 18 articles of the Universal Declaration of Human Rights (1948). Examples are the right to a name and to acquire a nationality (Article 7) and the right to an identity (Article 8); the right to life (article 6) and the principle of non-discrimination

(Article 2). But there are also the so-called "integrity rights", such as the ban on torture (Article 37), the right to protection from physical violence (Articles 19 and 34); from arbitrary arrest (Articles 37 and 40), the right to privacy (Article 16), ...

(b) *Political rights:* These cover freedom of opinion (Article 12), freedom of association (Article 15), freedom of opinion, religion and conscience (Article 14), freedom of access to information (Article 17). Note should be taken that in the Universal Declaration the heading Political Rights also covers the right to vote and the right to stand for election.

(c) *Economic rights:* Article 4 states in general terms that states parties shall take all appropriate legislative, administrative and other measures regarding economic, social and cultural rights. More specifically this involves the right to be protected from exploitation (Articles 32 and 36).

(d) *Social rights:* Again Article 4. This heading also covers the right to education (Articles 28 and 29), health care (Article 24), and social security (Article 26).

(e) *Cultural rights:* In addition to Article 4 once again, in this context we need to mention Article 31, recognizing the right Co rest and leisure, to engage in play and to participate fully in cultural and artistic life. The rights recognized by the Convention clearly coincide with traditional human rights.

## 2. Subdivision According to Objectives

The Convention has 3 main objectives:

(a) *Right of Self-determination:* A number of universal human rights are now explicitly recognized and therefore confirmed as applying to children. This was uncontroversial in the case of certain rights, such as the right to protection form torture. Others were much contested (sec above on debate during preparation of the Convention).

(b) *Right to protection:* The Convention contains a number

of provisions addressing the special needs or children and especially of their vulnerability, e.g. conditions of employment for children (Article 32). A number or these provisions impose more stringent requirements in the case of children than general human rights instruments,

(c) *Specific rights:* There are rights which apply specifically or even exclusively to children: the right not to be separated from then parents (Articles 9, 10 and 11), and provisions regarding adoption (Article 21), The best example under this heading is Article 31, recognizing the right to engage in play.

The Convention also aims to afford protection for specific categories of children: refugees (Article 22), handicapped children (Article 23), minorities (Article 30) and children caught up in armed conflicts.

**3. The three P's**

It is possible to subdivide in other ways, *e.g.* one commonly used, the 3 P's.

— *Provision*: Rights providing access to certain goods and services (education, healt care, ...).
— *Protection*: The right to be protected from certain activities (maltreatment, exploitation, ...).
— *Participation:* The right to act in certain circumstances and the right to participate.

Each subdivision throws a different light on the Convention. The first demonstrates that children have very few political rights. The three P's approach shows that the lions share of their rights are to social services and protection. If one looks at the Convention from the point of view of its objectives, the right to self-determination is placed at the forefront. It is also important to note Article 41, which states that if provisions of the Convention coincide with those of other international laws, or the laws of states parties, it is in all circumstances those provisions offering the highest standard which shall take precedence.

**SECTION 2. Entry into Force and Monitoring**

Although the Articles on monitoring (Articles 42-45) and entry into force of the Convention (Articles 46-54) are obviously an integral part of it, we will deal with them separately from the substantive articles. This should not, however, be regarded as an implication that they are of less importance, as we shall soon see.

**1. Entry into Force**

A convention can only become legally binding after certain conditions have been met. These conditions are indicated in the Convention. The Convention on the Rights of the Child, like other such texts, had also to complete the essential procedure of ratification by states parties. Ratification is the legal procedure, whereby the competent body of the state party—in most cases its Head of State-confirms the international agreement and accepts the obligations it imposes. Ratification involves a number of steps.

It goes without saying that the convention must first of all be adopted. The Convention on the Rights of the Child was adopted by the UN General Assembly on 20th November, 1989, whereupon it was opened for signature, ratification or accession.

Owing to active lobbying by the NGO Group which had already been closely involved in drafting the text, during the official ceremony in New York on 26th January, 1990 the Convention was immediately signed by 61 countries. In accordance with Article 46, the Convention remained open for signature by other states.

However, signing a Convention entails no more than a moral obligation. By signing it, the state indicates its intention to ratify the convention and hence to take all necessary steps in line with national legislation. The state also accepts a moral obligation not to take measures in breach of the convention in the period between signature and formal ratification.

Obviously formal ratification is the more important step.

In the case of the Convention on the Rights of the Child, instruments of ratification are lodged by States Parties with the UN Secretary General.

Article 49, 2 states that the Convention shall enter into force in a particular country on the thirtieth day after that state lodges its instruments of ratification. Furthermore Article 49, 1 state that the Convention will enter into force only on the thirtieth day following the date on which the twentieth set of instruments of ratification is lodged. Again owing, in part, to intensive lobbying by the NGO's, this minimum number was quickly reached, and on September 2nd, 1990 the Convention officially entered into force.

Since that date it has been ratified by 191 countries. Obviously the Convention remains open for accession by other states even now.

As we have said, after formal adoption of the Convention, the NGO Ad Hoc Group members began lobbying to speed up ratification, (to teach the number of 20 ratifications as soon as possible).

UNICEF and DCI played an important pare in this process. Article 51 stipulates that states are allowed enter make reservations on ratification, although reservations incompatible with the object and purpose of the Convention are not permitted. It is also important to note that states parties may propose amendments. Any amendment adopted by a majority of states parties shall be submitted to the UN General Assembly for approval. When accepted by a two-thirds majority of states parties, amendments become binding only on those states parties who Voted in favour (see art. 50).

## 2. Monitoring

We have already said that conventions are so-called "hard law", in other words legally binding. When a state joins a convention (*i.e.* ratifies it), it enters into an international agreement with the other states parries. Along with the others, it accepts the obligation to put into practice the provisions of the convention. The legal principle "pacta sum servanda" therefore also applies to international treaties between states.

A problem arising here, is in other areas of international law is monitoring. Because there is no supra-national body (yet) effectively monitoring implementation of international law, each convention contains provisions on monitoring. In fact, if there is no provision for effective monitoring of a convention, it remains binding only on paper.

Each convention being only as effective as its monitoring system, the Convention on the Rights of the Child also provides its own system to ensure implementation by states parties.

The Convention provides for monitoring of implementation to be carried out by a special body, the Committee on the Rights of the Child (Articles 42-45). The Committee- made up of ten independent experts- is to monitor "progress made by states parties in achieving the realization of the obligations undertaken in the Convention. For this purpose, within two years after ratification (and thereafter every fife years) states parties have to report to the Committee on the rights of the child in their country (Article 44, 1). Moreover, the authors of the Convention on the Rights of the Child opted for advice and assistance to support implementation, in order to achieve one of their main objectives: bringing about a "positive" monitoring climate. Thus, in their reports, states parties can request technical advice and assistance to enable them to apply certain provisions of the Convention. This was meant to turn reporting into an active means of improving children's situation rather than just a passive means of monitoring implementation.

**SECTION 3. Normative Value**

As we have already said, most international conventions require transposition into national legislation, since they are binding only on states parties and not on their citizens. Self-executing international conventions (such as the ECHR) are an exception to this rule: they can be invoked directly in national courts, without the need for national legislation. This is only the case if the national constitution provides the self-executing force.

We have already discussed the fact that the text approved in 1989 is a convention: unlike the 1959 Declaration, it is therefore binding on states parties, who have an obligation to implement the Convention within their own borders. If necessary, they must take legislative measures.

The situation is different when individual citizens attempt to enforce rights guaranteed by the Convention in a national court. This is where the question arises of the Convention's *direct effect, i.e.* its self-executive nature, arises. Whether the Convention can be applied directly depends on a number of factors, including some outside the Convention itself. First of all to be directly enforceable in a national court die Convention must have been *ratified.* Therefore ratification of the Convention is important both in a national and in an international context. Secondly, the state involved must have recognized the principle of direct applicability of international conventions in its own legislation. States recognizing this principle can express this in different ways.

Finally, the convention has to be suitable for direct application.

Therefore, to find out whether individuals can directly invoke the Convention on the Rights of the Child, we must examine the text more closely.

If a convention is to be directly applicable, its content must meet a number of conditions, *e.g.* it must be clear and comprehensive. If the text requires further elaboration before it can be used in a national court, this is work to be done by the national legislator.

Subjective rights guaranteed by the Convention will therefore be closely studied in every state party to determine whether they can be invoked directly. Because the terminology used in convention texts varies considerably, we must now take a closer look at terminological differences.

**Binding Declarations**

In the Convention there are a number of provisions which are obviously legally binding. These are the provisions which can be invoked in court in those countries which recognize the Convention's direct effect. Te text's binding nature comes out in expressions such as "recognize", "undertake", "respect", "ensure" and "guarantee". These expressions are used mostly in Articles which confirm existing rights or freedoms (e.g. the non-discrimination principle in Article 2).

**Statement of Intent**

Provisions containing expressions such as "promote"', "encourage", "use their best efforts", "strive" are to be considered statements of intent rather than binding measures.

**Appropriate Measures**

Many provisions refer to undertakings by states parties to take "appropriate" measures Terminology may even vary: appropriate measures, appropriate legislative and administrative measures", "appropriate legislative, administrative and other measures", etc.

The Convention on the Rights of the Child contains provisions referring both to first generation human rights and to those of the second generation. Hence the differences in terminology. Binding provisions refer to traditional first generation freedoms. They impose bans on states, requiring them to abstain from doing certain things. Provisions governing social, economic and cultural rights refer to positive obligations on states, which undertake to do certain things. These are so-called "appropriate measures".

We find the same terminological distinction between first and second generation human rights in other human rights instruments. The 1966, Covenant on Civil and Political Rights, for instance, contains mainly binding provisions, while the Covenant on Social, Economic and Cultural Rights refers mainly to intentions.

Attentive readers will have noticed that in some cases the three terminological categories appear in one and the same Article. In the case of economic, social and cultural rights, for instance, there are both expressions entailing obligations for states parties and others calling for appropriate measures to be taken. We find the same combination in Articles covering special categories of children. Where the Convention deals with specific rights, we find both declarations of intent and legally binding expressions.

Very often in the end it is case law which determines whether certain provisions can be invoked in national courts by individuals.

There is in fact no the same enthusiastic reception everywhere for the idea that the Convention should be directly enforceable. First of all, there are very few provisions which can be enforced directly. Secondly, those provisions which are binding seem to do very little more than reconfirm rights and freedoms already enshrined in other conventions in other words they add nothing.

There is nothing wrong per se with reaffirming existing rights in a new convention. Indeed, in certain cases, provisions in the Convention on the Rights of the Child may shed new light on existing rights and freedoms. The Convention does not, of course, exist in a legal vacuum, it is quite possible to invoke the Convention on the Rights of the Child *together* with other conventions. In this way, the Convention on the Rights of the Child can make an important contribution to legal practice. Fundamental .rights, translated into national law can be refined and added to on the basis of its provisions. Article 12, quoted many times in this Article, giving children the right to express their views in all matters which affect them, is an example of such a possible case.

Much depends on the willingness and creativity of lawyers and magistrates in making the Convention enforceable by individuals. In this sense, the theoretical debate on the Conventions normative value can lead to practical application of children's rights, through accurate and careful interpretation of the Convention. Case law is expanding rapidly in a number of countries, offering hope for the future.

**Conclusion**

If children were regarded as people, and it was therefore regarded as normal for human rights to apply to them, there would be no problems. In principle all human rights conventions would also apply to children. A separate convention on children's rights would be superfluous, because children could refer to existing instruments to assert their rights. However this is not the case.

If children's competence were generally recognized, it would be sufficient to add "age" as a non-discrimination criterion to existing human rights instruments. Article 14 of the ECHR, covering non-discrimination, offers ample possibilities to do so: the text contains a reference to "other status", which could also be read as meaning "children". Were the European Court for Human Rights to interpret or use Article 14 in this way, the controversy over human rights and children would be considerably closer to being resolved. So far, however, this has not happened.

New universal and regional children's rights instruments are still being drafted while, simultaneously, both in law and in the courts, children's rights ate gradually being integrated into existing human rights.

The Convention on the Rights of the Child does not stare explicitly that human rights apply to children. However, for the first time in history, it does grant a number of fundamental human rights to children (Articles 12 to 16). This recognition of fundamental human rights for children is an important new element in the debate on children's right to self-determination. The debate on the distinction between human rights and children's rights is clearly still in its infancy.

The Convention is not the final word, but only the beginnings of a solution, though at the same time it is an important strategic factor giving new impetus to the debate.

Generally, it is assumed human rights "in principle" also apply to children, but there is no agreement on the principle of children's legal competence. In other words, the fundamental friction between *separate children's rights* and *general human rights* will be with us for some time to come.

Our changing child-image and the fledgling (even threatened) exploration of the human rights project appear to demonstrate growing respect for children. I am convinced that only re-acting to deficiencies in our relationship with children is insufficient; what we need is a pro-active approach aimed at improving our relationship with children. In this respect, the Convention on the Rights-of the Child offers an unprecedented challenge. By its almost universal ratification, by its comprehensiveness and by its legally binding character, it is even a never seen *global binding social contract.*

Monitoring in particular offers unique opportunities, both nationally and internationally, to make children's rights the focus of wide-ranging social and political debate.[10]

**References**

1. Text based on E. Verhellen, *Convention on the Rights of the Child. Background, Motivation, Strategies, Main Theme,* Leuven, Garant, 1997 - 2nd edition.
2. See also E. Verhellen, 'Changes in the Images of the Child', in M. Freeman and Ph. Veerman (eds.)., *The Ideologies of Children's Rights,* Dordrecht, Martimis Nijhoff Publishers (1992), pp. 79-94.
3. See among others: J. Korczak, *Das Rechtdes Kindes auf Achtung* (Herausgegeben von Elisabeth Heimpel and Mans Roos), Gottigen, Vandenhoeck und Ruprecht (1994),
4. This became clear during the first international Congress on Children's Ombudswork, See: E. Verhellen and F. Spiesschaert (eds.), *Ombudswork for Children: A Way of Improving the Position of Children in Society.* Leuven, Acco (1989).
5. See e.g. Resolution 72 (29) on die lowering of the age of full legal capacity, adopted by the Committee of Ministers of the Council of Europe on 19 September, 1972.
6. This approach is found mainly in the Anglosaxon Free

School Movement. See inter alia ADAMS, P., e.a., *Children's Rights, Towards the Liberation of the Child,* New York, Praeger, 1972.

COHEN, H., *Equal Rights for Children* Towata, Littlefield, Adams 6C Co, 1980.

FRASON, R., *Birth-Rights,* Harmondsworth, Penguin, 1974. GOODMAN, P., *Growing-up Absurd.* New York, Random House, 1960.

GOTTLIEB, D. (ed.), *Children's liberation,* Prentice Hall, Englewood Cliffs, 1973.

GROSS, B. and GROSS, R. (eds.). *The Children's Rights Movement,* New York, Anchor Press, 1977.

HOLT, J., *Escape from Childhood,* Harmondsworth, Penguin, 1975.

7. Sec e.g.: C. Ross, 'Of children and liberty: an historian's view, in *American Journal of Orthopsychiatry* (1982), vol. 52, nr. 3, pp. 470-480.

   V. Wordfold, 'A philosophical justification for children's rights', in *Harvard Educational Review,* (1974), vol. 44, nr. 1, pp. 142-157.
8. E. Verhellen, Convention on the Rights of the Child, Background, motivation, strategies main themes, Garant, Leuven/Apeldoorn, 1997 - 2nd edition.
9. See: C. Price-Cohen, 'The United Nations Convention on the Rights of the Child: the drafting process', in F. Verhellen (ed.), *Rechten van be Kind: Lezngenbundel* 2, Gent, Centrum voor de Rechten van het Kind, (1992), pp. 5-19.
10. See: E. Verhellen and F Spiesschaert (eds.). *Children's Rights: Monitoring Issues,* Gent, Publishers Mys en Breesch (1994).

    E. Verhellen, *Monitoring Children's Rights,* Kluwer Law International, The Hague, 1996.

*ANNEXURE VIII*

## THE REPORTING PROCEDURE OF THE CONVENTION ON THE RIGHTS OF THE CHILD(1)(2)

### Introduction

1. On November 20th, 1989, exactly thirty years after the adoption of the "Declaration of the Rights of the Child" (November 20, 1959), the General Assembly of the United Nations unanimously adopted the "Convention on the Rights of the Child". Whereas the Declaration of 1959 was only a statement of principles in which 10 main guidelines on the protection of the child were put forward,[3] the Convention of 1989 constituted a legally binding instrument. In some forty Articles, certain civil, political, social, economic and cultural rights of the child were guaranteed. The Convention entered into force on the 2nd September, 1990 having been ratified by 20 countries.

2. A treaty is a legally binding instrument. The agreeing countries undertake to fulfill the obligations of the treaty. To ensure the actual implementation of the agreement there are many possible means of control. The effectiveness of a "treaty will largely depend on the chosen control system:[4] a treaty is as effective as its monitoring system. This choice will be largely determined by the general aims of the treaty concerned. A system of control may indeed be purely sanctioning, but it may also have a stimulating, informative or helpful effect.

3. In this text we will discuss the monitoring system of the Convention on the Rights of the Child, as drawn up in Articles 42 to 45. This system, like every other monitoring mechanism, was established to verify the effective compliance of the States Parties with their legal international obligations. The States Parties are monitored by an international medium to see if they fulfill their established legal obligations. In this way, the monitoring system is a judicial mechanism. From the relevant Articles, the "travaux repertoires" and the viewpoints adopted by the Committee on the Rights of the

Child with respect to these, it appears however that more is expected from the monitoring system. It is hoped that the monitoring system will actively contribute to the improvement of the position of the child in general and that it will give occasion to a broad, social discussion within the various countries themselves. From the study of the Conventions' Articles and the working methods of the Committee, it will be clear that the Convention on the Rights of the Child offers many possibilities for the fulfillment of these objectives.

4. The framework in which the Convention on the Rights of the Child situated, deserves to be outlined before further examination of the monitoring system. The Convention on the Rights of the Child is, after all, only one instrument enacted by the United Nations concerning human rights. Alston writes "(...) sichaque regime conventional doitétre examiné individuellement compte tenu de ses normes et de ses procédures propres, les divers régimes ne peuvent pas étre, a certains égards, envisages indépendamment les uns des autres ou hors du programme plus large concernant les droits de I'homme dans lequel ils s'integrent".[5] This especially applies to an evaluation of the monitoring system for two reasons. On the one hand, the former human rights treaties often serve as an inspiration for the newer treaties. On the other hand, more and more people wish to coordinate the several procedures and organs, which were developed to monitor human rights, thus creating a more effective and more efficient unit.[6]

## I. The Implementation of Human Rights

### A. *The Activities of the UN Concerning Human Rights*

5. Traditionally, there are a number of phases recognized in the activities of the United Nations with respect to the human rights issue[7]. In the first phase (from 1947 to 1954) the "standard-setting" was most important. In the second phase, the promotion of human rights formed the most important agenda-point (1955–1966). In the third phase

attention was drawn mainly to the protection of human rights. Since the end of the eighties the efficiency and the effectiveness of the monitoring of the implementation of human rights comes more and more on the agenda of the United Nations; "In the 1990s, the pre-eminent human rights concern of the international community will be the establishment and development of effective procedures and mechanisms for sustained monitoring and for rapid and constructive responses to violations"[8]. This concern appears, among others, in the agenda of the "World Conference on Human Rights", which took place from the 14th to the 25th of June, 1993.[9] It is however clear that this evolution does not give an overall image of the human rights activities of the United Nations. The setting of standards, promotion and protection still remain important UN-activities, which for example is clear from the recent adoption of 2 Optional Protocols to the Convention on the Rights of the Child[10].

6. The recent attention drawn to the efficiency and effectiveness of the monitoring procedures is explained by the fact dint the United Nations, after a period of upwards development, now has reached a point of reflection where the objectives and means of the human rights program must be evaluated.[11] Parmentier speaks of the "mid-life crisis" of the United Nations.[12-13] This development is sharpened, according to the same author, by 1 number of important political developments on a world-wide level. After the fall of the Berlin wall, the international authorities did not appear to be able to guarantee human rights in Eastern Europe that has now become the battlefield of ethnic conflicts and civil wars. Neither in the young democracies of Latin-America (not to speak of Africa) does respect for human rights appear to gain support without problems.[14] The UN had to face recently its failures in dealing with the events in Somalia, Rwanda (and Sierra Leone).

7. The attention paid to the monitoring of the implementation of human rights is mainly focused on two topics: (1) the important increase in the number of UN control bodies and (2) the functioning (or malfunctioning) of the

several control bodies and monitoring methods.[15] It is indeed the case that more and more control mechanisms and control bodies have been established since 1947. Some consider this increase as a positive development, whereas other people think that this increase has led to less clarity and a lower efficiency.[16]

8. Quite recently, a lot of attention is being paid to the efficiency of the monitoring systems. This is why this study aims to screen the monitoring mechanisms of the Convention on the Rights of the Child. Before this study is undertaken, however, we must state that it will never be possible to completely examine to what degree a control system can have a positive influence on human rights: "too many factors influence progress in human rights to make it possible to document precisely the role of international supervisory systems."[17] The Convention on the Rights of the Child does however offer us, thanks to its recent development, a good opportunity to find out what the United Nations have already learned from the past and how the efficiency of the supervisory systems can be increased-in the future.

**B. *The Implementation of Human Rights and Monitoring Human Rights***

9. A treaty is an agreement made between States. From a judicial point of view, a State fulfills its international obligations towards other States and not towards individuals; the State is not responsible to the victim of the violation, but to other States Parties.[18] The provisions of a treaty can nevertheless have their influence on the national legal system. As far as States with a dualist constitutional system are concerned, a provision of a treaty can only acquire a judicial meaning in the national legal system once the provision is transformed into national law. In States with a monist constitutional system however, the treaties are directly integrated into the national legal system. International provisions can moreover gain a self-executing character in the latter type of countries. This implies chat individuals

can appeal to the provisions of a treaty when appearing in a national court.

10. The implementation of human rights accepted in international treaties is basically a national concern.[19] This is only natural for those States with the dualist constitutional system. Indeed, the provisions of a treaty must always be converted into internal law before they can have any legal meaning in the internal legal system of the country. The implementation, however, is also basically a national matter for those countries with a monist constitutional system. If is indeed the case that not all provisions of a treaty can acquire a self-executing character. The ratification of a treaty does not only involve the obligation of a State to enter the provisions in national law (as far as this is necessary), but the State is also obliged—to attune its national policy to the ratified provisions of the treaty (the so-called 'subsidiary principle').[20]

11. As a result, the implementation of human rights is first of all a matter of national legislation and policy. However, lots of mechanisms have been developed on an international level to make sure that the States do actually comply with their obligations. The role played by these international procedures is subsidiary in relation to the implementation of human rights by the national authorities.[21]

12. These international procedures have different objectives and functions. On the one hand, there are procedures through which legal enforcement of human rights is made possible on an international level. This is the less developed kind of procedure within the United Nations. Parmentier states that only the procedure for the international Court of Justice matches this description to a certain degree.[22] This category is more extended on a regional level. The European Court of Human Rights is for example qualified to pronounce judgments which are legally binding for the States that have ratified the European Convention on Human Rights. A person who cannot enforce his rights before a national judge can hence appeal to an international judge.

13. The intention of the other procedures is not to

judicially enforce human rights on an international level but to check and encourage the implementation by the States. UN activities concerning human rights are characterized by an amalgamation of similar procedures, such as: reporting procedures,[23] country procedures,[24] thematic procedures,[25] communications procedures[26] and confidential procedures such as e.g. procedure 1503[27]. Van Boven makes a distinction between the regular and the special supervisor' procedures'. The reporting system is a regular supervisory procedure. Thematic procedures, country procedures, communications procedures and procedure 1503[26] are special procedures.

14. Not only a great number of methods but also a large collection of bodies that are active in the field of human rights can be distinguished within the United Nations. Alston classifies these bodies, depending on their judicial basis.[28] He comes up with two kinds of bodies. On the one hand, there are the so-called "Charter-based organs". The 6 principal organs[29], the functional commissions of the Economic and Social Council[30] and the sub-commissions founded by these functional commissions[31] are classified in this group. The other group consists of those bodies that were established through specific treaties. This group constitutes the so-called "treaty-based organs". The latter group has gone through a huge expansion over the past thirty years and contains the following organs: the Committee on Elimination of Racial Discrimination, the Committee on Elimination of Discrimination against Women, the Human Rights Committee, the Committee against Torture, the Committee on Economic, Social and Cultural Rights, the Committee on the Protection of the Rights of All Migrant Workers and Members of their Families (the latter has not been composed because the Convention itself has not entered into force yet) and the Committee on the Rights of the Child. The "treaty-based organs" have a number of characteristics in common and, according to Alston, mainly distinguish themselves from the "Charter-based organs" as for as their mandate and attitude wide regard to the States are concerned.[32] The "treaty-based organs" bear the responsibility for monitoring the

implementation of the provisions of the treaties concerned. The "Charter-based organs" have a much broader mandate to promote awareness, to foster respect, and to respond to violations of human rights standards. The "treaty-based organs" mainly take a non-conflicting stance vis-a-vis the States Parties, whereas the "Charter-based organs" take strongly conflicting stances whenever needed.

15. The UN human rights apparatus hence consists of a rather opaque ensemble of procedures and organs. Quantity does however not necessarily entail quality. On the contrary. "The main difficulty is created by the pluralism of the systems. Many organs apply similar rules in a different manner. The same rule is interpreted differently. This creates a lack of confidence on the part of all those who place their trust in human rights,"[33] as Ermacora stares. The recent attention paid to die improvement of monitoring systems has therefore a lot to do with the vague nesses and overlaps that have arisen due to the extension of the control organs and monitoring systems. This is exactly the reason why a more intensive coordination is more and more being advocated.[34] Some people even advocate a complete reform of the reporting procedures by means of a fusion of all the different reporting obligations into one single reporting obligation.[35] In the latter case, the monitoring would be taken care of by one monitoring organ. As a result, the various "treaty-based organs" could be dissolved.[36]

16. According to Meron, the United Nations' human rights system is characterized by a weak and sporadic implementation.[37] This shortcoming could, in his opinion, be remedied by a precise formulation of human rights; "The weaker the implementation system, the greater the importance of a more precise formulation of human rights instruments."[38] An exact and clear formulation could indeed ensure that the provisions concerned acquire a self-executing character. Individuals would thus be able to enforce their rights in national court. It goes without saying that this is not possible for all rights and freedoms. This situation is in most cases only feasible for civil and political rights. More

problems will rise when social, economic and cultural rights are concerned.[39] A precise formulation of these rights will in many cases turn out to be impossible, since the economic possibilities of the potential States Parties must be taken into account.[40]

17. The nature of the rights that will constitute the subject of the implementation will also have to be taken into consideration when choosing a monitoring system. Civil and political rights can be formulated in a more precise way. The development of a "more jurisdictional" monitoring system will therefore not be excluded. A stimulating monitoring system will rather be opted for when the treaty contains social, economic and cultural rights. This became clear, for example, in the two Covenants of 1966. Valticos states: "The difference between the procedures laid down in the two Covenants has been explained by the face that the Covenant on Civil and Political Rights involves precise and immediate obligations, whereas that relating to economic, social and cultural rights is considered to be aiming at promoting the progressive observance of the recognized rights to the extent that the means available to the State permit. A procedure for consideration of claims had not, therefore, seemed appropriate for rights of this kind."[41] However, it should be noted that some evolutions have occurred in this field. Nowadays, the principle of indivisibility, interdependence and interrelatedness of the two sets of rights (civil and political, and economic, social and cultural) is stressed. The Committee on Economic, Social and Cultural Rights advocates for example the installation of a procedure for consideration of communications concerning non-compliance with the International Covenant on economic, social and cultural rights, and quite recently the Committee on the Rights of the Child seems to move in the same direction (see Para. 59).

18. The above shows that the way in which monitoring is carried out on the international level cannot be separated from both the nature and the formulation of the rights concerned. It is within this framework quite understandable

that the monitoring system of the Convention on the Rights of the Child, that comprises both civil and political rights on the one hand and social, economic and cultural rights on the other hand, is based on a reporting obligation for the States involved.

## II. The Monitoring Mechanism of the Convention on The Rights of the Child

### A. *General Philosophy of the Monitoring Mechanism*

19. The monitoring mechanism of the Convention on the Rights of the Child is included in Articles 42 to 45. The authors of the Convention did not consider it appropriate to develop a chastising and reprimanding control system. The stances taken by the non-governmental organizations, organized in an "ad hoc group", had a lot to do with this. The "ad hoc" group indeed wished to create a "positive atmosphere" surrounding implementation. The monitoring system had to be based on the idea of mutual help, support and cooperation.[42] This is why a complaints procedure was not developed in this convention. A monitoring mechanism, based on a reporting obligation for the States, was opted for. The Committee that was founded for this purpose does not only act in a controlling but also in an advising way. The dynamic character of the monitoring system of the Convention was stressed more than once in the course of the "travaux prepnratoires". For example: there were originally two proposals regarding the description of the general task of the Committee on the Rights of the Child: 1st "monitoring the implementation of the provisions of the obligations undertaken in the present Convention"; and 2nd "examining the progress made by States Parties in achieving the realization of the obligations undertaken in the present Convention". The authors finally adopted the second proposal since the dynamic character ("examining the progress") of the obligation to report would thus be explicitly entered in the Convention.[43]

20. The States Parties do not only have the obligation

to report but also an obligation to inform. Article 42 says that the States are to make the provisions of the convention public, both to adults and to children.[44] A real and actual exercise of rights by children presupposes in the first instance a certain knowledge of these rights. This is why it is of paramount importance to inform children of their rights on the one hand and to raise public awareness relating to a larger respect for the rights of the child on the other hand. This obligation to inform, which is an essential part of the provisions of the Convention, is quite original since the other treaties on human rights never mentioned a similar dissemination duty.[45] Moreover, Article 44 § 6 obliges the States to put their reports at the disposal of everybody in their country.[46] The population, the non-governmental organizations and other associations will thus be well-informed. This will enable them to contribute strongly to the improvement of the effective application of the Convention. The Committee was moreover resolved to encourage the States to publish the results of the dialogue with the Committee: "Recognizing the importance of this measure to encourage popular participation and to achieve a comprehensive national approach to the implementation process of the Convention, (...) the Committee decided to encourage States Parties to inform it about the steps taker, to ensure the widespread dissemination of the results of the dialogue with the committee.[47] The report drawn up by the States is to mention in which way their information duty is accomplished. The "concluding observations" on the reports of those countries that have not yet (sufficiently) published the provisions of the Convention[48] and the general guidelines regarding the periodic reports[49] clearly show that the Committee considers this duty to inform as an essential part of the obligations entailed by the Convention.

**B. *The Committee on the Rights of the Child***

*1. The Foundation of the Committee*

21. By virtue of Article 43 of the Convention, a Committee

on the Rights of the Child was installed to assess the progress made by the States regarding the fulfillment of their obligations. The "travaux preparatoires" of the Convention show that not every country gave its downright approval to develop a specific children's committee. A lot of countries were indeed aware of the problems (such as financial implications[50], problems due to vagueness and overlaps, strains put on national administrations,..,) that are implied by an increase in the number Decontrol organs within the United Nations. As a matter of fact, it was the Belgian delegate who suggested leaving the monitoring of the implementation of the Convention on the Rights of the Child to the existing Committees. He more specifically meant the monitoring organs of the two Covenants of 1966[51]. Poland had suggested having the reports examined by a "Group of Governmental Experts", founded by the Economic and Social Council[52]. These proposals arose as a consequence of the recent concern regarding the increase in the number of UN organs that are to monitor human rights.

22. Neither proposal was adopted, however. The foundation of a separate Committee on the Rights of the Child was finally opted for. This Committee is financed through the UN-budget.[53] The argument that no UN-body has an overall view on the rights of the child has had a decisive influence on the discussion.[54]

2. *The Composition of the Committee*

23. The Committee on the Rights of the Child, just tike the other "treaty-based organs", consists or "experts of high moral standing and recognized competence in the field covered by this Convention" (in casu the rights of the child). The Committee consists of 10 members[55]. It is thus, together with the Committee against Torture, the smallest of the "treaty-based organs[56, 57]. Article 43 provides a specific procedure (or the election of the Committee members[58]. The first election of the Committee members took place between the 27th of February and the 1st of March, 1991[59]. The members of the Committee are elected for a period of four

years, but the term of office of five of the members[60] who were elected during the first elections comes to an end after two years. The Committee (or at least half of it) can thus have a different composition every two years. However, the members are eligible for re-election if they are renominated (Art. 43, § 6).[61]

24. The experts act in their personal capacity and are hence not dependent on the State of which they have the nationality (Art. 43, § 2): "(...) the Committee members are solely accountable to the children of the world"[62] It is for this reason that the Committee decided that the members will not participate in the discussion on the country report of their own government.[63]

*3. Official and Informal Meetings*

25. Initially, the Committee would meet once a year. The duration of the sessions is determined by a meeting of the States Parties of die Convention (Art. 43, § 10). During its first session (1991) the Committee already noted one session a year would not be enough to meet the requirement for example, that the initial reports of some 100 States Parties would need to considered by the Committee between 1992 and 1996, before the second periodic reports became due, and that a single annual session of three weeks duration would clearly not permit timely and thorough action on those reports even if the Committee devoted its time exclusively to that one activity. Additionally, the Committee would be unable to effectively address its other important responsibilities including chose regarding technical assistance under Article 45, the 'consideration of special studies and other reports submitted to it, the formulation of general recommendations on the implementation of the Convention, and the formulation of general comments to assist States Parties in fulfilling their reporting obligations"[64]. This is why the Committee deemed it necessary to ask the General Assembly to authorize the Secretary General to organize at least two sessions a year. Moreover, the Committee asked the General Assembly's permission to found a "Processional Working Group."[65] This

"Pre-sessional Working Group" would examine the country reports for a first time two months before the session would actually take place. Some questions regarding die country reports would be drawn up. These possible questions could then be put to the representatives of the States concerned. "This would facilitate the task of States Parties by providing advance notice of the principal issues arising from the examination of their reports and would significantly improve the efficiency of the reporting system."[66] The "Pre-sessional Working Group" could also pay some attention to the international cooperation and the technical support, as dealt with in Article 45 of the Convention. The General Assembly of the United Nations has approved both demands of the Committee in resolution 46/112.

26. Nevertheless, the main problem of the Committee remained the lack of time. Indeed, the Convention on the Rights of the Child had, in a very short period, become the UN convention with the largest number of ratifications.[67] It was in the course of its fourth session (1993) that the Committee decided to organize a special session in 1994.[68] At the fifth session (1994), the Secretary General was asked co organize a meeting of the States Parties at which the duration of the meetings would be discussed. He was at the same time asked to increase the number of both the annual sessions and of the meetings of the "Pre-sessional Working Group" from two to three.[69] Since 1994, the Committee is indeed meeting three times a year (3 sessions).

27. In spite of these administrative troubles, the Committee the not throw in the towel. The Committee itself took the initiative to promote both its activities and the children's Convention. Indeed, apart from the official sessions, the Committee has organized a number of informal regional meetings.[70] These meetings intend to promote the provisions of the Convention on a regional level, to encourage international cooperation in the field of children's rights and to offer its members the opportunity to examine the situation of the rights of the child on the spot.[71] The Committee on the Rights of the Child thus became the first UN human rights

body to study the situation of human rights on the spot in certain countries. "The regional meetings had constituted an innovative method of work and might be regarded as a first step in action by any treaty body useful tool for better promotion of children's rights."[72, 73] The Committee does however stress the fact that the regional informal meetings have no control function at all: "It was important to bear in mind that the Quito meeting had not been a monitoring operation by the Committee but simply an educational and training exercise. In future meetings, that fact should be made clear at the outset."[74] By means of listening to children on the spot and by getting in touch with non-governmental organizations, the Committee has given shape to one of the most important reasons of the Convention's existence: the participation of the children themselves.[75]

## *C. The Reporting Procedure*

### *1. The Content of the Reports*

#### *(a) Article 44 of the Convention*

28. In accordance with Article 44 of the Convention, the States are to regularly report on the measures they have taken to protect and promote the rights of the child and on the progress they have made with regard to the enjoyment of the rights concerned. This reporting obligation is to be complied with for a first time within two years after ratification of the Convention. Afterwards, a report is to be submitted once every five years[76]. The reports are addressed to the Secretary General, who communicates them to the Committee on the Rights of the Child, The States have the obligation to make sure that the reports are publicly available in their own country (Art. 44, § 6).

29. The Convention does not give a clear definition of what exactly is to be included in the report. According to the first paragraph of Article 44, the following is to be mentioned: "the measures they have adopted which give effect to the rights recognized herein." This is of course not sufficient. At the same time, information is to be given on

"the progress made on the enjoyment of those rights". It is hence not sufficient to list the measures taken; it also has to be checked to what degree these new measures (and the already existing regulations) have contributed to the actual enjoyment of human rights. The Convention does not only force the States to take measures, but also to assess the effect of these measures and to check whether they really contribute to the realization of the rights of the child.

30. Within this framework, the second paragraph of the same Article specifies that the reports are to mention the factors and the possible difficulties chat have their influence on the compliance with the obligations entailed by the Convention. States that, m one way or an other, experience some difficulties with the implementation of the Convention, have the opportunity to communicate these difficulties to the Committee. The Committee will then give its advice on the matter concerned. Article 44 mentions that the reports are to contain sufficient information in order to provide the Committee with a comprehensive understanding of the implementation of the Convention in the country concerned. In order not to strain the States too much, the third paragraph of Article 44 finally stipulates that a State, which has submitted a comprehensive initial report to the Committee need not, in its subsequent reports repeat basic information previously provided.

31. In spite of all these stipulations, this matter remains rather vague. How are the reports to be drawn be? How exhaustive and specific should the reports be? How is it to be checked whether progress has been made relating to the enjoyment of human rights? When is the information considered to be "sufficient" as implied by Article 44, § 2? The Committee on the Rights of the Child drew up some "general guidelines" on the 15th of October 1991 in order to better specify the requirements for the reports. The States are to meet these guidelines when drawing up their reports[77] . The introductory part of the report is to be based on the so-called "consolidated guidelines."[78] In the introductory part the States have to inform the Committee about the population

and the general institutional and judicial framework of the country. The description of this institutional framework is allowed to be the same for each report under an international treaty on human rights. It should be Finally noted that the "'general guidelines" of 1991 only relate to the initial reports. Another set of guidelines were adopted (during the thirteenth session) for the submission of the periodic reports.[79] These guidelines should lead to an assessment of measures adopted, progress achieved and difficulties encountered in implementing the Convention during the period under consideration, while giving particular emphasis on the follow-up to the suggestions and recommendations of the Committee as reflected in the Committee's. concluding observations on the previous report."[80] In Finalizing the new guidelines, the Committee had in mind the need for a dynamic approach to the situation of children, and the catalytic role played by the concluding observations adopted following the consideration of the initial reports submitted by States parties. It also stressed the importance of data and information collection, as well as the development of appropriate indicators in order to monitor progress, difficulties encountered and benchmarks established for future action in the various areas covered by the Convention.[81]

*(b) The General Guidelines*

32. According to the "general guidelines" the report is to be split up into eight sections. This classification entails char the Articles of the Convention are grouped per topic. A similar approach does not only offer the advantage that the Committee will receive better-structured reports. It also facilitates the participation of specialized agencies and non-governmental organizations that are well-skilled in certain aspects of the Convention on the Rights of the Child.[82] However, the Committee did stress that this classification is not a classification based on the importance of the rights. All rights remain equally important. The eight sections of the report are listed below:

(1) *General measures of implementation',* this section is to contain the description of the measures taken by the States to harmonize national law and policy with the provisions of the Convention. At the same time, all mechanisms that have been or that will be established on a national or a local level for coordinating policies relating to children and for monitoring the implementation of the Convention are to he described. The way in which the report will be made public in the country concerned and the way in which the population will be informed of the provisions of the Convention are to be mentioned as well.

(2) *'Definition of tin- child-,* the States are asked to inform the Committee about what is meant by child (Art. 1 of the Convention) in their legislation.

*General principles:* the Stares are to supply ail useful information concerning the non-discrimination principle (Art. 2), the best interest of the child (Art. 3), the right to life, survival and development (Art. 6) and respect for the views of the child (Art. 12). The Committee considers the above four principles as essential provisions, that are, as it were, incorporated in each other provision of the Convention.

(4) *Civil right and freedoms:* This section contains information on the civil rights and freedoms of the Convention.[83]

(5) *Family environment and alternative care:* The rights of the child in relation to his or her family are to be described in this section.[84]

(6) *Basic health and welfare:* This section contains information on a number of social and economic rights of the Convention.[85]

(7) *Education, leisure and cultural activities.*[86]

(8) *Special protection measures:* This section is split up into four sub-sections. The four sub-sections concern: (1) children in situations of emergency; (2) children in conflict with the law; (3) children in situations of exploitation (including physical and psychological recovery and social reintegration) and (4) children belonging co a minority or an indigenous group.

33. It should be noted that States are asked to describe the mechanisms at national or local level for coordinating policies relating to children and for monitoring the implementation of the Convention. Sections 6 (basic health and welfare) and 7 (education, leisure and cultural activities) also mention a similar monitoring mechanism. The Convention does not explicitly mention a similar national monitoring and coordinating mechanism. If is however obvious that when the States take the reporting seriously, a national follow-up is indispensable. This is especially so since the States, in accordance with Article 44, are not only supposed to give information on the measures taken but also on the progress that was made concerning the enjoyment of the rights of the child. Moreover, several "concluding observations" on the country-reports, show that the Committee sets great store by a national follow-up structure of this kind. The countries are either congratulated with the existence of a national follow-up structure, or they are urged to organize one.[87]

34. The success of the reporting procedure largely depends on the clearness of the guidelines.[88] When drawing up these guidelines, the Committee is to take into account the two following important elements: (I) on the one hand, the reports are to be sufficiently detailed and elaborated in order to enable the Committee to thoroughly evaluate the situation of human rights; (2) on the other hand, the Committee is to take into account its own possibilities and workload. Indeed, reports that are too detailed can give rise to some problems when the Committee tries to get an overall view of the situation of the rights of the child in the country concerned. As a consequence, the dialogue with the delegate of the State will not turn out to be very efficient. However, in the opinion of several authors, the general guidelines set by the Committee 1991 still lack some specification. Abramson, for example, states: "One glaring inadequacy of the guidelines is that they do not ask. States for any information on spending. Even the most elementary questions about what percentages of the budget go to children's health

or education are omitted. States merely "are encouraged" to provide relevant statistical information and indicators. The State is given total freedom to decide what is relevant."[89] This situation has led to a large diversity in the quality of the reports.[90] The Committee was pleased to see that the bulk of reports met the quality standards. Nevertheless, some reports turned out to contain insufficient information.[91] When the country reports lack the most elementary information such as the percentages of the Gross National Product that go to children's health care or education then the Committee cannot but spend most of the meeting on the gathering of additional information.[92] Thus, only little time remains to hold a debate. Nevertheless, the gaps in the guidelines are quite understandable. Indeed, at the time when these guidelines were drawn up, the Committee did not have a clear view on what the reports and the "constructive dialogue" would lead to. It was obvious that the Committee still had to derive the necessary and useful lessons from the initial reports of the countries. With this regard, it was decided to add a commentary to the guidelines, asking the States for a number of supplementary specifications.[93] To help ensure more effective implementation of the Convention, the Committee should also define an implementation strategy and appropriate indicators to measure achievement in het progressive realization of economic, social and cultural rights.[94] In the general guidelines of 1996 (regarding the periodic reports) the Committee has done so. According to these guidelines the States are asked to give information about (I) the steps undertaken to ensure coordination between economic and social policies; (2) the proportion of the budget devoted to social expenditures for children, including health, welfare and education, .it the central, regional and local levels, and where appropriate at the federal and provincial levels; (3) the budget trends over the period covered by the report; (4) arrangements for budgetary analysis enabling the amount and proportion spent on children to be clearly identified; (5) the steps taken to ensure that all competent national, regional and local authorities are guided by the best interests of the child in their budgetary decisions and evaluate the priority given to children in their policy-making; (6) the measures taken to ensure that disparities between different regions and groups of children are bridged in relation to the provision of social services; and (6) the measures taken to ensure that children, particularly those belonging to the most disadvantaged groups, are protected against the adverse effects of economic policies, including the reduction of budgetary allocations in the social sector.[95]

*2. The Study of the Reports by the Committee*

*(a) The Pre-sessional Working Croup*

35. The Committee decided during its first meeting that each report should be responded to within one year after submission.[96] In view of the very large number of reports and the limited time for meetings, this decision requires a thorough organization of the activities'.[97]

36. The Committee considers the reports in two steps.[98] In a first stage, the reports are studied by a Pre-sessional Working Group. This working group normally meets immediately after a plenary session of the Committee, in a closed meeting[99] to prepare for the next one. Representatives of the UN bodies and agencies can take part in the meeting. The working group can also invite representatives of non-governmental organisations.[100] The principal purpose of the working group is to facilitate the Committee's work under Articles 44 and 45 of the Convention, primarily by reviewing State party reports and identifying in advance the main questions that would need to be discussed with the representatives of the reporting States. It also provides an opportunity co consider questions relating to technical assistance and international cooperation. The resulting questionnaire ('List of Issues') is sent to the State in order to enable the representative to prepare himself for the Committee's dialogue, thus avoiding die possibility that the representative would make no reply to the questions. The State has to provide the answers in written form before the

dialogue will take place. Another advantage of this way of proceeding is that non-governmental organizations can be efficiently involved in the monitoring process[101] (see also Para. 49). In that regard, it should be noted that the Committee has quite recently (1999) adopted 'guidelines' to facilitate and encourage the process of written submission of NGO reports as well as the participation of NGOs and individual experts in Its pre-sessional working group meetings.[102] The Committee has stressed that the written contributions made by non-governmental organizations (or national coalitions or committees of NGOs) and individual experts and requests of non-governmental organizations to participate in the pre-sessional working group are to be submitted to the Committee through its Secretariat at least 2 months before the pre-session starrs.[103] When doing so, the Committee members have the time to examine the remarks delivered by the nongovernmental organizations and to compare these to the reports drawn up by the several States. Based on the written information submitted, the Committee will issue a written invitation to selected non-governmental organizations[104] to participate in the pre-sessional working group.[105]

37. In the opinion of Abramson, this way of working (the study of the reports by the Committee in two steps) did not turn out to be efficient in all cases. This is due to the fact that the Pre-sessional Working Group has had to spend too much time gathering additional information.[106] Some of the States did not have sufficient time to prepare the additional information. In many cases, the information has been submitted on the day of the discussion, which made it necessary for the- representatives to present the information orally. However, on the basis of a decision taken at the Pre-sessional Working Group of the fifth session of the Committee, the working group establishes informal contacts with the Permanent Missions of States whose reports are scheduled for consideration at the forthcoming session, in order to inform them of the procedure followed by the Committee for the consideration of reports and clarify the purposes of the dialogue with representatives of the States.[107]

*(b) A Constructive Dialogue*

38. The Committee examines the reports submitted by the various countries on the basis of the Pre-sessional Working Groups' preparations and the contributions made by the non-governmental organizations. The Committee considers the reporting as a means of coming to a constructive dialogue with the States.[108] It is not only· the Committee's intention to check what rights the States have not implemented, but also to check whether those that have been implemented so far have been done so successfully.[109] It is, however, not easy to have, a profound and constructive dialogue on the basis of the—in most cases - exhaustive and complex reports. The quality of the dialogue will always depend on several elements: the quality of the report, the document knowledge of the Committee's members, the relevance of the questions asked, the available time, the priorities set. The ability of the representatives of the States is an important condition for a constructive dialogue. Hence, the Committee has more than once stressed that the States should delegate expert representatives in order to hold as efficient a dialogue as possible.[110] Apart from some exceptions,[111] the Committee seemed to be pleased with the delegates representing the several States.

39. On the one hand, and as a result of the discussion of the first reports, it was clearly seen that the Committees way of proceeding is at some points in need of improvement. On the other hand, and in view of the large number of ratifications of the Convention on the Rights of the Child,[112] it was also obvious that the Committee does not have sufficient time at its disposal to hold a dialogue with the States. The Committee, being aware of this problem, has taken a number of measures to spend the time available as efficiently as possible. It was in the course of the fifth session (1994) chat the Committee decided to spend at the most 9 hours on the discussion of each single country report.[113] This measure is at present probably a necessary evil if the Committee wishes to limit the backlog to a minimum. But

then again, the Committee should not forget its own point basic principle: the first objective pursued through the reporting is to come to a constructive dialogue with the States. As a matter effface, the study of the reports is the first and foremost task of the Committee. In some cases, and in the opinion of Theytaz-Bergman, the time limit has had some baleful influences on the Committees activities: "This (the time limit) proved to be disastrous in the case of Mexico where the. Committee barely had time to even touch upon the serious problems that the country is facing including street children, torture and the uprising in the Chiapas region.[114] In another attempt to reduce its backlog, the Committee decided during its twenty-first session (May-June 1999) to increase the number of- States parties' reports considered to at least 8 per session as from January 2000.[115] A few months later, in the course of the twenty-second session, the Committee confirmed its intention to review 8 reports in its 23rd session (January 2000) and even 9 reports per session thereafter.[116] During the twenty-first session the Committee decided to re-establish the system of 'country-rapporteurs.'[117]

40. In order to lose less time, the Committee has requested the States to write down their answers to the questions of the Pre-sessional Working Group and to send them co the Committee before hand.[118] The gaps in the report could in this way be treated in writing. This way of proceeding did not turn out to be very efficient. Indeed, most of the States did not have sufficient time (only I month) to prepare the additional information. This is why the answers were not submitted before the day of the session.[119] Moreover, there is a real danger that the States will ask to postpone the discussion on their reports, because they have to give additional written information.[120]

41. Considering that the Committee's composition and the UN budget are limited, it is obvious that the Committee will never be able to examine each single aspect of the implementation of the Convention. This is why the Committee will have to get its priorities right and why the Committee

will have to deal thoroughly with flagrant problems. These will obviously differ from country to country. The Committee seems to share the same vision. During its sixteenth session (1997) it was decided that the States parties should focus on a limited range of issues in their periodic reports, in particular those issues identified in the concluding observations adopted by the Committee in relation to the previous report.[121] Priorities will also have to be established when drawing up the questions of the Pre-sessional Working Group. In the course of the twenty-second session, die Committee decided that in the future the List of Issues adopted following the pre-session should be mainstreamed and limited to the most significant issues.[122] Reporting can in this case be restricted to certain aspects of the Convention, thus facilitating a thorough examination. A following report could then deal with other aspects, including a follow-up of the previously examined report. This way of proceeding does bring along the disadvantage, however, that the interrelations between the several rights undertaken in the Convention will be paid less attention to.[123]

*(c) Concluding Observations*

42. The deliberation over the reports results in "concluding observations."[124] As pointed out in Article 45 of the Convention, the Committee is indeed allowed to formulate suggestions and general recommendations, based on information received pursuant to Articles 44 and 45. These suggestions and recommendations are sent to any State Party concerned and reported to the General Assembly. The information will possibly be accompanied by comments, if any, from the State parties (Art. 45, (d). The "concluding observations" enter the Committees main points of discussion. The Committee also indicates the topics that require a special follow-up. Thus, the documents constitute the basis for the discussion of the reports that follow. The "concluding observations" concerning the initial reports are always structured in one and the same way: (1) introduction; (2) positive aspects; (3) factors and difficulties impeding the

implementation of the Convention; (4) principal subjects of concern; ('5) suggestions and recommendations.[125] Since the nineteenth session however, the distinction until then made between (4) principal subjects of concern and (5) suggestions and recommendations has disappeared and has been replaced by the single (4) (principal) subject(s) of concern and the Committees recommendations.[126]

The 'concluding observations' concerning the periodic reports are structured as follows: (1) introduction; (2) follow-up measures undertaken and progress achieved by the State party; (3) factors and difficulties impeding further progress in the implementation of the Convention; and (4) principal subjects of concern and the Committees recommendations.[127]

43. The exact formulation of the "concluding observations" is a very important condition for the success of the reporting procedure.[128] 'On the one hand, the "concluding observations" encourage the States to take their reporting obligation seriously[129] whereas, on the other hand, the credibility of the Committee will in the long run be determined by the contents of the observations regarding the dialogues and the reports. "Concluding observations" that are drawn up too cautiously may lead to the indifference of States with regard to the Committees recommendations. But then again, the Committee is to make sure that the "concluding observations" do not turn into convictions. Indeed, the Committee does not have the authority to do so.[130] It is not only the formulation of the "concluding observations" but also the follow-up of suggestions and recommendations that is of paramount importance if the Committee wishes to encourage the States to take their reporting duties seriously.[131, 132]

### (d) *The Evaluation of the Operating Procedure of the Committee when Examining the Reports*

44. The above clearly indicates that a Committee on the Rights of the Child can also have its teething problems. The cause is to be found in the large number or reports[133] to be dealt with and in the limited meeting time. The Committee

is well-aware of this and has made one of its members responsible for the preparation of a "working paper". This working paper is to contain the ways in which the activities can be better organized.[134] When it is assumed that the Committee cannot possibly carry out an in-depth study for each report, then it is absolutely recommendable to establish priorities. Pursuing one's priorities often results in incompleteness. But then again, when the monitoring system of the Convention on the Rights of the Child is not only considered as a purely judicial tool, but also as an awareness-raising process then there can hardly be any objections at all.

*3. The "Positive Atmosphere" Urrounding Implementation: "Cooperative Attitude"*

45. As we have already pointed out above, the expectations of the monitoring mechanism are high: indeed, the monitoring system is to be more than just a control mechanism. This turns out a.o. in Article 45 of the Convention. This Article adds an original procedure to the reporting mechanism. The monitoring of the implementation of the rights is to be accompanied by help and support: "(....) the Convention envisages a much more active role for the Committee with respect for technical advice or assistance than is the case with other human rights treaty bodies." The authors of the Convention have seized the reporting procedure as a tool in order to act in an advisory or assisting way wherever needed. They do so on the basis of the information given in the reports: "The aim is that the Committee - together with the reporting government and any aid agencies involved- should attempt to define the problems and discuss what remedies are necessary."

*(a) From Reporting to Development Aid*

46. As Article 44, § 2, points out, the reports are to indicate the factors and possible difficulties that have their influence on the compliance with the obligations implied by the Convention. Reports showing a need for technical advice

or technical support can be sent to specialized agencies, UNICEF, and other competent bodies. The Committee can possibly add remarks and suggestions [Art. 45, (a)]. The Convention en the Rights of the Child goes a step further than other treaties. The reports cannot only be transmitted to a larger number of organs, it is moreover the Committee itself that decides whether the reports will be transmitted or nor. The Covenant on Political and Civil Rights (Art. 40, § 3) and the Covenant on Economic, Social and Cultural Rights [Art. 16, § 2, (b)] also provide the opportunity to submit the reports to specialized agencies. However, for these two Covenants, it is the United Nations Secretary General who is to take the initiative. It is obvious that the procedure adopted by the Convention on the Rights of the Child is less complex. However, in order to optimally seize this opportunity, it is necessary to inform the Committee of the existing programs concerning technical assistance on a national level and of the problems involved. Whenever a specific technical assistance program is recommended, the Committee will always encourage the State concerned to discuss the suggested program with the aid agency. When drawing up the "Rules of Procedure", the Committee on the Rights of the Child was also resolved to closely follow the transmitted reports. Doing so, the Committee can see what kind of technical help has been rendered and what progress" has been made (Rule 74).

47. Article 4 of the Convention also embodies the idea of mutual help and support: "(...) With regard to economic, social and cultural rights, States Parties shall undertake such measures to the maximum extent of their available resources and, where needed, within the framework of international cooperation". No other Convention on Human Rights links the reporting with development aid to such a large extent.[141] But then again, development aid is often used to enforce respect for human rights. "The link established by the Convention between the reports by the states and discussions about development aid may become a dynamic element in aid policies. States can ask for help through their reports.

At the same time, they can prove that they respect human rights. Moreover, through the "concluding observations of the Committee on the Rights of the Child, States are encouraged to look for, or to render, international assistance."[144] This way, the reporting procedure can develop into an important basis for well-founded development policies. The main condition is that the States release the necessary information on their expense policy. It is indeed important for the aiding States to know the priorities of the States that call for assistance and where their money goes to exactly. According to the guidelines regarding the form and contents of the periodic reports the reports should be accompanied by information about changes in the extent of international cooperation received or contributed for the realization of children's rights.

48. One has to be rather cautious when linking respect for human rights with development aid. According to De Feyter development aid soon adopts a compulsive characrer, if the donor and the receiver do not share the same beliefs towards human rights. Still according to the same author, there will arise no problems when development aid is joined to respect for human rights by the States. Indeed, by ratifying the Conventions on Human Rights, the State has assumed a judicial obligation to achieve the realization of human rights. When, on the contrary, cultural traditions are envisaged, De Feyter thinks it advisable to act cautiously, due to the fact that donor and receiver might possibly have differing opinions on human rights. This is even more the case when principles such as "the best interests of the child" are under discussion. After all, the ideas about what is or isn't in the best interests of the child differ depending on the cultural tradition.

*(b) A Broad Basis for Participation*

49. The cooperative spirit of the Convention is also seen in the fact that the specialized agencies, UNICEF and other United Nations organs have acquired the right to be represented at the deliberation on the application of those

provisions that fall within the scope of their mandate [Art. 45, (a)]. What's more, the Committee can invite the specialized agencies, UNICEF and other competent bodies that turn out to be useful, to give their expert advice on the implementation of the Convention. They can also be asked to submit "reports (see Paras. 33-36). In view of the workload and the limited financial resources of the Secretariat, the Committee will have to use this possibility efficiently in order to be well-informed. The "travaux preparatoires" clearly show that the term "other competent bodies" is to be understood in the broadest sense of the word. It was in the course of the first session (1991) of the Committee on the Rights of the Child that a delegate from Defense for Children International suggested a whole range of "other competent bodies": amongst others non-governmental organizations, the Organization of African Unity, the Organization of American States, the Council of Europe, the International Labour Organization, national research institutions,..... Thus, the Convention constitutes a broad basis for the participation of all kinds of organizations in the monitoring process. In view of the increase in the number of treaties on human rights,—of control bodies and control procedures, both within the United Nations and on a regional level, the Convention on the Rights of the Child offers an important opportunity to come to a certain degree of coordination and cooperation. The explicit inclusion of this matter is an important and innovative aspect of the reporting procedure. The success will however depend on the way in which the Committee uses the opportunities offered by the Convention. This is why it will be essential to develop procedures that can effectively guarantee this cooperation: "In regard to the work of the Committee, members pointed out that there should be effective coordination in the provision of relevant information from governmental and non-governmental sources on the implementation of the Convention in submitting reports." There was a lot of attention paid to this topic at the first session of the Committee (1991). The Committee listened for two days to the cooperation suggestions made by UNICEF, ILO, World Food Program and NGO's. The presentations did reveal A variety of ways in which such bodies can help the Committee in its work: (1) they can provide the Committee with information and documentation; (2) they can assist the Committee's Pre-sessional Working Group in identifying key issues in States parties' reports; (3) with respect to the Committee's role in the area of technical advice and assistance, they can give the Committee information about the type and appropriateness of assistance available (4) they can provide the Committee with reports and studies on topics or themes of particular interest to the Committee; and (5) they can help the Committee formulate general comments. It was also suggested to found a "technical advisory group." This group would consist of representatives from specialized agencies, UNICEF, other United Nations bodies and other competent bodies. Goodman sticks to the opinion that this technical advisory group would create lots of opportunities to steer the participation in the right direction. Still according to the same author, this group could act as the link between the Committee and the participating organs. The technical advisory group could for example assist the Committee when determining what organ is specifically skilled in a certain topic or in the situation of the children's right in a certain country. Hence, a similar structure would entail the advantage that the Committee would be able to determine in a fast and efficient way what organ can make a positive contribution to the Committees activities. All these proposals and initiatives have attracted the attention of the other "treaty-based organs". It was at its fifth session that die Committee on the Rights of the Child noted that "(...) the rights of the child had paved the way for a constructive dialogue between the different bodies of the United Nations system, non-governmental organizations and the Committee in such a decisive field as that of information."

### *D. Other Activities of the Committee*

#### *1. Urgent Actions*

50. During the second session (1992) the members of the

Committee agreed upon the fact that the Committee, apart from the periodical study of the country reports, should also be authorized to undertake urgent actions in serious situations. It was nevertheless stressed that the urgent actions ought to embody the spirit of the constructive dialogue. The Committee will therefore rake a non-conflicting attitude regarding this matter. Moreover, a number of conditions will have to be met, before the Committee will be allowed to take so-called "urgent actions":

1. The action is to be based on reliable information. This information can be passed on by anybody (*e.g.* non-governmental organizations), provided char it is accurate and trustworthy: "The situations justifying the urgent procedure would either be brought to the attention of the Committee by United Nations bodies and other competent bodies, or taken up ex office by the Committee."

2. A violation of die rights undertaken in the Convention is to be involved. The problematic situation is to fall within the jurisdiction or one or die States Parties.

3. The violation concerned must be blatant. There must be a real danger that more violations will take place. It must be possible to avoid a deterioration of the situation by taking the urgent action.

The Committee has charged a working group with the further and more detailed development of the procedure.[167]

51. The "urgent actions"—procedure is considered to be a part of the obligation to report: indeed, the Committee can ask a State at any time to draw up a report relating to the implementation of a specific provision of the Convention or to provide additional information.

52. Heedful of the cooperation idea, the Committee planned to pass on serious violations of human rights that fall within the competences of other organs, to the organs concerned. This has happened for example with a request for urgent actions (November 16, 1993) made by the Government of the Federal Republic of Yugoslavia. The Government asked the Committee to examine the violations of the Rights of the Child in Yugoslavia as a consequence

of the sanctions imposed by the United Nations. The Committee passed the case on to the Special Rapporteur on the former Yugoslavia, since it did not have sufficient information on this matter at its disposal.

53. The "urgent actions"—procedure authorizes the Committee to take actions, even if no report was received from the State involved. This way, the Committee can also offer its services at any moment between the consecutive reports. Although the Committee considers the urgent actions procedure to be an essential part of the obligation to report, the procedure could also be considered an alternative for the communications procedure, indeed, the Committee has stressed that apart from the United Nations organs also other competent bodies can pass on blatant violations of the Rights of the Child to the Committee. Since non-governmental organizations are generally accepted as competent bodies, they have the possibility to lodge a complaint with the Committee. Moreover, the conditions to start the "urgent actions-procedure are very similar to the admissibility requirements of "jurisdictional procedures": the violation must be blatant, it must be possible to avoid a deterioration of the situation and the action is to be based on reliable information. But then again, it remains unclear in which cases the Committee will declare a request for urgent actions admissible.

*2. Studies on Topics Concerning the Rights of the Child*

54. Article 45 (c) states that the Committee may recommend to the General Assembly of the United Nations to request the Secretary General to undertake on its behalf studies on specific issues relating to the rights of the child. The Committee has given this provision, in connection with Art. 45 (a) a broad interpretation. It can also ask specialized agencies, UNICEF, and other bodies to carry out studies. According to the Committee, similar Studies "would contribute to an increased awareness and better understanding of the provisions of the Convention and their implementation throughout the world."

55. During its first session (1991) the Committee also decided to dedicate one day of each session to the study of a well-determined topic. The following topics have already been discussed by now: children in armed conflict economic exploitation of children, the role of the family in the promotion of the rights of the child, the girl child, the administration of juvenile justice, the child and the media, the rights of the child with disabilitiesand children living in a world with HIV/AIDS. The thematic debate in September 2000 is co be dedicated co State violence against children. During these topical days the Committee listens for example to representatives of intergovernmental and non-governmental organizations. This is the way in which the Conventions idea of participation is given shape to.

56. The topical days constitute an important aid to come to a uniform interpretation of the provisions of the Convention on the Rights of the Child. This is more than ever the case when new developments in the area of human rights are concerned. The Committee will use these topical days as the basis for the publication of "general comments" on specific Articles undertaken in the Convention. What's more, these topical days can lead to the publication of additional protocols of the Convention. For example, the study day on "children in armed conflicts" has led to a proposal for and eventually an optional protocol (see para. 5).

## III. The Effectiveness of the Reporting Procedure

### *A. The Limitations of the Alternatives*

57. From a judicial angle, a State fulfills its international obligations cowards other States and not towards individuals. Nevertheless, it is obvious that States will nor be eager to lodge complaints relating to violations of human rights in order States.

- When the convention concerned provides a gradual implementation, then an individual complaints procedure cannot easily be followed, since States cannot (or very hardly) be held responsible for the fact that they have not yet achieved the realization of the ideal human rights situation.

- States take a very reluctant stance towards individual complaints mechanisms.
- Human rights are in most cases not violated by the State but by individuals or groups of individuals.
- According to Dimitrijevic, the main reason is that complaints procedures can never cover the entire range of human rights. "A modern human rights treaty aims at a generally favorable human rights situation, which includes creating the necessary conditions for the enjoyment of human rights and the elimination of factors that lead to violations, if a state is remiss, this very often cannot be related to an individual "victim" such as, for instance, when the cost of human life becomes low due to disease, uncontrolled and unrestricted use of dangerous installations and noxious substances, terrorism, poor police protection and other circumstances and the right to life is thus threatened and violated."

59. With regard to the two First limitations quoted by Dimitrijevic, a certain evolution should be noted. More and more attempts are made to increase the-normative character of the economic, social and cultural rights in this way the Committee on Economic, Social and Cultural Rights reflected its view in a "general comment" on the normative nature of the economic, social and cultural rights. According to the Committee the Covenant does impose various obligations which are of immediate effect. Moreover the Committee stresses that "(...) suggestions that the provisions of the Covenant are inherently non-self-executing would seem to be difficult to sustain." Moreover the Committee itself seems to advocate the installation of a complaints procedure. According to the Dutch Committee of Jurists for Human Rights a complaints procedure is precisely required to expose the normative implications of the Covenant. The Dutch Jurists' Committee thinks that the juridical nature of the economic, social and cultural rights constitutes no impediment for the

installation of the complaints procedure. The group of eminent experts on human rights from all over the world who came together in the Dutch city of Maastricht to make up the 'Maastricht Guidelines on Violations of Economic, Social and Cultural Rights' were also very much in favour of a swift adoption and ratification of a protocol providing for an individual and group complaints procedure to the above-mentioned Covenant ... and to the Convention on the Rights of the Child. Following the debates that took place during the commemorative meeting of the Convention on the Rights of the Child (1999), the Committee on the Rights of the Child itself decided to note and endorse the consideration of initiating discussions on an Optional Protocol to the Convention providing a mechanism for individual communications and asked the States parties to support its efforts in that respect.

60. Even if the first two impediments quoted by Dimitrijevic should somewhat be toned down, the other impediments still keep their value. Especially the small policy nature of the complaints procedure prevents a broad implementation of the human rights. Opsahl therefore states that the complaints procedure can only be a secondary aim. The author pleads for the installation of complaints procedures at a regional level and not so much for universal complaints procedures. For this the following reasons are given: "(...) the Committee will never be able to control violations in all parts of the world through complaints procedures. It would not be practical to develop its machinery to the extent which this control would require, since this would include hearings, fact-finding, visits, investigations, use of many languages, etc." Yet regional complaints procedures also offer the advantage that cultural traditions which seem to fie inconsistent with human rights can be judged in a more pragmatical way.

61. In order to achieve an implementation as complete as possible, the State can pass on their monitoring function to an international organ. The international organ then examines the international human rights situation based on

the reports that were submitted by the several States. These reports explain how the international obligations have been complied with. The main advantage of this kind of control is that the casuistic approach is no longer used. As a consequence, all human rights are getting a chance.

### B. The Limitations of the Reporting Procedure

There are a lot of doubts about the use and effectiveness of repotting procedures. The States' reports – it is said-are drawn up by national "officials", who try and draw as positive as possible a picture of the situation in their countries. Moreover, they will hardly ever draw the Committee's attention to flagrant violations of human rights. According to Robertson and Merrills, this criticism is justified to a certain extent. They add that the reporting system as such does not constitute an effective measure of control. Theodor Meron puts it in a more lyrical way: "(...) the reporting system, to paraphrase the title of Jacques Brel's play, is alive, but not well."

Robertson and Merrills think moreover that the efficiency and the effectiveness of the reporting system are largely dependent on the way in which the national reports are dealt with after submission: "What matters is how they (the national reports) are dealt with after they have been received. That is to say, whether there is an opportunity for critical examination, for drawing attention to gaps or inaccuracies in the information provided, and for comparing official statements with other sources of information on the same subject." The authors think that there are some four additional conditions that determine the effectiveness" of the reporting system: (I) the cooperation of the authorities Involved regarding the completeness of information; (2) the possibility to receive further ("and perhaps less flattering") information from other. sources; (3) the examination of gathered information by independent authorities or people; (4) a body's right to pass on suitable remarks and recommendations to the States concerned in view of the improvement of the law or the practice of human rights in the country involved.

It is remarkable that the authors pay this much attention to the gathering of additional information. The usual criticism is strongly countered by the possibility of the examining body to acquire additional and non-official information. For example, the official repot: can be compared to the information submitted by non-governmental organizations. This can give rise to the examining body asking the official authorities for additional information. It can also lead to a reaction to a number of "less flattering" data of the non-governmental organizations. What's more, the States Parties cannot back out of their obligations implied by the Convention by submitting reports that contain no relevant information: additional information can, after all, be requested. Mostly, representatives of the States are invited by the monitoring body to be present at the discussion of their countries reports, which gives cause for dialogue, whereby further clarifications and specifications of the country report will be discussed. Much will depend however on the manner in which the monitoring body makes use of the provided procedure.

Robertson and Merriils examine the reporting system purely from the point of view of control by the international organ, it is clear, however, that the reporting also has, in another way, effects concerning the application of the convention in question. The reporting obliges the Member States to check, within an arranged time limit, the national legislature and practices on the principles of the convention in question. Or, as Theodor Meron points out: 'The task of preparing reports focuses the attention of national administrations on weak points in internal compliance with international human rights obligations and encourages improvements". The States are in this way obliged to evaluate themselves, within a stipulated time limit Furthermore, when bodies other than the official ones we think for example of the NGO's—get the chance to study the country reports critically, the system can give cause to a broader social discussion and consciousness in the country concerned.

According to L.F. Zwaak the effectiveness of a legal,

international instrument can be worked our in two ways; (1) the universality, specifically the extent to which the convention is accepted by a large number of countries arid by public opinion; and (2) the readiness of the States to implement the provisions of the convention. In connection with the first factor, it has to be observed that the reporting mechanism has a stimulating effect. The reporting procedure is, after all, a non-contradictory procedure, so that countries will more quickly ratify a convention in which a reporting procedure is provided than a convention in which a complaints procedure is accepted. The universality is not only concerned with the number of ratifications but also with the extent to which the rights in question are accepted by public opinion. Since the reporting obligation forms a sound basis for coming to a social discussion within the different States, the public opinion too will become conscious more quickly of the importance of the concerned lights.

Zwaaks second criterion regarding the effectiveness of a human rights treaty deals with die willingness of the States to implement the treaty.

put forward in the convention. But then again, this is at the same time the weak point of the reporting procedure. The international controlling body cannot enforce the "concluding observations". The good-will of the States themselves will therefore be a decisive factor for the success of the reporting procedure. This second criterion, adopted by L.F. Zwaak, is consequently not only a standard to measure the effectiveness of the treaty, but also a standard to measure the effectiveness of the reporting procedure. The degree in which the States take their reporting obligation seriously will be decisive for the use, and effectiveness of the reporting duty: "(...) il semble exister une correlation positive entre l'efficacite des systems de presentation des rapports et la mesure dans laquelle les Etats parties prennent au serieux leurs obligations en la matiere."

It is however to be said that some States are not so fussy about the timely submission of their reports. Belgium for example, submitted its initial report regarding the Covenant on Civil and Political Rights after a delay of more than three years and its report regarding the Covenant on Economic, Social and Cultural Rights after a delay of almost 10 years. On the 1st of June 1988, there was an overall backlog of 626 reports. Eight years later, In 1996, the total of overdue reports has risen to 957. The heavy workload implied by the draft of these reports is usually mentioned as the main reason for this delay. Moreover," States have had to draw up increasingly more reports for the last couple of years. It is consequently harder for the national administrations to submit the various reports in due time. The United Nations themselves are also well-aware of this problem. By order of the General Assembly, Alston has formulated a number of proposals within this respect.

Another often voiced criticism on the reporting procedure concerns the fact that the controlling body is only authorized to act when it has a report at its disposal: "(...) it has compelled treaty bodies to behave, in situations where allegations of massive human violations were made, as if nothing had happened and to wait for years until the time for the submission of the report was due. Even when a government declared a state of emergency and then derogated some rights under the human rights treaty and duly notified the United Nations, the treaty body was supposed to remain inactive, not to speak of the more frequent de facto states of emergency." Some evolutions have however occurred in this field. When dealing with the situation in the former Yugoslavia, the Human Rights Committee has asked the governments of Croatia, Bosnia-Herzegovina and Yugoslavia, to urgently submit some specific reports on the implementation of certain Articles of the Covenant on Civil and Political Rights. At chat moment, Bosnia-Herzegovina and Croatia had not yet submitted their initial' reports (and still had some time left to do so). Yugoslavia had just submitted its third report. During its sixth session the Committee on Economic, Social and Cultural Rights went even further. The Committee requested the Dominican Republic "to suspend any actions which are not clearly in 'con form it with the provisions of the Covenant, and requests the government to provide additional information to it as a matter of urgency". So the Committee did not only ask for additional information, it also requested the State to stop the activities chat were inconsistent with the Convention. Within this framework, the Committee on the Rights of the Child decided at its third session that it is authorized to undertake urgent actions under serious circumstances.

Although the reporting procedure is not even close to perfection, it still appears to be the main method to keep on calling the people's attention to human rights through a non-casuistic approach. The effect of a similar procedure cannot be expected to show in the short run and is therefore to be assessed in the long run. Opsahl writes: "The long-term task of uniting nations in the cause of human rights should be seen in the first place as the constructive one of promoting respect of human rights and securing their observance. That is, after all, what the Universal Declaration calls for. It is, therefore, perhaps more important to convince and influence States than to condemn and expose them". An important condition for the success of the reporting procedure is that the participants cake their tasks seriously. More publicity will also be required concerning the activities of the Committee in order to increase the efficiency of reporting. The concluding observations issued by the Committee should give rise to a debate within the involved States. This task does not only concern the NGO's, but also the academics, if as much attention would be paid to these "concluding observations" as to for example the "views" of the Human Rights Committee, and, a.o. in Europe, to the decisions of the European Court on Human Rights, then a reporting procedure can also be accompanied by a certain "mobilization of shame".

## Evaluation of the Monitoring System of the Convention on the Rights of the Child

When studying the monitoring mechanism of the Convention on the Rights of the Child from a judicial angle, and when checking the degree to which the victim of a violation of human rights can call in the support of the Committee to cease the violation, one cannot but conclude that the control mechanism of the Convention offers only few possibilities. The meaning of the Convention however, is not in the first instance a judicial one. Opsahl thinks that all convention-based systems within the UN emphasize the promotion of human rights more than the protection of victims of potential human rights violations. It is rather a political instrument than an ensemble of judicially enforceable elements. Thomas Hammarberg states: "The Convention will in all probability result in increased political attention being given to children and young people. The Convention can from now on serve as an "agenda" for the discussion of the actual circumstances of children. The process required by the Convention, whereby reports have to be submitted on a regular basis and discussions held, should lead to regular examination in every country of issues relating to children and young people."

73. The Convention on the Rights of the Child will, in the first instance, give rise to a change in attitude. Children are for the very first time in history seen as subjects of rights and no longer only as objects of legal protection. The "implementation" of this viewpoint cannot occur just like that by means of legislation or regulation. A lot more is needed to do so and the effects will only show after quite some time. "Looking at legislative changes and economic issues is not enough because implementation is ultimately shaped by attitudes. The starting point of dialogue is the State's attitude towards children, and what the State is doing to change the public's attitude.

74. In our opinion, the monitoring system of the Convention offers a wide range of possibilities to implement this "change in attitude". The States are obliged to regularly submit reports to the Committee. The reporting duty of the State could result in a discussion in the country concerned, in which several participants could be involved. The Convention appears to .stimulate a similar discussion by

obliging the States to make their reports public m their country and to make the provisions of the Convention widely known to adults and children.

75. It is not only at a national level that a debate is pursued. The Committee on the Rights of the Child invites States to hold a dialogue on the reports they have submitted. They can always call in the technical assistance of the Committee. There is moreover a wide range of opportunities for other interested organizations and bodies to participate. This well-developed opportunity to participate constitutes an innovating aspect of the monitoring process within the United Nations. What's more, it can give rise to a better-coordinated and more uniform approach and interpretation of human rights. The Convention explicitly links development aid with respect for human rights. It can therefore develop into a new and dynamic element in development policies

76. The Committee organizes regional informal meetings and, by doing so, gets in touch with children living in problem areas, with regional nongovernmental organizations and government leaders. This way of working strongly contributes to the promotion of the Convention on the Rights of the Child and stimulates the awareness-raising process.

77. However, all of this does not mean that the Convention on the Rights of the Child would have no judicial meaning at all. Some rights are undoubtedly eligible for a self-executing character. In this respect, the elaboration of "General Comments" by the Committee can play an important-if not crucial- role. The Convention can moreover serve as the starting point for further national or international standardization: "The Convention could also serve as a starting-point for further standard-setting within the field of children's and young people's rights. (...) The Convention is obviously not a final product. Instead, it should be seen as the first and important milestone".

**References**

1. This contribution has been written within the framework

of the programme 'Inter universities Attractiepolen (nr. 94/27—Mensenrechten van kinderen, implemented en toezicht via participant)', financed by the Belgian State, Services of the Prime Minister—Federal Department of scientific, technical and cultural affairs.

2. The text has been updated—by using the official CRC-texrs- until the twenty-second session (September-October 1999) of the Committee on the Rights of the Child, and by using the CRC-Notes—until the twenty-fourth session (May-June 2000).
3. On the Declaration of the Rights of the Child of 1959. see; Vȃn Bueren, G:, *The international lane on the right of the child,* The Hague/Boston/London, Martinus Nljhoff Publishers (199S). pp. 9-1 2; Veerman. P *The Rights of the child changing image of childhood,Dondrect/ Boston/London* Martinus Nijhoff publishers (1992), p 159-180 Verheellen, F *convention of the right of the child,* Leuven /Apeldoorn, Garant (1994), pp. 59-64; Smith, "The Rights of the Child", in *The Role of the Nation-State in the 21st Century. Human Rights, International Organizations and Foreign Policy. Essays in Honour of Peter Baehr,* Castermans Holleman, M, Van Hoof, E and Smith, J, (eds), The Hague/Boston/Londoan. Kluwer law.
5. Alston, Ph., *Application effective des instruments internationaux relatifs aux droits de I,hmme, y compris I' obligation de presenter des rapports a ce titre,* A/44/668, para. 9.
6. See for example Nowak, M., "Proposals for Improving the UN Human Rights Programme", *NQHR2(1993),* p. 153-162. See also American Bar Association (ABA), "Recommendation towards consolidating into two committees the existing six UN committees currently monitoring UN human rights treaties (CCPR, CE5R. CERD, CEDAW CAT, CRC) (Draft recommendation adopted by the House of Delegates August 3-4, 1998), 20 *HRLJ.* (1999), p. 272.
7. See among others Alston, Ph., "Appraising the United Nations Human Rights Regime", in *The United Nations*

*and Human Rights - A Critical Appraisal,* Alston, Ph. (ed.), Oxford, Clarendon Press (1992), p. 3; Dormenval, A,, *Procedures onusiennes de wise en ueuvre des druits de I'homme; limites mi defauts,* Paris, Presses Universitaires de France (1991), p. 6; Parmentier, S., "Mensenrechten in de jaren negegtin", in *Mensenrechten tussen retoriek en realiteit - Tegenspark Cahier 14,* Parmentier, S, (ed.), Ghent, Mys and Breesch (1994), pp. 7-8.

8. Alston. Ph., "Preface", in *The United Nations and Human Rights -A Critical Appraisal,* Alston, Ph. (ed.), Oxford, Clarendon Press (1992), V. See also the study carried out by Alston, by order of the General Assembly or the U.N.; "De quelque maniere que Ton qualifie la situation presence, if esc admis en general que de systeme de surveillance cree par les instruments des Nations Unies relatifs aux droits de I'homme est parvenu a un point critique. Si l'on veut assurer son succes dans I'avenir, il faut reconnaitre la gravite des problemes actuels, reaffirmer I'importance cruciale du regime conventionnel dans son ensemble et poursuivre avec energie et determination la recherche de solutions creatrices et efficaces. II ne faudrait pas pour autant s'engager dans cetie recherche sans recounaitre qu'une oeuvre tres considerable a etc accomplie jusqu'ici et qu'il importe de proceder avec finesse et perspicacite de maniere a ne pas sacrifier I'integrite' fondamentale du systeme, et en particulier son aptitude a sauvegarder les droits tie 1'homme, a des notions illusoires de rationalization et de rendement. En d'autres termes, dans cette epoque de crise ou de defi, il faut voir aussi une epoque ou s'ouvreut des possibility's de reformc et d'amelioration constructives" (Doc. A/44/668, para. 8). See also: Opsahl, T, "Instruments of Implementation of Human Rights", 10 *HRL.J* (1989). p. 1'4.
9. In this respect, see Boerefijn, I. and Davidse, K., "Every Cloud...? I he World Conference on Human Rights and Supervision of Implementation of Human Rights, *NQHR* (1993), pp. 457 468; Vienna Declaration and Programme

of Action, UN Doc.A/Conf. 157/23, 12 July 1993, published in *NQHR.* (1993), pp. 346-368 and *NJCM-Bulletin,* (1993), pp. 716-738.

10. At its 97th plenary meeting, the General Assembly adopted 2 optional protocols to the Convention on the Rights of the Child on the involvement of children in armed conflict and on the sale of children, child prostitution and child pornography (UN Doc. A/54/ L.84 with Annexes).
11. Parmentier, S., "International control en implementing van mensenrechren" · in *Belgen over mensenrechten-Een bijdrage tot de Wereldconferentie Mensentecter, Vienna, 14-25 juni 1993,* Brussels, Ministerie van Buitenlandse Znken, Buitenlandse Handel en Ontwikkelings-samenwerking (1993), p. 26.
12. Parmentier, S., *op.cit,* p. 26.
13. A similar evolution does not only appear within the framework of the United Nations but is also seen within the Council of Europe. See: Roucounas. E., The reform of the human rights institutions of the Council of Europe", in *The reform of international institutions for the protenction of human rights.*
14. Parmentier, S., *op. cit.,* p. 26.
15. Parmentier, S., "International control en implementation van mensenrehten", in *Belgen over mensenrechten - Een bijdrage tot de Werldconferentie Mensenrechten, Vienna, 14-25 June 1993,* Brussels. Ministerie van Buitenlandse Zaken, Buitenlandse Handel en Ontwikkelings-samenwerking, (1993), p. 26. See also the study by Philip Alston, carried out by order of the General Assembly of the UN *(Application effective des instruments internationals relatifs aux drohits del'homme, y compris l'obligatin de presenter des rapports a ce titre.* Doc, A/4 4/668).
16. Sec for example for a negative point of view; American Bar Association (ADA), *op. cit.,* p. 272.
17. Virginia, A. Leary, "Lessons from the Experience of the International Labour Organization", in *The United*

*Nations and Human Rights. A Critical Appraisal,* Alston, P (ed.), Oxford, Clarendon Press (1992), p. 595.

18. Dimitrijevic, V, "The Monitoring of Human Rights and the prevention of human rights violations through reporting procedures", in *Monitoring Human Rights in Europe. Comparing International Procedures and Mechanisms,* Dordrecht/ Boston/London, Martinus Nijhoff Publishers (1993), p. 1.
19. Zwaak, L.F., *International Human rights procedures-Petitioning the ECHR, CCPR and CERD,* Utrecht, Ars Aequi Libri (1991), p. V; Opsahl. T., "Instruments of Implementation of Human Rights", 10 *HRLJ* (1989), p. 32; "One should never forget that national implementation must be the alpha and omega".
20. In the course of its twenty-second session (September-October, 1999) the Committee stressed the need to give itself detailed attention to a systematic approach to the issue of the legal status of the Convention: it identified the need to clarify the extent of applicability of the Convention in States where the principle of 'self-execution' is applicable, and the precise meaning of statements indicating that the Convention 'has a constitutional status' or 'has been incorporated' in the national legal order as of particular importance in this regard (CRC/C/90, para. 291, sub d).
21. "(...) although international control procedures are no substitute for means and methods of national implementation of human rights, international procedures have an important subsidiary or supplemental role to play" (Van Boven. T, "The international system of human rights: an overview", in *Manual on Human Rights Reporting* (Doc. HR/PUB/91/ 1), New York, United Nations (1991), p. 10).
22. Parmentier, S., *op. cit.,* p. 28. One can also assume that the respective *ad hoc* International Tribunals established to review events which have taken place in the former Yugoslavia and in Rwanda, and the future International

Criminal Court, at least to a certain extent match the same description.

23. The reporting procedure is laid down in Article 40 CCPR, Article 17 CESCR, Article 9 CERD, Article 18 OEDAW, Article 19 CAT, Article 44 CRC and in Article 73 International Convention on the Protection of the Rights of All Migrant Workers and Members of their Families.
24. The intention of country procedures is to thoroughly examine flagrant violations of human rights in a certain country. This can be realized by delegating special rapporteurs to the country concerned or by founding a permanent working group (e.g. the "Ad hoc Working Group of Experts on Southern Africa").
25. Thematic procedures are applied to examine the violation of certain human rights (such as torture, religious intolerance,...). They include special rapporteurs dealing with extrajudicial, summary or arbitrary executions; with the independence and impartiality of the judiciary; with jurors and assessors and the independence of lawyers; with torture; with the use of mercenaries; with the sale of children, child prostitution and child pornography; with religious intolerance; withs freedom of opinion and expression: with racism, racial discrimination.
26. By application of procedure 1503 (established in 1970 by the Economic and Social Council), in a first phase, a Working Group of the Sub-Commission on Prevention of Discrimination and Protection of Minorities reviews communications on gross and attested violations of human rights behind closed doors (this is if considered admissible) and then decides whether to transfer the communication to the Working Group of the Commission on Human Rights, which, in a second phase, discusses the communication once again behind closed doors. Communications remain confidential until such time the Commission on Human Rights may decide

to make recommendations to the Economic and Social Council.

27. Van Boven. T, *op, cit.*, p. 8. Parmentier, on the contrary, makes a distinction between mechanisms, a distinction which is based on a more procedural character, this is according to the object of the existing procedures, and irrespective of their judicial basis or their institutional context (reporting procedures, complaint procedures, enquiry procedures, other procedures) (Parmentier, , . S,, "De mechanismen voor de eerbiediging van de grondrechten en him belaog voor Belgie", in *50ste Verjaardag van de Universal Verklaring van de Recbten van de Mens,* Minsterie van Buitenlandse Zaken, Buitenlandse Handel en International Samenwerking-Ministerie van justitie (eds.), Brussels, (1999), p. 41-44).
28. Alston, Ph., "Appraising the .United Nations Human Rights Regime", in *The United Nations and Human Rights. A Critical Appraisal,* Alston, Ph. (ed.), Oxford, Clarendon Press (I 992), p. 4-5.
29. The General Assembly, the Economic and Social Council, Tin- Security Council, the international Court of justice, the Trusteeship Council and the Secretariat (Secret Genreal. The 'High Commissioner for Human Rights' (established by the General Assembly in December 1993) carries out the *good officer-* function of the Seceratary General in the field of human rights on behalf of the Secretary-General. The High Commissioner being the UN official with principal responsibility for human rights activities, is responsible for promoting and protecting human rights all over the world. The 'Centre for Human Rights' (Geneva), also part of the Secretariat, implements the policies of the High Commissioner.
30. There are nine functional commissions; Statistical Commission, Commission on Population and Development, Commission for Social Development, Commission on Human Rights, Commission on the Status of Women, Commission on Narcotic Drugs,

Commission on Science and Technology for Development, Commission on Crime Prevention and Criminal Justice and Commission on Sustainable Development.

31. The most important one is the Sub-Commission on Prevention of Discrimination and Protection of Minorities.
32. Alston, Ph., *op. cit.*, pp. 3-5.
33. Ermacora, R, "The reform of the human tights institutions of the United Nations", in *The reform of international institutions for the protection of human rights, First International Colloquium on Human Rights. La Laguna, Tenerife, 1st - 4th November 1992,* La Lacuna University, Brussels, Bruylant(1993), p. 140.
34. See for example Van Boven: "In order to maintain consistency in the interpretation of standards and in the assessment of facts and information, and with a view to avoiding duplication and confusion, there is much need for co-ordination between the various coexisting procedures and mechanisms. This co-ordination should be a constant concern of international secretariats and of the control mechanisms themselves" (Van Boven. T., *op. cit.*, p. 10). Sec also: Doc. *A/44/* 668, *Application effective des instruments international relntifs aux droits de I'homme, y compris I' obligation de presenter des rapports a ce titre.*
35. See for example: American Bar Association (ABA), *op. cit.*, p. 272. During its sixteenth session (1997), the Committee on the Rights of the Quid agreed on i he far; that such a reform would not be conducive to the implementation of the rights enshrined in each treatry: *"In view of the specificities of each of the six human rights treaties, the consolidation of reports to the six human rights treaty bodies into a single report would not be conducive to the implementation of the rights enshrined in each treaty, including the Convention on the Rights of the Child"* (Conclusions and recommendations adopted by the Committee on the Rights of the Child, CRC/C/69).

36. Nowak, M., "Proposals for Improving the UN Human Rights Programme", *NQHR2*(1993), p. 158.
37. Meron, Th.. *Human rights law-making in the United Nations – A critique of Instruments and Processes,* Oxford, Clarendon Press (1986), p, 2.
38. *Ibidem.*
39. "Now it is agreed that the economic, social and cultural rights set out in the other Covenant are to be implemented progressively. Indeed, it would obviously be impossible for a number of them- the right to work, for example-to be implemented immediately and completely anywhere. Civil and political rights, on the other hand, are as a general rule capable of immediate application, and a State should put its laws and administrative practice in compliance with the Covenant before ratifying it" (Robertson, A, H. and Merrill; J.G., *Human rights in the world. An introduction to the study of the international protection of human rights,* Manchester, Manchester University Press (1989), pp. 42-43).
40. This docs however not exclude social and economic rights from acquiring a self-executing character. Indeed, some social and economic rights can entail a so-called "standstill " – obligation.
41. Valticos, N., "International Mechanisms for the Protection of Human Rights", in *International Law: Achievements and Prospects,* Bedjaoui, M. (ed,), Dordrecht/Boston/Londen, Martinus Nijhoff Publishers (1991), p. 1152.
42. See Verhellen, E., *op. cit.,* p. 82. The author points out that the idea of mutual help, support and cooperation is at the same rime explicitly comprised in the substantial provisions of the Convention itself. Article 4, dealing with the economic, social and cultural rights, mentions that the States, whenever necessary, can look for the means to realize these rights, within the framework of the international cooperation.
43. Derrick, S. (ed.), *The United Nations Convention on the Rights of the Child. A Guide to the "Travaux paratoires",*

Dordrecht/Boston/London, Martinus Nijhoff Publishers (1992), p. 539. .

44. Article 42: "States Parries undertake to make the principles and provisions of the Convention widely known, by appropriate and active means, to adults and children alike".
45. Except a number of humanitarian conventions, that are applicable in situations of armed conflict.
46. The Belgian country reports arc to be found on the website of the Belgian Ministry of Justice: http://www.just.fgov.be/htmLdgl/kindnl.htm
47. CRC/C/20, para. 29.
48. See for example the "concluding observations" on the reports of Bolivia (CRC/C/20, para. 44). Vier Nam (CRC/C/20, para. 67), Costa Rica (CRC/C/20. para. 137), Peru (CRC/C/20, para, 75) and Egypt (CRC/C/I6, para. 108).
49. See: CRC/C/58, paras. 22-23.
50. In the course of the "travaux repertoires", a lot of attention was paid to the financial implications of the increase in the number of committees (see Detrick, S. (ed.), *op. cit.,* p. 555 and following).
51. Detrick, S. (ed.), *op. cit.* p. 555.
52. The Polish proposal was formulated as follows: "1. Reports submitted by the States Parties to the present Convention under Article 22 shall be considered by the Economic and Social Council, which may bring its observations and suggestions to the attention of the State Party concerned and of the General Assembly of the United Nations. The Council may also request a State Party to submit additional reports on specific issues relating to this Convention. To assist it in its task, the Economic and Social Council shall establish a Group of Governmental Experts entrusted with the responsibility of examining the reports submitted by States Parties...." (Detrick, S. (ed.), *op. cit.,* p. 552).
53. A lot of discussion on the manner of financing has arisen in the course of the "travaux repertoires". Some

countries, such as the United Kingdom and the United States of America, advocated financing by contributions made by the several States Parries. Other countries in their turn adhered to financing by the United Nations. This is why paragraph 12 of Article 43 has remained between square brackets for a longtime. Financing via the budget of the United Nations was finally opted for: "With the approval of the General Assembly, the members of the Committee established under the present Convention shall receive emoluments from United Nations resources on such terms and conditions as the Assembly may decide" (Art. 43, § 12).

54. "One representative expressed her belief that neither in the United Nations system nor among the non-governmental international organizations was there at present a legal entity which had an overall view of the rights of the child: it therefore believed that if it proved possible to establish a committee of specialists in this branch of the law, with expert knowledge of the serious problems that affect childhood today and with moral and legal authority to approach any governmental or private international agency to draw attention to the shortcomings in respect of children in the area of their different specialties (...), such a committee could be of considerable benefit to children and young people, in other words, minors" (Detrick, S. (ed.), *op. cit.* p. 539).

55. See http://www.unhchr.ch/tbs/doc.nsf

57. The Committee on Elimination of Racial Discrimination, the Human Rights Committee and the Committee on Economic, Social and Cultural Rights each consist of 18 experts. The Committee on Elimination of Discrimination against Women consists of 23 members. The Committee or; the Protection of the Rights of All Migrant Workers and Members of Their Families consist often members but, after the entry into force of the Convention for the forty-first State party, of fourteen experts.

57. It should however be pointed out that an amendment

to the Convention provides for an extension of the amount of members to 18. The amendment will only enter into force after the approval by 120 States parties. At the end of 1998, only half of the requisite States parties had approved the amendment (CRC/C/79, para. 11). Virtually no changes had occurred prior to the seventh meeting of the States parties (February 1999) (CRC/SP/25). After an extension of the members of the Committee from 10 to 18, the Committee could be divided in two working groups; as such, the amount of reports that could be reviewed would be doubled. This way of handling implies the risk that both 'parts' of the Committee could come to diverging interpretations, which would have its implications for the coherence of die Convention. This problem could, however, be countered by creating a 'bureau', consisting of the presidents of both working groups -as already exists in the European Court of Human Rights.

58. The procedure can be roughly outlined as follows:
1. Each State Party of the Convention may nominate one person from among its own nationals. The Secretary General of the United Nations invites the Stares Parties to .submit their nominations within a period of two months. He is to do so at least four months before the elections actually take place.
2. The Secretary General draws up an alphabetical list of all nominated persons, mentioning the countries they were nominated by. This list will then In: submitted to the States Parries of the Convention.
3. The elections are held at a meeting organized by the Secretary General. All States Parties are invited to this meeting. At least two thirds of the Stares Parties must attend the meeting. To be elected, a candidate must obtain an absolute majority of the votes of the attending delegates of voting States. Those who have the most voters are elected.

59. CRC/C/7, para. 3.

60. Those live members are appointed by the President of the Meeting by means of a lottery.
61. Six women and four men were elected at the first elections. Their countries of origin were the following: Egypt. Burkina Faso, Barbados, the Phlilipines, Sweden, Portugal, Russia, Brazil, Zimbabwe and Peru The female Brazilian member was replaced by a male Brazilian member at a second round of elections (CRC/C/10, para. 5). The term of office of four of the five members that expired at the 28th of February 1993 were renewed for another four years. The male Brazilin member was replaced by a female Brazilian member. On the 21th of February 1995 the Peruvian member was replaced by a female Israeli member. Alter the elections held at the 27th of February 1997, the countries of origin are the following: Italy, Israel, Russian Federation, Barbados, Indonesia, South Africa, Burkina Faso, Sweden, Lebanon and Brazil. And after the elections of the 1 6th February 1 999, the member of the Russian Federation, of Barbados and of Sweden were replaced by a Dutchman, a female Finnish member and a female Egyptian member. As the female Indonesian member has resigned at the twenty-second session (October 1999), another Indonesian female member has been recommended as a successor by her government. The Committee today consists of three men and seven women.
62. CRC/C/10, para. 33.
63. CRC/C/10), pant. 33.
64. CRG'C/7, para. 5.
65. CRC/C/7, *Recommendation concerning sessions of the Committee or its subsidiary bodies.*
66. CRC/C/7, para. 12.
67. Somalia is the only country that has not signed the Convention. The United States of America have signed the Convention on the 16th of February 1995, but haven't ratified it yet. The other countries have signed and ratified the Convention.

68. CCR/C/20, *Recommendation I.*
69. CRC/C/24, *Recommendation I.*
70. The first meeting was held in Quito, Ecuador between the 1st and the 5th of June 1992. The meeting was organized and financed by UNICEF and the Human Rights Centre (CRC/C/10, p. I ). The second meeting took place in Bangkok, Thailand, between the 23rd and the 29th of May 1993 (CRC/C/20, paras. 143-149). The third meeting took place in Africa, between the 11th and the 22e of July 1994 (CRC/C/34, paras. 156-159). The fourth informal meeting took place for two weeks in October 1995 in the South Asian region (CRC/C/46, paras. 186-194). The fifth informal meeting took place for two weeks in November 1996 in the Northern African region (CRC/C/62, para. 248-259). It is important to note that the visit to Egypt was the occasion of the holding, for the first time, of joint meetings between the Committee and the Committee on the Elimination of Discrimination against Women, It was agreed that the meetings had contributed to establishing a framework for more interaction between the two Committees and it was decided to follow up with periodic meetings to ensure further collaboration in the future on a regular basis (CRC/C/62, para. 257). From 29 May to 1 June 1998, the Committee was invited by the Italian authorities, with the support of the Italian National Committee for UNICEF. for an informal visit to Florence (CRC/C/79, para. 294).
71. CRC/C/10, para. 34; CRC/C/20, para. 143.
72. CRC/C/SR.29, para. 7.
73. It was at the second session (1992) that the Committee decided to call the attention of the "Fourth Meeting of persons chairing the human rights treaty bodies" to this work method: "The innovating experience of holding informal meetings at the regional level should be brought to the attention of the Fourth Meeting, in view of it relevance as a means to promote greater awareness of the Convention on the Rights of die Child

and its system of implementation, and to provide the Committee with a deeper knowledge and better understanding of the realities of a region" (CRC/C/10, *Recommendation* 5).

74. CRC/C/SR.29. para. 14.
75. Reid, R., "Children's Rights: Radical Remedies for Critical Needs, in *Justice for Children,* A5quith, S. and Hill, M. (ed.), Dordrecht/Boston/London, Martinus Nijhoff Publishers (1994), p. 21.
76. During its seventeenth session (1998), the Committee decided that it would start its consideration of periodic reports as from its nineteenth session in September-October 1998 (CRC/C/73, para. 146). During the nineteenth session only one periodic report had been considered, namely that of Bolivia. The discussion of the periodic report of Sweden, although on the agenda, was postponed on the request of the Swedish government (CRC/C/80, para. 20). During the twentieth session (January 1999), the Committee did consider the periodic reports of Sweden and Yemen (CRC/C/84, para. 128 and 151). The same has happened during the twenty-first (May-June 1999) (CRC/C/84, para. 95 and 205), the twenty-second (September-October 1999) (CRC/C/90, para. 63 and 160) and the twenty-third session.
77. *General guidelines regarding the form and content of initial reports to be submitted by States Parties under Article 44, paragraph I (a), of the Convention,* adopted by the Committee at its 22nd meeting (first session) on 1 5 October 1991 (CRC/C/7, Annex 111).
78. HRI/1991/1. Sec also *Manual relatifa I'etablissement des rapports sur les droits de I'homme,* New / York, Nations Unies (1992), pp. 33-34.
79. During its tenth session, the Committee decided to establish a working group with a view to preparing a working paper on the conceptual framework for guidelines regarding the form and content of periodic reports from States parties (CRC/C/46, para. 241).

During its eleventh session, the Committee decided to establish a working group to prepare a draft document for that purpose (CRC/C/50, para. 245). The guidelines were adopted by the Committee at its 343rd meeting (CRC/C/57, para. 222). See: CRC/C/58. See also: *Implementation Handbook fir the Convention on the /lights of the Child,* New York, Unicef (1998), p. 604-618.

80. CRC/C/54, para. 266.
81. CRC/C/57, para. 222.
82. Goodman, I)., "Analysis of the first session of the Committee on the Rights of the Child", NQHR 1(1992), p. 50.
83. Specifically: name and nationality (Art. 7), preservation of identity (Art. R). freedom of expression (Art. 13). access to appropriate information (Art. 17), freedom of thought, conscience and religion (Art. 14), freedom of association and of peaceful assembly (Art. 15), protection of privacy (Art. 16) and the right not to be subjected to torture or other cruel, in human or degrading treatment or punishment (Art. 37),
84. Specifically: art. 5 (parental guidance), Art. 18, $ 1 and 2 (parental responsibilities), Art. 9 (separation from parents), art, 10 (family reunification), Art. 27, $ -4 (recovery of maintenance for the child), Art. 20 (children deprived of a family environment), Art. 21 (adoption), art, 11 (illicit transfer and non-return), Art. 19 (abuse and neglect, including physical and psychological recovery and social reintegration), Art. 25 (periodic review of placement). The States are also to supply the Committee with the necessary information on the way in which the "best interest of the child" and the opinion of the child are being taken into account.
85. This section concerns the: following Articles: Art. 6, § 2 (survival and development), Art, 23 (disabled children), Art. 24 (health and health services), Art. 26 and 18, § 3 (social security and child care services and facilities) Art. § 1 to 3 (standard of living). Within this framework, the States are to describe a.o. the infrastructure of their health care policy.

86. Committee asks the States to supply some information on the provided infrastructure when carrying out their policies regarding education, including vocational training and guidance (Art. 28), aims of education (art. 29) and leisure, recrearion and cultural activities (art. 31)
87. See for example the "concluding observations" on the reports of Bolivia (CRC/C/16, para. 29), Vice Nam (CRC/C/16, para. 62), the Russian Federation (CRC/C/16, para. 85), Egypt (CRC/C/16, para. 96) Peru (CRC/C/20, para. 58), Sudan (CRC/C/20, para. 110), Costa Rica (CRC/C/20. para. 123), Denmark (CRC/C/38, para. 173) and Belgium (CRC/C/43. para. 103).
88. Goodman, D., "Analysis of the first session of the Committee on the Rights of the Child", *NQHR 1* (1992), p. 51.
89. Abramson. B., "First State reports; Sunny and... cloudy". *International children's rights monitor* (1993), Vol. 10, nos,. 1-2, p, 23. See also: Goodman, D., *op. cit.*, p. 51; Theytaz-Bergman, "Adjustments urgently needed. Fourth session of the Committee on the Rights of the Child", *International children's rights monitor* (1993), vol. 10, no. 4, p. 22; Smith, J., "The Committee on the Rights of the Child", *NQHR* (1994). p. 322; Himes, J.R., "Reflecting on indicators concerning the rights of the child - The development and human rights communities should get their acts together", in *Innocenti essays No* 5. *The United Nations Convention on the Rights of the Child: Three Essays on the Challenge of Implementation,* Unicef, Florence (1993), p. 20.
90. On the first reports, see: Abramson, B., "First State reports: Sunny and.., cloudy", *op. cit.,* pp. 22-37.
91. See the concluding observations on the reports of Rwanda (CRC/C/20, para. 139), Sudan (CRC/C/16, para. 111), Peru (CRC/C/20. para 56) and Indonesia (CRC/C/20, para 37).
92. However, it should be noted that in the guidelines regarding the periodic reports the States are asked to

give information about the change in budget allocation and expenditure for sectors serving children (CRC/C/58, pars, 7 and 20).

93. Theytraz-Bergman, L., 'Our of time 5th session of the Committee on the Rights of the Child", *International children's rights monitor* (1994), Vol. 11, No. 1. p. 10.
94. See: Himes, J.R., *op cit.* p. 13-20. See also: CRC/C/50, para, 244 en CRC/C/80, para. 200.
95. See: CRC/C/58. para. 20.
96. Hammarberg. T., "Justice for Children through the UN-Convention", *in justice for Children* Asquith, S. and Hill, M. (ed.), Dordrechr/Boston/London, Martinus Nijhoff Publishers (1994), p. 69.
97. During the twenty-second session (1999), it was decided that the pre-sessional meeting in the family would be country specific and strategically focused' (CRC/C/9(). para. 319).
98. CRC/C1/10, para. 39.
99. As the meeting is closed to die public, no observers are allowed *(Guidelines for the participation of partners (NGOs and individual experts) in the pre-sessional working group of the Committee on the Rights of the Child.* CRC/C/90, annex VIII. para. 6).
100. See a.o.: CRC/C/43, para. 12; CRC/C/46, para. 10; CRC/C/50, para. 10; CRC/C/54, para. 10; CRC/C/57, para. 11; CRC/C/62, para. 10.
101. See CRC/C/38, paras. 262-263: "Non-governmental organizations may (...) provide expert advice to the Committee, and they may submit reports, documentation or other information, both in writing and orally. Their cooperation has proved to be essential during the pre-scssional working group of the Committee. For that reason, the Committee decided that non-governmental organizations would be invited to the meetings or the working group with a view to providing it with expert advice. The Committee will address its invitations in the light of objective criteria, i.e. primarily based on written information previously

submitted by non-governmental organizations (...). Such organizations will be expected to provide factual information on specific aspects of each State parry report tinder consideration, in delight of the guidelines for reporting adopted by the Committee, including on the level of their involvement in the process of the preparation of the report, as well as on the implementation of the Convention".

102. CRC/C/90, para. 320. For the text to of these *Guidelines for the participation of partners (NGOs, and individual experts) in the pre-sessional working group of the Committee on the nights of the Child,* see: CRC/C/90, annex VIII.

103. See: *Guidelines for the participation of partners (NGOs and individual experts) in the pre-sessional working group of the Committee on the Rights of the Child,* CRC/C/90, annex VIII, paras. 2 and 3. Moreover, non-governmental organizations and individual experts wishing to provide written information to the Committee, should do so by providing twenty copies of each document to the Secretariat *(Ibidem,* para. 2).

104. The Committee will only invite NGOs whose information is particularly relevant to its consideration of the State's party's report. Priority will be given to partners who have provided information within the requested time-limit, who are working in the Stare party concerned and who can provide first-hand information that is complementary to information already available to the Committee *(Guidelines for the participation of partners (NGOs and individual experts) in the pre-sessional working group of the Committee on the Rights of the Child,* CRC/C/90. annex VIII, para. 4).

105. See: *Guidelines far the participation of partners (NGOs and individual experts) in the pre-sessional working group of the Committee on the Rights of the Child,* CRC/C/90. annex VIII, para. 4. The Committee strongly recommends that its partners limit their introductory remarks, which should be limited to highlights of the written submission, to a maximum if 15 minutes for NGOs

coming in-country and 5 minutes for others *(Ibidem,* para. 5).

106. Abramson, A.,"First State reports: Sunny and... cloudy", *op. cit.,* p. 26.
107. CRC/C/46. para. 13.
108. "Notwithstanding the desirability of such a dialogue, the Committee may use its right to examine reports even in the absence of a positive reaction on the part of a State party to the invitation to attend the meetings of the Committee. Such an approach is deemed necessary in order to enable the Committee to meet its mandate and heavy workload expeditiously and efficiently" (Conclusions and recommendations adopted by the Committee on the Rights of the Child, CROC/ 73).
109. HD. Goodman, D,, *op.cit.,* p. 48.
110. CRC/C/10, para. 40; Theytaz-Bergman, L *op. cit.,* p. 22.
111. See for example the "concluding observations" on the EI Salvador report (CRC/C/20, para. 77).
112. As at 1 July, 2000 there wore 191 Stares parties to the Convention.
113. Theytaz-Bergman, L., *op. cit.,* n. 11.
114. Theytaz-Bergman, L, *op. cit.,* p. 11; Smith, J., "The Committee on the Rights of thc Child", *NQHR*(1994), p. 322.
115. CRC/C/87, para. 255.
116. CRC/C/90, para, 318.
117. CRC/C/90. para. 318; CRC/C/87, para. 255. The country rapporteur is responsible: *(i)* for the contact with the staff member of the secretariat throughout the whole process; (2) for leading the discussion during the pre-session and the session; (3) for finalizing the List of Issues to be addressed to the State party after the pre-sessional working group meeting and (4) for finalizing and ensuring the quality of the concluding observations and recommendations (CRC/C/90, para, 318).
118. CRC/C/34, para. 12.

119. Mexico, Namibia, Romania and Belarus did comply with the request of the Committee but were not able to submit their written answers until the session actually took place. The information was moreover written in their own languages. Hence, the Committee members were not able to understand the information given. (Theyraz-Bergman, I.., *op.cit.,* p. 10).
120. Smith. J., the committee on the Rights of the Child", *NQHR*(1994), p. 32.
121. Conclusion and recommendations adopted by the Committee on the Rights of the Child (CRC/C/69).
122. CRC/C/90, para. 319.
123. CRC/C/16. annex VIII.
124. CROC/10, para. 41. For an entire overview of the concluding observations' from the 1th until the 17th session: Hohmtrom, L (ed.), *Concluding of the UN Committee on the Rights of the Child.* The Hague. Martinus Nijhoff Publishers (1999), 600 pages. See also the UN-Treaty Bodes Database' for the (remaining) concluding observations' and for all kinds of other documents: http://www.unchr.ch/tbs/doc.nsf
125. CRC/C/10. para. 42.
126. CRC/C/80 CRC/C/84; CRC/C/87; CRC/C/90. The concluding observations concerning the reports of Austria (CRC/C/84) and the Netherlands (CRC/C/90) -by chance two European States- do. however, contain only three parts (instead of four): (1) introduction; (2) positive aspects and (3) principal subjects of concern and the Committee's recommendations. The fourth part 'factors and difficulties impeding the implementation of the Convention has been omitted.
127. For the first concluding observations regarding a periodic report. see; CROC/80, paras. 88-118 (report of Bolivia); see also: CRC/C/84 (Sweden and Yemen); CRC/C/87 (Honduras and Nicaragua);CRC/C/90, (Russian Federation and Mexico). During the twentieth session, when considering periodic report of Sweden (CRC/C/84), and Liming the twenty-second session

(CRC/C/90). when considering the periodic report of the Russian Federation -once again two European States- the fourth element 'factors and difficulties impeding further progress in the, implementation of the Convention' has been omitted.

128. See also one of the principal recommendations in the study carried out by Philip Alston by order of the General Assembly of the UN: Alston, Ph., *Effective functioning of Bodies established pursuant to United Nations human right instruments, Final report on enhancing the long-term effectiveness of the United Nations human right treaty system, E/CN/4/1997/74, para* 122 "Treaty bodies must strive to further improve the quality, degree of detail, level of accuracy and specificity."
129. Goodman. 1)., *op. cit.,* 52.
130. For a case that can be discussed and in which the Committee nearly surpassed its authorities see concerting the Sudan report: Abramson, A., First State reports: Sunny and... cloudy", *op. cit.,* p. 24.
131. The Committee has emphasized that a follow-up of the suggestions and recommendations is really necessary (CRC/C/20, para. 28). See: "*Follow up to the consideration of initial reports by States Parties in the convention of the Rights of the Child us tit* 24 February 1994" (CRC/C/27, annex).
132. In the light of this, it should be noted that the representative of the International Labour Organization stated during the sixteenth session that the impact of the observations of the Committee at the national level was undeniable, as illustrated by the recent ratification by a number of Stare of ILO Convention No. 138 (CRC/C/69, para. 308).
133. As at 8 October, 1999, the Committee had received 134 initial and 25 periodic reports. A total of 110 reports have been examined by the Committee (CRC/C/90, para. 23).
134. The "working paper" is adopted as annex VIII with CRC/C/16. The following suggestions at that time were,

amongst others, formulated: the organization of an additional yearly session, in order to enable the Committee to spend two entire sessions on the study of the reports, and one session on specific topics, work organization, technical support,...; increase the number of Committee members to 18; only discuss the country reports for a certain period; restrict the time of discussion for each report; install sub-committees.

*ANNEXURE IX*

## UNITED NATIONS RULES FAR THE PROTECTION OF JUVENILES DEPRIVED OF THEIR LIBERTY ADOPTED BY GENERAL ASSEMBLY RESOLUTION 45/113 OF 14 DECEMBER 1990

### I. *Fundamental Perspectives*

1. The juvenile justice system should uphold the rights and safety and promote the physical and mental well-being of juveniles imprisonment should be used as a last resort.

2. Juveniles should only be deprived of their liberty in accordance with the principles and procedures set forth in these Rules and in the United Nations; Standard Minimum Rules for the Administration of Juvenile Justice (The Beijing Rules). Deprivation of the liberty of a juvenile should be a disposition of last resort and for the minimum necessary period and should be limited to exceptional cases. The length of the sanction should be determined by the judicial authority, without precluding the possibility of his or her early release.

3. The Rules are intended to establish minimum standards accepted by the United Nations for the protection of juveniles deprived of their liberty in all forms consistent with human rights and fundamental freedoms, and with a view to counteracting the detrimental effects of all types of detention and to fostering integration in society.

4. The Rules should be applied impartially, without discrimination of any kind as to race, colour, sex, age, language, religion, nationality, political or other opinion, cultural beliefs or practices, property, birth or family status, ethnic or social origin, and disability. The religious and cultural beliefs, practices and moral concepts of the juvenile should be respected.

5. The Rules are designed to serve as convenient standards of reference and to provide encouragement and guidance to professionals involved in the management of the juvenile justice system.

6. The Rules should be made readily available to juvenile justice personnel in their national languages. Juveniles who

are not fluent in the language spoken by the personnel of the detention facility should have the right to the services of an interpreter free of charge whenever necessary, in particular during medical examination and disciplinary proceedings.

7. Where appropriate, States should incorporate the Rules into their legislation or amend it accordingly and provide effective remedies for their breach, inducing compensation when injuries are inflicted on juveniles. States should also monitor the application of the Rules.

8. The competent authorities should constantly seek to increase the awareness of the public that the care of detained juveniles and preparation for their return to society is a social service of great importance, and to this end active steps should be taken to foster open contacts between the juveniles and the local community.

9. Nothing in the Rules should be interpreted as precluding the application of the relevant United Nations and human rights instruments and standards, recognized by the international community, that are more conducive to ensuring the rights care and protection of juveniles, children and all young persons.

10. In the event that the practical application of particular Rules contained in Sections II to V, inclusive, presents any conflict with the Rules contained in the present section, compliance with the latter shall be regarded as the predominant requirement.

### *II. Scope and Application of the Rules*

11. For the purposes of the Rules, the following definitions should apply:

- *(a)* A juvenile is every person under the age of 18. The age limit below which it should not be permitted to deprive a child of his or her liberty should be determined by law;
- *(b)* The deprivation of liberty means any form of detention or imprisonment or the placement of a person in a public or private custodial setting, from

which this person is not permitted to leave at will, by order of any judicial, administrative or other public authority.

12. The deprivation of liberty should be effected in conditions and circumstances which ensure respect for the human rights of juveniles. Juveniles detained in facilities should be guaranteed the benefit of meaningful activities and programs which would serve to promote and sustain their health and self-respect, to foster their sense of responsibility and encourage those attitudes and skills that will assist them in developing their potential as members of society.

13. Juveniles deprived of their liberty shall not for any reason related to their status be denied the civil, economic, political, social or cultural rights to which they are entitled under national or international law, and which are compatible with the deprivation of liberty.

14. The protection of the individual rights of juveniles with special regard to the legality of the execution of the detention measures shall be ensured by the competent authority, while the objectives of social integration should be secured by regular inspections and other means of control carried out according to international standards, national laws and regulations, by a duly constituted body authorized to visit the juveniles and not belonging to the detention facility.

15. The Rules apply to all types arid forms of detention facilities in which juveniles are deprived of their liberty. Sections I, II, IV and V of the Rules apply to all detention facilities and institutional settings in which juveniles are detained, and Section III applies specifically to juveniles under arrest or awaiting trial.

16. The Rules shall be implemented in the context of the economic, social and cultural conditions prevailing in each Member State.

### *III. Juveniles under Arrest or Awaiting Trail*

17. Juveniles who are detained under arrest or awaiting trial ("untried") are presumed innocent and shall be treated

as such. Detention before trial shall be avoided to the extent possible and limited to exceptional circumstances. Therefore, all efforts shall be made to apply alternative measures. When preventive detention is nevertheless used, juvenile courts and investigative bodies shall give the highest priority to the most expeditious processing of such cases to ensure the shortest possible duration of detention. Untried detainees should be separated from convicted juveniles.

18. The conditions under which an untried juvenile is detained should be consistent with the rules set out below, with additional specific provisions as are necessary and appropriate, given the requirements of the presumption of innocence, the duration of the detention and the legal status and circumstances of the juvenile. These provisions would include, but not necessarily be restricted to the following:

(*a*) Juveniles should have the right of legal counsel and be enabled to apply for free legal aid, where such aid is available, and to communicate regularly with their legal advisers. Privacy and confidentiality shall be ensured for such communications;

(*b*) Juveniles should be provided, where possible, with opportunities to pursue work, with remuneration, and continue education or training, but should not be required to do so. Work, education or training should not cause the continuation of the detention;

(*c*) Juveniles should receive and retain materials for their leisure and recreation as are compatible with the interests of the administration of justice.

### *IV. The Management of Juvenile Facilities*

#### *A. Records*

19. All reports, including legal records, medical records and records of disciplinary proceedings, and all other documents relating to the form, content and details of treatment, should be placed in a confidential individual file, which should be kept up to date, accessible only to authorized persons and classified in such a way as to be easily understood. Where possible, every juvenile should have the

right to contest any fact or opinion contained in his or her file so as to permit rectification of inaccurate, unfounded or unfair statements. In order to exercise this right, there should be procedures that allow an appropriate third party to have access to and to consult the file on request. Upon release, the records of juveniles shall be sealed, and, at an appropriate time, expunged.

20. No juvenile should be received in any detention facility without a valid commitment order of a judicial, administrative or other public authority. The details of this order should be immediately entered in the register. No juvenile should be detained in any facility where there is no such register.

*B. Admission, Registration, Movement and Transfer*

21. In every place where juveniles are detained, a complete and secure record of the following information should be kept concerning each juvenile received:

*(a)* Information on the identity of the juvenile;
*(b)* The fact of and reasons for commitment and the authority therefor;
*(c)* The day and hour of admission, transfer and release;
*(d)* Details of the notifications to parents and guardians on every admission, transfer or release of the juvenile in their care at the time of commitment;
*(e)* Details of known physical and mental health problems, including drug and alcohol abuse.

22. The information on admission, place, transfer and release should be provided without delay to the parents and guardians or closest relative of the juvenile concerned.

23. As soon as possible after reception, full reports and relevant information on the personal situation and circumstances of each juvenile should be drawn up and submitted to the administration.

24. On admission, all juveniles shall be given a copy of the rules governing the detention facility and a written description of their rights and obligations in a language they can understand, together with the address of the authorities competent to receive complaints, as well as the address of

public or private agencies and organizations which provide legal assistance. For those juveniles who are illiterate or who cannot understand the language in the written form, the information should be conveyed in a manner enabling full comprehension.

25. All juveniles should be helped to understand the regulations governing the internal organization of the facility, the goals and methodology of the care provided, the disciplinary requirements and procedures, other authorized methods of seeking information and of making complaints and all such other matters as are necessary to enable them to understand fully their rights and obligations during detention.

26. The transport of juveniles should be carried out at the expense of the administration in conveyances with adequate ventilation and light, in conditions that should in no way subject them to hardship or indignity. Juveniles should not be transferred from one facility to another arbitrarily.

*C. Classification and Placement*

27. As soon as possible after the moment of admission, each juvenile should be interviewed, and a psychological and social report identifying any factors relevant to the specific type and level of care and program required by the juvenile should be prepared. This report, together with the report prepared by a medical officer who has examined the juvenile upon admission, should be forwarded to the director for purposes of determining the most appropriate placement for the juvenile within the facility and the specific type and level of care and program required and to be pursued. When special rehabilitative treatment is required, and the length of stay in the facility permits, trained personnel of the facility should prepare a written, individualized treatment plan specifying treatment objectives and time-frame and the means, stages and delays with which the objectives should be approached.

28. The detention of juveniles should only take place

under conditions that take full account of their particular needs, status and special requirements according to their age, personality, sex and type of offence, as well as mental and physical health, and which ensure their protection from harmful influences and risk situations. The principal criterion for the separation of different categories of juveniles deprived of their liberty should be the provision of the type of care best suited to the particular needs of the individuals concerned and the protection of their physical, mental and moral integrity and well-being.

29. In all detention facilities juveniles should be separated from adults, unless they are members of the same family. Under controlled conditions, juveniles may be brought together with carefully selected adults as part of a special program that has been shown to be beneficial for the juveniles concerned.

30. Open detention facilities for juveniles should be established. Open detention facilities are those with no or minimal security measures. The population in such detention facilities should be as small as possible. The number of juveniles detained in closed facilities should be small enough to enable individualized treatment. Detention facilities for juveniles should be decentralized and of such size as to facilitate access and contact between the juveniles and their families. Small-scale detention facilities should be established and integrated into the social, economic and cultural environment of the community.

*D. Physical Environment and Accommodation*

31. Juveniles deprived of their liberty have the right to facilities and services that meet all the requirements of health and human dignity.

32. The design of detention facilities for juveniles and the physical environment should be in keeping with the rehabilitative aim of residential treatment, with due regard to the need of the juvenile for privacy, sensory stimuli, opportunities for association with peers and participation in sports, physical exercise and leisure-time activities. The design

and structure of juvenile detention facilities should be such as to minimize the risk of fire and to ensure safe evacuation from the premises. There should be an effective alarm system-in case of fire, as well as formal and drilled procedures to ensure the safety of the juveniles. Detention facilities should not be located in areas where there are known health or other hazards or risks.

33. Sleeping accommodation should normally consist of small group dormitories or individual bedrooms, while bearing in mind local standards. During sleeping hours there should be regular, unobtrusive supervision of all sleeping areas, including individual rooms and group dormitories, in order to ensure the protection of each juvenile. Every juvenile, should, in accordance with local or national standards, be provided with separate and sufficient bedding, which should be clean when issued, kept in good order and changed often enough to ensure cleanliness.

34. Sanitary installations should be so located and of a sufficient standard to enable every juvenile to comply, as required, with their physical needs in privacy and in a clean and decent manner.

35. The possession of personal effects is a basic element of the right to privacy and essential to the psychological well-being of the juvenile. The right of every juvenile to possess personal effects and to have adequate storage facilities for them should be fully recognized and respected. Personal effects that the juvenile does not choose to retain or that are confiscated should be placed in safe custody. An inventory thereof should be signed by the juvenile. Steps should be taken to keep them in good condition. All such Articles and money should be returned to the juvenile on release, except in to far as he or she has been authorized to spend money or send such property out of the facility, if a juvenile receives or is found in possession of any medicine, the medical officer should decide what use should be made of it.

36. To the extent possible juveniles should have the right to use their own clothing. Detention facilities should ensure that each juvenile has personal clothing suitable for the

climate arid adequate to ensure good health, and which should in no manner be degrading or humiliating. Juveniles removed from or leaving a facility for any purpose should be allowed to wear their own clothing.

37. Every detention facility shall ensure that every juvenile receives food that is suitably prepared and presented at normal meal times and of a quality and quantity to satisfy the standards of dietetics, hygiene and health and, as far as possible, religious and cultural requirements. Clean drinking water should be if available to every juvenile at any time.

*E. Education, Vocational Training and Work*

38. Every juvenile of compulsory school age has the right to education suited to his or her needs and abilities and designed to prepare him or her for return to society. Such education should be provided outside the detention facility in community schools wherever possible and, in any case by qualified teachers through programs integrated with the education system of the country so that, after release, juveniles may continue their education without difficulty. Special attention should be given by the administration of the detention facilities to the education of juveniles of foreign origin or with particular cultural or ethnic needs. Juveniles who are illiterate or have cognitive or learning difficulties should have the right to special education.

39. Juveniles above compulsory school age who wish to continue their education should be permitted and encouraged to do so, and every effort should be made to provide them with access to appropriate educational programs.

40. Diplomas or educational certificates awarded to juveniles while in detention should not indicate in any way that the juvenile has been institutionalized.

41. Every detention facility should provide access to a library that is adequately stocked with both instructional and recreational books and periodicals suitable for the juveniles, who should be encouraged and enabled to make fulf use of it.

42. Every juvenile should have the right to receive vocational training in occupations likely to prepare him or her for future employment.

43. With due regard to proper vocational selection and to the requirements of institutional administration, juveniles should be able to choose the type of work they wish to perform.

44. All protective national and international standards applicable to child labour and young workers should apply to juveniles deprived of their liberty.

45. Wherever possible, juveniles should be provided with the opportunity to perform remunerated labour, of possible within the local community, as a complement to the vocational training provided in order to enhance the possibility of finding suitable employment when they return to their communities. The type of work should be such as to provide appropriate training that will be of benefit to the juveniles following release. The organization and methods of work offered in detention facilities should resemble as closely as possible those of similar work in the community, so as to prepare juveniles for the conditions of normal occupational life.

46. Every juvenile who performs work should have the right to an equitable remuneration. The interests of the juveniles and of their vocational training should not be subordinated to the purpose of making a profit for the detention facility or a third party. Part of the earnings of a juvenile should normally be set aside to constitute a savings fund to be handed over to the juvenile on release. The juvenile should have the right to use the remainder of those earnings to purchase Articles for his or her own use or to indemnify- the victim injured by his or her offence or to send it to his or her family or other persons outside the detention facility.

*F. Recreation*

47. Every juvenile should have the right to a suitable amount of time for daily free exercise, in the open air whenever weather permits, during which time appropriate

recreational and physical training should normally be provided. Adequate space, installations and equipment should be provided for these activities. Every juvenile should have additional time for daily leisure activities, part of which should be devoted if the juvenile so wishes, to arts and crafts skill development, the detention facility should ensure that each juvenile is physically able to participate in the available programs of physical education. Remedial physical education and therapy should be offered, under medical supervision, to juveniles needing it.

*G. Religion*

48. Every juvenile should be allowed to satisfy the needs of his or her religious and spiritual life, in particular by attending the services or meetings provided in the detention facility or by conducting his or her own services and having possession of the necessary books or items of religious observance and instruction of his or her denomination. If a detention facility contains a sufficient number of juveniles of a given religion, one or more qualified representatives of that religion should be appointed or approved and allowed to hold regular services and to pay pastoral visits in private to juveniles at their request. Every juvenile should have the right to receive visits from a qualified representative of any religion of his or her choice, as well as the right not to participate in religious services and freely to decline religious education, counseling or indoctrination.

*H. Medical Care*

49. Every juvenile shall receive adequate medical care, both preventive and remedial, including dental, ophthalmologic and mental health care, as well as pharmaceutical products and special diets as medically indicated. All such medical care should, where possible, be provided to detained juveniles through the appropriate health facilities and services of the community in which the detention facility is located, in order to prevent stigmatization of the juvenile and promote self-respect and integration into the community.

50. Every juvenile has a right to be examined by a physician immediately upon admission to a detention facility, for the purpose of recording any evidence of prior ill-treatment and identifying any physical or mental condition requiring medical attention.

51. The medical services provided to juveniles should seek to detect and should treat any physical or mental illness, substance abuse or other condition that may hinder the integration of the juvenile into society. Every detention facility for juveniles should have immediate access to adequate medical facilities and equipment appropriate to the number and requirements of its residents and staff trained in preventive health care and the handling of medical emergencies. Every juvenile who is ill, who complains of illness or who demonstrates symptoms of physical or mental difficulties, should be examined promptly by a medical officer.

52. Any medical officer who has reason to believe that the physical or mental health of a juvenile has been or will be injuriously affected by continued detention, a hunger strike or any condition of detention should report this fact immediately to the director of the detention facility in question and to the independent authority responsible for safeguarding the well-being of the juvenile.

53. A juvenile who is suffering from mental illness should be treated in a specialized institution under independent medical management. Steps should be taken, by arrangement with appropriate agencies, to ensure any necessary continuation of mental health care after release.

54. Juvenile detention facilities should adopt specialized drug abuse prevention and rehabilitation programs administered by qualified personnel. These programs should be adapted to the age, sex and other requirements of the juveniles concerned, and detoxification facilities and services staffed by trained personnel should be available to drug or alcohol-dependent juveniles.

55. Medicines should be administered only for necessary treatment on medical grounds and, when possible, after

having obtained the informed consent of the juvenile concerned. In particular, they must not be administered with a view to eliciting information or a confession, as a punishment or as a means of restraint. Juveniles shall never be testers in the experimental use of drugs and treatment. The administration of any drug should always be authorized and earned out by qualified medical personnel.

*I. Notification of Illness, Injury and Death*

56. The family or guardian of a juvenile and any other person designated by the juvenile have the right to be informed of the state of health of the juvenile on request and in the event of any important changes in the health of the juvenile. The director of the detention facility should notify immediately the family or guardian of the juvenile concerned, or other designated person, in case of death, illness requiring transfer of the juvenile to an outside medical facility, or a condition requiring clinical care within the detention facility for more than 48 hours. Notification should also be given to the consular authorities of the State of which a foreign juvenile is a citizen.

57. Upon the death of a juvenile during the period of deprivation of liberty, the nearest relative should have the right to inspect the death certificate, see the body and determine the method of disposal of the body. Upon the death of a juvenile in detention, there should be an independent inquiry into the causes of death, the report of which should be made accessible to the nearest relative. This inquiry should also be made when the death of a juvenile occurs within six months from the date of his or her release from the detention facility and there is reason to believe that the death is related to the period of detention.

58. A juvenile should be informed at the earliest possible time of the death, serious illness or injury of any immediate family member and should be provided with the opportunity to attend the funeral of the deceased or go to the bedside of a critically ill relative.

*J. Contacts with the Wider Community*

59. Every means should be provided to ensure that juveniles have adequate communication with the outside world, which is an integral part of the right to fair and humane treatment and is essential to the preparation of juveniles for their return to society. Juveniles should be allowed to communicate with their families, friends and other persons or representatives of reputable outside organizations, to leave detention facilities for a visit to their home and family and to receive special permission to leave the detention facility for educational, vocational or other important reasons Should the juvenile be serving a sentence, the time spent outside a detention facility should be counted as part of the period of sentence.

60. Every juvenile should have the right to receive regular and frequent visits, in principle once a week and not less than once a month, in circumstances that respect the need of the juvenile for privacy, contact and unrestricted communication with the family and the defence counsel.

61. Every juvenile should have the right to communicate in writing or by telephone at least twice a week with the person of his or her choice, unless legally restricted, and should be assisted as necessary in order effectively to enjoy this right. Every juvenile should have the right to receive correspondence.

62. Juveniles should have the opportunity to keep themselves informed regularly of the news by reading newspapers, periodicals and other publications, through access to radio and television programs and motion pictures, and through the visits of the representatives of any lawful club or organization in which the juvenile is interested.

*K. Limitations of physical restraint and the use of force*

63. Recourse to instruments of restraint and to force for any purpose should be prohibited, except as set forth in Rule 64 below.

64. Instruments of restraint and force can only be used

in exceptional cases, where all other control methods have been exhausted and failed, and only as explicitly authorized and specified by law and regulation. They should not cause humiliation or degradation, and should be used restrictively and only for the shortest possible period of time. By order of the director of the administration, such instruments might be resorted to in order to prevent the juvenile from inflicting self-injury, injuries to others or serious destruction of property, in such instances, the director should at once consult medical and other relevant personnel and report to the higher administrative authority.

65. The carrying and use of weapons by personnel should be prohibited in any facility where juveniles are detained.

*L. Disciplinary Procedures*

66. Any disciplinary measures and procedures should maintain the interest of safety and an ordered community life and should be consistent with the upholding of the inherent dignity of the juvenile and the fundamental objective of institutional care, namely, instilling a sense of justice, self-respect and respect for the basic rights of every person.

67. All disciplinary measures constituting cruel, inhuman or degrading treatment shall be strictly prohibited, including corporal punishment, placement in a dark cell, closed or solitary confinement or any other punishment that may compromise the physical or mental health of the juvenile concerned. The reduction of diet and the restriction or denial of contact with family members should be prohibited for any purpose. Labour should always be viewed as an educational tool and a means of promoting the self-respect of the juvenile in preparing him or her for return to the community and should not be imposed as a disciplinary sanction. No juvenile should be sanctioned more than once for the same disciplinary infraction. Collective sanctions should be prohibited.

68. Legislation or regulations adopted by the competent administrative authority should establish norms concerning the following, taking full account of the fundamental characteristics, needs and rights of juveniles:

(*a*) Conduct constituting a disciplinary offence;
(*b*) Type and duration of disciplinary sanctions that may be inflicted;
(*c*) The authority competent to impose such sanctions;
(*d*) The authority competent to consider appeals.

69. A report of misconduct should be presented promptly to the competent authority, which should decide on it without undue delay. The competent authority should conduct: a thorough examination of the case.

70. No juvenile should be disciplinarily sanctioned except in strict accordance with the terms of the law and regulations in force. No juvenile should be sanctioned unless he or she has been informed of the alleged infraction in a manner appropriate to the full understanding of the juvenile, and given a proper opportunity of presenting his or her defence, including the right of appeal to a competent impartial authority. Complete records should be kept of all disciplinary proceedings

71. No juveniles should be responsible for disciplinary functions except in the supervision of specified social, educational or sports activities or in self-government programs.

*M. Inspection and Complaints*

72. Qualified inspectors or an equivalent duly constituted authority not belonging to the administration of the facility should be empowered to conduct inspections on a regular basis and to undertake unannounced inspections on their own initiative, and should enjoy full guarantees of independence in the exercise of this function. Inspectors should have unrestricted access to all persons employed by or working in any facility where juveniles are or may be deprived of their liberty, to all juveniles and to all records of such facilities.

73. Qualified medical officers attached to the inspecting authority or the public health service should participate in

the inspections, evaluating compliance with the rules concerning the physical environment, hygiene, accommodation, food, exercise and medical services, as well as any other aspect or conditions of institutional life that affect the physical and mental health of juveniles. Every juvenile should have the right to talk in confidence to any inspecting officer.

74. After completing the inspection, the inspector should be required to submit a report on the findings. The report should include an evaluation of the compliance of the detention facilities with the present rules and relevant provisions of national law, and recommendations regarding any steps considered necessary to ensure compliance with them. Any facts discovered by an inspector that appear to indicate that a violation of legal provisions concerning the rights of juveniles or the operation of a juvenile detention facility has occurred should be communicated to the competent authorities for investigation and prosecution.

75. Every juvenile should have the opportunity of making requests or complaints to the director of the detention facility and to his or her authorized representative.

76. Every juvenile should have the right to make a request or complaint, without censorship as to substance, to the central administration, the judicial authority or other proper authorities through approved channels, and to be informed of the response without delay.

77. Efforts should be made to establish an independent office (ombudsman) to receive and investigate complaints made by juveniles deprived of their liberty and to assist in the achievement of equitable settlements.

78. Every juvenile should have the right to request assistance from family members, legal counselors, humanitarian groups or others where possible, in order to make a complaint. Illiterate juveniles should be provided with assistance should they need to use the services of public or private agencies and organizations which provide legal counsel or which are competent to receive complaints.

*N. Return to the Community*

79. All juveniles should benefit from arrangements designed to assist them in returning to society, family life, education or employment after release. Procedures, including early release, and special courses should be devised to this end.

80. Competent authorities should provide or ensure services to assist juveniles in re-establishing themselves in society and to lessen prejudice against such juveniles. These services should ensure, to the extent possible, that the juvenile is provided with suitable residence, employment, clothing, and sufficient means to maintain himself or herself upon release in order to facilitate successful reintegration. The representatives of agencies providing such services should be consulted and should have access to juveniles while detained, with a view to assisting them in their return to the community.

***V. Personnel***

81. Personnel should be qualified and include a sufficient number of specialists such as educators, vocational instructors, counselors, social workers, psychiatrists and psychologists. These and other specialist staff should normally be employed on a permanent basis. This should not preclude part time or volunteer workers when the level of support and training they can provide is appropriate and beneficial. Detention facilities should make use of all remedial, educational, moral, spiritual, and other resources and forms of assistance that are appropriate and available in the community, according to the individual needs and problems of detained juveniles.

82. The administration should provide for the careful selection and recruitment of every grade and type of personnel, since the proper management of detention facilities depends on their integrity, humanity, ability and professional capacity to deal with juveniles, as well as personal suitability for the work.

83. To secure the foregoing ends, personnel should be

appointed as professional officers with adequate remuneration to attract and retain suitable women and men. The personnel of juvenile detention facilities should be continually encouraged to fulfi their duties and obligations in a humane, committed, professional, fair and efficient manner, to conduct themselves at all times in such a way as to deserve and gain the respect of the juveniles, and to provide juveniles with a positive role model and. perspective.

84. The administration should introduce forms of organization and management that facilitate communications between different categories of staff in each detention facility so as to enhance cooperation between the various between the various services engaged in the care of juveniles, as well as between staff and the administration, with a view to ensuring that staff directly in contact with juveniles are able to function in conditions favourable to the efficient fulfilment of their duties.

85. The personnel, should receive such training as will enable them to carry out their responsibilities effectively, in particular training in child psychology, child welfare and international standards and norm's of human rights and the rights of the child, including the present Rules. The personnel should maintain and improve their knowledge-and professional capacity by attending courses of in service training, to be organized at suitable intervals throughout their career.

86. The director of a facility should be adequately qualified for his or her task, with administrative ability and suitable training and experience, and should carry out his or her duties on a full-time basis.

87. In the performance of their duties, personnel of detention facilities should respect and protect the human dignity end fundamental human rights of all juveniles, in particular, as follows:

(*a*) No member of the detention facility or institutional personnel may inflict, instigate or tolerate any act of torture or any form of harsh, cruel, inhuman or degrading treatment, punishment, correction or discipline under any pretext or circumstance whatsoever;

*(b)* All personnel should rigorously oppose and combat any act of corruption, reporting it without delay to the competent authorities;

*(c)* All personnel should respect the present Rules. Personnel who have reason to believe that a serious violation of the present Rules has occurred or is about to occur should report the matter to their superior authorities or organs vested with reviewing or remedial power;

*(d)* All personnel should ensure the full protection of the physical and mental health of juveniles, including protection from physical, sexual and emotional abuse and exploitation, and should take immediate action to secure medical attention whenever required;

*(e)* All personnel should respect the right of the juvenile to privacy, and, in particular, should safeguard all confidential matters concerning juveniles or their families learned as a result of their professional capacity;

*(f)* All personnel should seek to minimize any differences between life inside and outside the detention facility which tend to lessen due respect for the dignity of juveniles as human beings.

*ANNEXURE X*

## UNITED NATIONS GUIDELINES FOR THE PREVENTION OF JUVENILE DELINQUENCY (THE RIYADH GUIDELINES)

## ADOPTED AND PROCLAIMED BY GENERAL ASSEMBLY RESOLUTION 45/112 OF 14 DECEMBER, 1990

### I. *Fundamental Principles*

1. The prevention of juvenile delinquency is an essential part of crime prevention in society. By engaging in lawful, socially useful activities and adopting a humanistic orientation towards society and outlook on life young persons can develop non-criminogenic attitudes.

2. The successful prevention of juvenile delinquency requires efforts on the part of the entire society to ensure the harmonious development of adolescents, with respect for and promotion of their personality from early childhood.

3. For the purposes of the interpretation of the present Guidelines, a child-centered orientation should be pursued. Young persons should have an active role and partnership within society and should not be considered as mere objects of socialization or control.

4. In the implementation of the present Guidelines, in accordance with national legal systems, the well-being of young persons from their early childhood should be the focus of any preventive program.

5. The need for and importance of progressive delinquency prevention policies and the systematic study and the elaboration of measures should be recognized. These should avoid criminalizing and penalizing a child for behavior that does not cause serious damage to the development of the child or harm to others. Such policies and measures should involve:

(*a*) The provision of opportunities, in particular educational opportunities, to meet the varying needs of young persons and to serve as a supportive framework for safeguarding the personal development of all young persons, particularly those who are demonstrably endangered or at social risk and are In need of special care and protection;

(*b*) Specialized philosophies and approaches for delinquency prevention, on the basis of taws, processes, institutions, facilities and a service delivery network aimed at reducing the motivation, need and opportunity for, or conditions giving rise to, the commission of infractions;

(*c*) Official intervention to be pursued primarily in the overall interest of the young person and guided by fairness and equity;

(*d*) Safeguarding the well-being, development, rights and interests of all young persons;

(*e*) Consideration that youthful behavior or conduct that does not conform to overall social norms and values is often part of the maturation and growth process and tends to disappear spontaneously in most individuals with the transition to adulthood;

(*f*) Awareness that, in the predominant opinion of experts, labeling a young person as "deviant", "delinquent" or "pre-delinquent" often contributes to the development of a consistent pattern of undesirable behaviour by young persons.

6. Community based services and programs should be developed for the prevention of juvenile delinquency, particularly where no agencies have yet been established. Formal agencies of social control should only be utilized as a means o last resort.

**II.** ***Scope of the Guidelines***

7. The present Guidelines should be interpreted and implemented within the broad framework of the Universal Declaration of Human Rights, the International Covenant on Economic, Social and Cultural Rights, the International Covenant on Civil and Political Rights, the Declaration of the Rights of the Child and the Convention on the Rights

of the Child, and in the context of the United Nations Standard Minimum Rules for the Administration of Juvenile Justice (The Beijing Rules), as well as other instruments and norms relating to the rights, interests and well-being of all children and young persons.

8. The present Guidelines should also be implemented in the context of the economic, social and cultural conditions prevailing in each Member State.

### III. *General Prevention*

9. Comprehensive prevention plans should be instituted at every level of Government and include the following:

*(a)* In-depth analyses of the problem and inventories of programs, services, facilities and resources available;

*(b)* Well-defined responsibilities for the qualified agencies, institutions and personnel involved in preventive efforts;

*(c)* Mechanisms for the appropriate coordination of prevention efforts between governmental and non-governmental agencies;

*(d)* Policies, programs and strategies based on prognostic studies to be continuously monitored and carefully evaluated in the course of implementation;

*(e)* Methods for effectively reducing the opportunity to commit delinquent acts;

*(f)* Community involvement through a wide range of services and programs;

*(g)* Close interdisciplinary co-operation between national. State, provincial and local governments, with the involvement of the private sector representative citizens of the community to be served, and labor, child-care, health education, social, law enforcement and judicial agencies in taking concerted action to prevent juvenile delinquency and youth crime;

*(h)* Youth participation in delinquency prevention policies and processes, including recourse to community resources, youth self-help, and victim compensation and assistance programs;

(*i*) Specialized personnel at all levels.

**IV. *Socialization Processes***

10. Emphasis should be placed on preventive policies facilitating the successful socialization and integration of all children and young persons, in particular through the family, the community, peer groups, schools, vocational training and the world of work, as well as through voluntary organizations. Due respect should be given in the proper personal development of children and young persons, and they should be accepted as full and equal partners in socialization and integration processes.

*A. Family*

11. Every society should place a high priority on the needs and well-being of the family and of all its members.

12. Since the family is the central unit responsible for the primary socialization of children, governmental and social efforts to preserve the integrity of the family, including the extended family, should be pursued. The society has a responsibility to assist the family in providing care and protection and in ensuring the physical and mental well-being of children. Adequate arrangements including day-care should be provided.

13. Governments should establish policies that are conducive to the bringing up of children in stable and settled family environments. Families in need of assistance in the resolution of conditions of instability or conflict should be provided with requisite services.

14. Where a stable and settled family environment is lacking and when community efforts to assist parents in this regard have failed and the extended family cannot fulfil this role, alternative placements, including foster care and adoption, should be considered. Such placements should replicate, to the extent possible, a stable and settled family environment, while, at the same time, establishing a sense of permanency for children, thus avoiding problems associated with "foster drift".

15. Special attention should be given to children of families affected by problems brought about by rapid and uneven economic, social and cultural change, in particular the children of indigenous, migrant and refugee families. As such changes may disrupt the social capacity of the family to secure the traditional rearing and nurturing of children, often as a result of role and culture conflict, innovative and socially constructive modalities for the socialization of children have to be designed.

16. Measures should be taken and programs developed to provide families with the opportunity to learn about parental roles and obligations as regards child development and child care, promoting positive parent-child relationships, sensitizing parents to the problems of children and young persons and encouraging their involvement in family and community-based activities.

17. Governments should take measures to promote family cohesion and harmony and to discourage the separation of children from their parents, unless circumstances affecting the welfare and future of the child leave no viable alternative.

18. It is important to emphasize the socialization function of the family and extended family; it is also equally important to recognize the future role, responsibilities, participation and partnership of young persons in society.

19. In ensuring the right of the child to proper socialization, Governments and other agencies should rely on existing social and legal agencies, but, whenever traditional institutions and customs are no longer effective, they should also provide and allow for innovative measures.

*B. Education*

20. Governments are under an obligation to make public education accessible to all young persons.

21. Education systems should, in addition to their academic and vocational training activities, devote particular attention to the following:

(*a*) Teaching of basic values and developing respect for the child's own cultural identity and patterns, for the social values of the country which the child is living, for civilizations different from the child's own and for human rights and fundamental freedoms;

(*b*) Promotion and development of the personality, talents and mental and physical abilities of young people to their fullest potential:

(*c*) Involvement of young persons as active and effective participants in, rather than mere objects of the educational process;

(*d*) Undertaking activities that foster a sense of identity with and of belonging to the school and the community;

(*e*) Encouragement of young persons to understand and respect diverse views and opinions, as well as cultural and other differences;

(*f*) Provision of information and guidance regarding vocational training, employment opportunities and career development;

(*g*) Provision of positive emotional support to young persons and the avoidance of psychological maltreatment;

(*h*) Avoidance of harsh disciplinary measures, particularly corporal punishment.

22. Educational systems should seek to work together with parents, community organizations and agencies concerned with the activities of young persons,

23. Young persons and their families should be informed about the law and their rights and responsibilities under the law, as well as the universal value system, including United Nations instruments.

24. Educational systems should extend particular care and attention to young persons who are at social risk. Specialized prevention programs and educational materials, curricula, approaches and tools should be developed and fully utilized.

25. Special attention should be given to comprehensive policies arid strategies for the prevention of alcohol, drug and other substance abuse by young persons. Teachers and

other professionals should be equipped and trained to prevent and deal with these problems. Information on the use and abuse of drugs, including alcohol, should be made available to the student body.

26. Schools should serve as resource and referral centres for the provision of medical, counseling and other services to young persons, particularly those with special needs and suffering from abuse, neglect, victimization and exploitation.

27. Through a variety of educational programs, teachers and other adults and the student body should be sensitized to the problems, needs and perceptions of young persons, particularly those belonging to underprivileged, disadvantaged ethnic or other minority and low-income groups.

28. School systems should attempt to meet and promote the highest professional and educational standards with respect to curricula, teaching and (earning methods and approaches, and the recruitment and training of qualified teachers. Regular monitoring and assessment of performance by the appropriate professional organizations and authorities should be ensured.

29. School systems should plan, develop and implement .extracurricular activities of interest to young persons, in co-operation with community groups.

30. Special assistance should be given to children and young persons who find it difficult to comply with attendance codes, and to "drop-outs".

31. Schools should promote policies and "rules that are fair and just; students should be represented in bodies formulating school policy, including policy on discipline, and decision-making.

*C. Community*

32. Community-based services and programs which respond to the special needs, problems, interests and concerns of young persons and which offer appropriate counseling and guidance to young persons and their families should be developed, or strengthened where they exist.

33. Communities should provide, or strengthen where

they exist, a wide range of community-based support measures for young persons, including community development centres, recreational facilities and services to respond to the special problems of children who are at social risk, in providing these helping measures, respect for individual rights should be ensured.

34. Special facilities should be set up to provide adequate shelter for young persons who are no longer able to live at home or who do not have homes to live in.

35. A range of services and helping measures should be provided to deal with the difficulties experienced by young persons in the transition to adulthood. Such services should include special programs for young drug abusers which emphasize care, counseling, assistance and therapy-oriented interventions.

36. Voluntary organizations providing services for young persons should be given financial and other support by Governments and other institutions.

37. Youth organizations should be created or strengthened at the local level and given full participatory status in the management of community affairs. These organizations should encourage youth to organize collective and voluntary projects, particularly projects aimed at helping young persons in need of assistance.

38. Government agencies should take special responsibility and provide necessary services for homeless or street children; information about local facilities, accommodation, employment and other forms and sources of help should be made readily available to young persons.

39. A wide range of recreational facilities and services of particular interest to young persons should be established and made easily accessible to them.

***D. Mass Media***

40. The mass media should be encouraged to ensure that young persons have access to information and material from a diversity of national and international sources.

41. The mass media should be encouraged to portray the positive contribution of young persons to society.

42. The mass media should be encouraged to disseminate information on the existence of services, facilities and opportunities for young persons in society.

43. The mass media generally, and the television and film media in particular, should be encouraged to minimize the level of pornography, drugs and violence portrayed and in display violence and exploitation disfavourably as well as to avoid demeaning and degrading presentations, especially of children, women and interpersonal relations, and to promote egalitarian principles and roles.

44. The mass media should be aware of its extensive social role and responsibility, as well as its influence, in communications relating to youthful drug and alcohol abuse. It should use its power for drug abuse prevention by relaying consistent messages through a balanced approach. Effective drug awareness campaigns at all levels should be promoted.

### V. *Social Policy*

45. Government agencies should give high priority to plans and programs for young persons and should provide sufficient funds and other resources for the effective delivery of services, facilities and staff for adequate medical and mental health care, nutrition, housing and other relevant services, including drug and alcohol abuse prevention and treatment, ensuring that such resources reach and actually benefit young persons.

46. The institutionalization of young persons should be a measure of last resort and for the minimum necessary period, and the best interests of the young person should be of paramount importance. Criteria authorizing formal intervention of this type should be strictly defined and limited to the following situations: *(a)* where the child or young person has suffered harm that has been inflicted by the parents or guardians; *(b)* where the child or young person has been sexually, physically or emotionally abused by the parents or guardians; *(c)* where the child or young person has been neglected, abandoned or exploited by the parents or guardians; *(d)* where the child or young person is

threatened by physical or moral danger due to the behavior of the parents or guardians; and *(e)* where a serious physical or psychological danger to the child or young person has manifested itself in his or her own behavior and neither the parents, the guardians, the juvenile himself or herself nor non-residential community services can meet the danger by means other than institutionalization.

47. Government agencies should provide young persons with the opportunity of continuing in full-time education, funded by the State where parents or guardians are unable to support the young persons, and of receiving work experience.

48. Programs to prevent delinquency should be planned and developed on the basis of reliable, scientific research findings, and periodically monitored, evaluated and adjusted accordingly.

49. 'Scientific information should be disseminated to the professional community and to the public at large about the sort of behavior or situation which indicates or may result in physical and psychological victimization, harm and abuse, as well as exploitation, of young persons.

50. Generally, participation in plans and programs should be voluntary young persons themselves should be involved in their formulation, development and implementation.

51. Government should begin or continue to explore, develop and implement policies, measures and strategies within and outside the criminal justice system, to prevent domestic violence against and affecting young persons and fair treatment to these victims of domestic violence.

## VI. Legislation and Juvenile Justice Administration

52. Governments should enact and enforce specific laws and procedures to promote and protect the rights and well-being of ail young persons.

53. Legislation preventing the victimization, abuse, exploitation and the use for criminal activities of children and young persons should De enacted and enforced.

54. No child or young person should be subjected to

harsh or degrading correction or punishment measures at home, in schools or in any other institutions.

55. Legislation and enforcement aimed at restricting and controlling accessibility of weapons of any sort to children and young persons should be pursued.

56. In order to prevent further stigmatization, victimization and criminalization of young persons, legislation should be enacted to ensure that any conduct not considered an offence or not penalized if committed by an adult is not considered it an offence and not penalized if committed by a young person.

57. Consideration should be given to the establishment of an office of ombudsman or similar independent organ, which would ensure that the status, rights and interests of young persons are upheld and that proper referral to available services is made. The ombudsman or other organ designated would also supervise the implementation of the Riyadh Guidelines, the Beijing Rules and the Rules for the Protection of Juveniles Deprived of their Liberty. The ombudsman or other organ would, at regular intervals, publish a report on the progress made and on the difficulties encountered in the implementation of the instrument. Child advocacy services should also be established.

58. Law enforcement and other relevant personnel, of both sexes, should be trained to respond to the special needs of young persons and should be familiar with and use, to the maximum extent possible, programs and referral, possibilities for the diversion of young persons from the justice system.

59. Legislation should be enacted and strictly enforced to protect children and young persons from drug abuse and drug traffickers.

### VII. *Research, Policy Development and Coordination*

60. Efforts should be made and appropriate mechanisms established to promote, on both a multidisciplinary and an interdisciplinary basis, interaction and coordination between economic, social, education and health agencies andservices,

the justice system, youth, community and development agencies and other relevant institutions.

61. The exchange of information, experience and expertise gained through projects, programs, practices and initiatives relating to youth crime, delinquency prevention and juvenile justice should be intensified at the national, regional and international levels.

62. Regional and international cooperation on matters of youth crime, delinquency prevention and juvenile justice involving practitioners, experts and decision-makers should be further developed and strengthened.

63. Technical and scientific cooperation on practical and policy-related matters, particularly in training, pilot and demonstration projects, and on specific issues concerning the prevention of youth crime and juvenile delinquency should be strongly supported by all Governments, the United Nations system and other concerned organizations.

64. Collaboration should be encouraged in undertaking scientific research with respect to effective modalities for youth crime and juvenile delinquency prevention and the findings of such research should be widely disseminated and evaluated.

65. Appropriate United Nations bodies, institutes, agencies and offices should pursue close collaboration and coordination on various questions related to children juvenile justice and youth crime and juvenile delinquency prevention.

66. On the basis of the present Guidelines, the United Nations Secretariat, in cooperation with interested institutions, should play an active role in the conduct of research, scientific collaboration, the formulation of policy options and the review and monitoring of their implementation, and should serve as a Source of reliable information on effective modalities for delinquency prevention.

***ANNEXURE XI***

## NATIONAL: CHARTER FOR CHILDREN, 2003

*The Government of India have had .for consideration the question of adopting a National Charter for Children to reiterate its commitment to the cause of the children in order to see that no child remains hungry, illiterate or sick. After the consideration, it has been decided to adopt the National Charter for Children enunciated below:-*

**National Charter for Children 2003.** Whereas the Constitution of India enshrines both in Parts III and IV the cause and the best interest of children, insofar that:

The State can make special provisions for children, [Art. 15(3)].

The State shall provide free and compulsory education to all children of the age of six to fourteen years, (Art. 21A).

No child below the age of 14 years shall be employed to work in a factory, mine or any other hazardous employment, (Art. 24).

The tender age of children is not abused and that citizens are not forced by economic necessity to enter avocations unsuited to their age or strength (Art. 39e).

Children are given opportunities and facilities to develop in a healthy manner and in conditions of freedom and dignity and that youth are protected against exploitation and against moral and material abandonment (Art. 39f).

The State shall endeavor to provide early childhood care and education for all children until they complete the age of six years, (Art. 45).

Whereas it is a Fundamental Duty of a parent or guardian to provide opportunities for education to his child or ward between the age of six and fourteen years, (Art. 51A)

Whereas through the National Policy for Children, 1974, we are committed to providing for adequate services to children, both before and after birth and throughout the period of growth, to ensure their full physical, mental and social development,

Whereas we affirm that the best interest of children must

be protected through combined action of the State, civil society, communities and families in their obligations in fulfilling children's basic needs.

Whereas we also affirm that while State, Society, Community and Family have obligations towards children, these must be viewed in the context of intrinsic and attendant duties of children and inculcating in children a sound sense of values directed towards preserving and strengthening the Family, Society and the Nation.

And whereas we believe that by respecting the child, society is respecting itself.

Now, therefore, in accordance with our pledge in the National Agenda of Governance, the following National Charter for Children, 2003 is announced.

Underlying this Charter is our intent to secure for every child its inherent right to be a child and enjoy a healthy and happy childhood, to address the root causes that negate the healthy growth and development of children, and to awaken the conscience of the community in the wider societal context to protect children from all firms of abuse, while strengthening the family, society and the Nation.

**1. Survival, Life and Liberty**

*(a)* The State and community shall undertake all possible measures to ensure and protect the survival, life and liberty of all children.

*(b)* In particular, the State and community will undertake all appropriate measures to address the problems of infanticide and foeticide, especially of female child and all other emerging manifestations that deprive the girl child of her right to survive with dignity.

**2. Promoting High Standards of Health and Nutrition**

*(a)* The State shall take measures to ensure that all children enjoy the highest attainable standards of health, and provide for preventive and curative facilities at all levels especially immunization and prevention of micronutrient deficiencies for all children.

*(b)* The State shall take measures to cover, under primary health facilities and specialized care and treatment,

all children of families below the poverty line.

(*c*) The State shall take measures to provide adequate pre-natal and post-natal care for mothers along with immunization against preventable diseases.

(*d*) The State shall undertake measures to provide for a national plan that will ensure that the mental health of all children is protected.

(*e*) The State shall take steps to ensure protection of children from all practices that are likely to harm the child's physical and mental health.

**3.** The State shall take steps to provide all children from families below the poverty line with adequate supplementary nutrition and undertake adequate measures for ensuring access to safe drinking water and environmental sanitation and hygiene.

**4. Assuring Basic Minimum Needs and Security**

(*a*) The State recognizes that the basic minimum needs of every child must be met, that foster full development of the child's faculties.

(*b*) In order to ensure this, the State shall in partnership with the community provide social security for children, especially for abandoned children and street children.

(*c*) State and community shall try and remove the fundamental causes which result in abandoned children and children living on streets, and provide infrastructure and material support by way of shelter, education, nutrition and recreation.

**5. Play and Leisure.** The State and community shall recognize that all children require adequate play and leisure for their healthy development and must ensure means to provide for recreational facilities and services for children of all ages and social groups.

**6. Early Childhood Care for Survival, Growth and Development**

(*a*) The State shall in partnership with the community provide early childhood care for all children and encourage programs which will stimulate and develop their physical and cognitive capacities.

*(b)* The State shall in partnership with the community aim at providing a child care centre in every village where infants and children of working mothers can be adequately cared for,

*(c)* The State will make special efforts to provide these facilities to children from SCs/STs and marginalized sections of society.

**7. Free and Compulsory Primary Education**

*(a)* The State recognizes that all children shall have access to free and compulsory education. Education at the elementary level shall be provided free of cost and special incentives should be provided to ensure that children from disadvantaged social groups are enrolled, retained and participate in schooling.

*(b)* At the secondary level, the State shall provide access to education for all and provide supportive facilities from the disadvantaged groups.

*(c)* The State shall in partnership with the community ensure that all the educational institutions function efficiently and are able to reach universal enrolment, universal retention, universal participation and universal achievement.

*(d)* The State and community recognize that a child be educated in its mother tongue.

*(e)* The State shall ensure that education is child-oriented and meaningful. It shall also take appropriate measures to ensure that education is sensitive to the healthy development of the girl child and to children of varied cultural backgrounds.

*(f)* The State shall ensure that school discipline and matters related thereto do not result in physical, mental, psychological harm or trauma to the child

*(g)* The Stale shall formulate special programs to spot, identify, encourage and assist the gifted children for their development in the field of their excellence.

**8. Protection from Economic Exploitation and All Forms of Abuse**

(*a*) The State shall provide protection to children from economic exploitation and from performing tasks that are hazardous to their well-being.

(*b*) The State shall ensure that there is appropriate regulation of conditions of work in occupations and processes where children perform work of a non-hazardous nature and that their rights are protected.

(*c*) The State shall move towards a total ban of all forms of child labor.

**9.** (*a*) All children have a right to be protected against neglect, maltreatment, injury, trafficking, sexual and physical abuse of all kinds, corporal punishment, torture, exploitation, violence and degrading treatment.

(*b*) The State shall take legal action against those committing such violations against children even if they be legal guardians of such children.

(*c*) The State shall in partnership with the community set up mechanisms for identification, reporting, referral, investigation and follow-up of such acts, while respecting the dignity and privacy of the child.

(*d*) The State shall in partnership with the community take up steps to draw up plans for the identification, care, protection, counseling and rehabilitation of child victims and ensure that they are able to recover, physically, socially and psychologically, and re-integrate into society.

**10.** (*a*) The State shall take strict measures to ensure that children arc not used in the conduct of any illegal activity, namely, trafficking of narcotic drugs and psychotropic substances, begging, prostitution, pornography or violence. The State in partnership with the community shall ensure that such children are rescued arid immediately placed under appropriate care and protection.

(*b*) The State and community shall ensure protection of

children in distress for their welfare and all round development.

*(c)* The State and community shall ensure protection of children during the occurrence of natural calamities in their best interest.

**11. Protection of the Girl Child**

*(a)* The State and community shall ensure that crimes and atrocities committed against the girl child, including child marriage, discriminatory practices, forcing girls into prostitution and trafficking are speedily eradicated.

*(b)* The State shall in partnership with the community undertake measures, including social, educational and legal, to ensure that there is greater respect for the girl child in the family and society.

*(c)* The State shall take serious measures to ensure that the practice of child marriage is speedily abolished.

**12. Empowering Adolescents.** The State and community shall take all steps to provide the necessary education and skills to adolescent children so as to equip them to become economically productive citizens. Special programs will be undertaken to improve the health and nutritional status of the adolescent girl.

**13. Equality, Freedom of Expression, Freedom to Seek and Receive Information, Freedom of Association and Peaceful Assembly.** The State and community shall ensure that all children are treated equally without discrimination on grounds of the child's or the child's parents or legal guardian's race, colour, caste, sex, language, religion, political or other opinion, national, ethnic or social origin, disability, birth, political status, or any other consideration.

**14.** All children shall be given every opportunity for all round development of their personality, including expression of creativity.

**15.** *(a)* Every child shall have the freedom to seek and receive information and ideas. The State and community shall provide opportunities for the child to access information that will contribute to the child's development.

(*b*) The State and community shall undertake special measures to ensure that the linguistic needs of children are taken care of and encourage the production and dissemination of child friendly information and material in various forms.

(*c*) The State and community shall be responsible for formulating guidelines for the mass media in order to ensure that children are protected from material injuries to their well-being.

**16.** All children shall enjoy freedom of association and peaceful assembly, subject to reasonable restrictions and in conformity with social and family values.

**17. Strengthening Family**

(*a*) Every child has a right to a family. In case of separation of children from their families, the State shall ensure that priority is given to reunifying the child with its parents. In cases where the State perceives adverse impact of such a—reunification, the State shall make alternate arrangements immediately, keeping in mind the best interests and the views of the child.

(*b*) All children have a right to maintain contact with their families, even when they are within the custody of the State for various reasons.

(*c*) The State shall undertake measures to ensure that children without families are either placed for adoption, preferably intra-country adoption, or foster care or any other family substitute services.

(*d*) The State shall ensure that appropriate rules with respect to the implementation of such services are drafted in a manner that are in the best interest of the child and that regulatory bodies are set up to ensure the strict enforcement of these rules.

(*e*) All children shall have the right to meet their parents and other family members who may be in custody.

**18. Responsibilities of Both Parents.** The State recognizes the common responsibilities of both parents in rearing their children.

**19. Protection of Children with Disabilities**

*(a)* The State and community recognize that all children with disabilities must be helped to lead a full life with dignity and respect. All measures would be undertaken to ensure that children with disabilities are encouraged to be integrated into the mainstream society and actively participate in all walks of life.

*(b)* State and community shall also provide for their education, training, health care, rehabilitation, recreation in a manner that will contribute to their overall growth and development.

*(c)* State and community shall launch preventive programs against disabilities and early detection of disabilities so as to ensure that the families with disabled children receive adequate support and assistance in bringing up their children.

*(d)* The State shall encourage research and development in the field of prevention, treatment and rehabilitation of various forms of disabilities.

**20. Care, Protection, Welfare of Children of Marginalized and Disadvantaged Communities.** The State and community shall provide care, protect and ensure the welfare of children from marginalized and disadvantaged communities, support them in preserving their identity, and encourage them to adopt practices that promote their best interest.

**21.** The State recognizes that children from disadvantaged communities and weaker/vulnerable sections of the society are in need of special interventions and support in all matters pertaining to education, health, recreation and supportive services. It shah make adequate provisions for providing such groups with special attention in all its policies and programs.

**22. Ensuring Child Friendly Procedures.** All matters and procedures relating to children, *viz.*, judicial, administrative, educational or social, should be child friendly. All procedures laid down under the juvenile justice system for children in conflict with law and for children in need of special care and protection shall also be child-friendly.

*ANNEXURE XII*

## THE COMMISSIONS FOR PROTECTION OF CHILD RIGHTS ACT, 2005 NO. 4 OF 2006

[20th January, 2006]

An Act to provide for the constitution of a National Commission and State Commissions for Protection of Child Rights and Children's Courts for providing speedy trial of offences against children or of violation of child rights and for matters connected therewith or incidental thereto.

WHEREAS India participated in the United Nations (UN) General Assembly Summit in 1990, which adopted a Declaration on Survival, Protection and Development of Children;

AND WHEREAS India has also acceded to the Convention on the Rights of the Child (CRC) on the 11th December, 1992;

AND WHEREAS CRC is an international treaty that makes it incumbent upon the signatory States to take all necessary steps to protect children's rights enumerated in the Convention;

AND WHEREAS in order to ensure protection of rights of children one of the recent initiatives that the Government have taken for Children is the adoption of National Charter for Children, 2003;

AND WHEREAS the UN General Assembly Special Session on Children held in May, 2002 adopted an Outcome Document titled "A World Fit for Children" containing the goals, objectives, strategies and activities to be undertaken by the member countries for the current decade;

AND WHEREAS it is expedient to enact a law relating to children to give effect to the policies adopted by the Government in this regard, standards prescribed in the CRC, and all other relevant international instruments;

**BE** it enacted by Parliament in the Fifty-sixth Year of the Republic of India as follows:

## Chapter I
## Preliminary

***Short Title, Extent and Commencement***

1. This Act may be called the Commissions for Protection of Child Rights Act, 2005.

2. It extends to the whole of India except the State of Jammu and Kashmir.

3. It shall come into force on such date as the Central Government may, by notification in the Official Gazette, appoint.

***Definitions***

2. In this Act, unless the context otherwise requires,-

*(a)* "Chairperson" means the Chairperson of the Commission or of the State Commission, as the case may be;

*(b)* "child rights" includes the children's rights adopted in the United Nations convention on the Rights of the Child on the 20th November, 1989 and ratified by the Government of India on the 11th December, 1992;

*(c)* "Commission" means the National Commission for Protection of Child Rights constituted under Section 3;

*(d)* "Member" means a Member of the Commission or of the State Commission, as the case may be, and includes the Chairperson;

*(e)* "notification" means a notification published in the Official Gazette;

*(f)* "prescribed" means prescribed by rules made under this Act; (g) "State Commission" means a State Commission for Protection of Child Rights constituted under Section 17.

## Chapter II
## The National Commission for Protection of Child Rights

### *Constitution of National Commission for Protection of Child Rights*

**3.** 1. The Central Government shall, by notification, constitute a body to be known as the National Commission for Protection of Child Rights to exercise the powers conferred on, and to perform the functions assigned to it, under this Act.

2. The Commission shall consist of the following Members, namely:

*(a)* a Chairperson who is a person of eminence and has done outstanding work for promoting the welfare of children; and

*(b)* six Members, out of which at least two shall be women, from the following fields, to be appointed by the Central Government from amongst persons of eminence, ability, integrity, standing and experience in,

- *(i)* education;
- *(ii)* child health, care, welfare or child development;
- *(iii)* juvenile justice or care of neglected or marginalized children or children with disabilities;
- *(iv)* elimination of child labour or children in distress;
- *(v)* child psychology or sociology; and
- *(vi)* laws relating to children.

3. The office of the Commission shall be at Delhi.

### *Appointment of Chairperson and Members*

4. The Central Government shall, by notification, appoint the Chairperson and other Members: Provided that the Chairperson shall be appointed on the recommendation of a three member Selection Committee constituted by the Central Government under the Chairmanship of the Minister in-charge of the Ministry of Human Resource Development.

Term of office and conditions of service of Chairperson and Members.

5. (1) The Chairperson and every Member shall hold office as such for a term of three years from the date on which he assumes office:

Provided that no Chairperson or a Member shall hold the office for more than two terms:

Provided further that no Chairperson or any other Member shall hold office as such after he has attained-

*(a)* in the case of the Chairperson, the age of sixty-five years; and

*(b)* in the case of a Member, the age of sixty years.

(2) The Chairperson or a Member may, by writing under his hand addressed to the Central Government, resign his office at any time.

### *Salary and Allowances of Chairperson and Members*

6. The salary and allowances payable to, and other terms and conditions of service of, the Chairperson and Members, shall be such as may be prescribed by the Central Government:

Provided that neither the salary and allowances nor the other terms and conditions of service of the Chairperson or a Member, as the case may be, shall be varied to his disadvantage after his appointment.

### *Removal from Office*

7. (1) Subject to the provisions of sub-section (2), the Chairperson may be removed from his office by an order of the Central Government on the ground of proved misbehavior or incapacity.

(2) Notwithstanding anything contained in sub-section (1), the Central Government may by order remove from office the Chairperson or any other Member, if the Chairperson or, as the case may be, such other Member, -

*(a)* is adjudged an insolvent; or

*(b)* engages during his term of office in any paid employment outside the duties of his office; or

*(c)* refuses to act or becomes incapable of acting; or

(*d*) is of unsound mind and stands so declared by a competent court; or

(*e*) has so abused his office as to render his continuance in office detrimental to the public interest; or

(*f*) is convicted and sentenced to imprisonment for an offence which in the opinion of the Central Government involves moral turpitude; or

(*g*) is, without obtaining leave of absence from the Commission, absent from three consecutive meetings of the Commission.

(3) No person shall be removed under this section until that person has been given an opportunity of being heard in the matter.

***Vacation of Office by Chairperson or Members***

8. (1) If the Chairperson or, as the case may be, a Member, (*a*) becomes subject to any of the disqualifications mentioned in section 7; or

(*b*) tenders his resignation under sub-section (2) of section 5, his seat shall thereupon become vacant.

(2) If a casual vacancy occurs in the office of the Chairperson or a Member, whether by reason of his death, resignation or otherwise, such vacancy shall be filled within a period of ninety days by making afresh appointment in accordance with the provisions of Section 4 and the person so appointed shall hold office for the remainder of the term of office for which the Chairperson, or a Member, as the case may be, in whose place he is so appointed would have held that office.

Vacancies, etc., not to invalidate proceedings of Commission.

9. No act or proceeding of the Commission shall be invalid merely by reason of-

(*a*) any vacancy in, or any defect in the constitution of, the Commission; or

(*b*) any defect in the appointment of a person as the Chairperson or a Member; or

(*c*) any irregularity in the procedure of the Commission not affecting the merits of the case.

***Procedure for Transaction of Business***

10. (1) The Commission shall meet regularly at its office at such time as the Chairperson thinks fit, but three months shall not intervene between its last and the next meeting.

(2) All decisions at a meeting shall be taken by majority: Provided that in the case of equality of votes, the Chairperson, or in his absence the person presiding, shall have and exercise a second or casting vote.

(3) If for any reason, the Chairperson, is unable to attend the meeting of the Commission, any Member chosen by the Members present from amongst themselves at the meeting, shall preside.

(4) The Commission shall observe such rules of procedure in the transaction of its business at a meeting, including the quorum at such meeting, as may be prescribed by the Central Government.

(5) All orders and decisions of the Commission shall be authenticated by the Member- Secretary or any other officer of the Commission duly authorized by Member-Secretary in this behalf.

Member-Secretary, officers and other employees of Commission.

11. (1) The Central Government shall, by notification, appoint an officer not below the rank of the Joint Secretary or the Additional Secretary to the Government of India as a Member-Secretary of the Commission and shall make available to the Commission such other officers and employees as may be necessary for the efficient performance of its functions.

(2) The Member-Secretary shall be responsible for the proper administration of the affairs of the Commission and its day-to-day management and shall exercise and discharge such other powers and perform such other duties as may be prescribed by the Central Government.

(3) The salary and allowances payable to, and the other terms and conditions of service of the Member-Secretary, other officers and employees, appointed for the purpose of

the Commission shall be such as may be prescribed by the Central Government.

Salaries and allowances to be paid out of grants.-

12. The salaries and allowances payable to the Chairperson and Members and the administrative expenses, including salaries, allowances and pensions payable to the Member-Secretary, other officers and employees referred to in Section 11, shall be paid out of the grants referred to in sub-section (1) of Section 27.

## Chapter III
## Functions and Powers of the Commission

### *Functions of Commission*

13. (1) The Commission shall perform all or any of the following functions, namely:-

*(a)* examine and review the safeguards provided by or under any law for the time being in force for the protection of child rights and recommend measures for their effective implementation;

*(b)* present to the Central Government, annually and at such other intervals, as the Commission may deem fit, reports upon the working of those safeguards;

*(c)* inquire into violation of child rights and recommend initiation of proceedings in such cases;

*(d)* examine all factors that inhibit the enjoyment of rights of children affected by terrorism, communal violence, riots, natural disaster, domestic violence, HIV/AIDS, trafficking, maltreatment, torture and exploitation, pornography and prostitution and recommend appropriate remedial measures;

*(e)* look into the matters relating to children in need of special care and protection including children in distress, marginalized and disadvantaged children, children in conflict with law, juveniles, children without family and children of prisoners and recommend appropriate remedial measures;

*(f)* study treaties and other international instruments and undertake periodical review of existing policies, programmes and other activities on child rights and make re-

commendations for their effective implementation in the best interest of children;

*(g)* undertake and promote research in the field of child rights;

*(h)* spread child rights literacy among various sections of the society and promote awareness of the safeguards available for protection of these rights through publications, the media, seminars and other available means;

*(i)* inspect or cause to be inspected any juvenile custodial home, or any other place of residence or institution meant for children, under the control of the Central Government or any State Government or any other authority, including any institution run by a social organization; where children are detained or lodged for the purpose of treatment, reformation or protection and take up with these authorities for remedial action, if found necessary;

*(j)* inquire into complaints and take suo motu notice of matters relating to,-

*(i)* deprivation and violation of child rights;

*(ii)* non-implementation of laws providing for protection and development of children;

*(iii)* non-compliance of policy decisions, guidelines or instructions aimed at mitigating hardships to and ensuring welfare of the children and to provide relief to such children, or take up the issues arising out of such matters with appropriate authorities; and

*(k)* such other functions as it may consider necessary for the promotion of child rights and any other matter incidental to the above functions.

(2) The Commission shall not inquire into any matter which is pending before a State Commission or any other Commission duly constituted under any law for the time being in force.

### *Powers Relating to Inquiries*

14. (1) The Commission shall, while inquiring into any matter referred to in clause (j) of sub-section (1) of Section 13 have all the powers of a civil court trying a suit under

the Code of Civil Procedure, 1908 and, in particular, in respect of the following matters, namely:-

*(a)* summoning and enforcing the attendance of any person and examining him on oath;

*(b)* discovery and production of any document;

*(c)* receiving evidence on affidavits;

*(d)* requisitioning any public record or copy thereof from any court or office; and

*(e)* issuing commissions for the examination of witnesses or documents.

(2) The Commission shall have the power to forward any case to a Magistrate having jurisdiction to try the same and the Magistrate to whom any such case is forwarded shall proceed to hear the complaint against the accused as if the case has been forwarded to him under Section 346 of the Code of Criminal Procedure, 1973 (2 of 1974).

### *Steps after Inquiry*

15. The Commission may take any of the following steps upon the completion of an inquiry held under this Act, namely:

*(i)* where the inquiry discloses, the Commission of violation of child rights of a serious nature or contravention of provisions of any law for the time being in force, it may recommend to the concerned Government or authority the initiation of proceedings for prosecution or such other action as the Commission may deem fit against the concerned person or persons;

*(ii)* approach the Supreme Court or the High Court concerned for such directions, orders or writs as that Court may deem necessary;

*(iii)* recommend to the concerned Government or authority for the grant of such interim relief to the victim or the members of his family as the Commission may consider necessary.

***Annual and Special Reports of Commission***

16. (1) The Commission shall submit an annual report to the Central Government and to the State Government concerned and may at any time submit special reports on any matter which, in its opinion, is of such urgency or importance that it should not be deferred till submission of the annual report.

(2) The Central Government and the State Government concerned, as the case may be, shall cause the annual and special reports of the Commission to be laid before each House of Parliament or the State Legislature respectively, as the case may be, along with a memorandum of action taken or proposed to be taken on the recommendations of the Commission and the reasons for non-acceptance of the recommendations, if any, within a period of one year from the date of receipt of such report.

(3) The annual report shall be prepared in such form, manner and contain such details as may be prescribed by the Central Government.

## Chapter IV
## State Commissions for Protection of Child Rights

***Constitution of State Commission for Protection of Child Rights***

17. (1) A State Government may constitute a body to be known as the ..........(name of the State) Commission for Protection of Child Rights to exercise the powers conferred upon, and to perform the functions assigned to, a State Commission under this Chapter.

(2) The State Commission shall consist of the following Members, namely:

*(a)* a Chairperson who is a person of eminence and has done outstanding work for promoting the welfare of children; and

*(b)* six Members, out of which at least two shall be women, from the following fields, to be appointed by the State

Government from amongst persons of eminence, ability, integrity, standing and experience in,

*(i)* education;

*(ii)* child health, care, welfare or child development;

*(iii)* juvenile justice or care of neglected or marginalized children or children with disabilities;

*(iv)* elimination of child labor or children in distress;

*(v)* child psychology or sociology; and

*(vi)* laws relating to children.

(3) The headquarter of the State Commission shall be at such place as the State Government may, by notification, specify.

### *Appointment of Chairperson and Other Members*

18. The State Government shall, by notification, appoint the Chairperson and other Members:

Provided that the Chairperson shall be appointed on the recommendation of a three Member Selection Committee constituted by the State Government under the Chairmanship of the Minister in-charge of the Department dealing with children.

### *Term of Office and Conditions of Service of Chairperson and Members*

19. (1) The Chairperson and every Member shall hold office as such for a term of three years from the date on which he assumes office:

Provided that no Chairperson or a Member shall hold the office for more than two terms:

Provided further that no Chairperson or any other Member shall hold office as such after he has attained-

(a) in the case of Chairperson, the age of sixty-five years; and (b) in the case of a Member, the age of sixty years.

(2) The Chairperson or a Member may, by writing under his hand addressed to the State Government, resign his office at any time.

Salary and allowances of Chairperson and Members.

20. The salaries and allowances payable to, and other

terms and conditions of service of, the Chairperson and Members shall be such as may be prescribed by the State Government:

Provided that neither the salary and allowances nor the other terms and conditions of service of the Chairperson or a Member, as the case may be, shall be varied to his disadvantage after his appointment.

*Secretary, Officers and Other Employees of the State Commission*

21. (1) The State Government shall, by notification, appoint an officer not below the rank of the Secretary to the State Government as the Secretary of the State Commission and shall make available to the State Commission such other officers and employees as may be necessary for the efficient performance of its functions.

(2) The Secretary shall be responsible for the proper administration of the affairs of the State Commission and its day-to-day management and shall exercise and discharge such other powers and perform such other duties as may be prescribed by the State Government.

(3) The salary and allowances payable to, and the other terms and conditions of service of the Secretary, other officers and employees, appointed for the purpose of the State Commission shall be such as may be prescribed by the State Government.

*Salaries and Allowances to be Paid Out of Grants*

22. The salaries and allowances payable to the Chairperson and Members and the administrative expenses, including salaries, allowances and pensions payable to the Secretary, other officers and employees referred to in Section 21, shall be paid out of the grants referred to in sub-section (1) of section 28.

*Annual and Special reports of State Commission.*

23. (1) The State Commission shall submit an annual

report to the State Government and may at any time submit special reports on any matter which, in its opinion, is of such urgency or importance that it should not be deferred till submission of the annual report.

(2) The State Government shall cause all the reports referred to in sub-section (1) to be laid before each House of State Legislature, where it consists of two Houses, or where such Legislature consists of one House, before that House along with a memorandum explaining the action taken or proposed to be taken on the recommendations relating to the State and the reasons for the non-acceptance, if any, of any of such recommendations.

(3) The annual report shall be prepared in such form, manner and contain such details as may be prescribed by the State Government.

***Application of Certain Provisions Relating to National Commission for Protection of Child Rights to State Commissions***

24. The provisions of Sections 7, 8, 9, 10, sub-section (1) of Section 13 and Sections 14 and 15 shall apply to a State Commission and shall have effect, subject to the following modifications, namely:

*(a)* references to "Commission" shall be construed as references to "State Commission";

*(b)* references to "Central Government" shall be construed as references to "State Government"; and

*(c)* references to "Member-Secretary" shall be construed as references to "Secretary".

## Chapter V
## Children's Courts

***Children's Courts***

25. For the purpose of providing speedy trial of offences against children or of violation of child rights, the State Government may, with the concurrence of the Chief Justice

of the High Court, by notification, specify at least a court in the State or specify, for each district, a Court of Session to be a Children's Court to try the said offences:

Provided that nothing in this section shall apply if –

*(a)* a Court of Session is already specified as a special court; or *(b)* a special court is already constituted, for such offences under any other law for the time being in force.

### *Special Public Prosecutor*

26. For every Children's Court, the State Government shall, by notification, specify a Public Prosecutor or appoint an advocate who has been in practice as an advocate for not less than seven years, as a Special Public Prosecutor for the purpose of conducting cases in that Court.

## Chapter VI
## Finance, Accounts and Audit

### *Grants by Central Government*

27. (1) The Central Government shall, after due appropriation made by Parliament by law in this behalf, pay to the Commission by way of grants such sums of money as the Central Government may think fit for being utilized for the purposes of this Act.

(2) The Commission may spend such sums of money as it thinks fit for performing the functions under this Act, and such sums shall be treated as expenditure payable out of the grants referred to in sub-section (1).

### *Grants by State Governments*

28. (1) The State Government shall, after due appropriation made by Legislature by law in this behalf, pay to the State Commission by way of grants such sums of money as the State Government may think fit for being utilized for the purposes of this Act.

(2) The State Commission may spend such sums of money as it thinks fit for performing the functions under Chapter

III of this Act, and such sums shall be treated as expenditure payable out of the grants referred to in sub-section (1).

*Accounts and Audit of Commission*

29. (1) The Commission shall maintain proper accounts and other relevant records and prepare an annual statement of accounts in such form as may be prescribed by the Central Government in consultation with the Comptroller and Auditor-General of India.

(2) The accounts of the Commission shall be audited by the Comptroller and Auditor-General at such intervals as may be specified by him and any expenditure incurred in connection with such audit shall be payable by the Commission to the Comptroller and Auditor-General.

(3) The Comptroller and Auditor-General and any person appointed by him in connection with the audit of the accounts of the Commission under this Act shall, have the same rights and privileges and the authority in connection with such audit as the Comptroller and Auditor-General generally has in connection with the audit of Government accounts and, in particular, shall have the right to demand the production of books, accounts, connected vouchers and other documents and papers and to inspect any of the offices of the Commission.

(4) The accounts of the Commission as certified by the Comptroller and Auditor-General or any other person appointed by him in this behalf, together with the audit report thereon shall be forwarded annually to the Central Government by the Commission and the Central Government shall cause the audit report to be laid, as soon as may be after it is received, before each House of Parliament.

*Accounts and Audit of State Commission*

30. (1) The State Commission shall maintain proper accounts and other relevant records and prepare an annual statement of accounts in such form as may be prescribed by the State Government in consultation with the Comptroller and Auditor-General of India.

(2) The accounts of the State Commission shall be audited by the Comptroller and Auditor-General at such intervals as may be specified by him and any expenditure incurred in connection with such audit shall be payable by the State Commission to the Comptroller and Auditor-General.

(3) The Comptroller and Auditor-General and any person appointed by him in connection with the audit of the accounts of the State Commission under this Act shall, have the same rights and privileges and the authority in connection with such audit as the Comptroller and Auditor-General generally has in connection with the audit of Government accounts and, in particular, shall have the right to demand the production of books, accounts, connected vouchers and other documents and papers and to inspect any of the offices of the State Commission.

(4) The accounts of the State Commission as certified by the Comptroller and Auditor-General or any other person appointed by him in this behalf, together with the audit report thereon shall be forwarded annually to the State Government by the State Commission and the State Government shall cause the audit report to be laid, as soon as may be after it is received, before the State Legislature.

## Chapter VII
## Miscellaneous

### *Protection of action taken in good faith*

31.No suit, prosecution or other legal proceeding shall lie against the Central Government, the State Government, the Commission, the State Commission, or any Member thereof or any person acting under the direction either of the Central Government, State Government, Commission or the State Commission, in respect of anything which is in good faith done or intended to be done in pursuance of this Act or of any rules made thereunder or in respect of the publication by or under the authority of the Central Government, State Government, Commission, or the State Commission of any report or paper.

***Chairperson, Memebrs and other officers to be public servant***

32. Every Member of the Commission, State Commission and every officer appointed in the Commission or the State Commission to exercise functions under this Act shall be deemed to be a public servant within the meaning of section 21 of the Indian Penal Code (45 of 1860).

***Directions by Central Government***

33. (1) In the discharge of its functions under this Act, the Commission shall be guided by such directions on questions of policy relating to national purposes, as may be given to it by the Central Government.

(2) If any dispute arises between the Central Government and the Commission as to whether a question is or is not a question of policy relating to national purposes, the decision of the Central Government thereon shall be final.

***Returns or Information***

34. The Commission shall furnish to the Central Government such returns or other information with respect to its activities as the Central Government may, from time to time, require.

Power to Central Government to make rules.-

35. (1) The Central Government may, by notification, make rules to carry out the provisions of this Act.

(2) In particular, and without prejudice to the generality of the foregoing power, such rules may provide for all or any of the following matters, namely:-

*(a)* terms and conditions of service of the Chairperson and Members of the Commission and their salaries and allowances under Section 6;

*(b)* the procedure to be followed by the Commission in the transaction of its business at a meeting under sub-section (4) of Section 10;

*(c)* the powers and duties which may be exercised and performed by the Member- Secretary of the Commission under sub-section (2) of section 11;

(*d*) the salary and allowances and other terms and conditions of service of officers and other employees of the Commission under sub-section (3) of section 11; and

(*e*) form of the statement of accounts and other records to be prepared by the Commission under sub-section (1) of Section 29.

(3) Every rule made under this Act shall be laid, as soon as may be after it is made, before each House of Parliament, while it is in session for a total period of thirty days which may be comprised in one session or in two or more successive sessions, and if, before the expiry of the session immediately following the session or the successive sessions aforesaid, both Houses agree in making any modification in the rule or both Houses agree that the rule should not be made, the rule shall thereafter have effect only in such modified form or be of no effect, as the case may be; so, however, that any such modification or annulment shall be without prejudice to the validity of anything previously done under that rule.

***Power of State Government to Make Rules***

36. (1) The State Government may, by notification, make rules to carry out the provisions of this Act.

(2) In particular, and without prejudice to the generality of the foregoing power, such rules may provide for all or any of the following matters, namely:-

(*a*) terms and conditions of service of the Chairperson and Members of the State Commission and their salaries and allowances under section 20;

(*b*) the procedure to be followed by the State Commission in the transaction of its business at a meeting under sub-section (4) of section 10 read with section 24;

(*c*) the powers and duties which may be exercised and performed by the Secretary of the State Commission under sub-section (2) of section 21;

(*d*) the salary and allowances and other terms and conditions of service of officers and other employees of the State Commission under sub-section (3) of Section 21; and (*e*) form of the statement of accounts and other records to be prepared by the State Commission under sub-section (1) of Section 30.

(3) Every rule made by the State Government under this section shall be laid, as soon as may be after it is made, before each House of the State Legislature where it consists of two Houses, or where such State Legislature consists of one House, before that House.

*Power to Remove Difficulties*

37. (1) If any difficulty arises in giving effect to the provisions of this Act, the Central Government may, by order published in the Official Gazette, make such provisions, not inconsistent with the provisions of this Act, as may appear to be necessary for removing the difficulty:

Provided that no order shall be made under this section after the expiry of the period of two years from the date of commencement of this Act.

(2) Every order made under this section shall be laid, as soon as may be after it is made, before each House of Parliament.

# Index